DEUTSCHES
BUSINESS-MAGAZIN

Tristam Carrington-Windo and Katrin Kohl

General Editor
Iris Sprankling

Hodder & Stoughton

LONDON SYDNEY AUCKLAND TORONTO

The authors and publishers are grateful to the following for permission to reproduce copyright photographs and other visual material:

Artra Verlag, Peter Beug page 25 (bottom/col. 2). Barclays Bank Plc page 15 (top). BASF Aktiengesellschaft pages 20-21. Bayerische Vereinsbank AG page 17. Beiersdorf AG pages 54, 55 (top). Bertelsmann Lexikon Verlag GmbH page 32 (bottom). BMW AG pages 24 (top), 28, 44 (top/col. 2), 51 (bottom), 55 (bottom/cols 1-2), 59 (middle, bottom), 69 (bottom/col. 2), 77 (top/col. 3, middle, bottom), 89. Robert Bosch Hausgeräte GmbH pages 84-85. British Steel plc page 24 (bottom). Bundesverband deutscher Banken e.V. page 15 (bottom). Burberrys of London page 35. Tristam Carrington-Windo pages 9 (middle), 11 (top/col. 1), 13 (top), 30 (top), 55 (bottom/cols 1-2 inset & col. 3), 58, 60 (top), 69 (top/col. 1, middle/col. 3), 77 (top/col. 2), 79 (bottom). CBF Electronics Vertriebs GmbH page 76. Marliese Darsow pages 26-27 (photograph from *Düsseldorf Kaleidoskop*, Greven Verlag Köln). Davy Bamag GmbH page 23. Deutsche Airbus GmbH pages 62, 63, 64. Deutsche Bank AG pages 14, 16 (top/col. 1). Deutsche Presse-Agentur pages 44-45 (bottom), 53 (top). Deutscher Gewerkschaftsbund page 32 (top). Edeka Zentrale AG page 52 (top). Elfema GmbH pages 78, 79 (top). ELNA Elektro-Navigation und Industrie GmbH page 59 (top/col. 1). Flughafen Frankfurt Main AG pages 8, 9 (top, bottom). Food from Britain page 51 (top/col. 1). Fotografie am Hofgarten GmbH page 41 (middle/col. 2 right). Fremdenverkehrsamt der Landeshauptstadt München pages 66-67 (inset, coat of arms), 90. Gardenex (The Federation of Garden and Leisure Manufacturers Ltd.) page 30 (top/col. 1). Gesamtverband der Deutschen Versicherungswirtschaft e.V. pages 82, 83. Globus Kartendienst GmbH pages 3 (map), 16 (top/col. 3), bottom), 33 (bottom), 52 (bottom), 53 (bottom), 72 (top). Hapag-Lloyd AG pages 48, 49. IGEDO Internationale Modemesse Kronen KG page 34. International Stock Exchange Photo Library cover photograph. Knürr - Mechanik für die Elektronik AG pages 70, 71. Katrin Kohl pages 19 (top/col. 1), 29 (bottom), 31, 50 (bottom), 65 (middle/col. 3). KölnMesse Messe- und Ausstellungs-Ges.m.b.H. Köln page 29 (middle). Lydmet Ltd page 13 (middle, bottom). Mannesmann AG pages 42, 43. Gundhard Marth pages 6-7, 25 (middle/cols 1-2). Messe Frankfurt GmbH pages 6-7 (inset), 18. Münchner Hybrid Systemtechnik GmbH pages 80 (top/col. 3), 81 (top). Münchner Technologiezentrum Betriebsgesellschaft mbH page 80 (top/cols 1-2). OBI Heimwerker- und Freizeitbedarf Handels GmbH & Co. KG pages 38, 39. Portex Ltd pages 60 (bottom), 61. Großversandhaus Quelle Gustav Schickedanz KG pages 72 (bottom), 73. Raumtechnik Gesellschaft für Messebau und Produktpräsentationen mbH page 19 (top/col. 2). Rowenta-Werke GmbH pages 10 (top/col. 3, middle/cols 1 & 3, bottom/col. 3), 11 (top/col. 3, bottom), 12. Salzgitter Stahl GmbH pages 40, 41 (top, middle/col. 2 left). Schmidt & Schneemilch GmbH page 50 (top). Hans Schwarzkopf GmbH pages 56, 57. Siemens AG pages 66-67, 86, 87, 88. Tourismus-Zentrale Hamburg GmbH pages 46-47, 65 (coat of arms, top/col. 2, bottom). VEDES Vereinigung der Spielwaren-Fachgeschäfte eG pages 74, 75. Verband der Technischen Überwachungs-Vereine e.V. page 10 (bottom/col. 1 left). Verband Deutscher Elektrotechniker e.V. page 10 (bottom/col. 1 right). Verkehrsamt der Stadt Frankfurt am Main pages 7 (coat of arms), 25 (coat of arms). Klaus Wechselberger page 81 (bottom). Werbe- und Wirtschaftsförderungsamt Düsseldorf pages 27 (coat of arms), 45 (coat of arms). Westward Technology Ltd page 68 (top/col. 1). Wirtschaftsprüferkammer pages 36 (top), 37 (bottom). Zahlenbilder, Erich Schmidt Verlag GmbH & Co. page 33 (top). Zimmer AG page 22.

The authors and publishers are grateful to the following for permission to reproduce written copyright material:

Artra Verlag, Peter Beug page 25 (extract from *Wohin in Frankfurt und Drumherum*). BASF Aktiengesellschaft page 20 (extracts from *BASF Ludwigshafen*). Bayerische Vereinsbank AG page 17 (extract from *Schnell und bequem: VEREINSBANK Geld & Service AUTOMATEN*). Beiersdorf AG page 54 (extract from *Hauskurier*). BMW AG page 13 (extract from *Zeitmotor. Auf den Spuren der Zukunft*), 28 (extract from *Logistik und Einkauf bei BMW*), 51, 55, 59, 69 and 77 (extracts from *Zum Thema BMW*). Robert Bosch Hausgeräte GmbH pages 84-85 (extracts from *Bosch Küche Collection*). CBF Electronics Vertriebs GmbH page 76 (extract from *CBF Programm-Übersicht*). City-Schlachterei Martin Höfner page 65 (extract from menu). Davy Bamag GmbH page 23 (extract from *Davy Bamag GmbH Wasser Abwasser Abluft Elektrolyse*). Deutsche Airbus GmbH pages 63 (extracts from *High-Tech aus Hamburg* and *MBB Hamburg Heute*), 81 (extract from *MBB Nachrichten*). Ernst & Young GmbH Wirtschaftsprüfungsgesellschaft page 36 (*Kurzmitteilung*). Financial Times page 16 (extract from the *Financial Times*). Flughafen Frankfurt Main AG pages 8 (extracts from *Flughafen Frankfurt Parken* and *Airport FRA - Porträt des Flughafens Frankfurt/Main*), 9 (extract from *Airport Conference Center*). Fremdenverkehrsamt der Landeshauptstadt München page 90 (extract from *München*). Gardenex (The Federation of Garden and Leisure Manufacturers Ltd.) page 30 (extract from *Internationale Gartenfachmesse Köln Katalog 1990*). German Chamber of Industry & Commerce pages 28 and 62 (extracts from *British-German Trade*), 81 (extract from *Features of the German Market*). Gruner + Jahr AG & Co page 67 (extract from © *GEO-Special "München" 1984*). Handelsblatt page 27 (extract from *Handelsblatt*). Hapag-Lloyd AG pages 48 (extract from *Weltweite Liniendienste*), 49 (extract from *Geschäftsbericht 1987*). HMSO pages 49, 82 and 89 (extracts from *British Business* with permission of the Controller of Her Majesty's Stationery Office). IDW Verlag GmbH page 37 (extract from Brooks/Mertin, *Neues deutsches Bilanzrecht*). IGEDO Internationale Modemesse Kronen KG page 34 (extract from *Düsseldorf Fashion House 2*). Knürr - Mechanik für die Elektronik AG pages 70-71 (extracts from *Knürr direkt* and *Dacomobile*). KölnMesse Messe- und Ausstellungs-Ges.m.b.H. Köln pages 29 (extract from *Messen nach Maß*), 30 (extracts from *Internationale Gartenmesse Köln Katalog 1990* and *Fragebogen für Aussteller*), 38 (extract from *Presse-Information*). Mannesmann AG pages 42 (extract from *Mannesmann-Illustrierte*), 43 (extracts from *Mannesmann-Post*). Münchner Hybrid Systemtechnik GmbH page 81 (extract from *Münchner Hybrid Systemtechnik*). Münchner Technologiezentrum Betriebsgesellschaft mbH page 80 (extracts from *Münchner Technologiezentrum*). OBI Heimwerker- und Freizeitbedarf Handels GmbH & Co. KG page 39 (extracts from newspaper insert). Patzer Verlag GmbH u. Co. KG page 31 (extract from *Garten- und Freizeitmarkt*). Großversandhaus Quelle Gustav Schickedanz KG page 73 (extract from *Quelle Katalog Herbst/Winter 88/89*). Raumtechnik Gesellschaft für Messebau und Produktpräsentation mbH page 19 (extract from advertisement). Salzgitter Stahl GmbH page 41 (extract from *Salzgitter Stahl Kurier*). Schmidt & Schneemilch GmbH page 50 (extract from *Tee?? Wußten Sie schon ...*). Steigenberger Parkhotel Düsseldorf page 45 (extract from menu). Süddeutscher Verlag GmbH pages 17 and 87 (extracts from *Süddeutsche Zeitung*). Tourismus-Zentrale Hamburg GmbH 65 (extract from Meyer-Marwitz, *Das Hamburg Buch*). VEDES Vereinigung der Spielwaren-Fachgeschäfte eG page 75 (extracts from *VEDES Buch der Wünsche* and *Geschenke zum Küssen*). Verkehrsamt der Stadt Frankfurt am Main page 7 (extract from *Frankfurt Live*). Werga-Tools GmbH pages 31 (extract from *Werga-Katalog*), 73 (extract from speech given by Heinz Leyerle at *Gardening Equipment and Supplies Seminar*, London). Westward Technologie GmbH page 68 (business letter).

It was not possible to identify the source of all the material used, and in such cases the publishers and authors would welcome information from copyright owners.

Whilst every effort has been made to ensure that the information given in this publication is accurate at the time of writing, no legal responsibility is accepted for any errors, omissions or misleading statements in this information whether caused by negligence or otherwise, and no responsibility is accepted in regard to the standing of any firms, companies, organizations or individuals mentioned. The authors and publisher welcome any corrections from readers.

To
Peggy
and
Alice

British Library Cataloguing in Publication Data

Carrington-Windo, Tristam
Deutsches Business Magazin.
I. Title II. Kohl, Katrin
438.6
ISBN 0-340-55540-8

First published 1991

© 1991 Tristam Carrington-Windo and Katrin Kohl

All rights reserved. No part of this publication may be reproduced or transmitted in any form or by any means, electronic or mechanical, including photocopy, recording, or any information storage and retrieval system, without permission in writing from the publisher or under licence from the Copyright Licensing Agency Limited. Further details of such licences (for reprographic reproduction) may be obtained from the Copyright Licensing Agency Limited, of 90 Tottenham Court Road, London W1P 9HE.

Design by Design Revolution.
Printed in Great Britain for the educational publishing division of Hodder & Stoughton Ltd., Mill Road, Dunton Green, Sevenoaks, Kent by Page Bros, Norwich

DEUTSCHES BUSINESS-MAGAZIN
Table of Contents

Page	
4	Acknowledgements
5	Introduction
	User Guide

Finanzmetropole – Frankfurt
6	Finanzmetropole – Frankfurt
8	Weltflughafen – Frankfurt Rhein-Main
10	Service, Export, Kooperation
12	Nüchtern und sachlich
13	Vom Coil zum Kunden 1
14	Bankfurt – Finanzzentrum Deutschlands
18	Messe Frankfurt
20	„Das größte Chemieareal der Welt"
22	Spezialisten für Anlagenbau
24	Vom Coil zum Kunden 2
25	Frankfurter Spezialitäten

Schreibtisch des Ruhrgebiets – Düsseldorf
26	Schreibtisch des Ruhrgebiets – Düsseldorf
28	Vom Coil zum Kunden 3
	Kommunikationsmittel Deutsch
29	Alles für den Garten
30	First Encounters
32	Demokratisierung der Wirtschaft
34	Modemetropole Düsseldorf
36	Beratung und Prüfung
38	Mit Abstand an der Spitze
40	Handel mit Stahl
42	Millimetergenau – mitten in der Nordsee
44	Vom Coil zum Kunden 4
	Düsseldorfer Spezialitäten

Das Tor zur Welt – Hamburg
46	Das Tor zur Welt – Hamburg
48	Container in alle Welt
50	Kaffee oder Tee?
51	Top Quality and Choice
	Vom Coil zum Kunden 5
52	Geschmackserlebnis mit neuen Ideen
53	Das Gesamtwohl der Wirtschaft
54	Ein Markenartikler mit Tradition
55	Vom Coil zum Kunden 6
56	Geänderte Umweltbedürfnisse
58	Navigation, Kommunikation, Automation
59	Vom Coil zum Kunden 7
60	Mit sehr hohem Einsatz
62	„Made in Europe"
65	Hamburger Spezialitäten

High-Tech an der Isar – München
66	High-Tech an der Isar – München
68	Die Feinheiten des deutschen Marktes
69	Vom Coil zum Kunden 8
70	Elektronik im Baukastensystem
72	Schnell und bequem
74	Ein anspruchsvoller Endverbraucher
76	Ein starker Konkurrenzkampf
77	Vom Coil zum Kunden 9
78	Der Produktkontakt zur Spitze
80	Zukunftsorientierte Technologien
81	Babylonisches Sprachgewirr?
82	Maßgeschneiderter Versicherungsschutz
84	Alles aus einem Haus
86	In 127 Ländern
89	Vom Coil zum Kunden 10
90	Münchner Spezialitäten

91	Feedback
95	Spelling and Pronunciation
96	Grammar
109	Glossary

ACKNOWLEDGEMENTS

The authors would like to thank the BBC, the Department of Education and Science, the Department of Trade and Industry, Hodder & Stoughton, Managed Learning and the Open College, who made this course possible.

The authors are also indebted to the following companies, organizations and people, whose contributions form the substance of *Deutsches Business-Magazin*. The positions given are generally those occupied at the time of interview:

Auswärtiges Amt, Abteilung für auswärtige Kulturpolitik
Ministerialdirektor Dr. Barthold Witte, Leiter der Kulturabteilung.
Barclays Bank Plc
Robert Becker, Risk Manager; John Connell, General Manager's Assistant; Christopher H. Davis, Assistant General Manager; Norbert A. Schramm, Manager.
BASF Aktiengesellschaft
Dr. Matthias Hensel, Pressesprecher.
Beiersdorf AG
Roland Glagowski, Marketing Medical International; Klaus Herre, Leiter Werbung; Dr. Simon Leadbeater, Management-Trainee; Hartwig Poppelbaum, Tesa Programm Marketing- und Vertriebsleiter Europa/Nordamerika; Dr. Sabine Sommerkamp-Vogel, Öffentlichkeitsarbeit.
BMW AG
Rainer Asch, Gruppenleiter mechanische Fertigung Motorkernteile; Klaus Bareuther, Hauptabteilungsleiter Karosserie-Rohbau; Friedrich Fichtner, Leiter des Physiklabors; Dr. Rudolf Harlfinger, Leiter Werkstofftechnik; Jakob Knieling, Hauptabteilungsleiter Preßwerk; Uwe Mahla, Leiter Inlandspresse; Angela Möller, Presseabteilung; Franz Schobert, Leiter Motorenbau; Hans Paul Thienel, Leiter Einkauf Rohmaterial und Verbindungselemente; Veit-Rüdiger Thomas, Werkstofftechnik; Kai Woiwod, Leiter Einkauf Großbritannien; Karl Wolf, Werksführung.
Robert Bosch Hausgeräte GmbH
Pierre Aschauer, Vertriebsleiter Export Küche; Karin Pfeiffer, Presse und Information; Gerd Strobel, Leiter Produktvertrieb Küche.
British Chamber of Commerce in Germany
Joe Parr, Director.
British Consulate-General Düsseldorf
Peter G.F. Bryant, Consul-General; Robert Calder, Consul (Commercial); Stuart Strong, Vice-Consul (Commercial).
British Consulate-General Frankfurt
Roger Thomas, Consul (Commercial).
British Consulate-General Hamburg
David J. Brown, Information Assistant; Ewen Mearns, Consul (Commercial); Heinz-Gerhard Wilkens, Information Officer.
British Consulate-General Munich
Charles Pattinson, Vice-Consul (Commercial); Neil Rothnie, Vice-Consul (Commercial).
British Steel plc
John E. Tune, Sales Manager, Automotive, British Steel Strip Products; Philip Wolfenden, Public Relations.
Bulldog Tools Ltd
Ian Hall, Export Manager.
Bundesverband deutscher Banken e.V.
Dr. Bernd Sprenger.
Burberrys of London
Dave de Boer, Central European Wholesale Manager; Christa Kellermann, Leiterin Öffentlichkeitsarbeit Deutschland; Hans Schar, Leiter Marketing Deutschland.
CBF Electronics Vertriebs GmbH
Claus B. Fritz, Geschäftsführer; Bernard C. Rodden, Produktmanager.
Davy Bamag GmbH
Karlheinz Dores, Geschäftsführer.
Davy McKee AG
Franz Dittrich, Leiter Stabsstelle Vorstand.

Department of Trade and Industry
John Barrass, Language Portfolio; Paul Isolani-Smyth, Focus Germany Campaign; Rosemary Rochester, Overseas Trade Division 3.
Deutsche Airbus GmbH
Heinz Kuckuck, Programmkoordinator; Bernhard Preuß, Leiter Ausstattungmontage und Flugbetrieb; Sigrid Schütz, Leiterin Presse und Information.
Deutsche Bank AG
Manfred ten Brink, General Manager (London); Dr. Jochen Degkwitz, Presseabteilung; Walther Weber, Presseabteilung.
Deutscher Gewerkschaftsbund
Dr. Dieter Schuster, Leiter der Bibliothek, des Archivs und der Dokumentation beim Bundesvorstand.
Edeka Zentrale AG
Folker des Coudres, Leiter Öffentlichkeitsarbeit.
Elfema GmbH
Klaus Michaelis, Geschäftsführer.
ELNA Elektro-Navigation und Industrie GmbH
Frank Braun, Serviceleiter; Wolfgang Grube, Marketing-Manager; Peter Schick, Geschäftsführer.
Ernst & Young GmbH Wirtschaftsprüfungsgesellschaft
Helmut Becker, Managing Partner; Manfred Masur, Partner in Charge.
Financial Times
Andrew Fisher, Frankfurt Correspondent.
Flughafen Frankfurt Main AG
Udo Brinkmann, Leiter Airport Conference Center.
Food from Britain
Roy G. Edleston, Director, Europe.
Fremdenverkehrsamt der Landeshauptstadt München
Gottfried L. Linke, Stellvertretender Direktor; Jasmin Zellner, Pressestelle.
Gardenex (The Federation of Garden and Leisure Manufacturers Ltd.)
Yvonne Slade, Secretary.
Gesamtverband der Deutschen Versicherungswirtschaft e.V.
Jörn H.-E. Badenhoop, Stellvertretender Verbandsdirektor.
Gruner + Jahr AG & Co
Detmar Grosse-Leege, Leiter Öffentlichkeitsarbeit.
Handelskammer Hamburg
Jutta Thormann, Geschäftsführerin, Abteilung Berufsbildung; Reinhard Wolf, Geschäftsführer, Abteilung Berufsbildung.
Hapag-Lloyd AG
Eva Gjersvik, Presse- und Informationsabteilung; Burkhard Jäckel, Leiter Frachtdienst Mittlerer Osten; Gerhard Simonsen, Leiter Presse- und Informationsabteilung.
Hillian Interlog Ltd
Hilary Greer, Director; Ian T. Greer, Director.
Industrie- und Handelskammer zu Düsseldorf
Joachim Wischermann, Geschäftsführer, Leiter des Dezernates Außenwirtschaft.
Industrie- und Handelskammer Frankfurt am Main
Dr. Heinz Kremp.
Industrie- und Handelskammer für München und Oberbayern
Inge Schifferer, Referentin der Abteilung Außenwirtschaft.
Inhome Ltd
Ken Dartington, Marketing Director; David Kirby, Group Product Manager.
Knürr - Mechanik für die Elektronik AG
Dr. Dietmar Mrosek, Vorstand Finanzen.
KölnMesse Messe- und Ausstellungs-Ges.m.b.H. Köln
Friedrich Wilhelm Bertram, Mitglied der Geschäftsleitung; Ulrike Hoberg, Pressereferentin.
Linguarama GmbH
Rosemary Annandale-Steiner, Geschäftsführerin.
Lydmet Ltd
Barrie Giles, Deputy Sales Manager.
Mannesmann AG
Dr. Hartmut Graf Plettenberg, Leiter Öffentlichkeitsarbeit.

Medic-Eschmann GmbH
Michael Endriat, Kaufmännischer Leiter; Lukas Garabet, Geschäftsführer; Sylvia Nieland, Innendienstleiterin Verkauf.
Messe Frankfurt GmbH
Rolf Hardy Pulina, Stabsbereichsleiter Presse und Public Relations.
Mill Automotive Group Ltd
Paddy Hopkirk, Director.
Münchner Hybrid Systemtechnik GmbH
Kornelia Huber, Gesellschafterin.
Irmgard Nohr-Wechselberger
Konferenzdolmetscherin.
OBI Heimwerker- und Freizeitbedarf Handels GmbH & Co. KG
Dr. Brigitte Hommerich, Leitung Öffentlichkeitsarbeit; Dr. Utho Creusen, Mitglied der Geschäftsleitung.
Großversandhaus Quelle Gustav Schickedanz KG
Wolfgang Keck, Leiter Import.
RaBe - Rad- und Bergsport
Gebhard Immler, Inhaber.
Rowenta-Werke GmbH
Gottfried Dodt, Leiter Öffentlichkeitsarbeit; Hugo Goldbach, Betriebsratsvorsitzender; Michael Tachenberg, Marketing-Manager International.
Saatchi & Saatchi Advertising GmbH
Dieter Kirschner, Client Services Director.
Salzgitter Stahl GmbH
Hermann Lohmar, Leiter der Offshore-Abteilung; Erhard Seeger, Bereichsleiter Controlling, Betriebswirtschaft, Organisation.
Schmidt & Schneemilch GmbH
Hans Otto Grelck, Geschäftsführer.
Hans Schwarzkopf GmbH
Inken Dabelstein, Auszubildende; Peggy Fischer, Auszubildende; Andreas Fuchs, Leiter Marketing; Hans-Jürgen Howind, Leiter Marketing, Handelsdivision; Ulrich Kaftanski, Leiter Handelsdivision; Viola Kassel, Leitung Öffentlichkeitsarbeit.
Siemens AG
Doris Lasch, Sekretärin, Vertrieb Ausland; Achim Meilenbrock, Leiter Auslandswerbung; Dr. Klaus Möller, Direktor Zentralverwaltung Ausland; Dr. Gerhard Vilsmeier, Zentralstelle Information.
South Down Trugs & Crafts Ltd
Robin Tuppen, Managing Director.
Steigenberger Parkhotel Düsseldorf
Hans-Joachim Kraß, Wirtschaftsdirektor.
Tourismus-Zentrale Hamburg GmbH
Helmut Cauer, Pressestelle.
VEDES Vereinigung der Spielwaren-Fachgeschäfte eG
Brigitte Beck, Sachbearbeiterin; Tanja Franke, Auszubildende; Rainer Loch, Geschäftsführer Vertrieb; Ursula Safar, Substitutin, Einkauf; Werner Schwarz, Leiter Import; Klaus Schwarzmann, Leiter Werbung.
Verkehrsamt der Stadt Frankfurt am Main
Günther Hampel; Wolfgang Kuldschun, Leiter.
Werbe- und Wirtschaftsförderungsamt Düsseldorf
Sabine Niemczyk; Wolfgang Röhl, Werbeabteilung.
Werga-Tools GmbH
Heinz Leyerle, Geschäftsführer.
Westward Technologie GmbH
Wilhelm J. Lohn, Geschäftsführer; Roland Pfister, Serviceleiter.

The authors are further grateful to the following for their help and advice: Michael Capone, Bruce Carrington-Windo, Christine Conlin, Catriona Dawson, Charles Foot, Shani Henty, Marianne Howarth, Margaret Kohl, Verena and Wolfgang Lehwald, Franziska and Alexander Limberg, Sheridan Maguire, David Playfair, Mark Roberts, Society of Authors and Gordon Fielden, Liz Weston, Richard Wheatley, Rachel Wood. We are indebted to Wynne Brindle, Tim Gregson-Williams and Robert Taylor for their encouragement and commitment to publishing this course. Special thanks are due to Günter Kohl for his thorough proof-reading, Judith Cunningham for her constructive criticism, and in particular to Iris Sprankling for her unstinting efforts and creative ideas.

INTRODUCTION

Deutsches Business-Magazin is a German reading course with a twin-track approach. It aims to help users understand the German business environment – one of the most successful in the world – and develops the skills necessary for reading about it in German. The course is a flexible network of articles, interviews and other authentic material which enables users to learn at their own pace.

The material for *Deutsches Business-Magazin* was gathered in more than 40 companies in Germany and the UK. Trade fairs, chambers of commerce and umbrella organizations were also visited and consulted. The authors carried out over 100 interviews with business people operating in the German market, who provided a personal perspective. The four sections of *Deutsches Business-Magazin* explore the business centres Frankfurt, Düsseldorf, Hamburg and Munich, to give an overview of different regions and sectors. These four business centres constitute some of the powerhouses of Germany's export-led economy and look set to retain their favoured status into the next millennium. Events in the autumn of 1989 set in train a process which has created a single German state, but the collapse of the east German economy following monetary union in 1990 ensured that the business patterns and practices of west Germany prevail.

Deutsches Business-Magazin was developed by the authors and the general editor in response to the need for German business language-learning materials identified by the Department of Education and Science and the BBC. Financial support was provided by the Open College and Managed Learning. The Department of Trade and Industry identified key sectors of interest to British exporters.

USER GUIDE

Do you think you're ❏ Good ❏ Bad ❏ Indifferent at languages? The answer's irrelevant. Everybody masters their mother tongue, together with ideas it can express, so why not make the most of your skills and expand into a new culture?

Deutsches Business-Magazin assumes no previous knowledge of German, although the interviews and articles are intended to stretch you from the start. They've been selected for their intrinsic interest rather than strictly graded according to the language. This is German in a business context, which means you can make full use of your background knowledge. Look on any difficulties you may come up against as a challenge rather than an ordeal! Because all the material relates to the German work environment, it's ideally suited to help you apply the skills you acquire.

Each piece of German is usually accompanied by an introduction in English to give you an idea of what it's about. Various activities and hints are designed to help you understand what you're reading and to suggest reading strategies:

FILAWORD	Useful German business words in context, with English translations. It's a good idea to write each new German word you come across on a card with a translation on the reverse. That way you can learn words in odd moments and put aside the cards when you think you know the word. Check through your cards at a later stage to refresh your memory.
FACTFINDER	Questions which direct you to specific facts in what you're reading. These questions have been graded according to the effort you'll be likely to need to find the answer: * basic input ** medium input *** concentrated input. (Answers in *Feedback*.)
DATABASE	Selected words or phrases that occur in the German, with context-specific translations.
EXECUTIVE SKILLS	Exercises to help you understand what you're reading and practise what you've learnt. They're graded to indicate the amount of effort you'll be likely to require: * basic input ** medium input *** concentrated input. (Answers in *Feedback*.)
EXECUTIVE PUZZLE	Teasers to develop your powers of analysis in German. (Answers in *Feedback*.)
ACTIONPACK	Suggestions to help you build up an outline of yourself and your company in German. (Example answers in *Feedback*.)
PROFILE	Short notes give guidance on locating important facts to build up a picture of companies or processes. (Answers in *Feedback*.)
FALLSTUDIE	Problems encountered in companies which the authors visited provide case studies (*Fallstudien*). They demonstrate how German companies approach a challenge, and train you to analyse management situations in German. (Answers in *Feedback*.)
FILAFACT	Examples are taken from the interview or article to highlight a point about the German language. A page reference ➡ P 00 points to a more detailed explanation in the *Grammar* section.
FILASKILL	Some hints on what you can do to make the most of your knowledge and improve your German reading skills.
T i P	Gives information on the German business environment, dos and don'ts, advice from the people we talked to.

The following four sections will provide you with help when reading *Deutsches Business-Magazin*:

Spelling and Pronunciation	A brief guide to the relationship between the letters you read and the sounds they represent.
Feedback	Key to *Factfinder, Executive skills, Executive puzzle, Actionpack, Profile* and *Fallstudie*.
Grammar	A summary of essential grammar points to give you guidance for detailed reading. Page references in *Filafact* refer you to the relevant section of the *Grammar*.
Glossary	A complete list of all German words in *Deutsches Business-Magazin*, and selected phrases. English equivalents apply to the words and phrases as they're used in *Deutsches Business-Magazin*.

You'll probably find it rather daunting to be faced by written German, if you allow yourself to be put off by unfamiliar words. Make the most of your powers of analysis and deduction! Read the English introductions carefully to find out as much background information as you can, and then see if you can find the answer to *Factfinder* using *Database* if necessary. Then have a good look at any *Filafact* and work through any activities like *Executive skills* for detailed understanding. The *Glossary* gives additional assistance for words that you still want to find out about. Read an interview or article several times, and if you still find it difficult – come back to it later.

Learning strategies

- Adopt a step-by-step approach to reading
- Make a regular commitment
- Take your time and don't expect too much of yourself
- Never give up!

Remember that you're dealing here with authentic material of the kind you'll come across in any dealings you may have with Germany. Don't approach it expecting to understand everything immediately. Concentrate on getting an overview, and leave detail to fit into place as your knowledge base expands.

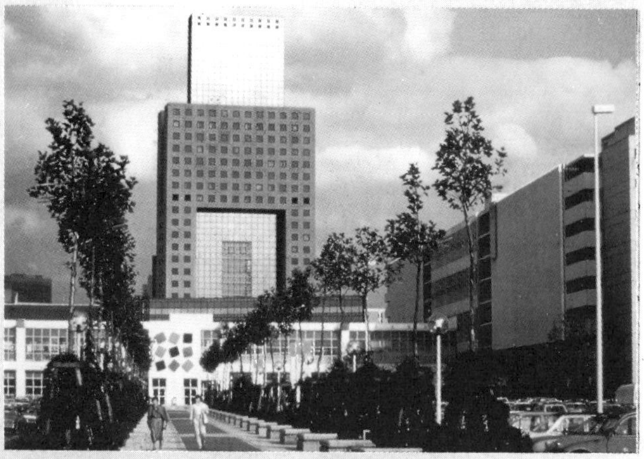

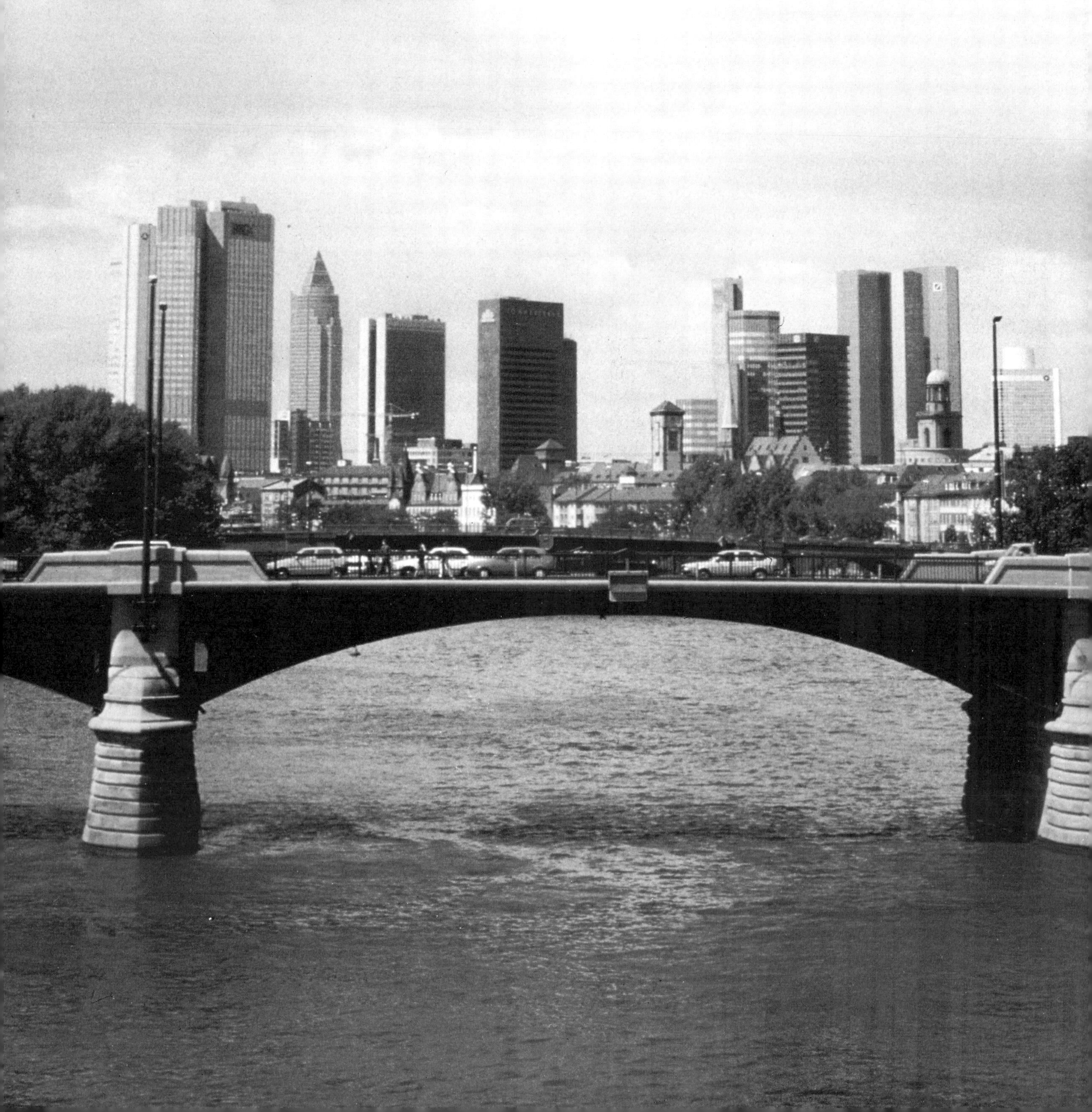

Frankfurt

Finanzmetropole

Frankfurt's central position in Europe has made it a centre for trade and commerce since the Middle Ages. Church dignitaries and rulers met at synods and other great events. These attracted merchants, and the first mention of the 'Frankfurt Fair' occurred as far back as 1240. Today's trade-fair complex is a monumental fairground of glass and concrete hosting the spring and autumn consumer fairs, the world-famous Frankfurt Book Fair, the Frankfurt Motor Show, and many other specialist trade fairs.

Banking has always been Frankfurt's speciality. Today the skyline of continental Europe's financial centre is dominated by gleaming skyscrapers, not least Deutsche Bank's twin towers, nicknamed Debit and Credit, *Soll und Haben,* and the *Messeturm* (Europe's tallest building). The city is said to have some 411 banks in all. Although not the German capital, Frankfurt is home to the country's central bank, the *Bundesbank,* and to its largest stock exchange. Decentralization is typical of Germany's strong federal structure – and is likely to remain so.

FILAWORD
der Handel *trade, commerce*
die Wirtschaft *economy, trade and industry*
die Industrie *industry*
die Messe *trade fair*
arbeiten *to work*

FILASKILL
The first piece of German might well look daunting, but don't be put off by unfamiliar words. Try some guesswork, make good use of the English introductions to help understanding, and start by finding the answer to the *Factfinder* questions. Then use *Database* for extra help, and work through the tasks in *Executive skills.* When you read the German again, you'll find you understand more. *Deutsches Business-Magazin* has a *Glossary* to help you with words that are unclear.

Mainhattan

FACTFINDER
*1 What kind of reputation does Frankfurt have?

Handelszentrum. Finanzmetropole. Die imposante Skyline verdeutlicht es sofort – im harten Big Business setzt Frankfurt Akzente. Der Ruf der Stadt ist international.

Einige hundert Kreditinstitute und Banken arbeiten in der Mainmetropole mit Geld und Devisen. Und zu Messezeiten trifft sich hier die Welt. (*Frankfurt Live*)

DATABASE
verdeutlicht es *sets the scene*
sofort *immediately*
setzt ... Akzente *... sets trends*
Der Ruf der Stadt *the reputation of the city*
Geld (*n*) *money*
Devisen (*f, pl*) *foreign exchange/ currency*
zu Messezeiten *when trade fairs are on*
trifft sich *congregates*
Welt (*f*) *world*

EXECUTIVE SKILLS
*1 Guesswork often yields dividends. What do these German words mean?
  a Zentrum *b* Finanz *c* Metropole *d* imposant *e* Skyline *f* hart *g* Big Business *h* ist *i* international *j* hundert *k* Kredit *l* Institut *m* und *n* Bank *o* hier.

*2 With the help of *Mainhattan*, try and match up the words in these two lists to make compound words:

a Finanz   *i* Institute
b Kredit   *ii* Metropole
c Messe   *iii* Metropole
d Main   *iv* Zeiten

*3 Some compound words need to be joined up with an extra element in the middle. Look carefully at *Mainhattan* to see which letter has been added to make *Handel* and *Zentrum* into a compound word.

*4 Why do you think that Frankfurt is nicknamed 'Mainhattan'?

FILASKILL
Many German words are borrowed from English or are similar to English. They're particularly popular in business, so you can deduce a lot simply by being on the ball.

DEUTSCHES BUSINESS-MAGAZIN **7**

Frankfurt

WELTFLUGHAFEN — FRANKFURT RHEIN-MAIN

Frankfurt's airport is a town in its own right, with over 50,000 employees. Including freight, the airport is the biggest in Europe, and it offers all the facilities of a bustling metropolis, with hotels, more than 100 shops and boutiques, over 30 cafés and restaurants, cinemas, a medical centre, and even somewhere to house your pet elephant!

Täglich 900 Starts und Landungen

FILAWORD
der Flughafen *airport*
das Flugzeug *aeroplane*
fliegen *to fly*
die Fracht *freight*
das Geschäft *shop, business*
die Klinik *medical centre, hospital*

Parken

Once you've come down to earth, underground and multi-storey car parks provide over 10,000 parking spaces, 24 hours a day. Parking fees (*Parkgebühren*) are given below.

FILAWORD
die Tiefgarage *underground car park*
das Parkhaus *multi-storey car park*
1 Stunde/1. Stunde *1 hour/1st hour*
2 Stunden/2. Stunde *2 hours/2nd hour*

Parkgebühren	
1 Stunde	DM 3,-
1.-7. Tag (pro Tag)	DM 20,-
ab 8. Tag (pro Tag)	DM 10,-
1 Woche	DM 140,-
2 Wochen	DM 210,-

EXECUTIVE SKILLS
*1 How many minutes in an hour, hours in a day, days in a week? Fill in the missing words:
   a 1 _____ = 60 Minuten
   b 1 _____ = 24 Stunden
   c 1 _____ = 7 Tage
*2 Which of the following are true? *a* 24 Stunden kosten DM 72,- *b* 1 Woche kostet DM 140,- *c* 10 Tage kosten DM 170,-.

Zahlen und Fakten

FACTFINDER
**1 How many companies run scheduled flights here?
*2 How many take-offs/landings are there per day?

- Durchschnittlich 82.000 Passagiere jeden Tag
- Etwa 95 Fluggesellschaften im Linienverkehr und ca. 200 Chartergesellschaften
- Rund 900 Starts und Landungen täglich
- Arbeitsplatz für mehr als 50.000 Menschen

DATABASE
jeden Tag *every day*
Fluggesellschaften (*f, pl*) *airline companies*
Arbeitsplatz (*m*) *workplace*

FILAFACT *numbers*
German use of stops and commas in figures is opposite to English usage:
   zweiundachtzigtausend: 82.000
   eighty-two thousand: 82,000
   acht Komma zwei: 8,2
   eight point two: 8.2

Often, though, you'll simply see *82 000*, with a space instead of a stop. For German numbers ➡ P 108. And here are some ways of giving approximate numbers: *durchschnittlich* (an average of), *etwa / ca. / rund* (approximately, around), *mehr als* (more than).

Jede Art von Service

There doesn't seem to be much you can't do at the airport! Herr Udo Brinkmann, director of the *Airport Conference Center*, gave a rundown.

FACTFINDER
***3 How many facilities does Herr Brinkmann mention?

Herr Brinkmann: Der Frankfurter Flughafen ist eine komplett ausgestattete Stadt. Wir haben Harrods. Wir haben einen Kindergarten und sogar eine Zahnklinik. Wir haben Tierstationen hier, die Hunde, Hauskatzen oder sogar Elefanten kurzfristig aufnehmen – jede Art von Service.

DATABASE
ausgestattet *equipped*
Zahnklinik (*f*) *dental clinic*
die ... kurzfristig aufnehmen *which accept ... for short-term stays*
jede Art von *every kind of*

FILAFACT *sein, haben*
Notice how Herr Brinkmann uses the German equivalents of the English verbs *is* and *have*:
   Der Flughafen *ist* eine komplett ausgestattete Stadt.
   Wir *haben* Harrods.

Have a look at the various forms of *sein* (to be) and *haben* (to have). ➡ P 102

FILASKILL
To get the gist of written German, it helps to concentrate on words with a capital letter. They are nouns, e.g. *der Flughafen* (the airport), *eine Zahnklinik* (a dental clinic).

Symbole - die internationale Sprache

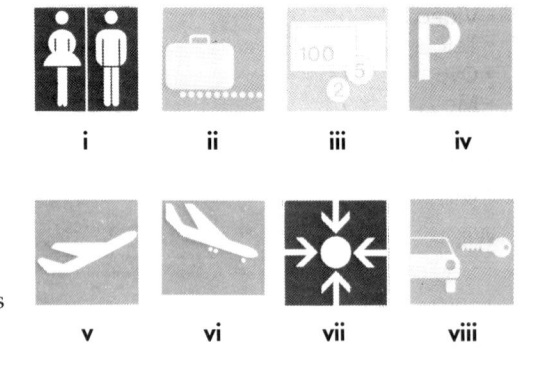

i ii iii iv

v vi vii viii

EXECUTIVE PUZZLE
1 Match these labels to the pictograms *i-iv*:
a Geldwechsel/Bank *b* Toiletten *c* Parkhaus *d* Gepäckausgabe.

2 Now work out where these labels belong in pictograms *v-viii*. The *Glossary* will help:
a Treffpunkt *b* Abflug *c* Mietwagen *d* Ankunft.

Frankfurt

Airport Conference Center

At the *Airport Center* you can rent an office for a day, hire a secretary or interpreter, or hold an international business meeting. And if the sales manager from Chicago can't make it – the *Airport Conference Center* has the latest facilities for video conferencing.

FILAWORD
der Kongreß *congress*
die Tagung *conference*
das Seminar *seminar*
die Besprechung *meeting*
das Büro *office*
mieten *to rent*

FILAFACT *gender*
Each German noun has a particular gender: masculine, feminine or neuter. It's gender determines the form of an accompanying definite article, equivalent to 'the' in English:

der Kongreß (*m*)
die Tagung (*f*)
das Seminar (*n*)

The plural of the definite article is always *die*. Usually gender has nothing to do with sex, and there's no easy way of telling what gender a noun is likely to be. It simply has to be learnt.
➡ P 97

Tagen am Flughafen

FACTFINDER
*1 How many types of business meeting are catered for at the *Airport Conference Center*?

Das Büro- und Kommunikationszentrum für die internationale Geschäftswelt. Tagungen, Seminare, Konferenzen oder kurze Meetings. Im Flughafen Frankfurt.

> **Ein Konferenzzentrum mit modernster Konferenztechnik:**
>
> • Video
> • Telefon
> • Overhead-Projektor
> • Media-Turm
> • Diaprojektor
> • Filmprojektor
> • Flip-Chart
>
> Wir informieren Sie gerne über Preise.

FILAFACT *hyphens*
If two compound words have an element in common, this can be replaced by a hyphen in the first word:

das Büro- und Kommunikations*zentrum*
= das Büro(*zentrum*) und Kommunikations*zentrum*

ACTIONPACK
Start building up your company's profile in German. Write down which of the above technical conference facilities you have.

Udo Brinkmann
Leiter
Airport Conference Center

Öffentlichkeitsarbeit und Marktforschung

6000 Frankfurt 75

Frankfurt Airport Center
Telefon (0 69) 6 90 - 70 0 65
Telex 417940

Visitenkarte

FACTFINDER
*2 What's a word for director (*literally* leader)?

Herr Brinkmann: Ich heiße Udo Brinkmann und bin Leiter des Airport Conference Centers auf dem Frankfurter Flughafen.

DATABASE
Ich heiße *My name is, I'm called*
(ich) bin *(I) am*

FILAFACT *spelling*
The letter ß (as in *heiße*) is equivalent to *ss*. Above *a, o, u*, you may find two dots (an umlaut or sound shift): *ä, ö, ü*. For pronunciation ➡ P 95.

ACTIONPACK
Start building up your personal profile in German by working out how to give your name.

Treffpunkt Flughafen

Herr Brinkmann defined several types of meeting held at the *Airport Conference Center*. A *Tagung* usually goes on for several days. A *Seminar* might be for management trainees learning the tricks of the trade. A *Meeting* (also *Besprechung*) is short and sweet!

FACTFINDER
*3 How long does the Mitsubishi conference last?
*4 What might you learn about human-resource management at a seminar?
*5 What are the words for 'fly in' and 'fly out'?

Die Tagung: „Jetzt ist hier zum Beispiel eine Tagung von Mitsubishi Deutschland. Die tagen vom 25. bis 29. Juli."
Das Seminar: „Wenn Sie zum Beispiel eine Führungskraft werden sollen, lernen Sie in einem Seminar das Know-how, wie man Mitarbeiter motiviert."
Das Meeting: „Kurze Meetings, das ist: reinfliegen, kurz treffen, darstellen und wieder rausfliegen."

DATABASE
zum Beispiel *for example*
Die tagen *They're holding a conference*
Wenn Sie ... werden sollen *If you're to become ...*
Führungskraft (*f*) *manager, executive*
Mitarbeiter (*pl*) *personnel, staff*
kurz *brief(ly)*
treffen *meet*
darstellen *give a presentation*

> **T i P**
>
> Shaking hands is part of the social ritual, except among young people. Generally you will find that colleagues shake hands each morning before starting work, and you should shake hands when you meet someone for the first time or meet a colleague again.

Videokonferenzraum

Frankfurt

SERVICE, EXPORT, KOOPERATION

The quality of electrical goods made in Germany reflects stringent standards and demanding consumers who expect the best and can afford to pay for it. Products bearing the approved VDE sign (*VDE-Zeichen*) conform to the exacting specifications laid down by the Association of German Electrical Engineers (*Verband der Deutschen Elektrotechniker*). This sign is a valuable selling point. The prestigious GS seal of approval stands for *geprüfte Sicherheit*, safety-tested. It is awarded by the *Technische Überwachungsverein* (TÜV), the German Technical Inspectorate, best known for the German equivalent of the MOT test. Style is also important, and design centres in Stuttgart, Essen and Hanover give awards for good design.

FILAWORD
das Elektrogerät *electrical appliance*
die Zulassung *approval, certification*
die Vorschriften (*f, pl*) *specifications, standards*
die Sicherheit *safety*
der Kundendienst *after-sales service*
die Gewerkschaft *trade union*

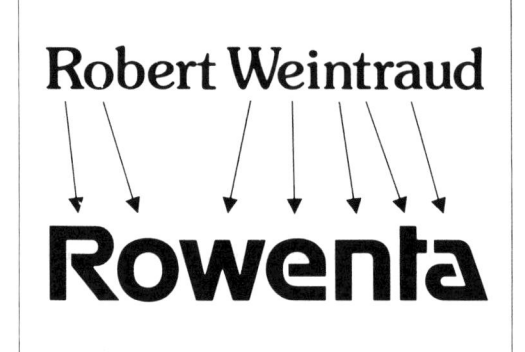

Zahlen und Fakten

Gründung: 1884
Gründer: Robert Weintraud
Stammwerk: Offenbach
Mitarbeiterzahl: Rowenta Deutschland: 2680
Branche: Elektrogeräte

TiP
The German seal of technical approval – "You're dead over there without it." Mr Paddy Hopkirk, of the Mill Automotive Group, says that his company ensures its exports are passed by the TÜV, even when it is not legally obliged to do so on safety grounds

Visitenkarte

At Rowenta we talked to Herr Tachenberg, international marketing manager, Herr Dodt, head of advertising and public relations, and Herr Goldbach, chairman of the works council (*Betriebsrat*).

FACTFINDER
*1 How many years have Herr Dodt and Herr Goldbach been at Rowenta?

Herr Tachenberg: Mein Name ist Michael Tachenberg, und ich bin Marketing-Manager International im Hause Rowenta in Offenbach.

Herr Dodt: Ich heiße Gottfried Dodt, und ich bin verantwortlich für Werbung, für Public Relations, für Messen und für den Bereich Kommunikation. Ich bin 58 Jahre alt und seit 18 Jahren in diesem Unternehmen.

Herr Goldbach: Mein Name ist Hugo Goldbach. Ich bin 51 Jahre alt und bin 30 Jahre hier im Betrieb. Ich bin jetzt Betriebsratsvorsitzender hier in der Firma.

EXECUTIVE SKILLS
*1 Find two ways of saying your name.
**2 How do two of the interviewees say how old they are?
*3 Three words are used for 'company'. Can you find them with the help of the *Glossary*?
***4 Find two ways of saying 'I've been in this company for X years'.

FILASKILL
When you're learning a language it's important to keep trying. *Executive skills* have been graded for the amount of input needed (➡ P 5). If you find some of the questions difficult, move on and come back to them later. *Executive skills* are designed to help you understand the German and develop reading strategies, not to test your knowledge.

ACTIONPACK
1 Using the interviews as models, write down your name and age.
2 Now write down two ways of introducing your job.

Der Service

Kundenberatung

Kundendienstwerkstatt

Ersatzteillager

EXECUTIVE PUZZLE
Each of the three captions above is a compound noun (➡ P 97). The following jumbled letters give the words that make up the compounds. Can you sort them out?
1 DUNKEN 2 GUTEBARN 3 LITE 4 SINTED
5 TRAZES 6 NEDNUK 7 TWARSKETT 8 GRELA.

Gottfried Dodt

Der Kundendienst

Although Rowenta has been in foreign hands since the 1960s, it is a typical German company with strong emphasis on service and exports. We asked Herr Dodt about customer service.

FACTFINDER
*1 What is essential for a brand-name manufacturer?

Herr Dodt: Ein einwandfrei funktionierender Kundendienst ist essentiell für einen Markenhersteller. Wir haben Vertragswerkstätten, mit denen wir praktisch das ganze Bundesgebiet abdecken. Oder aber der Kunde schickt das Gerät hier ins Werk. Wir haben hier im Werk einen zentralen Kundendienst. Das ist ein 24-Stunden Service.

DATABASE
einwandfrei funktionierend *smooth-running*
Markenhersteller (*m*) *brand manufacturer*
Vertragswerkstätten (*f, pl*) *authorized service centres*
mit denen wir praktisch das ganze Bundesgebiet abdecken *with which we more or less cover the whole Federal Republic*
Oder aber *Or alternatively*
Werk (*n*) *company, factory*

FILAFACT *gender*
The form of the indefinite article in German (equivalent to 'a(n)') varies according to the gender of the noun:

ein Kundendienst (*m*)
eine Stunde (*f*)
ein Gerät (*n*)

The indefinite article also occurs as *einen, eines, einer, einem*. As in English, there's no plural form. ➡ P 97-98

EXECUTIVE SKILLS
***1 Can you supply the verb to complete each sentence? These verbs are among the most widely used in the German language:

a Kundendienst ___ essentiell. *b* Wir ___ Vertragswerkstätten. *c* Wir ___ einen zentralen Kundendienst.

Die Verbindung vom Kollegen zur Geschäftsleitung

The workforce of any company with more than five employees is entitled to establish a works council, which can be a contentious issue in small businesses. Works councils are independent of the unions, although members may well belong to a union. The works council's brief is to represent the interests of the workforce on matters such as working practices and conditions, health and safety, and redundancy, whilst promoting the welfare of the company as a whole. This gives it a vital mediating role between employees and employers, and works councils have been instrumental in maintaining stable industrial relations.

FACTFINDER
**2 What is the works council responsible for?
**3 How does Herr Goldbach indicate he's about to give examples?

Herr Goldbach: Der Betriebsrat ist zuständig für die Probleme der Mitarbeiter. Wir müssen wissen, was wo im Tarifvertrag oder im Betriebsverfassungsgesetz steht. Zum Beispiel, wenn jemand kommt, der mit dem Meister nicht zufrieden ist, oder die Arbeit ist zu schwer, oder eine Frau sitzt zu krumm oder zu niedrig, oder wenn eine Kündigung ansteht. Der Betriebsrat ist die Verbindung vom Kollegen zur Geschäftsleitung.

DATABASE
Betriebsrat (*m*) *works council*
zuständig für *responsible for*
was wo ... steht *what's laid down and where ...*
der ... nicht zufrieden ist *who isn't satisfied ...*
wenn eine Kündigung ansteht *if a dismissal is imminent*
Verbindung (*f*) *link*
Geschäftsleitung (*f*) *management*

In schneller Folge montieren geschickte Hände aus vielen Einzelteilen Rowenta Kaffeeautomaten.

Partner

Ultimately, the works council is legally obliged to consider the company's financial welfare:

Herr Goldbach: Der Chef muß was verdienen. Wenn die nichts verdienen, geht's uns allen schlecht, das ist klar.

DATABASE
was verdienen *earn something*
der Chef ... die *the boss ... they (i.e. the company bosses)*
geht's uns allen schlecht *it's bad for us all*

FILASKILL
If you haven't read the *User Guide* (➡ P 5), have a look at it now for some guidance on how to set about reading the German in *Deutsches Business-Magazin*.

Hugo Goldbach

Frankfurt

Rowenta in England

England Nummer drei

Herr Tachenberg outlined the marketing strategy for Rowenta's range of electrical goods. We asked him about subsidiaries and product ranges abroad, and he emphasized the importance of tailoring sales to individual countries.

FACTFINDER
**1 Which three countries does Herr Tachenberg mention?
 *2 What product has a strong tradition in the UK?

Herr Tachenberg: In Hauptmärkten haben wir eigene Töchter, und in kleineren und mittleren Märkten haben wir ein Netz von Distributoren. Deutschland ist der größte Bereich, hier ist ja das Stammhaus. Nummer zwei ist Frankreich, wo wir auch Fabrikation haben. England ist dann Nummer drei; das ist eine Vertriebsgesellschaft.

Man muß das Vertriebsprogramm immer auf das einzelne Land ausrichten. In England konzentrieren wir uns zur Zeit auf Bügeleisen. Dann verkaufen wir sehr stark Toaster, wir verkaufen Kaffeemaschinen, wir verkaufen Staubsauger. Ein typisch englisches Produkt ist der Wasserkessel. Der *Kettle* hat in England eine sehr starke Tradition.

DATABASE
In Hauptmärkten *In principal markets*
eigene Töchter *our own subsidiaries*
hier ist ja das Stammhaus *after all, the parent company is here*
Vertriebsgesellschaft (f) *sales company, distributor*
Man muß ... immer auf ... ausrichten *You always have to gear ... to ...*
konzentrieren wir uns zur Zeit auf *we're concentrating on*

EXECUTIVE SKILLS
 *1 If *Staub* means 'dust' and *saugen* 'suck', what's a *Staubsauger*?
**2 When talking about the product range, Herr Tachenberg gives specific examples and a general statement. Which does he give first?
 *3 Make a list of the nouns in Herr Tachenberg's interview (remember nouns start with a capital). Try and work out the meanings and then check the *Glossary*.
***4 What's the subject of Herr Tachenberg's *a* first sentence and *b* last sentence?

Michael Tachenberg

FILAFACT *word order*
When you're reading German, you'll need to develop a flexible approach to word order. In English, the subject of a sentence usually comes before the main verb (e.g. 'we' is the subject in '*we* **sell** toasters'). German sentences often start with an element other than the subject, and this affects word order:

Wir	**verkaufen**	Kaffeemaschinen.
Dann	**verkaufen**	*wir* sehr stark Toaster.
Wir	**haben**	Vertragswerkstätten.
In Hauptmärkten	**haben**	*wir* eigene Töchter.

Try getting used to recognizing the verb. It's generally the second element, though the first element may be quite a long word group. ➡ **P 106-107**

NÜCHTERN UND SACHLICH

Magazines and newspapers are still the preferred medium for advertising in Germany, television advertising being strictly regulated by law. Herr Dieter Kirschner, client services director at Saatchi & Saatchi in Frankfurt, emphasized that Germans like to see the product and hear the facts, in contrast to British consumers who appreciate a humorous advertisement requiring lateral thinking. It seems, though, that the Germans are gradually being teased away from their rational approach.

FILAWORD
die Werbung *advertising*
werben *to advertise*
die Zeitung *newspaper*
die Zeitschrift *magazine*
das Fernsehen *television*
die Agentur *agency*

Werbung in Deutschland und Großbritannien

FACTFINDER
**3 What does a German beer advert usually show in addition to a bottle?

Herr Kirschner: Wir haben in Deutschland eine sehr nüchterne Mentalität: eher sachlich orientiert, weniger emotional, mehr rational. Das wirkt sich natürlich auch in der Werbung aus. Während zum Beispiel in England der Biermarkt eher humorvoll beworben wird, wird in Deutschland in aller Regel eine Flasche mit einem gefüllten Glas vor irgendeinem Hintergrund abgebildet. Es gelingt uns aber in zunehmendem Maße, auch in Deutschland über diesen rationalen Anspruch hinauszukommen und zusätzliche Dimensionen in die Werbung zu bekommen.

DATABASE
eher ... weniger ... mehr *more ... less ... more*
Das wirkt sich ... aus *That affects ...*
Es gelingt uns *We're succeeding*
in zunehmendem Maße *increasingly*
über ... hinauszukommen *to get away from ...*
Anspruch (m) *approach*

FILAFACT *wird/werden*
Notice how Herr Kirschner makes impersonal statements:

Während in England der Biermarkt humorvoll *beworben* **wird** ...
(While in Britain the beer market *is* targetted humorously ...)
... **wird** in Deutschland eine Flasche *abgebildet*
(... in Germany, a bottle *is* depicted)

Look out for *wird* (is) and *werden* (are).
➡ **P 102-104**

Vom Coil zum Kunden 1

With more than 300,000 BMWs on Britain's roads, the blue and white propeller emblem is a familiar sight. UK sales rose during the 1980s to top 50,000 units in 1990, and this steady growth has ensured that BMW seeks to expand countertrade.

Although BMWs are unmistakably 'Made in Germany', the company aims to concentrate on core competences like design and development, and buys in around 50% of its components, including many from abroad. Lydmet and British Steel are two suppliers for the BMW 3 Series. In a ten-part survey, **Deutsches Business-Magazin** traces the progress of two components from production in the UK, through processing and fitting in Munich, to export back to the UK – as components of an upmarket saloon.

Chilled-Iron Camshafts

Lydmet operates in the highly specialized field of chilled iron camshafts. With automotive manufacturers switching to chilled iron, and the advent of four-valve technology requiring two camshafts instead of one, demand outstrips supply. Production facilities are therefore being expanded to double capacity.

Mr Barry Giles, deputy sales manager, was initially employed to provide sales support, after-sales service and quality liaison in Germany. His background in languages and his previous post as technical translator at Mercedes-Benz in Stuttgart gave him the requisite skills for tackling a competitive market where closeness to the customer is vital: "When I started, the companies were grateful that they could liaise with somebody who actually spoke German. A lot of barriers came down very suddenly, and business increased considerably during that period, especially with BMW." Customers will generally feel more comfortable if there is a contact on their doorstep, and consequently Lydmet runs two agents in Germany, one specifically for BMW.

The final inspection process. As the camshafts are being packed into crates for dispatch to Munich, experienced operators check them by eye against BMW's inspection criteria.

Zulieferer

Ein Automobilwerk kann nicht alles allein herstellen. Es wird daher von tausenden spezialisierten Betrieben im In- und Ausland beliefert. Rund die Hälfte des Fahrzeugwertes stellt die Belegschaft von BMW her, die anderen 50% kauft BMW zu. Etwa 15% der Teile stammen aus dem Ausland. *(Zeitmotor)*

Filaskill

Of course, when you read German in the 'real world' you won't have **Filafact** and **Database** to help you. **Vom Coil zum Kunden** gives you practice in working out gist on your own. Read through each part several times, then use the *Glossary* for help with individual words. And remember – you can always come back later and try again once you've worked through later sections of **Deutsches Business-Magazin**.

Metal from the melting furnace is being transferred to a holding furnace where it is adjusted to the customer's specifications before being poured.

TiP

"You couldn't really operate the way we do in Germany if you didn't have somebody here in the company who can speak German. It's a must. Most of the buyers can speak English, but people looking after supplies want to speak to somebody in their own language if they have a problem."
(Barry Giles, Lydmet)

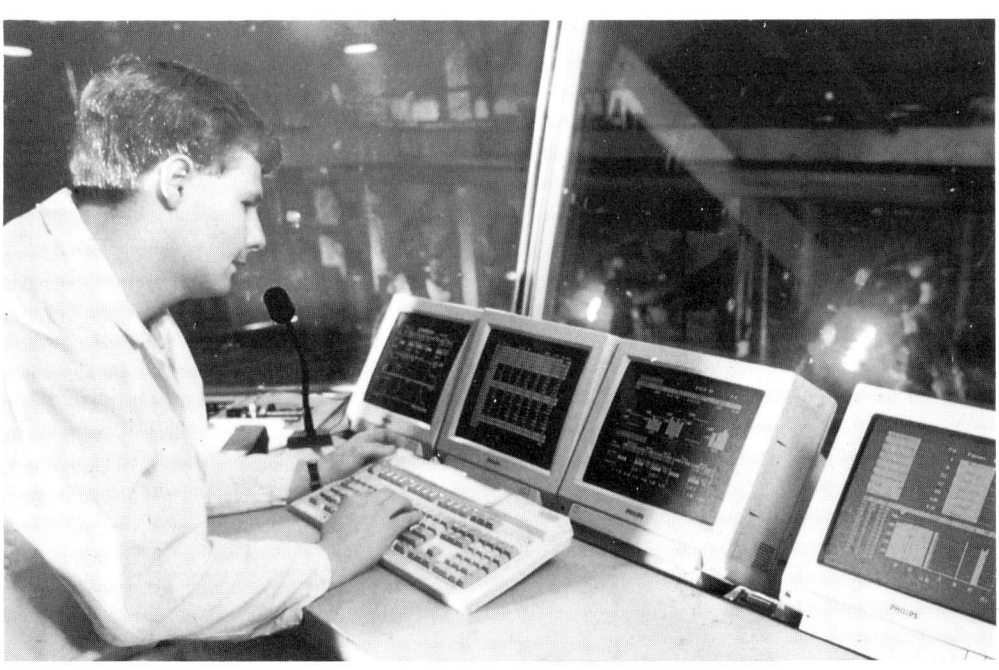

The main foundry control cabin is equipped for on-line data acquisition. Extensive use is made of statistical process control techniques to ensure product consistency and compliance with quality expectations.

„Soll und Haben" - das Gebäude der Deutschen Bank in Frankfurt

BANKFURT - FINANZZENTRUM DEUTSCHLANDS

German banking has traditionally been tightly regulated, and conservative. The principal concern has been to ensure that banks are financially sound. The banking scene is dominated by universal banks offering a complete range of services. There are well over 4000 banks operating at regional and local level, but the 'big three' are the main players, with branches throughout the country: Deutsche Bank, Dresdner Bank and Commerzbank.

The universal banks fall into three main categories: private commercial banks (*private Geschäftsbanken*), public-sector banks (*öffentlich-rechtliche Kreditinstitute*), comprising savings banks and their central clearing houses, and cooperative banks (*genossenschaftliche Kreditinstitute*), e.g. *Volksbanken, Raiffeisenbanken*. Additionally there are a large number of specialist banks, e.g. mortgage banks (*Hypothekenbanken*) and building societies (*Bausparkassen*).

The exclusive right to issue banknotes resides with the *Deutsche Bundesbank*, Germany's independent central bank in Frankfurt. It regulates the money supply and amount of credit available to the economy. Overall responsibility for policing Germany's strict banking regulations lies with the *Bundesaufsichtsamt für das Kreditwesen* in Berlin. Beyond ensuring the banks' solvency, its remit covers the way banks go about their business.

German banks are big shareholders in German industry, and the power of the banks is an evergreen theme for discussion. Private investors in Germany are more cautious than their Anglo-Saxon counterparts, and favour safe fixed-interest savings rather than shares.

Universalbanken

Dr Bernd Sprenger of the *Bundesverband deutscher Banken* outlined the range of services offered by universal banks.

FACTFINDER
**1 What two activities are not undertaken by the universal bank itself?

Dr. Sprenger: Universalbank heißt, daß diese Bank praktisch alle Bankgeschäfte durchführt mit Ausnahme von zwei Geschäften: Banknoten darf heutzutage nur die Notenbank ausgeben, und die meisten Institute haben für das Hypothekengeschäft Tochtergesellschaften. Aber die gesamte übrige Palette, das heißt Kredite, Spareinlagen, Wertpapiere, Zahlungsverkehr – alle diese Dinge führen hier die meisten Banken unter einem Dach durch.

DATABASE
heißt, daß *means that*
mit Ausnahme von *except for*
darf ... ausgeben ... *may issue*
Notenbank (*f*) *central bank, bank authorized to issue banknotes*
das heißt *that is, i.e.*
alle diese Dinge *all these things*
unter einem Dach *under one roof*

FILAFACT *verbs*
Notice how the verb *durchführen* (carry out) can be split up into two components:

..., daß diese Bank alle Bankgeschäfte *durchführt*.
Alle diese Dinge *führen* die meisten Banken *durch*.

Some German verbs have separable prefixes (*sep.*): the first part may separate and appear at the end of the sentence or clause. ➡ P 102, 107

FILASKILL
All the material in *Deutsches Business-Magazin* was collected in Germany. It's language you'll come across in a magazine, in a brochure or out and about. Whenever you're having difficulties, move on to something else or have a rest and read through the German later. As in real life, it's usually not necessary to understand every word.

FILAWORD
das Geld *money*
die Währung *currency*
die deutsche Mark, die D-Mark *Deutschmark, German mark, D-Mark*
die Bank *bank*
die Zentrale *headquarters*
die Filiale *branch*
die Börse *stock exchange*
der Kredit *credit, loan*
die Aktie *share*
das Wertpapier *security*

Frankfurt

Internationaler Partner

Barclays' target market in Germany consists of the top 500 German companies plus other selected middle-market companies with strong export-related activities. According to Mr Chris Davis, assistant general manager in Frankfurt, Barclays concentrates on niche activities, as it cannot compete with the larger German banks on their home ground: "One of the perpetual complaints we receive from companies further down the scale is that they might like to do a bit more business with us, but they have to give it to the Deutsche Bank, the Dresdner, or the Commerz, as their principal minority shareholder." Barclays has been seeking to develop its profile in Germany through the purchase of private banking house Merck Finck & Co., the opening of a branch office in east Germany, and entry into the German credit-card market.

BARCLAYS
BARCLAYS BANK PLC

Chris Davis
Robert Becker 
Norbert Schramm 

Der Tanz auf dem Vulkan

Herr Robert Becker, risk manager, sees his job as a "dance on the edge of a volcano".

FACTFINDER
**1 What two sides of the business are separated?
***2 What are Herr Becker's two main aims in his job?

Herr Becker: Wir haben hier bei uns im Hause klar getrennt zwischen der Marketing-Seite und der Risikobetrachtung. Die Kollegen haben die Aufgabe, den Kunden zu identifizieren. Meine spezielle Aufgabe ist es, die Kreditanträge zu prüfen. Die Zielrichtung ist ganz klar: so viel Geschäft wie nur möglich zu machen und möglichst das Risiko zu verhindern. Das ist halt immer ein Tanz auf einem Vulkan.

DATABASE
Wir haben ... klar getrennt *There's a clear division ...*
Aufgabe (f) *task, function*
die Kreditanträge zu prüfen *to examine the credit applications*
so viel ... wie nur möglich *as much ... as possible*
Geschäft ... zu machen *to do ... business*
zu verhindern *to avoid*

FILAFACT *zu + infinitive*
Notice how Herr Becker uses the infinitive form of a verb, after *zu*:

die Aufgabe, ... *zu identifizieren.*
(the task *to identify* ...)

In German you need to look for the infinitive at the end of a sentence or clause. ➡ P 108

TIP
As Norbert Schramm stressed, you have to be on your toes when you meet a prospective client. Most Germans like a bit of initial chitchat, but some find it a waste of time and expect your presentation right away.

Was ist wo auf deutschen Eurochecks?

EXECUTIVE PUZZLE
1 Which do you fill in first, the amount or the payee?
2 What do you have to fill in on a Eurocheque that you wouldn't have to fill in on a normal British cheque?
3 What is the German for: *a* bank sort code *b* account number *c* cheque number?

Eine Präsentation

Manager Herr Norbert Schramm outlined how to approach your prospective client.

FACTFINDER
*3 What two examples of small talk does Herr Schramm give?

Herr Schramm: Man kommt ins Zimmer, begrüßt sich und versucht so ein bißchen über Smalltalk das Gespräch in Gang zu halten, guckt aus dem Fenster, „das Wetter ist schön", redet über den Urlaub, der vielleicht gerade bevorsteht, und versucht dann so langsam ins Geschäft hineinzukommen. Es gibt auch die Erfahrung, daß man dann ganz schnell abgeblockt wird, so nach dem Motto: „Wir wollen uns doch nicht gegenseitig die Zeit stehlen. Zehn Minuten haben Sie bei mir, nun erzählen Sie doch mal, was Sie besser machen können als andere Banken." Und dann steht man ziemlich alleine da und soll sich in relativ kurzer Zeit präsentieren.

DATABASE
Man ... begrüßt sich *You ... greet each other*
... in Gang zu halten *to keep ... going*
den Urlaub, der vielleicht gerade bevorsteht *the holiday which may be coming up*
daß man ... abgeblockt wird *that you're cut short ...*
Wir wollen uns doch nicht gegenseitig die Zeit stehlen *We surely don't want to waste each other's time*

FILAFACT *es gibt*
Es gibt or *gibt es* is generally equivalent to 'there is/are'. To express 'there was/were', people use *es gab* or *gab es*. ➡ P 99-100

Frankfurt

Verläßlichkeit und Solidität

Deutsche Bank maintained a presence in London even before the first world war, but the confiscation of all assets twice over led to a period of domestic consolidation in the fifties and sixties. Since then it has regained the leading place in international business appropriate to a bank which handles around 20% of Germany's foreign trade. The opening of a capital markets subsidiary in 1987 in London and the purchase of Morgan Grenfell in 1989 are indicators of its strategy for a global future.

Global Player mit europäischer Basis

Herr Manfred ten Brink, general manager at Deutsche Bank in London, discussed the strategy for the nineties.

FACTFINDER
***1 Does Deutsche Bank expect to have an identical approach for all countries?

Herr ten Brink: In den neunziger Jahren würden wir uns gerne als einen *Global Player* sehen wollen, mit einer sehr starken europäischen Basis und dem Ursprung einer deutschen Bank. Wir können aber nicht erwarten, daß wir in allen Ländern immer das gleiche machen. Was man vielleicht erreichen kann, ist wenigstens den Kernteil dessen, was wir unsere *Corporate Culture* nennen, nämlich *Dependability*, Verläßlichkeit, Solidität.

DATABASE
würden wir uns gerne ... sehen wollen *we'd like to see ourselves ...*
daß wir ... machen *that we do ...*
den Kernteil dessen, was wir ... nennen *the core of what we call ...*

FILAFACT *verbs*
Notice the vowel change in the verb *können* when the verb is in the singular (I, you, he/she/it/one):

wir *können* erwarten (*plural*)
(we *can* expect)
man *kann* erreichen (*singular*)
(one *can* achieve)

Some of the most common German verbs have a vowel change. ➡ **P 102**

TiP

Cheques and credit cards are less widespread in Germany than in the UK and the US. Bills are generally paid by credit transfer or direct debit. The Eurocheque enjoys greater popularity than in the UK, but you will still need to carry some cash. And you cannot rely on finding a cash dispenser which accepts a British Visa card.

Macht oder Einfluß

German banks have traditionally provided industry with capital and baled out ailing companies. This has given rise to complex interconnections, but to what extent it gives the banks power over industry is a moot point. The issue has been likened to the Loch Ness Monster: "widely rumoured, occasionally claimed to be spotted, but impossible to pin down when scientifically researched" (*Financial Times*).

FACTFINDER
*2 What does Deutsche Bank have, if not power?
**3 Which company is Daimler-Benz's biggest shareholder?

Herr ten Brink: Britische Banken werden dafür kritisiert, daß sie keine Industriebeteiligung haben, und deutsche Banken werden in Deutschland dafür kritisiert, daß sie welche haben. Wir haben Einfluß und sind auch stolz darauf, und den Einfluß möchten wir auch gelegentlich ausnutzen. Nicht als Macht – das können wir gar nicht; die Firmen sind heute viel zu selbständig. Selbst im Falle Daimler-Benz, wo wir immerhin mit über 28% der größte Aktionär sind, ist es nicht so, daß etwa das ganze Bankgeschäft der Daimler-Benz-Gruppe mit der Deutschen Bank gemacht würde.

DATABASE
werden dafür kritisiert, daß *are criticized that*
Industriebeteiligung (*f*) *industrial holdings*
Einfluß (*m*) *influence*
das können wir gar nicht *that's something we can't do anyway*
ist es nicht so, daß *it isn't the case that*
gemacht würde *is transacted*

FILAFACT *kein*
Notice how *kein* is used to make things negative:

keine Industriebeteiligung
(*no* industrial holdings)

k+*ein* has the same endings as *ein*. ➡ **P 97-98**

FILASKILL
If you've read through a piece of German a couple of times and are missing some key words (maybe *Macht*) try the *Glossary*. Check through its introduction first.

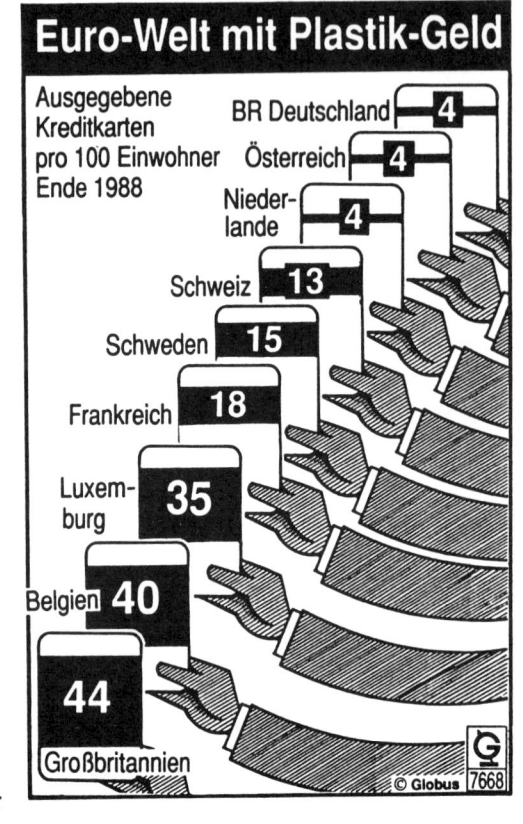

Euro-Welt mit Plastik-Geld

Ausgegebene Kreditkarten pro 100 Einwohner Ende 1988

- BR Deutschland 4
- Österreich 4
- Niederlande 4
- Schweiz 13
- Schweden 15
- Frankreich 18
- Luxemburg 35
- Belgien 40
- Großbritannien 44

EXECUTIVE PUZZLE
Have a look at the countries in the two charts *Euro-Welt mit Plastik-Geld* and *Wohnen unter eigenem Dach* and see if you can reconstitute the countries below. Remember to make the first letter a capital.

1 wchszei 2 rnhcifeark 3 leninedrade
4 irthesörec 5 inonibrengatßr 6 nasipen

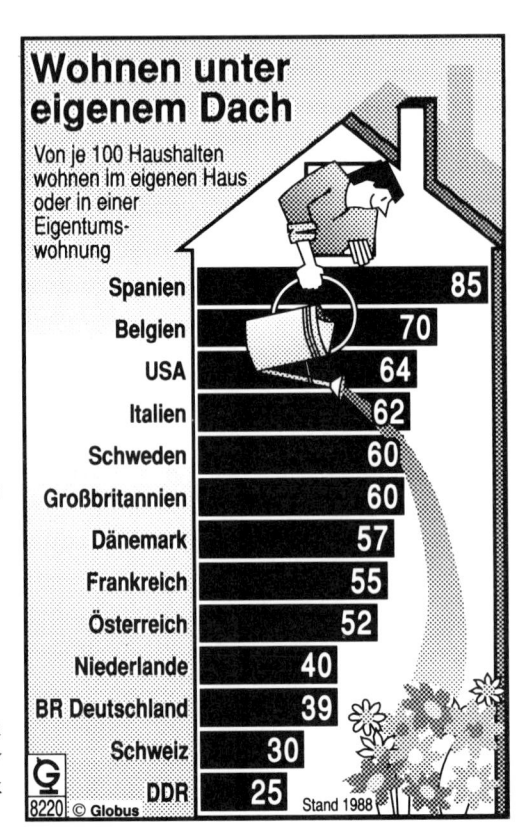

Wohnen unter eigenem Dach

Von je 100 Haushalten wohnen im eigenen Haus oder in einer Eigentumswohnung

- Spanien 85
- Belgien 70
- USA 64
- Italien 62
- Schweden 60
- Großbritannien 60
- Dänemark 57
- Frankreich 55
- Österreich 52
- Niederlande 40
- BR Deutschland 39
- Schweiz 30
- DDR 25

Stand 1988

Rund ums Geld

Although Germans tend to be free-spending when it comes to holidays, cars and clothes, there is a well-established tradition of saving. One prime incentive is home ownership. Houses and flats are expensive, and you need a hefty slice of your own money as deposit – a major reason for the relatively low percentage of home-owners.

Chancen für britische Bausparkassen?

This newspaper article highlights the difference between acquiring a home in Germany and the UK.

FACTFINDER
*1 How many hours does the average German earner have to work to buy a house?
*2 How does this compare with a British counterpart?

Auch Englands Bausparkassen blicken auf die Chancen, die sich für sie in dem europäischen Binnenmarkt bieten. In einer detaillierten Analyse stellte die Nationwide Anglia gravierende Unterschiede auf den verschiedenen Wohnungsmärkten der europäischen Gemeinschaft fest. Danach braucht der durchschnittliche Brite nur 9000 bis 10 000 Stunden für den Kauf einer durchschnittlichen Bleibe zu arbeiten, für den deutschen Durchschnittsverdiener dagegen sind es über 20 000 Stunden. (Süddeutsche Zeitung)

DATABASE
die sich ... bieten *which present themselves ...*
gravierende Unterschiede *substantial differences*
braucht ... zu arbeiten *... needs to work*
dagegen *by contrast*

FILAFACT *case*
The words *des*, *der* and *eines*, *einer* are forms of the definite/indefinite article which can be equivalent to 'of the'/'of an':

die Hälfte *des* Fahrzeugwerts
auf den Wohnungsmärkten *der* europäischen Gemeinschaft
für den Kauf *einer* Bleibe

This is called the genitive case. ➡ P 98

FILASKILL
You may come across unfamiliar grammar terms in *Filafact*. You'll find explanations in the *Grammar* (➡ P 96).

EXECUTIVE SKILLS
*1 Try and find German equivalents for the following: *a* average *b* single market *c* European Community.
***2 *fest* is part of a separable verb. Can you find the other part? You may need the *Glossary*.
*3 Which of the following refer to some kind of dwelling place? *a* Kauf *b* Bleibe *c* Verdiener *d* Wohnung.

FILAWORD
das Bargeld *cash*
der Scheck *cheque*
die Kreditkarte *credit card*
die Rechnung *bill, invoice*
die Überweisung *credit transfer*
die Lastschrift *direct debit*
der Geldautomat *cash dispenser, automatic teller*
die Hypothek *mortgage*
der Bausparvertrag *home-loan agreement*
sparen *to save*

Geld aus dem Automaten

EXECUTIVE PUZZLE
See if you can get some money out of a cash dispenser by matching up the captions and operations.

a Geheimzahl eintippen. Vertippt? Korrekturtaste drücken und gesamte Geheimzahl neu eingeben.
b Drücken Sie die Funktionstaste „Auszahlung", dann den gewünschten Auszahlungsbetrag eintippen.
c Eurocheque-Karte entnehmen. Dann erfolgt die Geldausgabe.
d Noch einfacher erhalten Sie Ihr Bargeld mit der Schnellauszahlungstaste „400 DM".
e Eurocheque-Karte so einstecken, wie es das Symbol am Geld & Service AUTOMATEN zeigt.

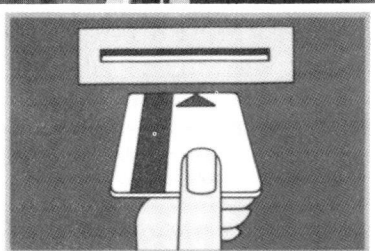

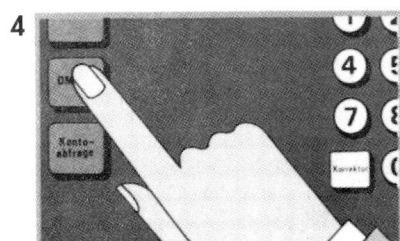

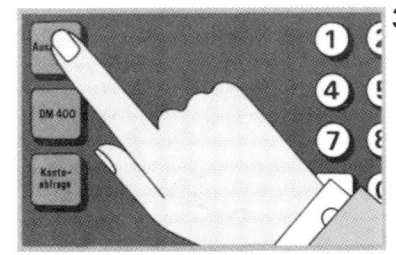

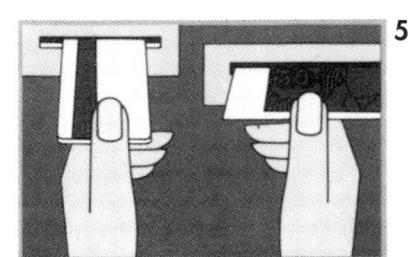

Frankfurt

Messeland Nr. 1

At a fair, you won't get far without asking questions. Start by working out what we asked Herr Rolf Hardy Pulina of the Messe Frankfurt. Most German questions begin with a verb (e.g. *Kommen viele britische Firmen?*) or with a W question word like the following:

Was ...?	What ...?
Was für ...?	What kind of ...?
Wie ...?	How ...?
Wie viele (or Wieviel) ...?	How many (or How much) ...?
Welche ...?	Which? or What?

FACTFINDER

***1 We asked Herr Pulina about the following topics. Can you put them in the order in which we asked about them?
  a The presence of British companies at fairs in Frankfurt.
  b What a fair offers to its exhibitors and visitors.
  c The costs involved.
  d The number of trade-fair complexes in Germany.
  e The international standing of German trade fairs.
  f The type of company exhibiting at Frankfurt.

Business-Magazin: Welche Stellung haben die deutschen Messen international?
Herr Pulina: Die Bundesrepublik ist Messeland Nummer eins in der Welt. Hier ist eine Tradition da: Die Messe Frankfurt, zum Beispiel, ist 750 Jahre alt.
Business-Magazin: Wie viele Messeplätze gibt es in der Bundesrepublik?
Herr Pulina: Wir haben hier fünf große Messeplätze: Frankfurt, München, Köln, Düsseldorf, Hannover. Und unter diesen Fünfen herrscht ein gesunder Konkurrenzkampf.
Business-Magazin: Was bietet eine Messe den Ausstellern und Fachbesuchern?
Herr Pulina: Messen sind das wichtigste Marketingmedium, das es überhaupt gibt. Die Messe Frankfurt verkauft heute im Prinzip keine Hallen, sondern Zugang zum Weltmarkt. Für Fachbesucher bieten wir nicht nur Produkte an, sondern auch Dienstleistungen und Information.
Business-Magazin: Was für Firmen stellen hier allgemein aus?
Herr Pulina: 90 Prozent unserer Aussteller kommen aus dem Mittelstand, eigentlich 99 Prozent.
Business-Magazin: Kommen viele britische Firmen?
Herr Pulina: Ja. Wir haben 1990 fast 1000 britische Aussteller gehabt, also Firmen; dann an die 9000 Fachbesucher.
Business-Magazin: Wie hoch sind die Kosten für den Aussteller?
Herr Pulina: Der Quadratmeter kostet durchschnittlich 250 Mark. Das ist die Miete für die nackte Fläche, hinzu kommen dann Standkosten.

DATABASE

ist ... da *there is ...*
unter diesen *amongst these*
herrscht *there's* (literally *reigns*)
das wichtigste ..., das es überhaupt gibt *the most important ... there is*
verkauft ... keine ... sondern Zugang zum *doesn't sell ... but access to the*
bieten wir ... an *we offer ...*
unserer Aussteller *of our exhibitors*
Mittelstand (m) *small and medium-sized companies*
haben ... gehabt *had ...*
also *i.e.*
an die *close on*
Das ist *That's*
hinzu kommen dann *then there are also*

Germany has an unrivalled position in staging major international trade fairs. The main centres are Hanover, Düsseldorf, Munich, Frankfurt and Cologne. Berlin, long restricted as a trade-fair centre by its location, is working hard to achieve similar status, while Leipzig, formerly eastern Europe's shop window, has some way to go before measuring up to western German standards.

Whatever your product may be, you can be fairly sure that there will be a specialist trade fair somewhere in Germany. Trade fairs are a way of life there, and you cannot expect to be taken seriously by prospective buyers unless you attend the right trade fairs regularly. Responses may be slow, and you may go for several years without any concrete results, but remember the British manufacturer who, after five years of exhibiting, received his first order from a man who had visited his stand every year. Asked some time later why he had waited five years to place an order, the reply was a firm: "I wanted to be sure you were serious about the German market"!

FILAWORD

die Fachmesse *(specialist) trade fair*
der Aussteller *exhibitor*
ausstellen *(sep.) to exhibit*
die Konkurrenz *competition*
der Markt *market*

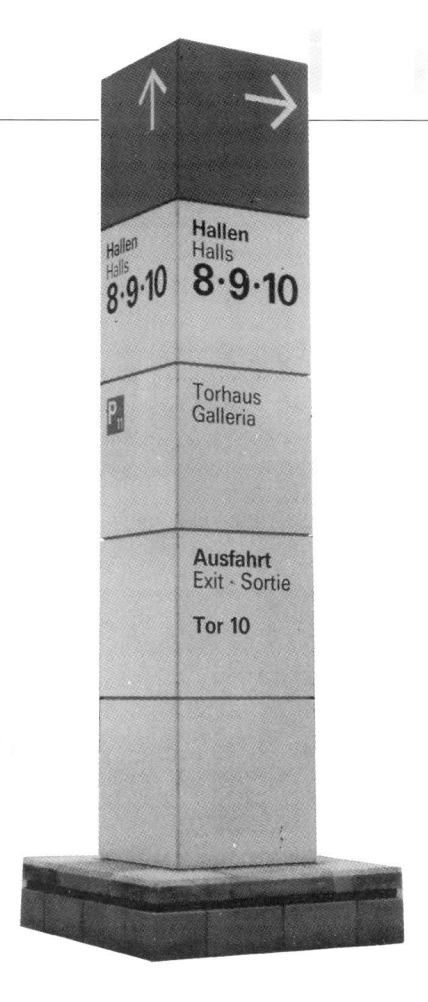

Die Raumtechnik®
Messebau

Macht Sie der Gedanke an Ihre nächste Messebeteiligung nervös?

Das muß nicht sein: Delegieren Sie! Wir bauen nicht nur Ihren Ausstellungsstand, sondern nehmen Ihnen auch alle mit der Messe zusammenhängenden Arbeiten ab, die Sie gerne loswerden wollen.

1  2
3  4 
5  6 

FILAFACT *verbs*

Look out for the verb-ending *-(e)t* in the singular form *er/sie/es/man* (he/she/it/one), and the ending *-(e)n* in the plural forms *wir/sie/Sie*:

der Quadratmeter kost**et** (*sing.*)	(the square metre *costs*)
ein Konkurrenzkampf herrsch**t** (*sing.*)	(competition *exists*)
wir biet**en** (*pl*)	(we *offer*)
die Aussteller komm**en** (*pl*)	(the exhibitors *come*)

If the verb is singular, its subject must be singular (e.g. *der Quadratmeter*, *ein Konkurrenzkampf*). If the verb is plural, its subject must be plural (e.g. *wir*, *die Aussteller*). ➡ **P 103**

EXECUTIVE SKILLS

*1 Get used to recognizing the components of compound words. Try splitting each of these into two words:
  a Messeplatz   *b* Konkurrenzkampf
  c Fachbesucher *d* Weltmarkt
  e Dienstleistung *f* Standkosten.

*2 Plural forms vary, depending on the noun (➡ **P 97**). Can you find the plural forms of these words in the interview:
  a Dienstleistung *b* Messe *c* Firma *d* Platz *e* Produkt.

**3 *Nicht nur*, 'not only', is often followed by the equivalent of 'but also'. Can you find the German for 'but also'?

*4 Can you spot the German equivalents for the numbers 'one' and 'five'? Check and learn the numbers (➡ **P 108**).

FILASKILL

Try some instant vocabulary expansion every now and then. When you come across a short noun, check the *Glossary* to see if it occurs in compounds. When you come across a long word, check in the *Glossary* whether it can be split into components.

T i P

Exhibiting at a trade fair is not a matter to be taken lightly. Herr Pulina stressed the importance of visiting a trade fair before deciding to exhibit, to see what goes on. Exhibition staff with language skills, and detailed follow-up are prerequisites for success.

DATABASE

der Gedanke an *the thought of*
Das muß nicht sein *It's not necessary*
nehmen Ihnen ... ab *relieve you of ...*
die Sie gerne loswerden wollen *which you want to get rid of*

FILAFACT *vocabulary*

German has a lot of verbs ending in *-ieren*. It's often easy to deduce their meaning:

deleg*ieren* (to delegate)	produz*ieren* (to produce)
export*ieren* (to export)	organis*ieren* (to organize)

EXECUTIVE PUZZLE

See if you can match these captions with the various aspects of organizing an exhibition at a fair depicted in the advertisement (1-6):
  a Messe-Werbung *b* Produkt-Präsentation
  c Entwurf des Messestandes *d* Stand-Organisation
  e Messestände in individueller Bauweise *f* Presse-Betreuung.

Frankfurt

„Das grösste Chemieareal der Welt"

Germany's three chemical giants are located within a 200 km radius of Frankfurt: Bayer in Leverkusen to the north, Hoechst in its own district in Frankfurt, and BASF to the south in Ludwigshafen. After demand failed to live up to expectations following expansion in the 1970s, Germany's chemicals industry moved quickly to cut excess capacity in bulk chemicals and diversify into speciality chemicals and pharmaceuticals. Heavy investment in research, and foreign acquisitions have internationalized an industry where sales outside Germany are now more than double the domestic turnover.

FILAWORD
die Chemie *chemistry, chemicals (industry)*
die Chemikalien (f, pl) *chemicals*
die Forschung *research*
die Umwelt *environment*
der Umweltschutz *environmental protection*

Zahlen und Fakten

Gründung:	1865 **B**adische **A**nilin- und **S**oda**f**abrik
	1925 Zusammenschluß mit Bayer und Hoechst zur IG Farben
	1953 Neugründung als BASF
Stammwerk:	Ludwigshafen
Gesellschaftsform:	AG
Mitarbeiter:	55 000 (Stammwerk)
Gewerkschaft:	IG Chemie
Branche:	Chemische Industrie

FACTFINDER
**1 How many kilometres of *a* rail track *b* pipeline and *c* road does BASF have in total?

Werk Ludwigshafen der BASF Aktiengesellschaft am Rhein: Stammwerk der BASF-Gruppe, zu der weltweit rund 330 Gesellschaften gehören. Mit 6,6 Quadratkilometern Werksfläche das größte zusammenhängende Chemieareal der Welt. Ein Komplex von 1600 Gebäuden, 100 Kilometern Straßen, 200 Kilometern Eisenbahnschienen, über 2000 Kilometern Rohrleitungen. Arbeitsstätte für 55 000 Mitarbeiter. *(BASF Ludwigshafen)*

DATABASE
zu der ... gehören *to which ... belong*
der Welt *in the world*

FILAFACT *prepositions*
The prepositions *an, bei, für, in, von, zu* can be fused with the following definite article:
  am Rhein = *an* de*m* Rhein
  zur IG Farben = *zu* de*r* IG Farben
Look out for the following forms:
  am/beim/im/vom/zum = *an/bei/in/von/zu* de*m*,
  zur = *zu* de*r*, *fürs* = *für* da*s*.
➡ P 106

FILASKILL
Filafacts are facts to file away in your memory. They'll help you build up a knowledge base which will enable you to make sense of German in other contexts. If you can't remember them easily, don't be discouraged – keep coming back to them and they'll gradually sink in as you find other examples. It's also a good idea to follow up cross-references to the *Grammar*.

Forschung und Entwicklung

FACTFINDER
 *2 What proportion of BASF's products has been developed recently?

Rund ein Fünftel der Mitarbeiter sind in der Forschung tätig. Rund ein Drittel des Sortiments der BASF besteht aus Produkten, die in den letzten zehn Jahren entwickelt wurden. *(BASF Ludwigshafen)*

FILAFACT *fractions*
Fractions are recognizable by the ending *-tel*, e.g. *Drittel* (third), *Viertel* (quarter), *Zehntel* (tenth). *Hälfte* (half) is an exception. ➡ P 108

TiP
There has always been an emphasis on training and quality in German companies, which goes hand-in-hand with a highly developed sense of corporate spirit and tradition. People have been trained in the company and have strong ties of loyalty.

Ludwigshafen und die BASF

Dr Matthias Hensel, press officer at BASF, stressed the loyalty of employees and the company's positive approach to training.

FACTFINDER
**3 What are the employees proud of?

Dr. Hensel: Eine Besonderheit der BASF ist die starke Verankerung mit Ludwigshafen und der Umgebung. Die Leute sind richtig stolz darauf, „Aniliner" (Mitarbeiter der **B**adischen **A**nilin- und **S**oda**f**abrik) zu sein. Man sagt hier: „Wenn man einmal bei der BASF ist, dann ist man immer bei der BASF."

Ausbildung

The training workshops at BASF are well equipped. Management does not believe in skimping when it comes to training the next generation.

FACTFINDER
 *4 Where does training bring results?

Dr. Hensel: Die Ausbildungswerkstätten sind phantastisch ausgestattet mit den neuesten Geräten. „Da ist uns die Mark nicht zu schade," sagen die Verantwortlichen, „je besser wir unsere jungen Leute ausbilden, desto besser sind sie hinterher in der Produktion."

DATABASE
Da ist uns die Mark nicht zu schade *We think every penny's well spent*
je besser ... desto besser *the better ... the better*

Frankfurt

Die Struktur des Unternehmens

There are not nearly as many companies quoted on the stock exchange in Germany as in the UK, and BASF Aktiengesellschaft is unusual in having a large number of small **shareholders**, many of them employees of the company. The employees are given an annual bonus either in cash or in shares at a slightly reduced rate. The **supervisory board** has twenty members; half are elected by the shareholders and half by the employees. It is answerable to the shareholders. The **board of management** is responsible for day-to-day business decisions and is answerable to the supervisory board.

In 1987, the chemicals industry abandoned the distinction between wage (*Lohn*) and salary (*Gehalt*) as barriers separating white-collar workers (*Angestellte*) and blue-collar workers (*gewerbliche Arbeitnehmer*) disappear. The neutral term *Entgelt* replaces *Lohn* and *Gehalt*.

FACTFINDER
*2 Match up the words in bold above with their German equivalents below.

Aktionäre: Etwa 400 000, überwiegend Kleinaktionäre. Viele Mitarbeiter sind Aktionäre.
Aufsichtsrat: 20 Mitglieder, 10 von den Aktionären gewählt, 10 von den Beschäftigten der BASF gewählt. Aufsichtsratsvorsitzender von den Vertretern der Kapitalseite gewählt. Der Aufsichtsrat ist den Aktionären verantwortlich.
Vorstand: Verantwortlich für die täglichen operativen Entscheidungen des Geschäftsbetriebes und für das Ergebnis. 11 Mitglieder. Vom Aufsichtsrat benannt. Der Vorstand ist dem Aufsichtsrat verantwortlich.

Umweltschutz - ein sensibler Bereich

Like all German chemical companies, BASF is keen to convince a critical public that it is concerned for the environment.

Hauptprobleme:	Luft und Abwasser
Ausgaben für Umweltschutz pro Jahr:	ungefähr 1,2 Milliarden Mark (1989)
Abteilung Umweltschutz und Arbeitssicherheit:	ca. 1000 Mitarbeiter
Umweltschutzüberwachungszentrale:	1988 fertiggestellt

EXECUTIVE SKILLS
*1 A word that seems familiar may not always mean what you think. What kind of 'area' is *ein sensibler Bereich*?
*2 Can you split up the noun *Umweltschutzüberwachungszentrale* into four nouns?

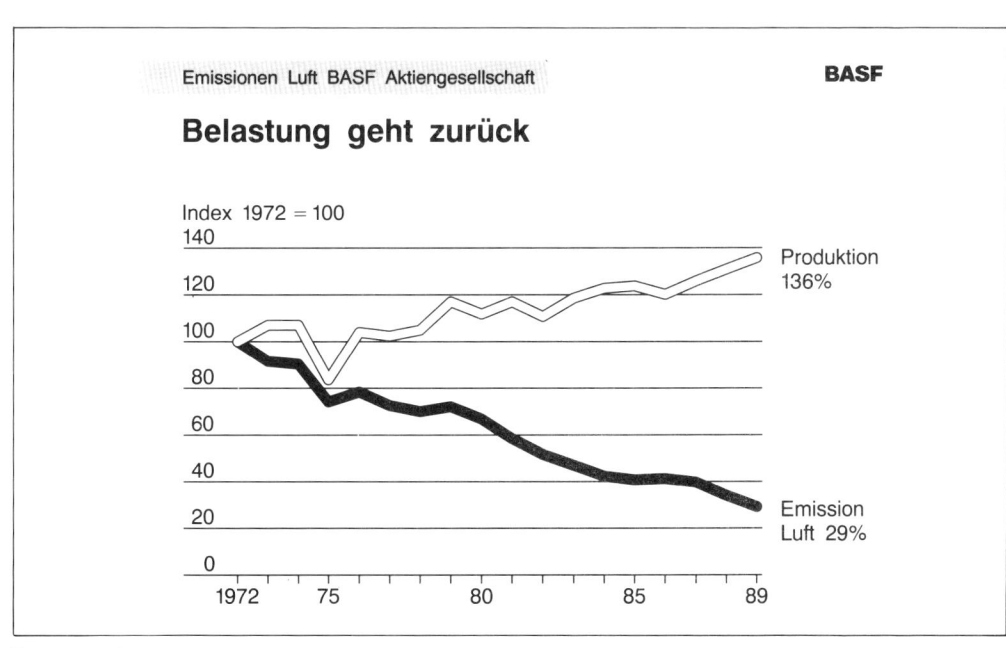

FILAFACT *past participles*
Verbs often appear in the form of past participles, e.g. sav*ed*, spen*t*, writt*en*. In English, most past participles end in -(e)d, -t or -(e)n. In German, they end in -(e)t or -en. You can recognize most of them by the syllable (-)*ge*- at the beginning or, in the case of separable verbs, after the prefix:

von den Aktionären *gewählt* (*elect*ed by the shareholders)
phantastisch *ausgestattet* (fantastically *equipped*)

But verbs with an inseparable prefix, e.g. *entwickeln, benennen*, and most verbs ending on -*ieren*, don't add (-)*ge*- in the past-participle form: *entwickelt* (develop*ed*), *benannt* (nominat*ed*), *delegiert* (delegat*ed*). ➡ P 103

FILASKILL
In German, you can't assume that it will be obvious if a noun is plural. For possible forms of the plural, check the *Grammar* (➡ P 97), and get used to checking the plural of nouns in the *Glossary*.

Emissionen Luft BASF Aktiengesellschaft — **BASF**

Belastung geht zurück

Index 1972 = 100

(Graph showing Produktion 136% rising and Emission Luft 29% falling from 1972 to 1989)

FACTFINDER
*1 Sind die Emissionen gestiegen oder gefallen?

DEUTSCHES BUSINESS-MAGAZIN **21**

Frankfurt

SPEZIALISTEN FÜR ANLAGENBAU

Zimmer AG and Davy Bamag GmbH were subsidiaries of Davy McKee AG, Frankfurt, until 1991. Zimmer specializes in planning and constructing polymer and synthetic-fibre plants. Davy Bamag designs and constructs water-purification and waste-water treatment plants. In 1991, both were bought up by Metallgesellschaft AG.

FILAWORD
die Anlage *plant*
bauen *to build, construct*
das Verfahren *process*
die Umwelttechnik *environmental technology*
die Tochtergesellschaft *subsidiary*
übernehmen *to take over*

Zahlen und Fakten

Gründung: 1951
Gründer: Hans J. Zimmer
Stammwerk: Frankfurt
Gewerkschaft: IG Metall
Branche: Anlagenbau

Polyester-Polykondensations-Anlage in Yizheng, Volksrepublik China – die größte der Welt

Von den Vorprodukten bis zur fertigen Faser

Herr Franz Dittrich, personnel coordinator for the board of management, gave a rundown of the products made by Zimmer plants.

FACTFINDER
*1 What are the main products manufactured by Zimmer plants?

Herr Dittrich: Die Bekanntheit von Zimmer basiert auf Synthesefasern. Das ist der Oberbegriff. Und dann gibt es Polyester. Dann gibt es Polyamid, und zwar das deutsche Perlon und Nylon 66 aus USA. Das sind die Hauptprodukte, die mit unseren Anlagen von den Vorprodukten bis zur fertigen Faser hergestellt werden.

DATABASE
die ... hergestellt werden *which are produced ...*
von ... bis zur *from ... through to the*

EXECUTIVE SKILLS
**1 Which is the odd one out and why?
  a Polyester *b* Synthesefaser *c* Polyamid.
*2 Which of these are plural?
  a Anlagen *b* Faser *c* Produkte.
  Check your answer in the *Glossary*.
***3 Can you find verbs belonging to the same 'family' as these nouns? *a* Basis *b* Herstellung. Now try to work out the infinitive form, which ends in *-en*.

Ein guter Kreislauf

Zimmer oversees the process of constructing a plant from the drawing board through to commissioning.

FACTFINDER
*2 Where does Zimmer buy some of the equipment?
*3 What does Zimmer guarantee?
**4 What is the last thing that Zimmer's specialists do before their return?

Herr Dittrich: Wir Anlagenbauer haben das Wissen, wie so eine Anlage zur Herstellung von Fasern ausschauen muß. Wir konzipieren sie hier bei uns, kaufen zum Teil die Ausrüstung hier in Deutschland oder in England und liefern sie an den Kunden aus. Dann gehen unsere Fachleute raus und überwachen die Montage der Anlage, denn wir garantieren ein Produkt. Wir garantieren Qualität und Quantität. Dann wird die Anlage angefahren, das Kundenpersonal wird geschult, und dann kommen unsere Leute wieder zurück. Wir machen dadurch einen guten Kreislauf.

DATABASE
wie so eine Anlage ... ausschauen muß *what such a plant ... has to look like*
sie *it (i.e.* die Anlage *(f))*

FILAFACT *passive*
Notice how Herr Dittrich makes general impersonal statements using the passive:

Die Anlage *wird* angefahren.
(The plant *is* started up.)
Das Kundenpersonal *wird geschult*.
(The customer's personnel *is trained*.)

In German, passives are formed with the verb *werden* and the past participle of another verb.
➡ P 102-104

EXECUTIVE SKILLS
***1 These verbs are each part of a separable verb (➡ P 102): *a* liefern *b* gehen *c* kommen.
  Try and find the other part in the interview.
**2 Company X has got its procedures mixed up. Can you put it on the right track by sorting out the correct order?
  a Die Anlage wird angefahren.
  b Dann liefern wir die Ausrüstung an den Kunden aus.
  c Dann kommen unsere Leute wieder zurück.
  d Wir konzipieren die Anlage.
  e Das Kundenpersonal wird geschult.
  f Unsere Fachleute überwachen die Montage der Anlage.
  g Wir kaufen die Ausrüstung.

Frankfurt

Über hundert Jahre Umwelttechnik

Davy Bamag has been specializing in environmental technology for water purification and waste treatment since 1872. We visited the company in Butzbach, a picture-book village amid Hesse cornfields about 30 kilometres from Frankfurt. Herr Karlheinz Dores, the managing director, talked about problems that necessitate complex water-purification processes.

Davy Bamag GmbH

Leistungsspektrum

Wirtschaftlichkeitsstudien
Forschung und Entwicklung
Planung und Beratung
Projektmanagement
Projektfinanzierung
Verfahrenstechnik und Konstruktion
Beschaffung und Lieferung
Errichtung und Inbetriebnahme
Personalschulung
Betrieb und Wartung
Anlagenmodernisierung

FILAFACT *nouns*
Nouns ending in *-ung* are feminine (*f*), e.g. *die Forschung*. ➡ **P 97**

EXECUTIVE SKILLS
***1 Expand your vocabulary by controlled experimentation. Try making verbs out of all the nouns in *Leistungsspektrum* ending in *-ung*. Simply remove the ending and add *-en* except in two cases, where it would help to read through *Forschung und Entwicklung* (➡ **P 20**) and *Ein guter Kreislauf* (➡ **P 22**). You'll have to split compound nouns.

ACTIONPACK
Build up a company profile by writing down in German any of the activities in *Leistungsspektrum* which your company carries out.

Eine wirtschaftliche Lösung

FACTFINDER
*1 What is a typical problem in Germany?
***2 What used to happen to many pollutants?

Herr Dores: Ein typisches Problem in der Bundesrepublik ist das Vorhandensein von Nitraten im Trinkwasser. Wir haben Verfahren entwickelt (und sind dabei, weitere zu entwickeln), um für diese Probleme in Zukunft eine wirtschaftliche Lösung anbieten zu können.

Heute stellt man fest, daß es sehr viele Probleme gibt, die in früheren Jahren dazu geführt haben, daß das Grundwasser verschmutzt wurde. Viele Schadstoffe, die früher unkontrolliert in den Boden gelangen konnten, werden heute mit modernen Meßgeräten festgestellt und zum Teil auch als krebserregende Stoffe klassifiziert. Sie müssen heute entfernt werden, ehe das Wasser in das Trinkwassernetz gegeben werden kann.

DATABASE
sind dabei, weitere zu entwickeln *are now developing others*
um ... anbieten zu können *in order to be able to offer ...*
stellt man fest, daß *people are realizing that*
die ... dazu geführt haben, daß ... verschmutzt wurde *which ... caused ... to be polluted*
die früher ... gelangen konnten *which used to be able to get ...*
Sie müssen ... entfernt werden *... they have to be removed*
gegeben werden kann *can be supplied*

FILAFACT *daß clauses*
When you see *daß* (that), you need to look for the *verb* at the end of the clause:

Heute stellt man fest,
daß es sehr viele Probleme *gibt*,
die in früheren Jahren dazu geführt haben,
daß das Grundwasser *verschmutzt wurde*.

Sometimes you'll find a word made up of *da-* plus *preposition* before the *daß* clause, e.g. *dazu* in the sentence above:

dazu ..., daß (*to the fact* that).
➡ **P 106-107**

EXECUTIVE SKILLS
*1 Try to find the plural forms for *a* Problem *b* Stoff *c* Verfahren. Check your answers in the *Glossary*.

T i P

Flexitime (Gleitzeit/gleitende Arbeitszeit) is widespread in Germany, and you may be unlucky if you want to contact someone after the core time (Kernzeit). On Fridays many offices close at lunchtime.

Trinkwasserwerk in Ägypten

Frankfurt

ⓑ Vom Coil zum Kunden 2

British Steel for the BMW Divider

In the early 1980s, when British Steel had gone through the major part of its rationalization process in the run-up to privatization, the company pursued a European strategy to compensate for the decline of the British motor industry. British Steel offices in major steel centres such as Düsseldorf help to ensure that the service offered from Britain is equivalent to that provided by local steel mills.

British Steel supplies steel for the divider that separates the saloon from the luggage compartment in the BMW 3 Series. The divider is specific, carrying its own quality and dimensions, and the steelmaking process is specified to producing the quality for that part. The steel coil is specially packed for shipping to ensure that it arrives at BMW's press shop in prime condition.

Mr John Tune, sales manager at Newport, is responsible for sales of British Steel strip products to the European car industry. Mr Tune stressed the close cooperation necessary with BMW before a new part is allocated: "BMW visit the steelworks to satisfy themselves of the plant capability. Following this, a sample quantity is pressed in their press shop, and we send a technical representative from the works to observe the pressing. Assuming the trial is successful and we have established our commercial position with regard to pricing and volume, we are then allocated a supply programme for the year."

Die Trennwand trennt den Gepäckraum vom Passagierraum.

The 25-ton coil is fully encased in a steel wrapping with waterproof paper on the inside. It is sent as a unit load and only removed at the warehouse in Munich.

BMW – Wer ist wer?

Hans Paul Thienel, Leiter Einkauf Rohmaterial und Verbindungselemente. Ausbildung: Studium Betriebswirtschaft. Hobbys: Fotografie, Bergsteigen, Skifahren.

500 Kilo Feinblech

Herr Hans Paul Thienel is head of purchasing for raw materials and fasteners at BMW's headquarters in Munich. *Deutsches Business-Magazin* asked him about steel procurement in general and for the divider in particular – one of those unglamorous but vital parts in a motor car.

Das Einkaufsvolumen

Herr Thienel: Das Einkaufsvolumen von BMW für Feinbleche liegt nahe bei 400 Millionen Mark im Jahr. BMW produziert 550 000 Autos im Jahr. Je nach Fahrzeug-Typ hat ein Auto 500 - 650 kg Feinblech.

Der Kontakt mit British Steel

Herr Thienel: Wir haben mit British Steel übers Jahr hinweg relativ oft Kontakt. Immer dann, wenn man einen neuen Auftrag an BS erteilt, werden Probelieferungen zusammen mit den Technikern von British Steel in den Preßwerken besprochen. Die Kaufleute treffen sich zirka ein- bis zweimal im Jahr, unter anderem, um ein Preis-Abschlußgespräch für das Folgejahr zu führen.

Die Trennwand

Herr Thienel: BMW bestellt von British Steel unter anderem auch Feinbleche für eine Trennwand, die im Fahrzeug den Gepäckraum vom Passagierraum trennt. Dieses Blech wird als Coil gekauft. Es hat eine Materialstärke von 0,7 mm und eine Coilbreite von 1400 mm. Der Werkstoff entspricht einer in der Stahlindustrie üblichen Materialqualität.

> **TiP**
>
> "In many ways we find it easy to deal with the Germans. They perhaps do things in a way we do. Once you have established good lines of communication, we find it very comfortable, very easy to deal with BMW and other German companies." (John Tune, British Steel Plc)

Frankfurter Spezialitäten

Frankfurt's old town hall, *Römer* (literally *Roman*), may have got its name from a house used by Italian merchants. The election of a new German emperor was debated here, and from 1562, when the emperor was first crowned in Frankfurt, the magnificent *Römersaal* became known as the *Kaisersaal*. The people of Frankfurt celebrated an imperial coronation in grand style. On the *Römerberg*, an ox was stuffed with chickens, suckling pigs and sausages, and roasted on a spit for the citizens, while red and white wine flowed from a fountain. The last coronation feast in the *Kaisersaal* was held in 1792, just before the emperor was forced to abdicate by Napoleon.

After centuries of imperial grandeur, Frankfurt became a stepping stone on Germany's path to democracy when the first democratic parliament was elected at the *Paulskirche* in 1848. During the second world war much of the *Altstadt* was destroyed, but the *Römer* has been painstakingly reconstructed.

Römer

FILAWORD
das Hotel *hotel*
das Zimmer *room*
das Bad *bath(room)*
die Toilette *toilet, lavatory*
das Frühstück *breakfast*

Sachsenhausen und „Ebbelwei"

No one's quite sure what makes *Apfelwein* (called *Ebbelwei* in local dialect) so popular in Frankfurt, but there's no doubt that this tart cider contributes to *Gemütlichkeit*, a typically German concept relating to a cosy get-together with friends. The place to go is Sachsenhausen, a district south of the Main and therefore strictly speaking in southern Germany, with all the attendant connotations of jolly conviviality.

FACTFINDER
*1 What season do opening times apply to?
*2 Can you get a hot meal on a winter Tuesday?
*3 When do you need to reserve a table?

Dauth-Schneider

– Apfelwein-Lokal –

Öffnungszeiten: Sommer (1.4. - 30.9.):

Dienstag bis Freitag von 16.00 bis 24.00 Uhr

Samstag, Sonntag, Feiertag von 12.00 bis 24.00 Uhr

Warme Küche: wie Öffnungszeiten

Ruhetag: Winter: Montag + Dienstag

Reservierung: für Gruppen nötig

Kreditkarten: –

Frankfurt auf einen Blick

Einwohnerzahl:	627 900
Fluß:	Main
Postleitzahl:	D/W-6000
Telefonvorwahl:	(0)69-
Flughafen:	Frankfurt Rhein-Main (10 km vom Zentrum); S-Bahn (S14, 15) zur Stadtmitte; Intercity-Verbindung.
Information:	Verkehrsamt, Kaiserstraße 52, Tel. 21 23 88 49; Hauptbahnhof Gleis 23.
Post:	Hauptpost, Zeil 110, geöffnet täglich 8-20 Uhr; Hauptbahnhof durchgehend geöffnet; Flughafen 6-22 Uhr.
Wichtige Messen:	**Internationale Frankfurter Messe** (Konsumgüter), **IAA** (Internationale Automobil-Ausstellung), **automechanika** (Auto-Ersatzteile und -Zubehör), **Frankfurter Buchmesse**
Sehenswürdigkeiten:	Römer, Altstadt, Zoo, Fernmeldeturm
Typisches Essen:	Handkäse mit Musik
Typisches Getränk:	Apfelwein

Hotels und Pensionen

EXECUTIVE PUZZLE
Try matching up each hotel facility with the right pictogram.
a Sauna *b* Kreditkarte *c* Zimmer mit Dusche
d Unterbringung von Hunden möglich
e Restaurant *f* Parkplatz *g* Zimmer mit Dusche und WC *h* Schwimmbad *i* Zimmertelefon
j Fitnessraum *k* Garage *l* Fernsehen
m Konferenzraum *n* Zimmer mit Bad und WC
o Behinderten-Service *p* Bar.

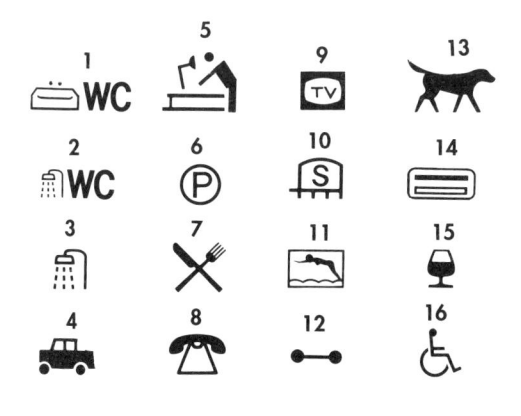

TiP

If you decide to go out to a restaurant, remember to check that it is open: a Ruhetag *can fall on any day of the week, and in the summer restaurants often close for* Betriebsferien.

Schreibtisch

Düsseldorf
des Ruhrgebiets

Düsseldorf started life as a fishing village on the Rhine, at the mouth of the River Düssel. Its close proximity to the Ruhr and the arrival of the railways acted as a magnet to industry. Around the mid-1800s, Belgian industrialists brought metal industries and machinery to Düsseldorf, and in 1893 the city became the headquarters of the Mannesmann brothers who had revolutionized the steel-tubing industry with their invention of seamless steel tubes. Düsseldorf's location favoured its development as the administrative centre, or *Schreibtisch*, of the Ruhr.

While the city lay in ruins at the end of the second world war, a company for organizing trade fairs was set up. The newcomer to the trade-fair scene went on to become a major centre for trade fairs in capital goods. Foreign companies have not been slow to recognize the city's advantages as an administrative headquarters. Düsseldorf is now a trading city with a large concentration of steel traders, and the *Japan-Center* is a monument to the scale of Japanese investment which has made Düsseldorf the home of the largest Japanese community in Europe.

Restructuring of traditional metal-based industries has involved cutbacks in capacity, slashed workforces and diversification. Today, the service sector continues to grow, and a reputation as capital of Germany's fashion industry reinforces the city's move away from the rust-belt industries of the Ruhr.

Strukturwandel

FACTFINDER
*1 Why has the service sector strengthened during the last decade and a half?
*2 What sectors have been most affected by restructuring?

Der Anteil des Dienstleistungssektors hat gerade in den letzten eineinhalb Jahrzehnten fortlaufend zugenommen, teils infolge eigenen Wachstums, teils infolge des Rückgangs der Industrie. So verschwanden alleine seit Mitte der 70er Jahre 15 000 industrielle Arbeitsplätze. Dieser Strukturwandel, der sich auch gegenwärtig noch fortsetzt, hat vor allem die metallverarbeitenden Bereiche wie Röhrenproduktion, Stahl-, Maschinen- und Anlagenbau erfaßt. (*Handelsblatt*)

DATABASE
hat ... fortlaufend zugenommen *has steadily increased ...*
infolge eigenen Wachstums *due to its own growth*
infolge des Rückgangs *due to the decline*
verschwanden *disappeared*
sich ... fortsetzt *is continuing ...*
hat vor allem ... erfaßt *has particularly affected ...*

Wußten Sie schon ...?

1 Düsseldorf hat die größte japanische Kolonie Europas.
2 Düsseldorf ist der zweitgrößte Banken- und Börsenplatz in der Bundesrepublik.
3 Der Pro-Kopf-Umsatz des Einzelhandels in Düsseldorf liegt etwa um 42% über dem Bundesdurchschnitt, und die Düsseldorfer verdienen etwa 23% über dem Bundesdurchschnitt (Netto-Einkommen Pro-Kopf).
4 Nordrhein-Westfalen (Landeshauptstadt: Düsseldorf) erzeugt über ein Viertel des Bruttosozialproduktes der Bundesrepublik.
5 In Düsseldorf erfand 1907 die Firma Henkel das „erste selbsttätige Waschmittel der Welt" – Persil.

FILAWORD
der Stahl *steel*
die Montanindustrie *coal and steel industry*
die metallverarbeitende Industrie *metal-processing industry*
die Investitionsgüter (*n, pl*) *capital goods*
die Verwaltung *administration*
der Strukturwandel *structural change, restructuring*
die Dienstleistung *service*
der Schreibtisch *(writing) desk*
der Arbeitsplatz *job, workplace*

TiP
Make sure you have plenty of business cards to hand in Germany – a first meeting is usually accompanied by a flourish of cards.

Düsseldorf

ⓘ Vom Coil zum Kunden 3

BMW Logistik und Einkauf

Der Unternehmensbereich Logistik und Einkauf umfaßt Planung, Beschaffung, Bereitstellung und Koordination des Materials für die gesamte BMW-Organisation.

Die langfristige Einkaufs-Strategie:
- In den Ländern, in denen unsere Fahrzeuge gekauft werden, mehr Stammlieferanten gewinnen.
- Auf dem Gebiet der Logistik mit unseren Lieferanten noch enger zusammenzuarbeiten, um den Materialfluß weiter zu optimieren und die Flexibilität noch mehr zu erhöhen.
- Die Vorteile ausländischer Märkte aufgrund ihrer Spezialisierung oder Rohstoffvorräte noch mehr zu nutzen.
- Kostenvorteile für einen sinnvollen Wettbewerb schaffen.
- Grundsätzlich mehr internationale partnerschaftliche Beziehungen. (*Logistik und Einkauf bei BMW*)

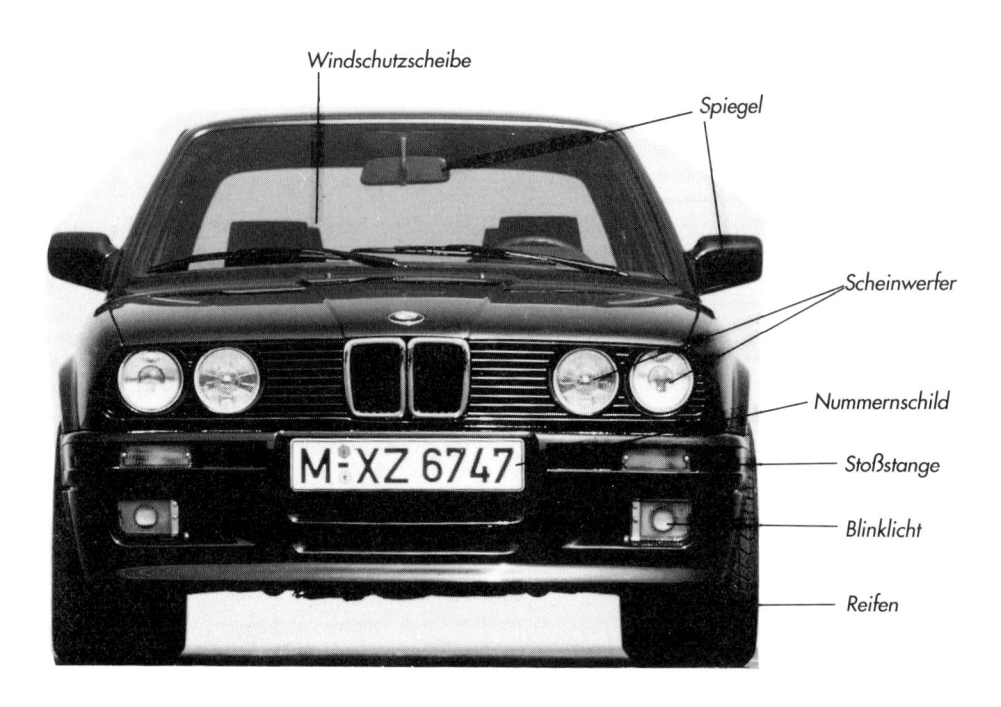

Windschutzscheibe — Spiegel — Scheinwerfer — Nummernschild — Stoßstange — Blinklicht — Reifen

Internationaler Einkauf

Herr Woiwod: BMW hat im Laufe der Jahre festgestellt, wie wichtig internationaler Einkauf ist. Aus verschiedenen Gründen, z.B. um restriktive Verkaufsmärkte überhaupt zu öffnen oder Währungsrisiken zu vermindern, ist der Einkauf im Ausland sehr wichtig. Großbritannien ist nach USA der zweitgrößte Exportmarkt für BMW und daher wichtig für den Einkauf.

Im Rahmen der positiven Entwicklung der britischen Industrie in den 80er Jahren hat sich auch die Zulieferindustrie sehr positiv entwickelt. Von Stahlblech über Gußteile, Motorenteile, Bremsteile bis hin zu Elektrik- und Elektronikteilen – die Stärken der Zulieferindustrie umfassen viele Produktgruppen. Wir suchen besonders Partner mit hoher Entwicklungs- und Fertigungstechnologie, für Einzelteile bis hin zu kompletten Systemen wie z.B. elektronischer Motorensteuerung.

BMW – Wer ist wer?

Kai Woiwod, Purchasing Manager bei BMW GB Ltd, verantwortlich für den Zentraleinkauf der Tochtergesellschaft und für den Einkauf bei englischen Lieferanten für die Muttergesellschaft in München. Ausbildung: kaufmännische Lehre; Studium Betriebswirtschaft. Hobbys: Tennis, englische Oldtimer.

Hohe Anforderungen

Herr Woiwod: Wir schauen uns die Fertigung an, wir schauen uns die Qualitätssicherung an, wir schauen uns den Produktionsablauf an, wir schauen auf den Maschinenpark. Man unterhält sich mit der Firmenleitung und dem Exportleiter. Unsere Anforderungen sind hoch hinsichtlich Qualitätssystemen, Design- und Entwicklungs-Know-how, Flexibilität und Zuverlässigkeit. Außerdem muß ein Hersteller natürlich vom Preis her wettbewerbsfähig sein.

Kommunikationsmittel Deutsch

While reading through **Finanzmetropole**, there may have been moments when you felt a little jaded with German, and wondered whatever made you want to learn it in the first place. Ministerialdirektor Dr Barthold Witte, head of the Foreign Ministry's cultural policy department in Bonn, has overall responsibility for the dissemination of the German language. He gave his views on the role of German in Europe.

Eine wichtige Lingua franca

Dr. Witte: Das Deutsche ist in einer Reihe von Regionen Europas als Kommunikationsmittel ganz unentbehrlich. Das ist natürlich zunächst einmal der muttersprachlich deutsche Raum in Mitteleuropa, der ja alleine über hundert Millionen Menschen umfaßt; dazu kommt dann das nachbarliche Umfeld. Vor allem in Ost- und Südosteuropa – in Polen, in Ungarn, in der Tschechoslowakei, in Bulgarien – ist das Deutsche nach wie vor eine wichtige Lingua franca, mit der man oft sehr viel besser zurechtkommt als mit Englisch oder Russisch. Russisch ist nicht beliebt, Englisch ist nicht sehr verbreitet; das Deutsche hat eine nach wie vor starke Stellung.

Im Wachsen begriffen

Dr. Witte: Die Bundesrepublik Deutschland ist im gemeinsamen Binnenmarkt der größte Anbieter von Waren und Dienstleistungen und der größte Markt dafür. Ich glaube, daß die Nachfrage nach dem Deutschen auch in Großbritannien wachsen wird. Wir haben insgesamt festgestellt, daß die Nachfrage nach dem Deutschen in den Mitgliedstaaten der europäischen Gemeinschaft im Wachsen begriffen ist, nachdem sie in einer Reihe von EG-Mitgliedsländern lange Zeit im Rückgang befindlich war.

DATABASE
das Deutsche (*the*) *German* (*language*)
unentbehrlich *indispensable*
nach wie vor *still, now as ever*
Nachfrage (*f*) *demand*
im Wachsen begriffen ist *is growing*
im Rückgang befindlich war *was declining*

TiP

"When exhibiting at a trade fair, brochures and vital information such as price lists should be in German as well as English, otherwise the exhibitor runs the risk of being regarded as unseriös and hence unworthy of being a business partner." (British-German Trade, *German Chamber of Industry & Commerce*)

> **Halle / hall 13.2**
> **Internationale Gartenfachmesse**
>
> Gartenausstattung, Gartenhäuser, Gewächshäuser und Zubehör, Licht- u. Wassertechnik, Heimtierbedarf
>
> Garden fittings, garden sheds, greenhouses and accessories, light and water technology, pet supplies
>
> Articles pour l'aménagement des jardins, abris de jardin, serres et accessoires, techniques d'éclairage et d'alimentation hydraulique, fournitures pour animaux domestiques

ALLES FÜR DEN GARTEN

Amateur gardeners in Germany are always on the look-out for a bargain, as long as it's not at the expense of reliability. Innovations are popular where they reduce the time spent on mundane, labour-intensive activities and satisfy heightened environmental awareness.

According to one German wholesaler, the typical amateur gardener in Germany is 40 years old, married, has children and earns net between DM 2000 and DM 3000 per month, belongs to the middle-class and lives in a small town with 5000 - 20,000 inhabitants. The Association of the German Gardening Industry (*Industrieverband Gartenbau* – IVG) has estimated that households with a garden spend an average of DM 500 on garden products every year.

The *Internationale Gartenfachmesse* in Cologne is universally acknowledged to be the major international trade fair for this sector.

Vier Arten von Ständen

Herr Friedrich Bertram of KölnMesse advised on the range of stands available and the costs involved in exhibiting at a fair.

FACTFINDER
*1 How many types of stand are there?
**2 What is the average price for a stand?
*3 What proportion of an exhibitor's total costs is the floorspace rental?

Herr Bertram: Sie haben die Wahl zwischen vier Arten von Ständen: Reihenstand (Row), Eckstand (zwei Seiten offen), Kopfstand (drei Seiten offen) oder Blockstand (alle vier Seiten offen). Der Durchschnittspreis liegt bei DM 140 pro Quadratmeter für die Gesamtzeit der Veranstaltung, also für Aufbau, Laufzeit der Messe und Abbau. Man kann davon ausgehen, daß die Miete maximal 20 Prozent der Gesamtkosten einer Messebeteiligung beträgt, also ein Fünftel.

DATABASE
Sie haben die Wahl *You have the choice*
für die Gesamtzeit der Veranstaltung *for the duration of the entire event*
Man kann davon ausgehen, daß ... *You can assume that ...*

FILASKILL
If you see *also*, look out for an explanation or expansion. It's equivalent to *i.e.* (or *so* or *therefore*).

FILAWORD
der Stand *stand*
die Halle *exhibition hall*
der Garten *garden*
der Schrebergarten *allotment*
die Blume *flower*
der Baum *tree*

Ausstellerberatung und Ausstellerservice

a Anreise-Informationen
b Aushilfspersonal, Standhilfen
c Aussteller-Befragung
d Aussteller-Verzeichnisse
e Besucher-Analysen
f Bewirtung von Gästen
g Bezugsfertige Stände
h Blumen und Grünpflanzen
i Fotografen
j Funk/Fernseh-Studio
k Gas- und Wasseranschlüsse
l Müllbeseitigung
m Pressekonferenzen, Pressekontakte
n Standreinigung
o Versicherung
p Werbeflächen im Messegelände
q Zimmervermittlung

EXECUTIVE SKILLS
Above is an extract from the list of services the Cologne Fair offers to exhibitors (use the *Glossary* for help). Which of the services

*1 help you get to the fair and find accommodation?
*2 affect the appearance and running of a stand?
*3 provide insurance?
*4 are concerned with publicity?
*5 give information about exhibitors and visitors?

Düsseldorf

Major International Show

British gardens and gardening equipment have a high reputation in Germany, Britain's second largest export market in this sector. GARDENEX, the export arm of the British garden industry, run an export award with the prize of a free stand at Cologne.

Gardenex

South Down Trugs & Crafts produces hand-crafted trugs – familiar to many British gardeners. After winning a GARDENEX export award, Robin and Peter Tuppen were confident of moving outside their traditional export market, the US: "We decided that, as we definitely wanted to get into the European market, the only thing to do was to go for it and get ahead of the competition."

Establishing a distributor for a new product can be tricky, but Hilary and Ian Greer of Hillian Interlog – specializing in interlocking-timber and water products – succeeded on their first day. A first-timer at Cologne, Ian Greer was convinced of the need to speak German: "Even though our distributor speaks fluent English, his 20 salesmen don't. The literature helps a little bit, but the final touch would have been to converse in German and tell them how to sell our product."

Inhome, producers of a range of hoses and hose accessories, was at Cologne for the second time, and marketing director Ken Partington was mainly interested in making international contacts at the fair: "It isn't just about a German garden show, it's a major international show. We've had Australians on this morning, Americans, and a lot of people from the Middle East." They had even had a German competitor trying to find out about the company's new Multibrush hose system! Before actually exhibiting at the fair, Inhome had come as visitors for several years, and Ken Partington emphasized the 'softly-softly' approach of German buyers: "A general rule of thumb is that you're here the first year, people say 'oh, that's interesting', you're here the second year, 'that's interesting, they mean business', you're here the third, 'that's interesting, let's go and do some business'."

Although Inhome's group product manager David Kirby maintained that "to exist in the German market you have to have good quality", Ian Hall, export manager at Bulldog Tools, has found it an uphill struggle to persuade otherwise quality-conscious German buyers to pay a premium for a garden spade. But after 10 years at the fair, he is optimistic about the prospects for top-of-the-range British garden tools: "Now we're making more headway. Virtually all German products are pressed, and of course ours are all forged. Our spades probably cost nearly 50% more than a German spade, but they have a guarantee for ten years and will probably last for 50."

Ian Hall, Bulldog Tools, at the Cologne Garden Fair

EXECUTIVE PUZZLE

Here is the GARDENEX entry in the catalogue for Cologne's 1990 Garden Fair. How would the secretary for GARDENEX have filled in the form below?

	Halle	Gang	Stand
GARDENEX - The Federation of Garden & Leisure Equipment Exporters Ltd,	13.2	C	10

☎ 886 534

96 Church Street, **Great Bedwyn**,
Marlborough (Wilts) SN8 3PF/Großbritannien,
Telefon 0672-870392, Telefax 0672-870788

Messe- und Ausstellungs-Ges.m.b.H. Köln, - Abteilung 220 -,
Postfach 21 07 60, D-5000 Köln 21

Fragebogen

Aussteller: **1** _____
Straße: **2** _____
Ort: **3** _____
Land: **4** _____
Telefon: **5** _____ Telefax: **6** _____
Halle: **7** _____ Gang: **8** _____
Stand: **9** _____ Standtelefon: **10** _____

FIRST ENCOUNTERS

The commercial services at the British consulates in Germany are a mine of information on all aspects of the German business scene and export opportunities to Germany.

Companies can get a full appraisal of the market prospects for a product through the Export Representative Service. Following visits to all their contacts in a particular sector of industry, the commercial services provide a report giving the British company details of the market for their goods. This includes the view of German industry on the product's quality, the relevant trade fairs, and the most appropriate means of advertising. Finally, they provide a list of German firms interested in the product and in representing the British firm in Germany. This is backed by a full report on the German company with such details as turnover and reputation.

The commercial consuls stressed the need to convince your customer, and your agent, that you really do mean business. According to Mr Peter Bryant, consul general in Düsseldorf, "you need to visit the market, support your agent, supply information, and give him whatever encouragement you can". Support, of course, includes delivering the products on time and making sure they work. Especially if a product is new, German customers will want to be sure that a foreign company is committed to the German market. Speaking the customer's language is part of showing your commitment, and Mr Bryant emphasized that "initial approaches should be made in German, with a letter in German, literature in German about the firm's product, or at least a summary of the product features in German".

Richtung Gartenschmuck

Werga-Tools GmbH (**Wer**kzeug und **Ga**rtengeräte) developed from a subsidiary of Spear and Jackson in a management buy-out by Herr Heinz Leyerle, head of Spear and Jackson Tools GmbH, in 1978. Now, Herr Leyerle is moving away from functional tools into garden accessories.

Eigenentwicklung - Tomatenspiralstäbe

FACTFINDER
*1 What colour is the plastic coating?

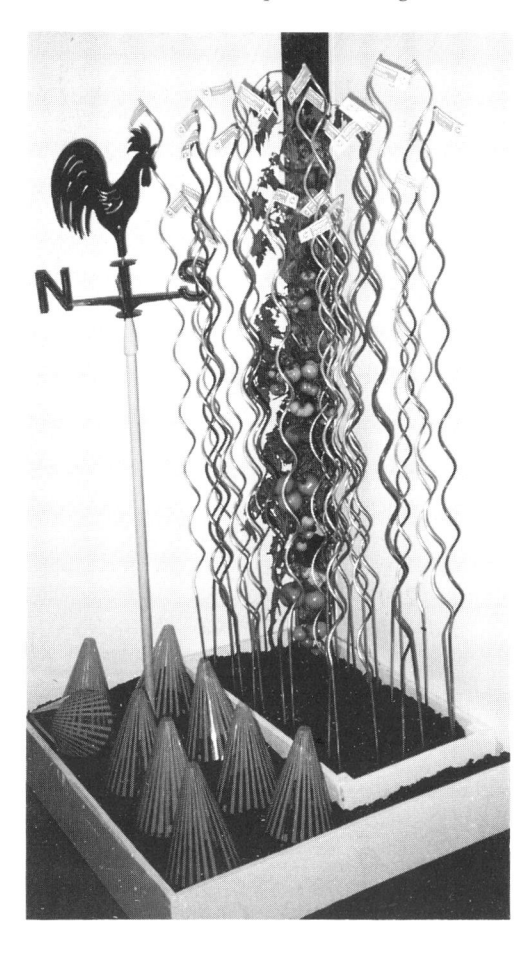

Verzinkt und kunststoffbeschichtet

Die grüne Kunststoffbeschichtung hat folgende Vorteile:

- Verminderte Erwärmung
- Noch größere Haltbarkeit
- Größerer Gesamtdurchmesser
- Geschmackvolles Gartengrün, dadurch ein schönerer Garten.

FILAFACT *adjectives*
Be prepared to find different endings on adjectives. They vary with the gender of the noun and according to whether the noun is singular or plural:

größerer Gesamtdurchmesser (*m*)
größere Haltbarkeit (*f*)
geschmackvolles Gartengrün (*n*)
folgende Vorteile (*pl*)

They also vary according to the noun's case, and any article before the noun! ➡ **P 100-101**

„Die Messe ist für mich jetzt eine reine Imagesache geworden, weil wir inzwischen in Deutschland eine sehr hohe Penetranz haben." (Heinz Leyerle, links)

Werga-Tools in Zahlen

EXECUTIVE PUZZLE
Here are some facts and figures about Werga from a trade magazine, but they are under the wrong headings. Can you match up the headings and the correct details, with the help of the *Glossary*?

1 **Betriebsfläche**
a 7 Länder, Schwerpunkte Schweiz und Österreich

2 **Mitarbeiterstamm**
b 27,5 Millionen Mark

3 **Messen**
c Komplettprogramm, Eigenentwicklungen, Innovationen, Markenimage

4 **Abwicklung**
d Aus aller Welt, momentan aus 16 Ländern

5 **Umsatz 1990**
e Aufträge über mobile Datenerfassung. Auslieferung in ganz Deutschland spätestens am dritten Werktag

6 **Export**
f Circa 6000 m²

7 **Import**
g Garten- und Fachmesse Köln

8 **Stärken**
h (Incl. Reisende) 40
Zusätzliche Mitarbeiter in der Saison: bis ca. 12

(*Garten- und Freizeitmarkt*)

Schnickschnack

FACTFINDER
**2 Which part of the country has the main conurbations?
***3 Is amateur gardening more popular in the south or the north?
**4 Why is Herr Leyerle moving away from traditional gardening equipment?

Herr Leyerle: Wir haben uns ganz auf den Amateurgärtner konzentriert. Das Amateurgärtnern ist in Deutschland mit einem Süd-Nord-Gefälle versehen: Wir haben im Norden wesentlich weniger Großstädte als im Süden, und wesentlich mehr ländliches Gebiet, wie Niedersachsen, Ostfriesland, Schleswig-Holstein; und je ländlicher ein Gebiet ist, desto weniger ist dieser Schnickschnack eigentlich gewünscht.

Ich werde in nächster Zeit immer stärker in Richtung Gartenschmuck gehen, weil da eine Innovation viel leichter zu finden ist als in den herkömmlichen Dingen.

DATABASE
Süd-Nord-Gefälle (*n*) *south-north divide ('falling off' from south to north)*
je ländlicher ... desto weniger *the more rural ... the less*
ist ... eigentlich gewünscht ... *is really in demand*
immer stärker *more and more*
Gartenschmuck (*m*) *garden accessories*
viel leichter zu finden ist *is much easier to find*

FILAFACT *comparisons*
Notice how Herr Leyerle says 'few**er** ... **than**' and 'easi**er** ... **than**' (➡ **P 101-102**):

Wir haben im Norden *weniger* Großstädte *als* im Süden.
..., weil da eine Innovation *leichter* zu finden ist *als* ...

EXECUTIVE SKILLS
*1 Try matching up the German words (*i-vi*) with their English equivalents (*a-f*):

i der Garten *ii* die Gärtnerin *iii* gärtnern
iv die Gärtnerei *v* der Gärtner
vi gärtnerisch

a gardener (*f*) *b* to garden *c* nursery
d horticultural *e* gardener (*m*) *f* garden.

***2 Can you work out the comparative form of the following words with the help of Herr Leyerle's comments?

a leicht *b* wenig *c* stark.

TiP

The name of a company must state the company's purpose. However, Herr Leyerle was permitted to call his company 'Werga-Tools GmbH' in place of the long-winded 'Werga Werkzeug- und Gartengeräte Vertriebs GmbH' because the official at the chamber of commerce recognized the English word 'tools'!

DEMOKRATISIERUNG DER WIRTSCHAFT

Industrialization started relatively late in Germany, and Bismarck tried to stifle the infant trade-union movement and avoid social conflict by instituting progressive welfare legislation. A patchwork of religious and political trade unions still emerged, but it was brutally suppressed under the Nazis. After the war the Allies, together with German trade unionists, were concerned to create a stable system of industrial relations as a bulwark against political upheaval. The result was a streamlined system of 16 trade unions under the umbrella of the *Deutsche Gewerkschaftsbund* (DGB).

Union membership stands at around 40% of the workforce. The power of German unions derives in part from the absence of demarcation; workers in the chemical industry join *IG Chemie* whether they are computer programmers, secretaries or technicians. Strict labour laws favour the employees and ensure that industry cannot ride roughshod over them, although the closed shop and politically motivated strikes are illegal.

The unions are responsible for negotiating centralized collective agreements with the employers or employers' associations, and the annual pay round starts well before current wage agreements expire. Such agreements are legally binding, and strikes are illegal while an agreement is in force or negotiations are proceeding. Any strike requires a 75% mandate from a secret ballot of the membership. *Beamte*, government employees, are not allowed to strike; they range from teachers through judges to train drivers. The legal framework, together with a strong sense of order and company loyalty, have combined with overall prosperity to ensure an enviable record of industrial relations in the social market economy.

Within companies, provision for worker participation in management through works councils and representation on company boards has sustained a remarkable degree of consensus. This consensus lies at the heart of Germany's enduring industrial success, although every now and then cracks appear in the cosy partnership.

Mitbestimmung

The *Betriebsverfassungsgesetz* (Industrial Constitution Act) of 1952 stipulated that in an *Aktiengesellschaft*, the employees should elect a third of the *Aufsichtsrat* (supervisory board). This regulation still holds for AGs with up to 2000 employees, and other companies with 500 to 2000 employees. The coal and steel industry forms an exception: since 1951 companies with more than 1000 employees have had parity between shareholders and employees on the supervisory board, with an additional neutral member agreed by both sides. The supervisory board also elects an *Arbeitsdirektor* (worker director) to represent the interests of the employees on the *Vorstand* (board of management). The unions have been keen to extend this model to other sectors, but have had to be content with the *Mitbestimmungsgesetz* (Co-determination Act) of 1976. This law gives the two sides parity in companies with more than 2000 employees, but the chairman, who is elected by the shareholders, has a casting vote.

FILAWORD
der Arbeitgeber *employer*
der Arbeitnehmer *employee*
die Sozialpartner/Tarifpartner (m, pl) *unions and management*
die Mitbestimmung *(worker) participation in management, co-determination*
der Tarifvertrag *collective agreement*
das Mitglied *member*
der Beitrag *contribution, sub*
die soziale Marktwirtschaft *social market economy*

TiP

"The main rules of doing business with a German company are essentially based on good manners, i.e. keeping the commitment you've made, producing the goods to the specification, the price and the date you agreed, and if anything goes wrong, picking up the telephone or sending a fax."
(Neil Rothnie, vice-consul (commercial), Munich)

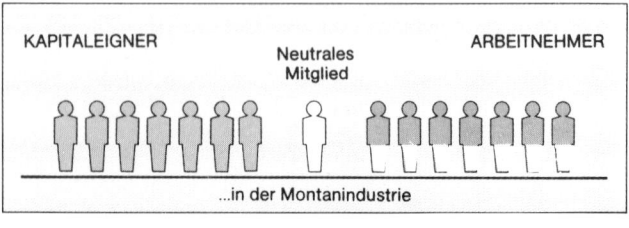

Tarifautonomie

Dr Dieter Schuster, head of the DGB archive in Düsseldorf, gave a brief outline of the relationship between the DGB and the individual unions.

FACTFINDER
*1 Where did Britain want power to be in the post-war union structure?
**2 Which three aspects of union autonomy does Dr Schuster mention?

Dr. Schuster: Nach 1945 gab es auf deutscher Seite die Vorstellung, das Dach muß sehr stark werden und die Gewerkschaften spielen nur eine kleinere Rolle. Da haben jedoch entscheidend die Briten eingegriffen und haben gesagt, „*No*, die einzelnen Gewerkschaften müssen ihre Machtposition behalten." Heute bestimmt jede Gewerkschaft, welchen Beitrag sie verlangt und welche Leistung sie für ihre Mitglieder liefert. Die Gewerkschaften haben auch die sogenannte Tarifautonomie, das heißt, jede Gewerkschaft ist völlig autonom in ihrer Tarifpolitik.

DATABASE
Dach (*n*) *umbrella organization* (literally *roof*)
haben ... entscheidend ... eingegriffen ... ... *decisively intervened*
haben gesagt *said*
welche Leistung sie ... liefert *which benefits it will provide* ...
Tarifpolitik (*f*) *policy for pay and working conditions*

FILAFACT *verbs*
Notice how *müssen* sends other verb(s) to the end of the sentence:

   Das Dach *muß* sehr stark *werden*.
   Die Gewerkschaften *müssen* ihre Machtposition *behalten*.

The same happens with *können, sollen, wollen, dürfen, mögen.* (➡ P 103)

EXECUTIVE PUZZLE
To get the correct statistics, fit the types of job to the pictures. Clue: Planning and research make up 4.9%. *a* Planen, Forschen *b* Büroarbeiten *c* Sichern *d* Allgemeine Dienstleistungen *e* Leiten *f* Herstellen *g* Maschinen einstellen, warten *h* Ausbilden, Informieren *i* Handel treiben *j* Reparieren

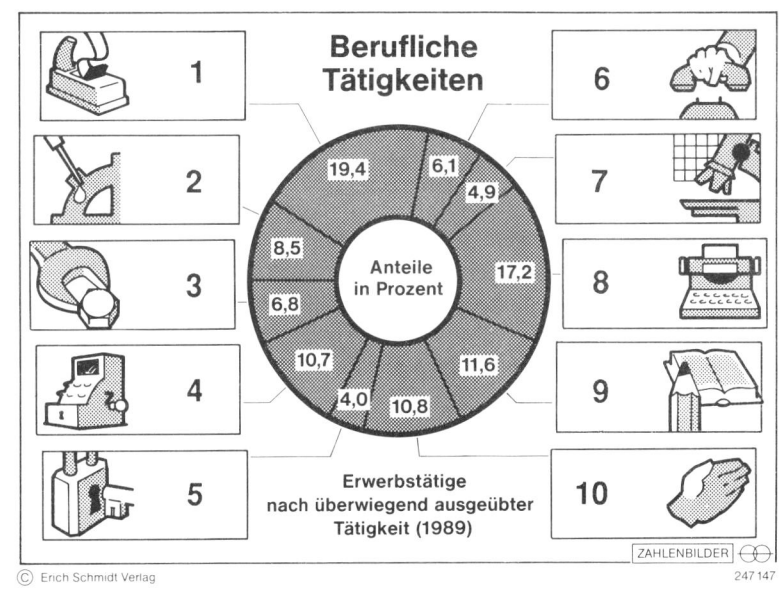

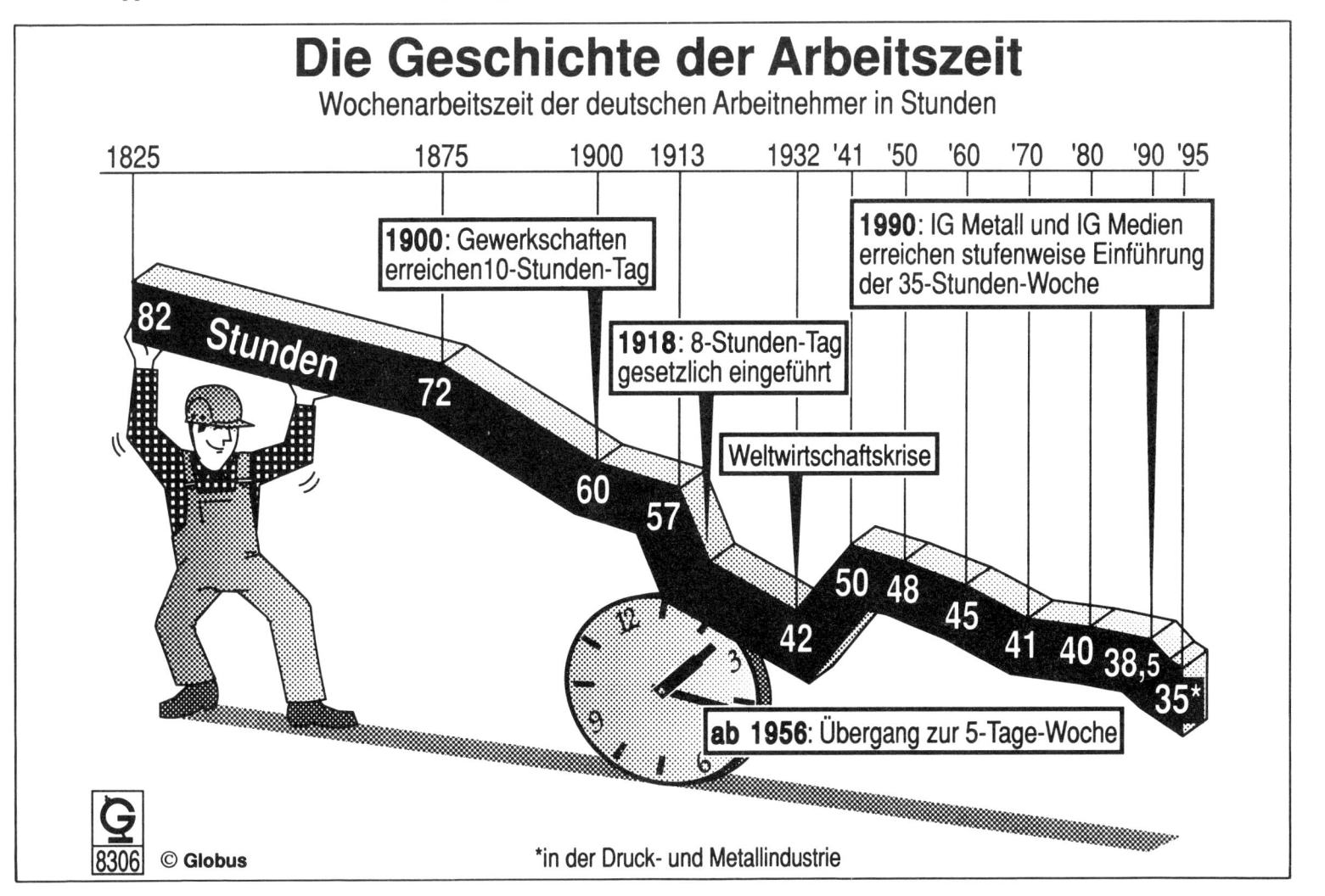

Berufliche Tätigkeiten

Anteile in Prozent: 19,4 — 6,1 — 4,9 — 17,2 — 11,6 — 10,8 — 4,0 — 10,7 — 6,8 — 8,5

Erwerbstätige nach überwiegend ausgeübter Tätigkeit (1989)

© Erich Schmidt Verlag

Die Geschichte der Arbeitszeit
Wochenarbeitszeit der deutschen Arbeitnehmer in Stunden

1825: 82 Stunden — 1875: 72 — 1900: 60 — 1913: 57 — 1932: 42 — '41: 50 — '50: 48 — '60: 45 — '70: 41 — '80: 40 — '90: 38,5 — '95: 35*

1900: Gewerkschaften erreichen 10-Stunden-Tag

1918: 8-Stunden-Tag gesetzlich eingeführt

Weltwirtschaftskrise

ab 1956: Übergang zur 5-Tage-Woche

1990: IG Metall und IG Medien erreichen stufenweise Einführung der 35-Stunden-Woche

© Globus

*in der Druck- und Metallindustrie

Fashion House 2

MODEMETROPOLE DÜSSELDORF

After the war, Düsseldorf and Munich succeeded Berlin as Germany's fashion centres. Although Munich is a strong contender for the title of designer metropolis, Düsseldorf, with its IGEDO fashion fair and central location, has achieved a leading role in the European fashion arena. The *Königsallee* is the city's shop window where Germany's most stylish women buy the latest in international design. Now the Düsseldorf fashion show comes to Berlin twice a year, and it remains to be seen whether Berlin regains its former pre-eminence.

FILAWORD
die Mode *fashion*
die Kleidung *clothing*
der Einzelhändler *retailer*
der Großhändler *wholesaler*
der Einkäufer *buyer*
das Schaufenster *shop window*
anspruchsvoll *sophisticated*

Düsseldorf Fashion House

Düsseldorf's futuristic Fashion Houses 1 and 2 are permanent extensions of IGEDO (*Interessengemeinschaft Damenoberbekleidungs-Industrie*), the world's biggest fashion fair.

FACTFINDER
*1 How many fashion fairs are held in Düsseldorf each year?
**2 What kind of fashion does Fashion House 2 cater for?

Die Mode prägt das Image der Stadt. Den stärksten Impuls von „fashion" gibt seit 1949 die IGEDO der Stadt Düsseldorf. Die IGEDO ist der Veranstalter von 6 Modemessen im Jahr mit über 7000 Ausstellern und mehr als 200 000 Einkäufern aus der ganzen Welt. Die IGEDO war auch Initiator des *Düsseldorf Fashion House 1*.

Düsseldorf Fashion House 2 ist die logische Konsequenz aus dem Marktbedürfnis des gehobenen Fachhandels nach zentralen Informations- und Ordermöglichkeiten im gesamten Bereich der anspruchsvollen Mode. *Düsseldorf Fashion House 2* bietet Mietern und Kunden die technische Voraussetzung für die optimale Abwicklung von Information, Order und Lagereinkauf. (*Düsseldorf Fashion House 2*)

DATABASE
prägt *shapes*
aus dem Marktbedürfnis des gehobenen Fachhandels *arising from the demands of the exclusive fashion trade*
die technische Voraussetzung *the technical prerequisite*
Lagereinkauf (*m*) *stock buying*

EXECUTIVE SKILLS
***1 Can you spot the subject in each of the four sentences in the first paragraph of *Düsseldorf Fashion House?* Be guided by context and sense, as well as cases!

FILAFACT *case*
German nouns have cases, which can define the noun's role in a sentence. Word-order may be flexible, so it's sometimes necessary to look at the form of the article that goes with the noun to see what role the noun is playing. The sentence *Den stärksten Impuls gibt die IGEDO der Stadt Düsseldorf* is equivalent to the English '**The IGEDO** gives the strongest impetus to the city of Düsseldorf':

	(*m*)	(*f*)	(*f*)
Nominative:	der	***die IGEDO***	die
Accusative:	***Den*** stärksten Impuls gibt	die	die
Genitive:	des	der	der
Dative:	dem	der	***der*** Stadt Düsseldorf.

***2 Check the explanation of the genitive case (➡ P 98) and then see if you can work out which three of these six nouns are in the genitive: *a* das Image der Stadt *b* aus dem Marktbedürfnis des Fachhandels *c* im Bereich der Mode.

***3 With the help of *Düsseldorf Fashion House*, can you find the right slot for these words – *nach, im, von, seit, aus* – in the following phrases? *a* Messebesucher ___ der ganzen Welt *b* die Abwicklung ___ großen Aufträgen *c* ___ 1980 *d* der Umsatz ___ High-Tech-Bereich *e* das Bedürfnis ___ anspruchsvoller Kleidung.

The writer might also have written: *Die IGEDO gibt der Stadt Düsseldorf den stärksten Impuls.* In English, the subject of a sentence (here 'the IGEDO') is usually the first noun. In German, it may not be the first, but it's always in the nominative case and agrees with the verb. ➡ P 97-98, 107

Düsseldorf

Ungestörter Einkauf

Burberrys no longer exhibit at IGEDO. Instead they have a permanent showroom in Fashion House 2, together with some 80 other prominent fashion businesses. Buyers are able to view the collections at a far more leisurely pace than at the fair, as Frau Christa Kellermann, responsible for PR in Germany, pointed out.

FACTFINDER
*1 How many product groups does Frau Kellermann refer to?

Frau Kellermann: Der Kunde arbeitet hier sehr viel ungestörter mit unserer großen Kollektion: Er geht von den Mänteln zu den Strickwaren und von da zu den Accessoires. Das ist hier sehr viel besser und übersichtlicher präsentiert als auf einem naturgemäß kleineren Messestand.

Eine 1ᵃ Lage

Burberrys make no compromises when it comes to choosing a site for one of their exclusive shops – in Hamburg the company had to wait five years for the right site. According to Herr Dave de Boer, wholesale manager for central Europe, only an A1 location will do.

FACTFINDER
*2 What are the locations in Hamburg and Munich?

Herr de Boer: Unsere Einzelhandelsgeschäfte sind immer auf einer 1ᵃ Lage und am liebsten noch auf einer 1ᵃᵃ Lage. In Hamburg auf dem Neuen Jungfernstieg, in München auf der Perusastraße – also immer da, wo die besten, hochwertigsten Geschäfte der jeweiligen Stadt sind.

DATABASE
am liebsten noch *best of all, ideally*
immer da, wo *always where*
die ... hochwertigsten Geschäfte *the ... most exclusive shops*

FILAFACT *comparisons*
Notice how you can compare things, as in the English 'well - bett**er** - be**st**':

gut	besser	am besten
gern	lieber	am liebsten
hochwertig	hochwertiger	am hochwertigsten

➡ P 101-102

Die Herren bevorzugen Baumwolle

Regional differences are very important in Germany. Frau Kellermann and Herr Hans Schar, who looks after the German market, find that regional tastes and sizes affect the length, colour and fabric of Burberry raincoats.

FACTFINDER
**3 Which part of the German market has a predominance of short women?
*4 Are olive-green coats more likely to be bought in Munich or Hamburg?
*5 Who prefers cotton?

Herr Schar: Wir produzieren vier verschiedene Längen für den deutschen Markt, immer im Abstand von vier Zentimetern. Das ist notwendig, denn im Süden gibt es viel mehr kleine Damen als im Norden. Und ich bin sicher, daß wir hier in Deutschland längere Mäntel verkaufen als in England.

Frau Kellermann: Von den Farben her gibt es ein starkes Nord-Süd-Gefälle. Olive Töne gehen besser im süddeutschen Raum als zum Beispiel im Hamburger Raum, wo sehr viel Beige und Dunkelblau getragen wird.

Herr Schar: Die Hanseatinnen lieben keine verknitterten Mäntel und tragen lieber Mischware, während das im Westen und Süden nichts ausmacht. Und die Herren bevorzugen generell Baumwolle.

Burberrys
OF LONDON

DATABASE
immer im Abstand *at intervals*
Das ist notwendig, denn *That's necessary, because*
Von den Farben her *Where colours are concerned*
gehen besser *sell better*
Hanseatinnen (f, pl) *women in the Hanseatic cities of Hamburg, Bremen and Lübeck*
verknittert *crumpled*
Mischware (f) *mixed fabrics*
während das ... nichts ausmacht *while that doesn't matter ...*

FILASKILL
If you see *denn* or *weil*, you can expect to find an explanation for a fact or opinion. *Weil* clauses have the verb at the end.

> **TiP**
>
> *Germany is very regionalized, and you might well need three or four agents to cover the country properly. Regional differences also play a major part in marketing in Germany, as consumers differ considerably from region to region.*

DEUTSCHES BUSINESS-MAGAZIN **35**

Beratung und Prüfung

German financial statements are viewed by the Anglo-Saxon world as extremely conservative. Dividends are kept to the minimum and profits are retained for growth, or salted away in undisclosed reserves. Many German companies are privately owned and obtain capital primarily from the banks. This means they are not dependent on capital markets for finance. The banks often base their lending on inside knowledge of the companies, since they may well have a shareholding and be represented on the board.

Implementation of the 4th EC directive (adopted in 1978), designed to harmonize accounting rules within the Community, has shaken up German accountancy. Before 1987 only *Aktiengesellschaften*, *GmbHs* with a turnover above DM 250 m., banks and insurance companies were obliged to have an annual audit and publish accounts. The 4th EC directive has excluded small *AGs* from this requirement, but included medium-sized as well as large *GmbHs*, thus increasing the number of companies that require an annual audit and have to publish their accounts. The profession of *Wirtschaftsprüfer* (auditor), traditionally highly elitist, is now having to open up in order to provide the manpower necessary to handle the increased workload.

FILAWORD
prüfen *to audit, inspect, examine*
der Steuerberater *tax adviser, book-keeper*
der Wirtschaftsprüfer *auditor (comparable with chartered accountant)*
der vereidigte Buchprüfer *certified accountant*
die Buchprüfung *audit*
die Buchführung *bookkeeping, accounting*
die Bilanz *balance sheet, annual accounts*
die Steuererklärung *tax return*
der Jahresabschluß *year-end accounts, annual accounts*

Berufsbilder

Herr Helmut Becker and Herr Manfred Masur, partners in accountants Ernst & Young GmbH, enumerated some of the tasks associated with their professions. Herr Becker is a *Steuerberater* who advises individuals and companies on their tax affairs. Herr Masur is a *Wirtschaftsprüfer*, and as such he is qualified to audit large companies.

FACTFINDER
**1 What can Herr Becker do for his clients' tax burden?

Herr Becker: Beratung von Einzelpersonen und Unternehmen jeder Rechtsform bei der Anfertigung von Steuererklärungen, Beratung mehr planerischer Art, wie man seine Steuerlast minimieren oder zumindest zeitlich verlagern kann. Hilfestellung bei steuerlichen Betriebsprüfungen, Prüfung von Bescheiden.

Herr Masur: Die klassischen Aufgaben: Abschlußprüfung von Unternehmen, Beratung im weitesten Sinne, Gutachtenerstellung, Bewertungsgutachten.

DATABASE
jeder Rechtsform *of any legal form*
zeitlich verlagern *spread over time*
Beratung im weitesten Sinne *consultancy in the widest sense*
Gutachten (n) *expert opinion, certification*

Kurzmitteilung

Ernst & Young GmbH
Wirtschaftsprüfungsgesellschaft

Kurzmitteilung vom _____

Betrifft:
❏ Ihr Schreiben vom _____
❏ Ihr Anruf vom _____
❏ Unser Gespräch am _____

Mit der Bitte um:

❏ Kenntnisnahme   ❏ zum Verbleib   Ihr Zeichen
❏ Erledigung   ❏ Fotokopie anbei
❏ Rückgabe   ❏ Irrläufer   Unser Zeichen
❏ Stellungnahme   ❏ siehe Rückseite
❏ Rückruf   ❏ Anlage

EXECUTIVE SKILLS
**1 Which boxes in the *Kurzmitteilung* would Herr Masur's secretary have to tick in the following situations? *a* Replying to a letter and sending a photocopy for information *b* Replying to a phone call by letter with enclosures and asking for comment *c* Sending a photocopy referring to a conversation and requesting a return phone call *d* Replying to a phone call relating to an enclosure and requesting that the matter be dealt with *e* Returning wrongly addressed mail.

*2 What is the German equivalent for *a* of (the) *b* on (the) *c* our ref. *d* your ref.?

***3 Does *Mit der Bitte um* refer to *a* both columns of boxes *b* the left-hand column?

FILASKILL
All the German words used in *Deutsches Business-Magazin* are given in the *Glossary*, but if you want to find German equivalents for English words you'll need to use a dictionary. This will also be useful when you read German newspapers, magazines etc.

> **TIP**
> The *GmbH* is the simplest form of company and enables any foreign company to be fully operational in Germany with a local managing director. According to Herr Becker, German companies prefer to deal with a legal entity registered in Germany itself.

Visitenkarte

FACTFINDER

**1 How many years did Herr Masur spend in the US?

**2 How long after his qualification as *Wirtschaftsprüfer* did he become a partner?

Herr Masur: Ich habe eine Standardausbildung. Ich habe in Marburg Volkswirtschaft studiert; ich bin Diplomvolkswirt. Ich habe dann bei Ernst & Whinney – jetzt Ernst & Young – angefangen und habe knapp zwei Jahre als Prüfungsassistent gearbeitet. Dann bin ich das erste Mal nach Amerika gegangen, für ein Jahr nach Milwaukee. Es war eine sehr gute Zeit. Ich bin dann zurückgekommen und bin hier ziemlich schnell befördert worden. Ich habe dann das Steuerberater-/Wirtschaftsprüferexamen gemacht. Nach zehn Jahren bin ich Partner geworden, und ich bin dann nochmal ein gutes Jahr in New York gewesen. Seitdem bin ich wieder hier und leite seit drei Jahren das Büro.

DATABASE

Diplomvolkswirt (*m*) *graduate in economics*
bin ... befördert worden *was promoted ...*
bin ich Partner geworden *I became a partner*

FILAFACT *the past*

Notice how Herr Masur talks about the past, using the verb *haben* or *sein* with the past participle (➡ **P 103**) of another verb (the form is similar to the English 'I **have** *started*', 'I **have** *studied*', or 'I **have** *gone*'):

Ich **habe** bei Ernst & Whinney *angefangen*.
(*I started at Ernst & Whinney.*)
Ich **habe** Volkswirtschaft *studiert*.
(*I studied economics.*)
Ich **bin** nach Amerika *gegangen*.
(*I went to America.*)

This is called the perfect tense. ➡ **P 104**

ACTIONPACK

With the help of Herr Masur's summary of his career, make a note of some key facts about your education and career:

1 Profession/occupation/trade 2 Education
3 First job 4 Career 5 Present position/responsibilities.

These phrases may help: **1** Ich bin (*X trade/profession*). **2** Ich habe (*1985*) (*name of O Levels/GCSE/A Levels*) gemacht. Ich habe in (*name of town*) (*name of subject*) studiert/gelernt. **3** Ich habe als (*name of job*) bei (*name of company*) angefangen. **4** Ich bin (*1990/dann/nach fünf Jahren*) (*job*) geworden. Ich bin (*1990/dann/nach fünf Jahren*) zu (*company*) gegangen. Ich bin (*1990/dann/nach fünf Jahren*) nach (*town/country*) gegangen. **5** Ich bin jetzt (*job*). Ich bin jetzt verantwortlich für (*area of responsibility*). Ich leite (*seit 1987/seit drei Jahren*) die Abteilung (*name of department*).

Die 4. EG-Richtlinie

The 4th EC directive has given a new official definition of *mittelgroßes Unternehmen*, but the lines are not quite so clearly drawn in practice, and many companies with three or four hundred employees may still look on themselves as *mittelständische Unternehmen*, i.e. part of the *Mittelstand*.

FACTFINDER

***3 Does company X have to submit a full annual financial statement? Its 15 employees generate annual sales around DM 7 million.

***4 GmbH Y has a balance-sheet total of DM 6.5 million, and 129 employees. Is it subject to a statutory audit (*abschlußprüfungspflichtig*)?

- Der Jahresabschluß besteht aus Bilanz und Gewinn- und Verlustrechnung mit einem ausführlichen Anhang.
- Außer kleinen Gesellschaften sind alle GmbHs abschlußprüfungspflichtig.
- Außer kleinen Gesellschaften müssen alle Kapitalgesellschaften ihre Jahresabschlußunterlagen einreichen bzw. publizieren.
- Kleine Gesellschaften hinterlegen verkürzte Bilanzen, keine Gewinn- und Verlustrechnungen.

Größenklassen für die Kapitalgesellschaften:

	Bilanzsumme	Umsatzerlöse	Arbeitnehmer
	Mio. DM	Mio. DM	
kleine	≤ 3,9	≤ 8	≤ 50
mittelgroße	> 3,9 ≤ 15,5	> 8 ≤ 32	51 ≤ 250
große	> 15,5	> 32	> 250

(Brooks/Mertin, *Neues deutsches Bilanzrecht*)

DATABASE

besteht aus *comprises*
Gewinn- und Verlustrechnung *profit and loss account*
mit einem ausführlichen Anhang *with comprehensive notes*
außer *except for*
müssen ... ... einreichen bzw. publizieren
 ... must submit or publish ...

FILASKILL

When you use *Filaword* – do just that! Make a card for each word and carry the cards with you until you know the words in German. Do this with every word you want to learn. This is also a useful way of remembering *Filafact*.

FILAWORD

die Firma *firm, company*
der Betrieb *business, company, operation*
die Gesellschaft *company, corporation*
das Unternehmen *company, enterprise*
die Kapitalgesellschaft *incorporated company*
die Personengesellschaft *partnership*
die GmbH (Gesellschaft mit beschränkter Haftung) *Ltd (limited company)*
die KG (Kommanditgesellschaft) *limited partnership*
die AG (Aktiengesellschaft) *Plc (public limited company)*
die Gruppe *group*
der Konzern *concern, group*

Mitglieder der Wirtschaftsprüferkammer

Altersstruktur der Mitglieder. Ende 1990 nahm die Wirtschaftsprüferkammer ihr zwölftausendstes Mitglied auf.

Düsseldorf

MIT ABSTAND AN DER SPITZE

Leisure is a growth area in Germany. Long holidays, reduced working hours and a rumoured decline in the work ethic prompt Germans to pay serious money for structured leisure. Home improvements are a popular pastime, making the DIY market the largest in Europe. A house of your own (*Eigenheim*) is often custom-built for life by its future occupants – DIY professionals looking for quality when they purchase tools and materials.

FILAWORD
die Freizeit *leisure*
das Heimwerken *do-it-yourself, DIY*
der Heimwerker *DIY enthusiast*
der Markt *market, (super)store, centre*
das Sortiment *range*
der Umsatz *turnover, sales*

Prognosen für die Freizeit

FACTFINDER
***1 What are the two biggest leisure sectors?

Bis 1995 wird die jährliche Freizeit in der Bundesrepublik Deutschland nochmals um 9,2% zunehmen, der private Freizeitkonsum wird um weitere 33% wachsen und die Ausgaben der privaten Haushalte für die Freizeit werden auf 300 Mrd. DM (1985: 226 Mrd. DM) ansteigen. Zu diesem Ergebnis kommt das Institut für Freizeitwirtschaft, München, in seiner jüngsten Marktuntersuchung „Wachstumsfelder im Freizeitbereich bis 1995". Das schnellste Wachstum wird dabei für den heute schon neben dem Tourismus größten Freizeitbereich – die Aktivitäten im Zusammenhang mit der „hauswirtschaftlichen Freizeit" – prognostiziert. (*Presse-Information KölnMesse*)

FILAFACT *werden*
As in the English 'leisure **will** increase by 1995', **werden** plus the *infinitive* of another verb forms the future:

Bis 1995 **wird** die Freizeit *zunehmen*.

It's easy to confuse the future with the passive, where *werden* is used with the past participle of another verb. On its own, *werden* is equivalent to the English 'become'. (➡ P 102-104)

EXECUTIVE SKILLS
***1 *Freizeitbereich* in the last sentence has a definite article. What is it?
**2 Find one or more expressions in *Prognosen für die Freizeit* consisting of a preposition + verb which mean *a* to increase to *b* to increase by.
***3 Can you find two more verbs in *Prognosen für die Freizeit* which refer to the future? *a* zunehmen *b* _____ *c* _____
***4 And can you find one verb which is in the passive?

Ein OBI-Markt

Visitenkarte

Dealing with the leisure market, it seemed appropriate to ask Dr Utho Creusen, personnel manager at DIY-franchiser OBI, about his hobbies.

FACTFINDER
**2 How many types of hobby does Dr Creusen mention?

Dr. Creusen: Ich heiße Utho Creusen. Ich bin in der OBI-Systemzentrale in der Geschäftsleitung tätig und zuständig für den Bereich Personal, Organisationsentwicklung und Franchising.
  Ich habe sehr viele Hobbys. Erstmal ist mein Beruf mein Hobby. Dann habe ich eine große Familie – ich habe vier Kinder. Dann treibe ich relativ viel Sport, um mich fit zu halten, das macht mir Spaß. Dann beschäftige ich mich unheimlich gerne mit wissenschaftlichen Dingen. Ich habe neben meiner Tätigkeit hier bei OBI in Soziologie promoviert, und im Augenblick versuche ich mich zu habilitieren. Heimwerken – das macht meine Frau!

DATABASE
um ... zu *in order to ...*
das macht mir Spaß *I enjoy that*
mit wissenschaftlichen Dingen *with academic things*
Ich habe ... promoviert *I did a doctorate ...*
mich zu habilitieren *to habilitate (i.e. write a thesis that will qualify me for university teaching)*

FILAFACT *verbs*
Verbs like 'I *occupy* **myself**' are known as reflexive verbs. German has more reflexive verbs than English, e.g.:

Ich *beschäftige* **mich** mit wissenschaftlichen Dingen.
Ich versuche **mich** zu *habilitieren*.

In the *Glossary*, you'll find reflexive verbs preceded by *sich*. ➡ P 100

Utho Creusen

ACTIONPACK
Use Dr Creusen's description as a basis for describing your hobbies. You'll probably need to use a dictionary.

38 DEUTSCHES BUSINESS-MAGAZIN

Marktführer in Deutschland

OBI, Germany's leading chain of DIY centres, is riding high on the home-improvement wave, with an enviable level of public awareness.

FACTFINDER
**1 What is OBI's position in the market?

Dr. Creusen: Im Bekanntheitsgrad steht OBI mit Abstand an der Spitze. Wir haben eine Reihe von ungestützten Untersuchungen gemacht, „Was fällt Ihnen ein bei dem Begriff Bau- und Heimwerkermarkt?", und etwa 97% sagten dann unter anderem „OBI". Das ist ein traumhaft hoher Wert. Mit 203 Märkten haben wir die meisten Verkaufsstellen und mit 1,8 Milliarden den größten Umsatz in der Bau- und Heimwerkermarktbranche. Wir können uns insofern also ganz getrost Marktführer in Deutschland nennen.

DATABASE
Bekanntheitsgrad (*m*) *level of awareness*
mit Abstand an der Spitze *top of the league by a long chalk*
Was fällt Ihnen ein *What do you think of*
ganz getrost *quite confidently*

Listung

OBI's central purchasing committee establishes a product range from which the individual DIY superstores can make their choice. They buy directly from the supplier at the agreed preferential rates.

FACTFINDER
*2 How many products does the average OBI superstore carry?
*3 How much is imported?

Dr Creusen: Wir haben eine Kommission: Das sind vier gewählte Marktleiter und zwei gewählte Franchise-Partner. Diese Kommission legt ein Gesamtsortiment fest, eine sogenannte Listung mit 150 000 Artikeln, die geführt werden können. In einem OBI-Markt werden aber durchschnittlich nur 20 000 bis 25 000 geführt. Das heißt, der Marktleiter hat die Möglichkeit, sich aus diesen 150 000 Artikeln sein Sortiment individuell zusammenzustellen. Dadurch können wir gewährleisten, daß wir diese 150 000 Artikel relativ günstig einkaufen können, aber auf der anderen Seite noch immer die hohe Flexibilität im Markt haben. Es wird zum größten Prozentsatz auf dem deutschen Markt eingekauft. Unter zehn Prozent wird importiert.

DATABASE
legt ... fest *decides on ...*
die geführt werden können *which may be carried*
sich ... zusammenzustellen *to put together ...*
Dadurch können wir gewährleisten *That way we can ensure*
relativ günstig *at a relatively good price*

FILASKILL
When you see *das heißt* (abbreviated *d.h.*, and equivalent to 'i.e.') you can expect an explanation or expansion of what's gone before.

a Montage- und Füllschaum

Nach DIN 4102/B2, zum Abdichten und Isolieren, zum Ausfüllen von Wandfugen und zum Kleben und Montieren von Türzargen usw.

600 ml bei OBI DM 8,95

EXECUTIVE SKILLS
***1 Find out what you can do with these products by looking for verbs disguised as nouns.
***2 What preposition introduces these verbal nouns here? It's equivalent to the English 'for (do)ing'.
***3 What gender are these verbal nouns? Clue: they're not masculine.

TiP

Inserts (Beilagen) in local, regional and national newspapers are a common form of advertising in Germany. OBI uses inserts for the main thrust of its advertising strategy.

OBI Bau+Heimwerkermärkte

b Blitzzement

Für die schnelle Montage, zum Verdübeln, Gießen, Verankern und Befestigen von Eisen und Rohren; für innen und außen.

10 kg bei OBI DM 16,95

c Spachtelmasse

Weiß, zum Schließen von Löchern und Rissen sowie zum Glätten von Unebenheiten; für innen und außen.

4 kg bei OBI DM	8,50
8 kg bei OBI DM	11,95

Düsseldorf

Blechwender am Kühl- und Inspektionsbett

HANDEL MIT STAHL

Until 1990 the Salzgitter Group was unusual in that it was 100% government-owned, having been founded in 1937 to exploit the ore deposits in the Salzgitter area. The steel crisis in the late seventies and early eighties forced Salzgitter to adopt an ambitious programme of modernization and restructuring to diversify out of reliance on steel production. In 1990 the Salzgitter Group was privatized and became a subsidiary of Preussag AG.

FILAWORD
die Stahlerzeugung *steel production*
die Stahlkrise *steel crisis*
die Umstrukturierung *restructuring*
staatlich *government-owned*
privatisieren *to privatize*
der Auftrag *order*
die Fachleute (pl) *experts*

FILASKILL
When you learn a noun, make sure you learn it with *der*, *die* or *das*, so that you can recognize the gender.

ACTIONPACK
Build up a short profile of your job by referring to *Visitenkarte*:

1 Ich bin (Sekretärin/Leiter der Abteilung_____ /Einkäufer bei der Firma_____).
2 Die tägliche Arbeit besteht darin, (die Post zu lesen/Briefe zu schreiben/Berichte zu schreiben).
3 Zu meinen Aufgaben gehört es auch, (_____ zu organisieren/ _____ zu besuchen).
4 Ich bin verantwortlich für (die Buchhaltung/ die Abwicklung von Aufträgen/die Schreibarbeit von Herrn|Frau_____ /die Post).

Visitenkarte

Herr Hermann Lohmar and Herr Erhard Seeger gave personal profiles and an outline of their activities at Salzgitter Stahl GmbH, the company's steel trading subsidiary in Düsseldorf.

FACTFINDER
*1 What is Herr Lohmar's job?
*2 What is Herr Seeger's job?

Herr Lohmar: Mein Name ist Hermann Lohmar. Ich bin kaufmännischer Angestellter mit dem Titel Prokurist bei Salzgitter Stahl, Leiter der Abteilung Offshore.

Die tägliche Arbeit besteht zunächst einmal darin festzustellen, wo es neue Projekte gibt, denn im Offshorebereich bekommt man nicht automatisch Anfragen. Zu meinen Aufgaben gehört es auch, Werbeaktionen zu starten, Messen zu besuchen, die Mitarbeiter zu kontrollieren, daß sie die Abwicklung von Aufträgen richtig durchführen. Die Tätigkeit ist mit sehr vielen Reisen verbunden.

Herr Seeger: Mein Name ist Erhard Seeger. Ich bin Mathematiker von der Ausbildung her. Ich leite die Controlling-Abteilung dieses Hauses und die Organisationsabteilung.

Ich sage immer, ich bin das betriebswirtschaftliche Gewissen des Unternehmens. Das heißt also, ich bin derjenige, der verantwortlich ist für die Wirtschaftlichkeitsrechnungen, für die Controlling-Maßnahmen, für die Ergebnisvergleiche, für die Planung der Ergebnisse, für die Berichterstattung innerhalb des Hauses und auch die Berichterstattung des Hauses an die Gesellschafter und an die Aufsichtsgremien.

DATABASE
besteht zunächst einmal darin festzustellen
 initially consists in ascertaining
das betriebswirtschaftliche Gewissen *the budgeting conscience*
derjenige, der *the person who*
Berichterstattung (f) *reporting*

FILAFACT *infinitive clauses*
Notice how Herr Lohmar says it's part of his job *to launch* advertising campaigns, *to visit* fairs, *to supervise* staff:

Zu meinen Aufgaben gehört es, Werbeaktionen *zu starten*, Messen *zu besuchen*, die Mitarbeiter *zu kontrollieren*.

The infinitive comes at the end of the clause. If the verb has a separable prefix, *zu* goes after the prefix, e.g. *festzustellen*. ➡ **P 108**

Düsseldorf

Gebogene Grobbleche für eine Druckrohrleitung

Das A und O des Geschäfts

Steel trading in the offshore sector is highly specialized, as an article in Salzgitter's in-house magazine emphasizes. Long lead times before contracts are signed are followed by demands for fast delivery.

FACTFINDER
**1 Why does delivery have to be fast?

Die Mitarbeiter der Offshore-Abteilung sind Fachleute auf ihrem Gebiet: Beratung und zeitraubende Gespräche mit den technischen Vertretern der Kunden sind das A und O des Geschäfts. Es vergeht manchmal ein Jahr und mehr, bis der Kunde den Auftrag plaziert. Dann fordert er schnellste Materiallieferung, denn jeder Tag Verspätung bei der Förderung von Öl und Gas kostet Geld. Entscheidend im Offshore-Geschäft ist allerdings ein hoher Qualitätsstandard.

Hermann Lohmar, der Leiter der Offshore-Abteilung, betont, daß man sich bei Salzgitter Stahl GmbH die Sache nicht leicht macht: "Wir verstehen uns nicht nur als Händler, sondern bieten unseren Kunden eine breite Service-Palette. Qualität und systematische Verfolgung der Termine werden großgeschrieben."
(Salzgitter Stahl Kurier)

Hermann Lohmar   *Erhard Seeger*

DATABASE
zeitraubende Gespräche *time-consuming discussions*
das A und O *the be-all and end-all*
daß man sich ... die Sache nicht leicht macht *that one doesn't just take the easy option ...*
Wir verstehen uns *We regard ourselves*
... werden großgeschrieben *We attach great importance to ...*

EXECUTIVE SKILLS
**1 Here are some points covered in *Das A und O des Geschäfts:* a quality b consultation and discussion c delivery d placing the order e systematic scheduling f wide range of services g extraction of oil and gas. Can you put them in the order in which they're mentioned?

FILAFACT *case*
When trying to understand a sentence or a clause, look **1** for the main verb **2** for the subject (in the nominative case and agreeing with the verb) **3** for any object:

..., bis der Kunde**(2)** den Auftrag**(3)** plaziert**(1)**.
(... until the customer**(2)** places**(1)** the order**(3)**.)

Den Auftrag is a direct object, and is in the accusative case. With some verbs, like *geben* (to give), *bieten* (to offer), *liefern* (to deliver) you may also have **4** an indirect object, which will be in the dative case:

Wir**(2)** bieten**(1)** unseren Kunden**(4)** eine breite Service-Palette**(3)**.
(We**(2)** offer**(1)** our customers**(4)** a wide range of services**(3)**.)

On how to work out the case of a noun ➡ **P 98**.

Die Mitarbeiter

Mitarbeiter (literally 'co-worker') is a term you'll meet frequently in German companies. It can mean 'colleague' or 'employee' depending on context, and refers to all employees in the company. Herr Seeger defined two general positions in company hierarchies which can often cause confusion. A *Prokurist* is a *leitender Angestellter*, i.e. a member of the middle management. This person is empowered to sign legal documents on behalf of the company and appears in a public register. A *Sachbearbeiter* is broadly speaking an employee carrying out clerical tasks, with a closely defined area of responsibility.

FACTFINDER
*2 Who can a *Prokurist* act for?
**3 Do *Sachbearbeiter* belong to management?

Herr Seeger: Ein Prokurist ist im Handelsregister eingetragen. Er kann für das Unternehmen handeln, das heißt, er kann für die Gesellschaft unterschreiben.

Sachbearbeiter sind in unserem Haus die Gruppe von Mitarbeitern, die das Tagesgeschäft entwickeln, die also keinerlei Führungsfunktionen haben. Der Sachbearbeiter hat normalerweise ein bestimmtes Arbeitsfeld, das er mehr oder weniger selbständig nach Anleitung betreut.

DATABASE
für ... handeln *act for ...*
Tagesgeschäft (n) *day-to-day business*
mehr oder weniger selbständig *more or less independently*
nach Anleitung *according to instructions*

FILAFACT *relative clauses*
Notice how Herr Seeger uses relative clauses to give additional information about nouns, just as one might say in English 'employees who ...' or 'an area of responsibility which ...':

die Gruppe von *Mitarbeitern* (m, pl), **die** (m, pl) das Tagesgeschäft **entwickeln**,
ein bestimmtes *Arbeitsfeld* (n, sing.), **das** (n, sing.) er **betreut**.

You can recognize a relative clause by the relative pronoun at the beginning (*der, die, das, den, dem, dessen, deren*) and the verb at the end of the clause. ➡ **P 99, 107**

T i P

When German speakers refer to halb neun, *they mean 8.30, not 9.30. You need to be extra careful when making appointments. It pays to be on time, otherwise you may find you have been edged out of a busy person's schedule. Anything over a quarter of an hour late is considered extremely impolite.*

Düsseldorf

MILLIMETERGENAU - MITTEN IN DER NORDSEE

Mannesmann was the first of the big German steel producers to diversify into areas such as communications systems and electronics. One of the group's most spectacular technical achievements must surely be the jacking operation to raise six drilling platforms in the North Sea Ekofisk oilfield. A Mannesmann subsidiary carried out the operation which is reviewed in the following accounts.

In einer beispiellosen Aktion hob Mannesmann Rexroth im vergangenen Jahr sechs Nordsee-Bohrinseln im norwegischen Ekofisk-Feld samt der zugehörigen Verbindungsbrücken, Produktions- und Versorgungsleitungen um 6 m in die Höhe. Dadurch wurde der Sicherheitsabstand der Plattformen zum Meer, der sich durch das Absinken des Meeresbodens verringert hatte, wiederhergestellt. Um den Komplex mit einem Gesamtgewicht von 40 000 t zum Teil gleichzeitig anheben zu können, setzte Rexroth 122 Hydraulikzylinder (aus Rohren der Mannesmannröhren-Werke) und 212 Hydraulikaggregate ein. (Mannesmann-Illustrierte, 1988)

„**Mannesmann Rexroth** erhielt von der Phillips Petroleum den Auftrag, sechs Gasbohrplattformen in der Nordsee hydraulisch anzuheben. Diese Plattformen hatten sich im Laufe ihres Betriebes abgesenkt, und es bestand die Gefahr, daß bei einer großen Welle, einem großen Sturm, die Plattformen mit ihren Einrichtungen überschwemmt würden.

Mannesmann Rexroth hat dann gleichzeitig diese Plattformen hydraulisch angehoben. Das geschah folgendermaßen: An die Plattformbeine, mit denen die Plattformen auf dem Meeresboden stehen, wurden seitlich Hydraulikzylinder angeschraubt; zwischen diesen Hydraulikzylindern wurden dann die Beine der Plattformen durchgetrennt. Anschließend wurden die Plattformen hydraulisch angehoben, und in die entstehenden Lücken von etwa sechs Metern neue Stahlstücke eingesetzt und verschraubt. Das ganze Unternehmen mußte gleichzeitig erfolgen, da die Plattformen dabei weiter betriebsbereit blieben. Es geschah innerhalb weniger Stunden, und diese Gleichzeitigkeit wurde erreicht durch einen Computer, der die ganzen Vorgänge millimetergenau steuerte."

(Dr. Hartmut Graf Plettenberg, Leiter Öffentlichkeitsarbeit, Mannesmann AG, 1988)

„Insel-Stadt im Meer" hochgehoben

Vor einigen Wochen sorgte ein spektakuläres Ereignis nicht nur bei der Fachwelt für beträchtliches Aufsehen: Inmitten der tosenden Nordsee wurden sechs Plattformen der Phillips Petroleum Company Norway im Öl- und Erdgas-Bohrfeld Ekofisk um sechs Meter angehoben. Experten hatten in letzter Zeit ein stetiges Absinken des Meeresbodens (und damit auch der Bohr- und Förderinseln) festgestellt. Sicherheit vor einer möglichen „Jahrhundertwelle" bestand nach dieser Beobachtung weiterhin weder für die Plattformen noch für die darauf arbeitenden Menschen, so daß unbedingt etwas zur Lösung dieses Problems geschehen mußte. Man entschloß sich schließlich zu diesem Hebeversuch. Mit der Durchführung der auf den ersten Blick „unmöglichen Aktion" wurde die Mannesmann Rexroth-Gruppe beauftragt, die in der Hydraulik-Anwendung über das größte Know-how verfügte. Schier Unglaubliches wurde von den Hydraulik-Spezialisten aus Deutschland, Holland und Frankreich verlangt. Nicht nur ein Gesamtgewicht von über 40 000 t mußte mit den sechs Plattformen in die Höhe gehievt werden – allein 10 500 t wog die Hotelplattform –, vier der sechs miteinander verbundenen Inseln mußten wegen diverser Brücken, Produktions- und Versorgungsleitungen auch noch gleichzeitig und gleichmäßig angehoben werden.
(Mannesmann-Post, November 1987)

DATABASE
hob ... in die Höhe *raised*
Bohrinsel (f) *drilling platform*
Sicherheitsabstand (m) *safety distance*
das Absinken des Meeresbodens *the subsidence of the sea bed*
Um ... anheben zu können *In order to be able to raise ...*
gleichzeitig *simultaneously*
Welle (f) *wave*
Beine (n, pl) *legs*
sorgte ... für ... Aufsehen ... *caused a ... sensation*
Man entschloß sich ... zu *It was ... decided to carry out*
mußte ... in die Höhe gehievt werden *had to be lifted ...*
mußten ... angehoben werden *had to be lifted ...*
Zwischenstücke (n, pl) *spacers*
An ... erinnern jetzt nur noch *The only thing that still reminds one of ... are*

PROFILE *operation Ekofisk*
See if you can work out the details of the operation by reading the four accounts.

1. The owner of the platforms
2. The company carrying out the operation
3. The year in which the operation took place
4. The origin of the experts
5. The reason for the operation
6. The number of platforms raised simultaneously
7. Control of the operation
8. The number of hydraulic cylinders
9. The method of attachment to the platform legs
10. The total weight of the platforms
11. The material comprising the spacers
12. The cost of the operation
13. The duration of the operation

TiP
In 1919, the constitution of the new German republic decreed that nobility should lose their privileges, and titles should become part of the name. Most common is von, *e.g.* Herr von Sohlern. *Mannesmann's head of Public Relations is a count with a doctorate, who strictly speaking should be addressed as* 'Herr Dr. Graf Plettenberg'.

Die Aktion ist gelungen, die Ekofisk-Inseln stehen wieder auf ihren um 6 m verlängerten Beinen. Deutlich zu sehen sind die Zwischenstücke, mit denen die Inseln und die Menschen darauf nunmehr sicher vor einer eventuellen „Jahrhundertwelle" sind. An die spektakuläre Hebe-Aktion, die einen Meilenstein in der Offshoretechnik darstellt und mehr als 350 Mill. Dollar kostete, erinnern jetzt nur noch die neuen Zwischenstücke. (Mannesmann-Post, November 1987)

FILAFACT *the past*
Notice three ways of referring to the past:

1) Perfect:
   Mannesmann Rexroth *hat* diese Plattform *angehoben*.
   ➡ P 104

2) Past tense:
   Ein Computer *steuerte* die Vorgänge. (regular verb *steuern*)
   Mannesmann Rexroth *hob* sechs Bohrinseln in die Höhe. (irregular verb *heben*)
   As in English, the past tense is recognizable by a particular ending on the verb (as in 'control' - 'controll**ed**') or by a vowel change in the verb stem (as in 'see' - '**saw**'). Past forms of verbs that change their vowel are listed as separate entries in the *Glossary*, and also indicated under the heading of the infinitive: e.g. *sehen (ie)*, *a, e* = sehen (si*e*ht), s*a*h, ges*e*hen. ➡ P 102, 104

3) Pluperfect:
   Diese Plattformen *hatten* sich *abgesenkt*.
   As in English ('the platforms *had subsided*'), the pluperfect refers further back in time to an event which took place before the event described in the past tense. ➡ P 104

EXECUTIVE SKILLS
Here are some infinitive forms of verbs referring to the past in *Millimetergenau* (some occur more than once). List the forms you can find:

***1 *Perfect* *a* anheben *b* gelingen.

***2 *Past* *a* heben *b* einsetzen *c* erhalten *d* bestehen (x2) *e* geschehen (x2) *f* müssen (x4) *g* bleiben *h* steuern *i* sorgen *j* sich entschließen *k* verfügen *l* wiegen *m* kosten.

***3 *Pluperfect* *a* sich verringern *b* sich absenken *c* feststellen.

***4 And finally, can you spot the verbs which are in the *past* and *passive*?
a wiederherstellen *b* anschrauben *c* durchtrennen *d* anheben (x2) *e* einsetzen *f* verschrauben *g* erreichen *h* beauftragen *i* verlangen.

Düsseldorf

VOM COIL ZUM KUNDEN 4
Wareneingangsprüfung

BMW – Wer ist wer?
Dr. Rudolf Harlfinger, Leiter Werkstofftechnik. Ausbildung: Mechanikerlehre; Studium Maschinenbau. Hobbys: Gartenarbeit, Basteln, Musik (spielt Klavier und Flöte, Jazz und Klassik), Segeln, Schwimmen, Skiwandern.

BMW – Wer ist wer?
Veit-Rüdiger Thomas, Werkstofftechnik, zuständig für das Preßwerk. Ausbildung: Lehre, Werkstoffprüfung. Hobbys: Radfahren, Theaterbesuch, Musik, Fotografie.

BMW – Wer ist wer?
Friedrich Fichtner, Leiter des Physiklabors. Ausbildung: Lehre bei BMW, Werkstoffprüfung; Studium Fachhochschule Maschinenbau. Hobbys: Reisen, Fotografie.

Werkstoffprüfung

Dr. Harlfinger: Die Werkstoffprüfung ist überwiegend zerstörend. Man kann also nur hin und wieder stichprobenmäßig prüfen, da sonst die ganze Ware zerstört ist. Aber zerstörungsfreie Röntgen-, Ultraschall- und magnetinduktive Prüfverfahren setzen sich mehr und mehr durch, wo man die Sicherheit braucht.

Stichproben im Sinne der Statistik können wir nicht betreiben. Wir können nur ein Audit machen, das heißt ab und zu mal ein Teil herausnehmen und prüfen. Wie viele Teile geprüft werden, hängt von verschiedenen Faktoren ab. Zunächst weiß man aus Erfahrung: Es ist ein guter Lieferant, bei dem wir nicht so oft prüfen müssen. Dann kennen wir die Schwierigkeit der Teile: Wir können sagen, bei diesem Teil kann überhaupt nichts schiefgehen, also werden wir die Prüfung sehr zurückschrauben. Es gibt auch Teile, die nicht stichprobenmäßig, sondern hundertprozentig geprüft werden, wie zum Beispiel Achsschenkel. Jeder Achsschenkel läuft über eine Prüfstrecke, wo die Festigkeit und das Material geprüft werden.

> **TiP**
> "If you're invited to someone's home, take a small gift, such as flowers, chocolates or tea. The wrapping paper should be taken off before you hand over the flowers. A bottle of British wine has novelty value!" (Roger Thomas, consul (commercial), Frankfurt)

Das BMW-Gebäude in München – der sogenannte "Vierzylinder"

Trennwand

Herr Thomas: Die Trennwand schließt den Gepäckraum zum Fahrgastraum ab. Das Blech für die Trennwand kommt in sogenannten Coils an. Die Ringe dürfen äußerlich nicht beschädigt sein. Sie müssen frei von Rost sein, damit das Material so, wie es hier abgeladen wird, an die Presse gehen und einwandfrei ohne Reklamation verarbeitet werden kann. Das Material wird bei Eingang auf Fehler begutachtet. Während der Abpressung wird verfolgt, ob sich das Material einwandfrei umformen läßt, also unseren Anforderungen entspricht.

Herr Fichtner: Es ist nicht möglich, die Coils vor dem Pressen aufzuschneiden und dann entsprechende Proben zu ziehen. Erst wenn an der Presse Umformschwierigkeiten in Form von Rissen auftreten, werden genaue Untersuchungen durchgeführt.

Nockenwelle

Herr Fichtner: Die Firma Lydmet ist, bevor sie an uns liefern durfte, von unserem Außendienst und auch von den Werkstoffleuten besichtigt worden. Man hat sich also davon überzeugt, daß dort richtig gegossen werden kann. Diese Firma hat auch ein ganz hervorragendes Qualitätssicherungssystem, so daß mögliche Fehler von vornherein ausgeschaltet werden können.

Die Nockenwelle ist eines der wenigen Teile, wo wir jede Lieferung prüfen. Wir können aber nur eine Nockenwelle prüfen und müssen dann auf das gesamte Lieferlos schließen. Bei dieser Prüfung brechen wir die Nocken, um zu sehen, wie weit diese weißerstarrt sind. Es sind aber dann in der Fertigung nachgeschaltet nochmal Härtemessungen vorgesehen, wo wir uns über mehrere Teile – fünf oder sechs – zerstörungsfrei überzeugen: Die Nockenwellen sind in Ordnung oder sind Ausschuß.

DÜSSELDORFER SPEZIALITÄTEN

Napoleon is reputed to have dubbed Düsseldorf a miniature Paris, and ever since then the city has been keen to live up to this accolade. Düsseldorf's *Champs-Élysées*, the *Kö*, was built in 1804 on the site of the old city walls. Its present name stems from 1848 when the visiting Prussian King Friedrich Wilhelm IV was pelted with horse dung by a Francophile citizen. To appease the King, local dignitaries named the site of his affront *Königsallee*.

Königsallee

Düsseldorf is an extrovert city, with a reputation for avant-garde art, and advertising. A stroll down the *Kö* reveals the Americanized glitz of a nouveau-riche society accustomed to an uninhibited display of wealth. The latest fashions are promenaded along the *Kö* in winter and summer.

If you are planning a visit to one of Düsseldorf's trade fairs, make sure you book your hotel in good time. For an international fair like DRUPA, held every four years, hotels are likely to be fully booked four years in advance. Check out the prices of your hotel during *Messezeiten* as they may be as much as DM 50 or DM 100 more than prices at other times.

Straßenkarneval

Steigenberger Parkhotel Düsseldorf
Ein kleiner Auszug aus der Speisenkarte des Restaurants

RÔTISSERIE

Vorspeisen

Angeräucherte Entenbrust, rosa gebraten,
mit Avocado und Papaya in süß-saurer Sauce .... DM 25,00

Norwegischer Lachs und Jakobsmuscheln
in Lauch-Trüffelgelee und Sauce Grelette 29,00

Suppen

Spargelcrème mit Parmaschinken 12,00

Suppe von Steinbutt, Garnelen
und Jakobsmuscheln mit Safran und Spinat 16,00

Fisch

Lachs und Petersfisch vom Grill in Basilikum-Sauce
mit Gemüsestreifen, Safrannudeln 30,00

Seezungenfilet, gebraten mit Champignons,
Speck und norwegischen Shrimps, Petersilienkartoffeln 42,00

Fleisch

Medaillons vom Schweinefilet in Estragon-Jus,
Brokkoli und Mandelbutter, Karotten-Kartoffelpurée 28,00

In Rotwein geschmorte Rinderroulade mit magerem Speck
und Kräuterpilzen gefüllt, tourniertes Saisongemüse,
Kartoffel-Krusteln 32,00

foto dpa

Düsseldorf à la Carte

FACTFINDER
*1 How many dishes in the menu include seafood?
*2 Which dish would you avoid if you don't like pork?
**3 Your guest is keen on fried fish. What could you recommend?

FILAWORD
das Essen *food, meal*
die Vorspeise *starter*
das Fleisch *meat*
der Fisch *fish*
die Nachspeise/der Nachtisch *dessert*

Düsseldorf auf einen Blick

Landeshauptstadt Nordrhein-Westfalen

Einwohnerzahl:	570 000
Flüsse:	Rhein, Düssel
Postleitzahl:	D/W-4000
Telefonvorwahl:	(0)211-
Flughafen:	Rhein-Ruhr-Flughafen (in Lohausen, 8 km vom Zentrum); S-Bahn (S7) zur Stadtmitte.
Information:	Verkehrsverein, Konrad-Adenauer-Platz (Immermann-Hof), Tel. 35 05 05
Hauptpostamt:	Charlottenstr. 61, geöffnet Mo-Fr 7-21 Uhr, Sa-So 12-20 Uhr.
Wichtige Messen:	**boot** (Bootsausstellung), **DRUPA** (Druck und Papier), **IGEDO** (Mode), **INTERKAMA** (Meß- und Automatisierungstechnik), **INTERPACK** (Verpackungsmaschinen, Packmittel, Süßwarenmaschinen), **K** (Kunststoff und Kautschuk)
Sehenswürdigkeiten:	Königsallee ('Kö'), Altstadt, Rheinturm (Rundsicht), Schloß Benrath, Kunstsammlung Nordrhein-Westfalen (20. Jahrhundert), Skulpturen in der Stadt
Typisches Essen:	Sauerbraten
Typisches Getränk:	Altbier
Wichtige Termine:	Karneval (Februar), Kirmes (Juli)

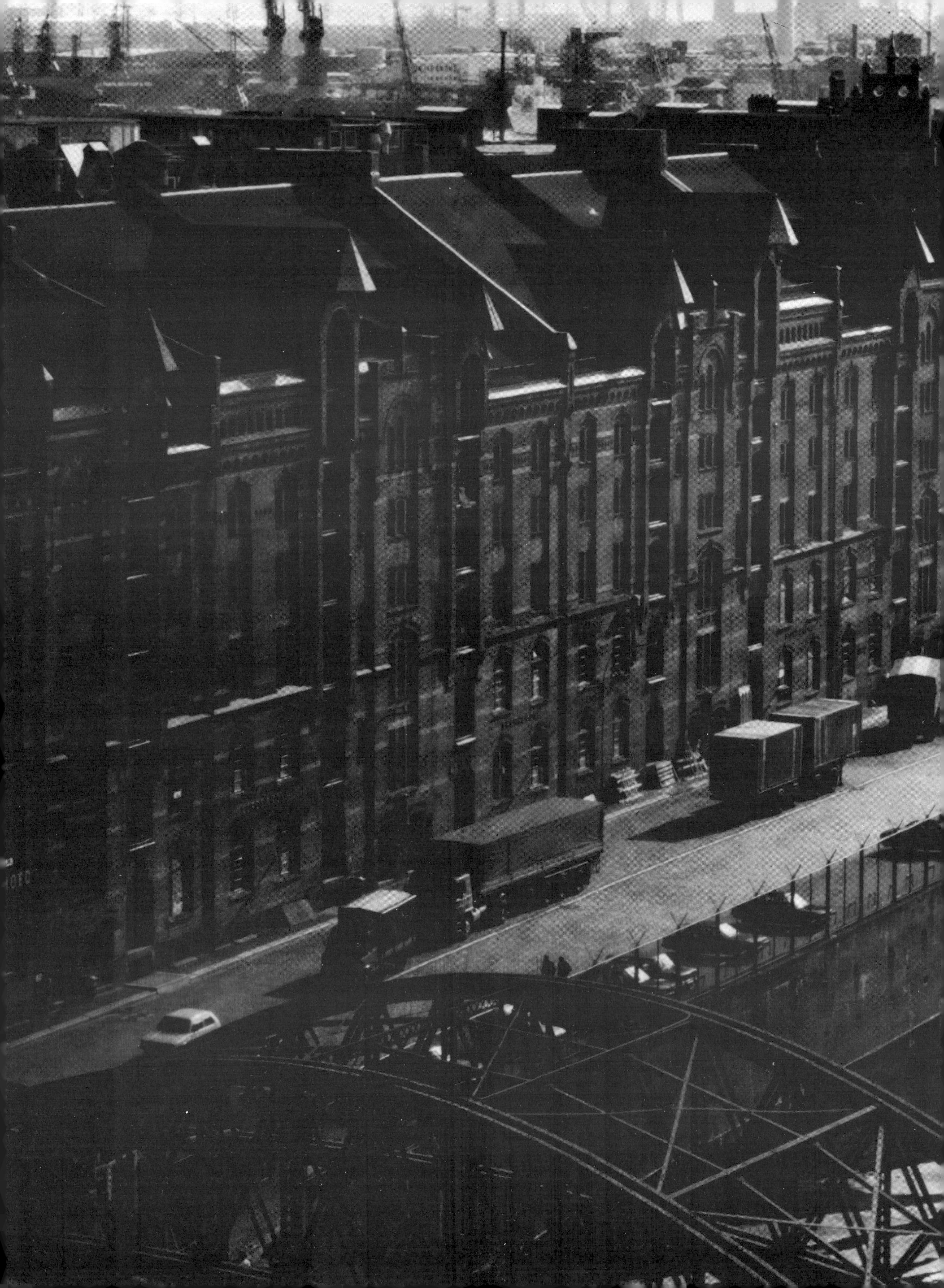

Hamburg

Das Tor zur Welt

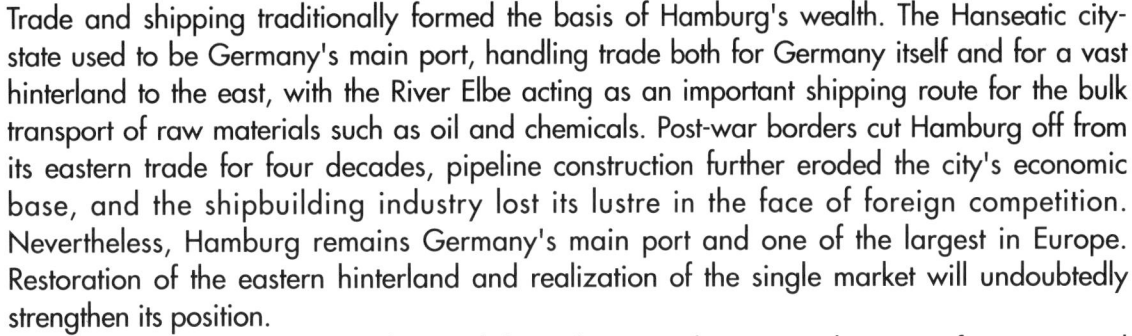

Trade and shipping traditionally formed the basis of Hamburg's wealth. The Hanseatic city-state used to be Germany's main port, handling trade both for Germany itself and for a vast hinterland to the east, with the River Elbe acting as an important shipping route for the bulk transport of raw materials such as oil and chemicals. Post-war borders cut Hamburg off from its eastern trade for four decades, pipeline construction further eroded the city's economic base, and the shipbuilding industry lost its lustre in the face of foreign competition. Nevertheless, Hamburg remains Germany's main port and one of the largest in Europe. Restoration of the eastern hinterland and realization of the single market will undoubtedly strengthen its position.

Hamburg was slow to diversify out of dependence on shipping and promote future-oriented industrial development. Traditional disdain for smokestack industry together with a heavy tax burden in this Social-Democrat stronghold combined to make companies slow to invest, although the city is breaking out of its established mould by refocusing on electronics. New industries require a highly-trained workforce, and millions are being poured into the new technical university to provide home-grown engineers for the new era.

Zukunftsträchtige Industrie

Herr Reinhard Wolf of the Hamburg Handelskammer reflected on the city's maritime past and painted an optimistic picture of the future.

FACTFINDER
**1 What branches of industry did Hamburg attract in the past?
*2 What type of industry does Hamburg now aim to attract?

Herr Wolf: Hamburgs Ursprünge sind eng verbunden mit dem Hafen. Dadurch war die Industrie natürlich branchenmäßig schon vorgeprägt: nämlich erstens durch Industriezweige, die mit Schiffbau verbunden waren, und zweitens durch Industriezweige, die Massengüter transportierten, wie zum Beispiel die Mineralölverarbeitung und die chemische Industrie.

Gerade diese Industriezweige haben aber an ' Bedeutung verloren. Dies hat dazu geführt, daß Hamburg als Industriestandort strukturelle Probleme zu lösen hatte. Wir müssen andere Industrien in Hamburg stark machen. Ich denke, daß wir es bis zum Ende dieses Jahrhunderts schaffen, auch im Norden weitere zukunftsträchtige Industriezweige anzusiedeln und die bereits vorhandenen weiterzuentwickeln. Für die Zukunft denke ich insbesondere an alle Bereiche, die mit Elektronik zu tun haben.

DATABASE
eng verbunden mit *closely bound up with*
war die Industrie ... branchenmäßig schon vorgeprägt *the industrial sectors were ... already predetermined*
haben ... an Bedeutung verloren *... have diminished in importance*
Dies hat dazu geführt *This meant*
zu lösen hatte *had to solve*
wir es ... schaffen, ... anzusiedeln *... we will manage to establish ...*
zukunftsträchtig *with growth potential*
die bereits vorhandenen *the existing ones*
denke ich insbesondere an *I'm particularly thinking of*

FILAWORD
der Hafen *harbour, port, docks*
die Schiffahrt *shipping*
die Werft *dock, shipyard, hangar*
Übersee *overseas*
die Güter (*pl*) *goods*

Wußten Sie schon ...?

1 Die Freie und Hansestadt Hamburg ist ein Stadtstaat.
2 Die Fläche von Hamburg (755 km²) ist etwa so groß wie München, Frankfurt und Düsseldorf zusammen.
3 Hamburg mit seinem über 800 Jahre alten Hafen ist der größte Außenhandelsplatz Deutschlands.
4 Hamburg ist mit 2484 Brücken die brückenreichste Stadt Europas.

T i P

It is not normal in Germany to use first names and the familiar du form of address, except with friends and among young people. Office colleagues may never get onto first-name terms even if they work together for years.

Container in alle Welt

Hapag-Lloyd AG was the result of a merger between the Hamburg-Amerikanische Packetfahrt-Actien-Gesellschaft (HAPAG) and the Bremen-based Norddeutscher Lloyd. Up to the first world war, HAPAG was the biggest shipping company in the world with 206 ships. Having lost all but five ships following the Versailles Treaty, the fleet was built up again in the interwar period, only to be reduced to a single coaster after the second world war. Today, Hapag-Lloyd is a shipping, airline, and travel group with a world-wide liner service for container transport.

Filaword

die Reederei *shipping company/line*
das Verkehrsmittel *means of transport*
der Güterfernverkehr *long-distance freight (road)*
die Eisenbahn/Bahn/Bundesbahn *rail, railway*
der Spediteur *freight forwarder*
die Vertretung *agent*
buchen *to book*
die Buchung *booking*
verladen *to load, ship*
die Ladung *cargo, consignment*

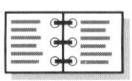

Fallstudie: Containerdienst

Herr Gerhard Simonsen, spokesman for Hapag-Lloyd, and Herr Burkhard Jäckel, head of freight shipping to the Middle East, provided information on container shipping. Find out the details by answering the questions.

Moderne Kommunikationssysteme im weltweiten Verbund

Data Processing and Communication

1 What was a common unit of loading for freight in the past?
2 What formed the basis for modern freight forwarding?
3 What are EDP and communications systems used for?
4 What two factors are important in the transport chain?

Die elektronische Datenverarbeitung

Herr Simonsen: Die elektronische Datenverarbeitung ist Voraussetzung für jeden Containertransport; ohne den Computer kann man keine Container dirigieren. Früher lud man den Sack in Hamburg ein und lud den Sack in New York aus. Heute geht der Container aber tief vom Inland in das andere Inland hinein, und diese Container müssen ja überwacht werden. Der Computer war Grundvoraussetzung für den gesamten Containerverkehr.

Zuverlässig und pünktlich

Wir nutzen die EDV und moderne Kommunikationssysteme weltweit und integriert. Als Instrument der Planung, Disposition, Kontrolle und Optimierung der Transporte. Damit in der Transportkette Zuverlässigkeit und Pünktlichkeit nicht zufällig sind. Alle, die an der Transportkette beteiligt sind, müssen zu jeder Zeit über den gleichen Informationsstand verfügen. Auch Ihre Dokumentation erstellen wir präzise und schnell, ganz nach Ihren Anforderungen.

(Weltweite Liniendienste)

Weltweite integrierte Nutzung der EDV

Database

müssen ja überwacht werden *have to be monitored, of course*
Zuverlässigkeit (f) *reliability*
zu jeder Zeit *at all times*
über ... verfügen *have access to ...*
ganz nach *in accordance with*

Filafact *prepositions*

The case of a noun may depend on the preposition that precedes it, e.g.:

für den Containerverkehr (accusative)
von dem (vom) Inland (dative)

Most prepositions are used with either the accusative (e.g. *bis, durch, für, gegen, ohne, um*) or the dative (*aus, außer, bei, gegenüber, mit, nach, seit, von, zu*). Some can be used with either case (*an, auf, hinter, in, neben, über, unter, vor, zwischen*), and with these, case affects meaning: accusative indicates directional movement from one place to another, answering the question 'where to', while dative indicates a state of rest or non-directional movement and answers the question 'where' (➡ P 106):

in das (ins) Inland (accusative)   (into the country)
in dem (im) Inland (dative)   (in the country)

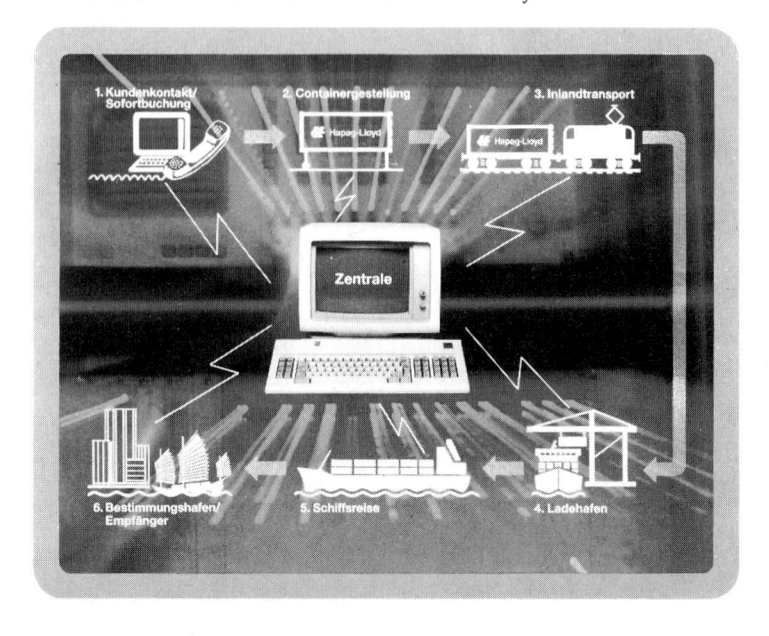

Ein Container für das Schiff X nach Dubai

SHIPMENT
1 Who does the prospective customer approach in Munich?
2 When is the cargo space for the container booked on the ship?
3 Where is the hypothetical container to be delivered for loading?
4 When does it have to be in Hamburg?
5 Where does the interchange take place?

Herr Jäckel: Der Ladungseigentümer wendet sich an unsere Vertretung in München und sagt, „ich möchte gerne zu der und der Zeit einen Container von Hamburg nach Dubai verladen". Dann wird er durch unseren dortigen Verkauf über Verlademöglichkeiten beraten, das heißt über Landverkehrsträger und über Schiffe, die in dem Zeitintervall, das er vorgibt, von Hamburg versegeln.

Nehmen wir an, es entsteht eine Buchung für einen Lkw-Landtransport und die Seeverladung des Containers von Hamburg nach Dubai. In dem Moment bucht unser Verkauf bei der entsprechenden Frachtabteilung den Schiffsraum für diesen Container für das Schiff X nach Dubai. Zum gleichen Zeitpunkt gibt der Verkaufskollege auch eine Buchungsvoranmeldung für den Container, daß beispielsweise per Gestellungsdatum 20.8. diesem Kunden bitte ein 20-Fuß Container morgens um acht auf den Hof der Fabrik gestellt werden soll. Zu gegebener Zeit wird die Leercontainergestellung in der Fabrik und der Landtransport für den Kunden organisiert und durchgeführt.

In aller Regel müssen Container, die mit einem Schiff ausgehend von Hamburg verladen werden, 24 Stunden vor Ankunft des Schiffes hier sein. Der Containertruck fährt an das Gate des Terminals, das wir benutzen. Dort wird ein Interchange gemacht zwischen dem Vorlauf und dem Seelauf, der nun beginnen soll. Nach Verladung des Containers auf das Schiff findet der Seetransport nach Dubai und die Auslieferung an den dortigen Empfänger statt.

DATABASE
Der Ladungseigentümer wendet sich an *The owner of the shipment contacts*
zu der und der Zeit *at such and such a time*
durch unseren dortigen Verkauf *by our sales office there*
Nehmen wir an *Let's assume*
per Gestellungsdatum 20.8 *on the delivery date 20 August*
diesem Kunden *for this customer*
gestellt werden soll *should be delivered*
Zu gegebener Zeit *In due course*
In aller Regel *Normally*

EXECUTIVE SKILLS
**1 What is the order in which these stages described by Herr Jäckel take place?
  a Ankunft des Containers in Hamburg *b* Containergestellung
  c Buchungsvoranmeldung für den Container *d* Beratung
  e Ankunft des Schiffes in Hamburg *f* Buchung.
*2 Does Herr Jäckel's hypothetical customer utilize the same means of transport to the freight terminal as the EDP diagram on the opposite page suggests?
**3 Can you match up the stages in the transport chain shown on the EDP diagram with the three paragraphs of *Ein Container für das Schiff X nach Dubai*? Stage 1 has two parts.
***4 Which of these clauses are relative clauses?
  a das heißt über Landverkehrsträger und über Schiffe *b* die in dem Zeitintervall versegeln *c* das er vorgibt *d* daß ein 20-Fuß Container auf den Hof gestellt werden soll *e* das wir benutzen *f* der nun beginnen soll.

Aus der Hapag-Lloyd Containerpalette

THE CONTAINER
1 What type of container would you order to ship these cargoes:
a frozen meat *b* shirts *c* cooking oil *d* soft toys *e* grain *f* combine harvesters *g* liquids?

Standard-Container 20' u. 40'
Geeignet für jede normale Ladung.

Platform 20' u. 40'
Speziell für Schwergut und übergroße Ladung.
Nicht containerisierbare Ladung kann auf mehreren zusammengestellten Platforms untergebracht werden.

Kühl-Container 20' u. 40'
Speziell für Ladung, die konstant gehaltene Plus- oder Minus-Temperaturen erfordert.
Mit eingebautem Kühlaggregat.

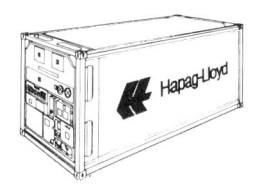

Bulk-Container 20'
Speziell für Schüttgut, wie z.B. Malz.

Tank-Container 20'
Speziell für flüssige Chemikalien.
Ausgewählte Container werden ausschließlich für den Transport von flüssigen Lebensmitteln eingesetzt.

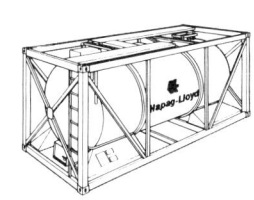

FILAFACT *subordinate clauses*
Remember that in *daß* clauses and relative clauses, the verb comes at the end (➡ **P 23, 41**):

..., *daß* ein Container auf den Hof **gestellt werden** *soll*.
Container, *die* mit einem Schiff **verladen** *werden*, ...

A subordinate clause is always separated off from the main clause by a comma. ➡ **P 106-107**

FILASKILL
An important part of learning a language is setting the right pace. Set aside a regular period each day if you can, and be patient with your progress.

TiP

"Germany is the land of pallets. All merchandise, storage and handling revolves around palletization. Germans deal in one type of pallet only: the Euro-Palette, *which measures 1.20 x 1.80 m."*
(Roy Edleston, Food from Britain, British Business)

Hamburg

KAFFEE ODER TEE?

Germany is primarily a nation of coffee drinkers, but tea has always been popular among the East Frisians in *Ostfriesland*, where average consumption is around 3 kg of tea a year, compared with the national average (including the East Frisians) of 240 g. Schmidt & Schneemilch have been importing British food and drink since the 1940s, and were taken over by Lyons in 1985.

FILAWORD
der Verbraucher *consumer*
der Abnehmer *purchaser*
die Lebensmittel (*n, pl*) *food(stuffs)*
das Getränk *drink*
der Kaffee *coffee*
der Tee *tea*
die Milch *milk*
der Zucker *sugar*
die Tasse *cup*
das Kännchen *(small) pot (of coffee/tea)*
essen *to eat*
trinken *to drink*

Lieferung von heute auf morgen

Herr Hans Otto Grelck, managing director of importers Schmidt & Schneemilch, talked about supplying the German food market.

FACTFINDER
**1 What type of delivery is the German retail trade used to?
***2 What role do department stores play for Schmidt & Schneemilch?

Herr Grelck: Der deutsche Handel ist gewohnt, relativ schnell beliefert zu werden, und die Importeure bilden da einen Puffer. Wir haben Ware auf Lager, die wir auf eigene Rechnung kaufen, und diese Ware bieten wir dem Kunden an. Wir können also von heute auf morgen liefern. Innerhalb Deutschlands ist eine Belieferung zwischen 24 und 72 Stunden hundertprozentig zu gewährleisten.

Hauptabnehmer sind traditionell die Kaufhäuser. Im Gegensatz zu ihrer allgemeinen Bedeutung im Lebensmittelhandel haben sie bei uns eine sehr starke Bedeutung. Zweiter Hauptabnehmerkreis sind die Verbrauchermärkte, „das Warenhaus auf der grünen Wiese". Die ungeheuer große Auswahl in einem Verbrauchermarkt reizt die Verbraucher.

DATABASE
bilden da einen Puffer *form a buffer*
ist ... ... zu gewährleisten *... can be guaranteed ...*
Kaufhäuser (*n, pl*) *department stores*
Im Gegensatz zu *In contrast to*
Verbrauchermärkte (*m, pl*) *superstores/hypermarkets*
Auswahl (*f*) *choice*

Wußten Sie schon, wie Tee zubereitet wird?

Man nehme dazu einen Teelöffel pro Tasse und einen für die Kanne. Über den Tee das sprudelnde, kochende Wasser gießen. Der Tee sollte zwischen 4 und 5 Minuten ziehen, denn danach hat sich das volle Aroma des Tees entfaltet. Je nach Geschmack Sahne, Zucker oder Kandis zugeben.

EXECUTIVE SKILLS
**1 There are certain stock phrases which it is useful to memorize. With the help of the extract from the interview with Herr Grelck, see if you can build three stock phrases out of these words: *auf, auf, auf, von, heute, eigene, morgen, Lager, Rechnung.* You should end up with phrases which are equivalent to these English phrases: *a* on my/our/their ... own account *b* in stock *c* from one day to the next.

FILASKILL
It's a good idea to give yourself a mental picture to go with a new word, or actually put labels on things round the home or in the office as you learn them.

FILAFACT *da + preposition*
You'll often find a preposition attached to the syllable *da(r)-*. This syllable can be equivalent to 'this' or 'that', e.g. *dazu, danach, dafür, daran, darauf*:

Man nehme *dazu* einen Teelöffel pro Tasse. (*for this*)
Danach hat sich das Aroma entfaltet. (*after that*)
➡ P 99, 106

FACTFINDER
*3 When should you keep your hands out?

50 DEUTSCHES BUSINESS-MAGAZIN

Top Quality and Choice

Teenage experiences in seaside boarding houses and the UK's general reputation have given many foreigners a jaundiced view of British cuisine, but the image of British food and drink as such is positive, particularly in the case of export classics like whisky, tea and jam.

Food from Britain is the official promotion agency paving the way for British food and drink companies who want to establish themselves in the market. Mr Roy Edleston, the managing director in Frankfurt, identifies product categories, communicates these to British manufacturers, provides information about the market and helps to find a distributor. He stressed that highly motivated personnel, an adequate command of German and a more international outlook were the key to increased market penetration.

The German consumer tends to be conservative when it comes to food, although Mr Edleston stressed that retailers were striving to change traditional attitudes: "The new buzz-word is *Erlebniseinkauf*. German retailers are starting to realize that you can get a lot more mileage out of the store by offering high quality and an atmosphere that's a pleasure to be in."

TiP

"One thing a German customer often won't forgive is not keeping your promises, i.e. if you say you'll deliver in 12 weeks, they expect you to deliver in 12 weeks." (Neil Rothnie, vice-consul (commercial), Munich)

Vom Coil zum Kunden 5

Preßwerk

Das Coil: Eine mannshohe Blechrolle. Von ihr bis zum fertigen Automobil ist es ein schwieriger Weg: Dreieinhalb Kilometer lang. Oder drei Schichten. Also eineinhalb Tage.

Im Preßwerk fängt alles an. Aus den Blechrollen werden Platten geschnitten, Teile gestanzt: Bodenbleche, Trennwände, Seitenrahmen, Türblätter, Dächer. Die haushohen Tiefziehpressen senken sich wie mühelos über das blanke Blech. Das knackt und knirscht. Abfall blättert wie Papier. *(Zum Thema BMW)*

BMW – Wer ist wer?
Jakob Knieling, Hauptabteilungsleiter Preßwerk. Ausbildung: Lehre Werkzeugmacher; Studium Fachhochschule Maschinenbau. Hobbys: Wandern, Schwimmen.

Fertigung in Pressenstraßen

Herr Knieling: Die Fertigung in einem Preßwerk läuft anders ab als in einer Bandfertigung. Wir fertigen im Stoß eine Losgröße für mehrere Tage, rüsten dann um und fahren in den gleichen Maschinen ein anderes Teil. Innerhalb von 17 Tagen müssen wir bis zu 25 verschiedene Teile je Pressenstraße abpressen.

Um ein Teil herstellen zu können, braucht man Betriebsmittel, das sind in erster Linie die Maschinen (also die Pressen) und in zweiter Linie Werkzeuge. Die Maschinen sind universell einsetzbar, das heißt, auf diesen Pressen kann man unterschiedliche Teile fertigen, während die Preßwerkzeuge teilbezogen sind. Um eine Fertigung, die aus mehreren Arbeitsfolgen besteht, sinnvoll durchziehen zu können, werden die Pressen in sogenannten Pressenstraßen aufgestellt. Das heißt, man stellt fünf bis acht Maschinen in eine Reihe, um die einzelnen Arbeitsfolgen hintereinander fertigen zu können. Die Trennwand hat fünf Arbeitsfolgen.

Die Trennwand ist zweiteilig und besteht aus einem Oberteil- und einem Unterteil-Trennwand: Im Oberteil der Trennwand (Hutablage) sind die Prägungen vorgesehen, in denen die Montage die Stereolautsprecher befestigt. Das Unterteil hat den vorgestanzten Durchbruch für die Sonderausstattung Skisack. Der Ausschnitt für den Skisack wird bis auf zehn kleine Stellen durchgeschnitten. Wenn ein Kunde die Sonderausstattung Skisack bestellt, wird der Ausschnitt im Rohbau an den zehn kleinen Befestigungspunkten herausgetrennt.

Die zwei Pressenstraßen im Münchner Werk

Hamburg

GESCHMACKSERLEBNIS MIT NEUEN IDEEN

German eating habits are changing, and *Abendbrot* has extended beyond the three slices of bread, with *Wurst*, cheese and jam. Purchasing power opens up new choices, and variety is in vogue. Consumer demand for healthy eating echoes the strict food laws (*Lebensmittelgesetze*) governing additives and preservatives.

The number of corner shops („*Tante-Emma*"-*Läden*) has been radically reduced over the past 20 years as retailing has concentrated, and retailers vie for custom with psychological pricing (69 Pfg., DM 1,99). Germany has nearly three times as many superstores as Britain, and rigid laws restrict opening times (*Ladenschlußgesetze*) although the introduction of late shopping on Thursdays marks a move towards liberalization.

FILAWORD
der Einzelhandel *retail trade*
der Großhandel *wholesale trade*
der Laden *shop*
das Sonderangebot *special offer*
mindestens haltbar bis *best before*

Edeka Geschäft

Qualitatives Wachstum

The Edeka Group is a voluntary cooperative of independent traders with around 12,500 retail outlets, the majority still being small shops in the provinces. Herr Folker des Coudres at Group headquarters in Hamburg sees the future in purveying up-market 'experiences for the palate'.

FACTFINDER
**1 Why has qualitative growth become important?
*2 In what types of product does Germany have record variety?
**3 What is special about the *Brotshops*?
***4 What is not a limiting factor for consumers?

Herr des Coudres: Das Langweiligste in Deutschland ist die Werbung des Lebensmitteleinzelhandels, weil man glaubt, daß man nur den Preis runtersetzen muß und damit bereits alles erreicht hat. Heute ist die Bevölkerung rückläufig, und es geht jetzt für uns darum, das durch qualitatives Wachstum auszugleichen. Qualitatives Wachstum heißt „neue Produkte", heißt „Geschmackserlebnis bringen mit neuen Ideen". Man muß dem Verbraucher Geschmackserlebnis verkaufen und nicht nur Edamer und Gouda als „Hollandkäse für 69 Pfennige".

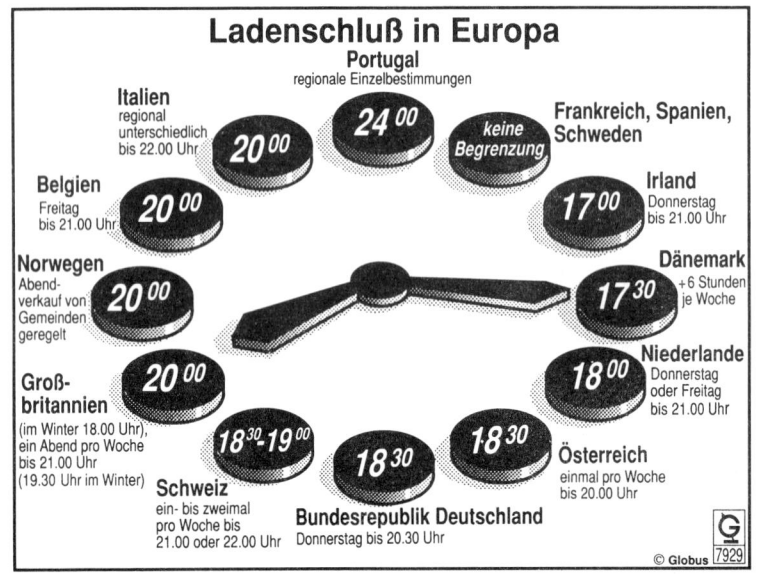

Deutschland ist das Land mit den meisten Brotsorten, mit den meisten Wurstsorten, mit den meisten Biersorten. Brot, zum Beispiel, ist eine Delikatesse, und die Leute machen jetzt „Brotshops", wo sie Brot scheibenweise verkaufen und sagen, „du kannst zwei Scheiben Vollkornbrot, zwei Scheiben Feinbrot, eine Scheibe Weißbrot und eine Scheibe Graubrot haben". Es ist doch viel schöner, wenn man morgens vier verschiedene Sorten hat und sagt, „zur Konfitüre nehme ich ein helleres Brot, und zur Wurst und zum Schinken nehme ich ein schwarzes Brot". Das ist es eben, was das Geschmackserlebnis und die Idee ausmacht. Das wird in allen Bereichen kommen, und es wird nicht mehr unbedingt der Preis als einziges Kriterium entscheidend sein. Man muß den Verbraucher nur sensibilisieren, Geld hat er ja.

DATABASE
Das Langweiligste *The most boring thing*
runtersetzen *to lower*
rückläufig *declining*
es geht jetzt ... darum ... *the issue now is*
das ... auszugleichen *to make up for that ...*
heißt ... bringen *means offering ...*
scheibenweise *by the slice*
Das ist es eben, was ... ausmacht *It's that which constitutes ...*
nicht mehr unbedingt *no longer necessarily*
... hat er ja *after all, he's got ...*

FILAFACT *comparisons*
Notice that these adjectives are both comparative, equivalent to the English 'nic*er*' and 'light*er*':

es ist doch viel **schön**er
ein **heller**es Brot

In the second example, *heller* has an added ending because it precedes a noun. ➡ **P 100-101**

T*i*P
Choose your words carefully when advertising in Germany. In English, preservatives are an ingredient of jam, but check the **Glossary** *to find the devastating effect* Präservative *might have in a German advert. Gift also has a sting in the tail.*

Das Gesamtwohl der Wirtschaft

There is a tripartite system for representation within German trade and industry. *Arbeitgeberverbände* are concerned with working conditions and social issues at the workplace, and they represent the employers in the annual round of collective-bargaining negotiations. *Wirtschaftsverbände* deal with all matters affecting business, e.g. investment, taxation, environmental legislation. Whereas such associations are interest groups with voluntary membership, which are organized according to sector, membership of the *Industrie- und Handelskammern* is mandatory for all companies in Germany.

The 83 chambers of industry and commerce are financed by a compulsory levy on their members, and the *Industrie- und Handelstag* is the umbrella organization for all the 83 chambers. Although a public law system, the chambers are independent and it is their duty to safeguard the interests of trade and industry in general and their own members in particular. In addition to their advisory role to local authorities and government departments, one of the main functions of the chambers is to administer and examine Germany's extensive vocational training programmes.

There are some 380 officially recognized vocations. Before a company is allowed to take on trainees, the local chamber establishes that the company has skilled personnel capable of giving adequate training. The chamber then ensures that each trainee has a proper contract with the employer. An obligatory part of training is attendance at a vocational training college for an average of twelve hours a week, either on two days of the week or in blocks of several weeks at a time. The chambers are also responsible for the examination process. Trainees are examined by a committee made up of representatives of the employers, employees and vocational training colleges.

The apprenticeship system in Germany has an unbroken tradition, and industry invests heavily in training a skilled workforce. The cost to the company for each training place has been estimated at around DM 20,000 per year. Many companies set their standards well above the legal requirements, and as competition becomes more intense a highly trained labour pool is likely to prove one of Germany's major assets.

Auszubildende an der Werkbank

FILAWORD
die Industrie- und Handelskammer *chamber of industry and commerce*
der Arbeitgeberverband *employers' association*
der Wirtschaftsverband *industrial association*
die Ausbildung *education, training*
die Berufsschule *vocational training college*
der Auszubildende/Lehrling *trainee, apprentice*

So hoch sind die Lehrlings-Gehälter

Durchschnittliche monatliche Ausbildungsvergütung 1990 in DM

- 255 Herrenschneiderin
- 453
- 550 Friseurin
- 567 Augenoptiker
- 622 Bäcker
- 629 Hauswirtschafterin
- 641 Kfz-Mechaniker
- 649 Gärtner
- 682 Elektroinstallateur
- 691 Gas- u. Wasserinstallateur
- 700 Maler, Lackierer
- 743 Koch
- 779
- 797 Verwaltungsfachangestellte
- 830 Einzelhandelskaufmann
- 837 Industriekaufmann
- 850 Energieelektroniker
- 1094 Industriemechaniker
- 1120 Versicherungskaufmann
- 1235 DM Maurer
- Bergmechaniker
- Arzthelferin

Quelle: bibb

FACTFINDER
*1 Does the chart give *a* weekly *b* monthly or *c* annual pay?
*2 Which of these apprentices earns the most? *a* medical-practice assistant *b* cook *c* insurance clerk *d* car mechanic

FILAFACT *male/female*
With German job designations, you'll often find the ending *-in* for women, e.g. *der Gärtner - die Gärtnerin, der Schneider - die Schneiderin*.

FILASKILL
Many of the companies we visited publish their company reports in both German and English. Why not try writing off to a company in your field to ask for the latest annual report in both languages?

Hamburg

Ein Markenartikler mit Tradition

Chemicals are among Hamburg's 'classical' industries, although the chemical companies are not in the same league as the giants on the Rhine. Ironically, while Beiersdorf had suffered the effects of being classified as a Jewish concern, trademarks such as *Nivea* and *Elastoplast* were confiscated with foreign assets after the war. Beiersdorf now has an impressive portfolio of brands, again headed by the *Nivea* flagship. However, it is having to work hard at projecting the corporate image behind the brand names under the banner *'Ideen fürs Leben'*.

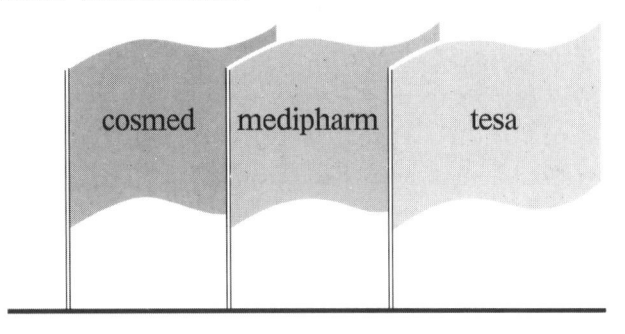

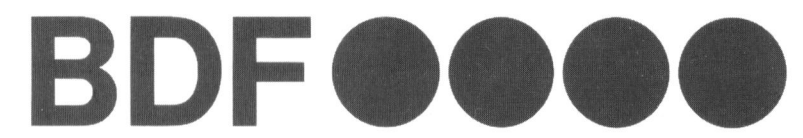

Oscar Troplowitz

1890 erwarb Oscar Troplowitz das Laboratorium von Paul Beiersdorf und begründete die industrielle Fertigung. Er führte als erster in Hamburg den 8-Stunden-Tag, bezahlten Urlaub, Mutterschutz, kostenloses Mittagessen und Altersversorgung ein.

Firmenprofil

Herr Klaus Herre, head of advertising at Beiersdorf, is responsible for corporate identity.

Factfinder
*1 Which company can Beiersdorf be confused with?
*2 What does the company logo consist of?

Herr Herre: Wir haben Anfang der siebziger Jahre erkannt, daß es notwendig ist, ein Firmenprofil aufzubauen. Der Firmenname Beiersdorf stand eigentlich nie im Vordergrund, sondern immer seine Marken, wie *Nivea*, *Hansaplast* oder *Tesafilm*. Das ging so lange gut, wie die Märkte noch wenig besetzt waren. Heute hat man andere Verhältnisse. Die Märkte sind sehr viel enger geworden, die Produkte sind ähnlich und unterscheiden sich eigentlich mehr oder weniger nur durch die Aufmachung.

Wir haben durch viele Untersuchungen festgestellt, daß man unsere Marken kennt, aber eigentlich nicht weiß, wer dahinter steht. Nach fast hundert Jahren hatte der Name Beiersdorf nur eine ungestützte Bekanntheit von 20 Prozent. Der Name ist mit der Firma Bayer verwechselbar, und er wird auch manchmal mit einem Dorf in Bayern in Verbindung gebracht: Da ist schon Post für uns angekommen, adressiert an die „Niveawerke in Beiersdorf"! Die Zusammengehörigkeit der Produkte ist nicht erkennbar.

Wir haben also beschlossen, daß wir ein Firmenprofil aufbauen müssen, um den Goodwill aller Bereiche zu einer Kraft zu bündeln. Bei der Größe des Hauses war es nötig, Profit Centers zu schaffen, und es entstanden Sparten: die Sparte *cosmed*, die Sparte *medipharm* und die Sparte *tesa*. Dann haben wir unser Symbol entwickelt: BDF – eine Abkürzung aus Beiersdorf – mit vier Punkten. Dies soll ein Erkennungssymbol sein für innovative Produkte von hoher Qualität. Außerdem brauchten wir einen Slogan. Das Döschen Niveacreme, der Katheter, der Tesafilmstreifen – sie helfen, das Leben ein bißchen angenehmer zu machen. Es sind alles „Ideen fürs Leben". Dieser Slogan drückt die Gesamtphilosophie unseres Hauses aus.

Database
daß es notwendig ist, ...zu... *that it's necessary to ...*
Das ging so lange gut, wie *That was fine while*
er wird ... ... in Verbindung gebracht *it's ... associated with ...*
um ... zu bündeln *in order to combine ...*
sie helfen, ... zu machen *they help to make ...*

Profile *corporate image*
Beiersdorf decided to build up a company profile to exploit the synergy effect of successful brands. Can you identify the order in which Herr Herre made the following points?

a Confusion of company with other names
b Development of slogan
c Development of logo
d Market research into level of awareness
e Decision to build up company profile
f Nature of present-day markets
g Formation of three divisions
h Relation of company name to brands
i Purpose of company profile

Filaword
die Marke *brand*
der Markenartikel *brand product*
der Markenartikler *brand manufacturer*
das Markenzeichen *trademark*
die Sparte *division, product group*
die Aufmachung *packaging, presentation*

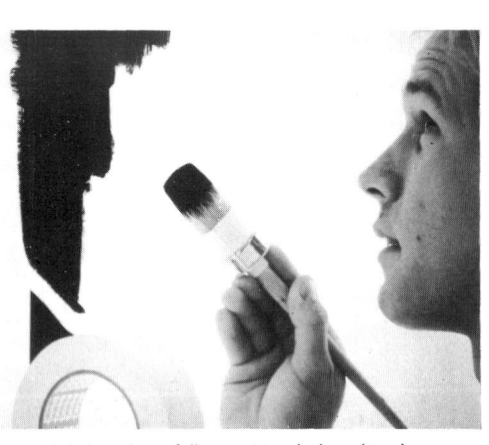

Tesaklebebänder erfüllen im Haushalt und in der Industrie die verschiedensten Aufgaben.

TiP
"The one difficulty we have with Germany is that each individual department and each individual group within each department tends to work on its own. So unless you're talking at the right level to the right person, you run the risk of not getting the message through." (Barry Giles, Lydmet Ltd)

Der Aufsichtsrat bei Beiersdorf

FACTFINDER
*1 How many union representatives are there on the *Aufsichtsrat* at Beiersdorf?
**2 How many people elect the chairman of the *Aufsichtsrat*?
***3 Who is the board of management responsible to?

FILAWORD
wählen *to elect*
bestellen *to appoint*
beaufsichtigen *to supervise*
beschließen *to approve*
der Vertreter *representative*
der Vorsitzende *chairman*
der Stellvertreter *deputy*

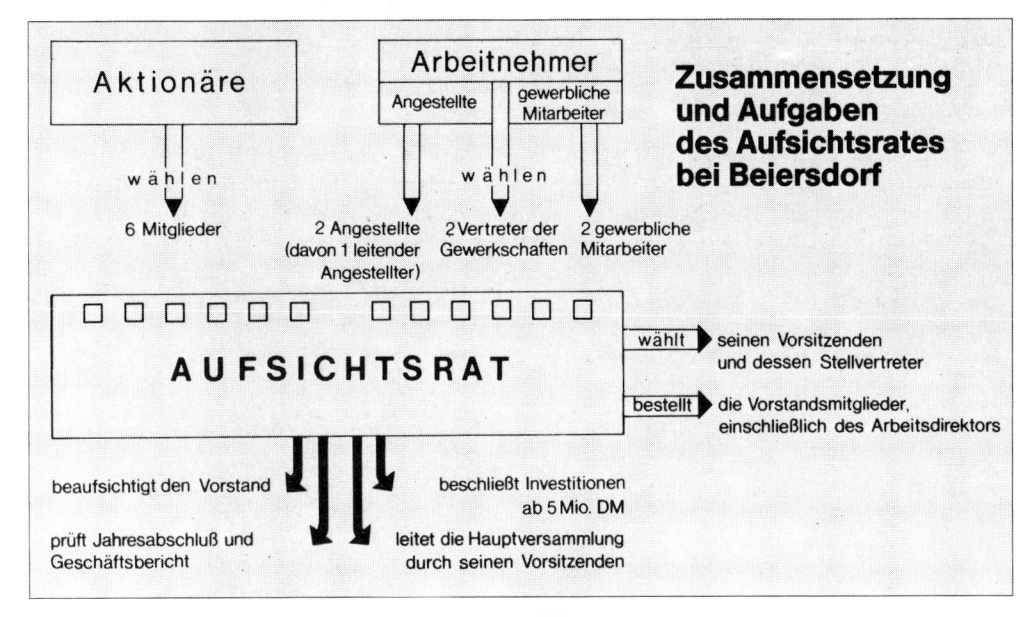

Zusammensetzung und Aufgaben des Aufsichtsrates bei Beiersdorf

Aktionäre wählen 6 Mitglieder

Arbeitnehmer (Angestellte, gewerbliche Mitarbeiter) wählen 2 Angestellte (davon 1 leitender Angestellter), 2 Vertreter der Gewerkschaften, 2 gewerbliche Mitarbeiter

AUFSICHTSRAT
- wählt seinen Vorsitzenden und dessen Stellvertreter
- bestellt die Vorstandsmitglieder, einschließlich des Arbeitsdirektors
- beaufsichtigt den Vorstand
- prüft Jahresabschluß und Geschäftsbericht
- beschließt Investitionen ab 5 Mio. DM
- leitet die Hauptversammlung durch seinen Vorsitzenden

VOM COIL ZUM KUNDEN 6

Rohbau

Die Blechteile werden verschweißt, verlötet, verschraubt oder geklebt. Einige tausend Schweißpunkte halten ein Karosseriegerippe sicher zusammen. Immer mehr Roboter und Vielpunktautomaten übernehmen diese wichtige Arbeit. Dieser Rohbau sieht anonym aus. Doch schon hier hat das Automobil seinen späteren Kunden; nach seinen Wünschen wird es weitergebaut. (*Zum Thema BMW*)

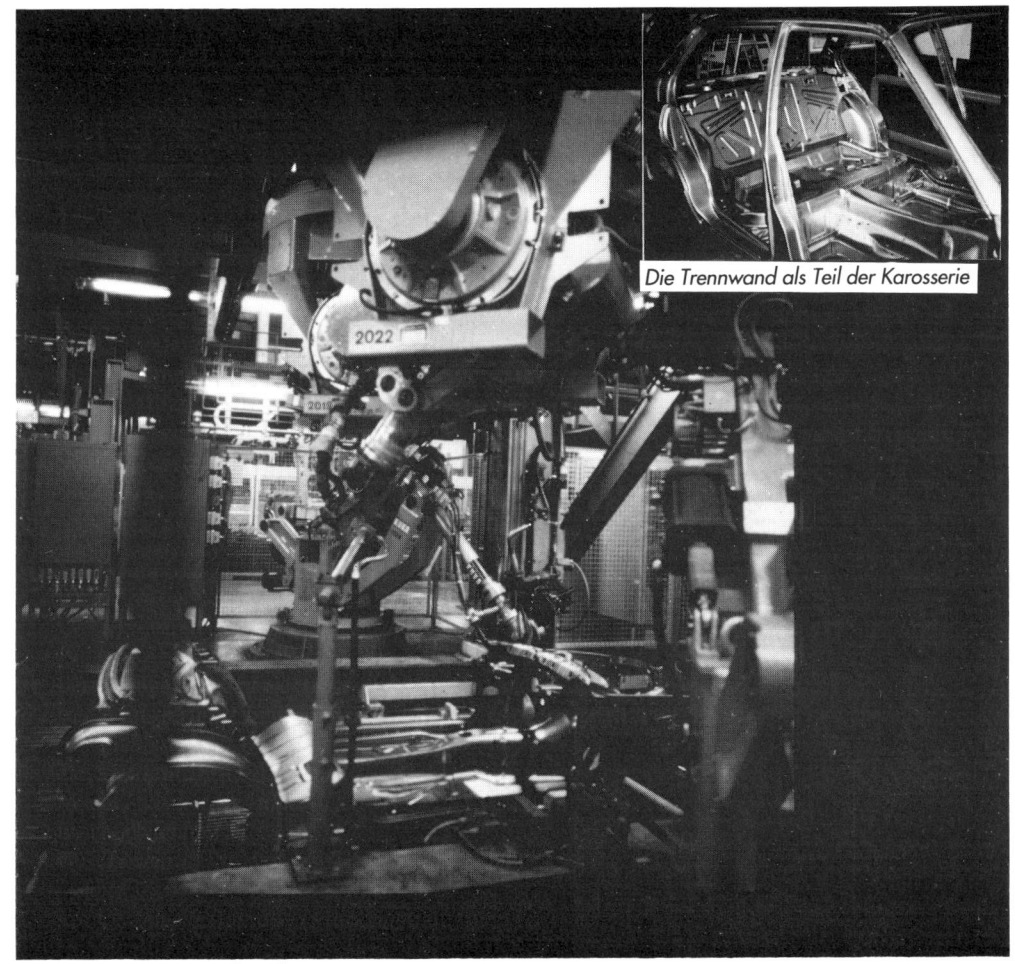

Die Karosserie wird geschweißt.

Die Trennwand als Teil der Karosserie

BMW – Wer ist wer?

Klaus Bareuther, Hauptabteilungsleiter Karosserie-Rohbau. Ausbildung: Lehre Maschinenbau; Studium Fachhochschule Maschinenbau, Fertigungstechnik, Schweißfachtechnik. Hobbys: Angeln, Jagd.

Ein hoher Automatisierungsgrad

Herr Bareuther: Wir haben im Rohbau einen sehr hohen Automatisierungsgrad. 95% der Schweißpunkte – und das sind immerhin 3600 – werden in irgendeiner Form automatisch geschweißt, entweder durch Roboter oder durch automatisierte Anlagen. Wir haben Roboter zum Schweißen, wir haben Roboter zum Bolzensetzen, wir haben aber auch Roboter, die versiegeln, und Roboter, die Handhabungstätigkeiten machen.

Die Trennwand ist eins von über 600 Teilen, aus denen eine Karosserie besteht. Sie befindet sich als Abschottung zum Gepäckraumbereich zwischen den hinteren Radhäusern. Sie macht den Innenraum schalldichter, weil Material aufgebracht werden kann. Außerdem sind Verankerungen für Sicherheitsgurte mitintegriert. An dieser Trennwand sind 188 Schweißpunkte. Insgesamt arbeiten vier Roboter daran. Für einen Schweißpunkt braucht ein Roboter knapp zwei Sekunden.

Die Trennwand wird geprüft.

GEÄNDERTE UMWELTBEDÜRFNISSE

If you are looking for your favourite shampoo, you might not find it in an *Apotheke*, which is mainly geared to medicines. *Drogerien* and *Parfümerien* are the usual outlet for cosmetic and body-care products, but self-service *Drogeriemärkte* are increasingly popular. A healthy lifestyle and enhanced environmental awareness mean that demand is increasing for 'natural' products which are friendly to the environment.

Verantwortlichkeit in Richtung Umwelt

Hans Schwarzkopf GmbH in Hamburg started as a *Drogerie* in Berlin, where Hans Schwarzkopf developed the idea of a shampoo in powder form. For today's consumers, environmentally sound packaging is as much of a selling point as the shampoo itself. Herr Ulrich Kaftanski, head of the trading division, and Herr Andreas Fuchs, marketing manager, discussed the company's commitment to an environmental range of products.

FACTFINDER
*1 What is the purpose of the checklist?
***2 What have Schwarzkopf changed about the packaging of *Schauma*?

Herr Fuchs: Verantwortlichkeit in Richtung Umwelt wird in diesem Hause sehr ernst genommen. Alle unsere Maßnahmen richten sich in diesem Bereich danach aus, die Produkte so zu machen, daß sie völlig unbedenklich für die Umwelt sind. Wir machen das ganz konkret, mit Checklist für jedes Produkt.

Herr Kaftanski: Unsere führende Marke ist *Schauma*, eine alte Marke unseres Hauses, die wir gerade im vergangenen Jahr gerelauncht haben, um sie den gestiegenen Verbraucherbedürfnissen, aber auch den geänderten Umweltbedürfnissen gerecht zu machen. Wir haben zum Beispiel die Flasche umgestellt von der sogenannten PVC-Verpackung auf eine Polyäthylenverpackung, die biologisch leicht abbaubar ist. Das geht konsequent bis in die Kartonnagen, Etiketten usw. Das war mit ein wesentlicher Punkt bei allen Relaunches, die wir in den letzten Jahren in unserem Haus durchgeführt haben.

DATABASE
Verantwortlichkeit *responsibility*
wird ... sehr ernst genommen *is taken very seriously ...*
richten sich ... danach aus, ... zu machen ... *are geared to making ...*
so ..., daß ... *in such a way that*
unbedenklich *safe*
Umweltbedürfnisse (n, pl) *environmental requirements*
Wir haben ... ... umgestellt von ... auf ... *we changed ... from ... to*
mit ein wesentlicher Punkt *one essential factor*

FILAFACT *um ... zu*
Notice how Herr Kaftanski uses *um ... zu*, the equivalent of 'in order to'. The verb is in the infinitive form and comes at the end of the clause:

..., *um* sie (die Marke) den geänderten Umweltbedürfnissen gerecht *zu machen*.
(... *in order to* make it appropriate to the changed environmental requirements.)
➡ P 108

Das absatzpolitische Instrumentarium

Marketing is vital for a company like Schwarzkopf, as Herr Hans-Jürgen Howind, marketing manager in the trading division, explains.

FACTFINDER
***3 What crucially distinguishes Schwarzkopf's products from others?
**4 Which two retail trade outlets does Herr Howind mention?

Herr Howind: Bei uns ist die Technologie nicht so wahnsinnig kompliziert. Die Rezepturen sind relativ leicht durchschaubar, und sie ähneln sich. Genau das ist der Grund, warum für uns Marketing so wichtig ist.

Es ist mein Job rauszukriegen, wie muß das aussehen, wie muß das riechen, was muß ich versprechen, wie muß es wirken, damit die Verbraucher sich dafür interessieren und das letztlich kaufen. Das geht los bei Rezeptur, über Packung, Preis, wo disponiere ich es – will ich mehr in den Fachhandel, will ich in den Lebensmittelhandel –, wie muß das werblich unterstützt werden, wie muß ich das promotionsmäßig unterstützen. Und das ist unser absatzpolitisches Instrumentarium. Das ist auf der ganzen Welt gleich.

FILAWORD
die Toilettenartikel (m, pl) *toiletries*
die Seife *soap*
das Shampoo *shampoo*
die Zahnbürste *toothbrush*
die Zahnpasta *toothpaste*

DATABASE
leicht durchschaubar *transparent*
ähneln sich *resemble each other*
rauszukriegen *to find out*
Das geht los bei *It starts with*
unterstützt werden *be supported*
gleich *the same*

FILAFACT *das*
When you see *das*, you need to find out what it's equivalent to:

1 'The' (definite article) – *das* is followed by a noun which is neuter, singular and in the nominative or accusative case. ➡ P 97–98
2 'Which'/'who' (relative pronoun) – *das* refers back to a noun of the same gender (i.e. neuter) and number (i.e. singular) in the preceding clause. It introduces a relative clause with the verb at the end. ➡ P 99, 107
3 'This'/'that'/'it' (demonstrative pronoun) – *das* usually stands for an earlier noun of the same gender and number, or for a phrase, sentence or idea. ➡ P 99

All three might be combined, e.g.:

Das(**3**) ist das(**1**) absatzpolitische Instrumentarium, das(**2**) wir benutzen.
(This(**3**) is the(**1**) marketing mix which(**2**) we use.)

EXECUTIVE SKILLS
***1 Herr Howind uses *das* nine times. Have a look at *Filafact das* and check each *das* to see whether it belongs to category **1**, **2**, or **3**.
***2 Check the *Glossary* to find out which of the verbs Herr Howind uses are
a reflexive (➡ P 100) *b* separable (➡ P 102).
***3 And which of his verbs is in the passive form (➡ P 104)?
**4 *a* Which of the following verbs doesn't refer to the effect of the product? *i* riechen *ii* wirken *iii* versprechen *iv* aussehen.
b Which of the following nouns isn't connected with the product?
i Verbraucher *ii* Packung *iii* Preis *iv* Rezeptur.

Auszubildende bei Schwarzkopf

Die Ausbildung

Frau Inken Dabelstein and Frau Peggy Fischer are trainees at Schwarzkopf. They are working their way through the departments and will come out qualified as *Bürokauffrauen*.

Factfinder
*1 How many departments does Frau Fischer mention?
*2 Is attendance at vocational college weekly or arranged in blocks?

Frau Fischer: Wir durchlaufen hier unwahrscheinlich viele Abteilungen: Personalabteilung, Personalentwicklung, Lohn- und Gehaltsbüro, Einkauf, Vertriebsinnendienst, Öffentlichkeitsarbeit, die ganze Abrechnung – das ist Kundenbuchhaltung und Finanzbuchhaltung –, dann Marketing und die Zentrale mit Telefonvermittlung.

Frau Dabelstein: Wir haben Berufsschule, und zwar fast alle Vierteljahre sieben Wochen, und danach richtet sich zum Teil auch der Ausbildungsablauf in der Firma. Die Ausbildung dauert zweieinhalb Jahre. Es wurde uns ein halbes Jahr durch die Vorbildung angerechnet.

Database
Wir durchlaufen *We go through*
danach richtet sich zum Teil ... *... is partly determined by that*
Es wurde uns ... angerechnet *We were credited with ...*
durch die Vorbildung *on the basis of our previous education*

Executive Skills
***1 The verb *sich richten* is accompanied by a preposition. Can you work out what it is? Use the *Glossary* to check your answer.

**2 Which of these departments doesn't Frau Fischer mention? *a* purchasing *b* export *c* personnel *d* R & D *e* PR *f* accounts *g* in-house sales department.

Filaskill
After *und zwar*, you can expect an explanation or specification. It means something like 'actually' or 'in fact', but has no real equivalent in English.

TiP

The concept of Fräulein *as an equivalent to* 'Miss' *has suffered a slow demise. In official contexts this title has been abolished and replaced by* Frau, *which is equivalent to Miss, Mrs or Ms. However, young women under 20 are sometimes still addressed as* Fräulein.

Hamburg

NAVIGATION, KOMMUNIKATION, AUTOMATION

ELNA specializes in supplying ships of all types with navigation and communication systems manufactured by foreign companies, although the company is now looking to expand into land-based automation and control systems. The company has a high level of technical expertise and cooperates closely with manufacturers.

Service und Vertrieb

After many years of marketing and servicing sophisticated instruments, technical cooperation with British manufacturers is still a must for managing director Herr Peter Schick.

FACTFINDER
- ****1** Herr Schick gives a short company profile. Outline the company's age, activities and product areas.
- ***2** What can make modifications necessary?

Herr Schick: Das Unternehmen ist 38 Jahre alt. Es befaßte sich von Anfang an mit der Aufgabenstellung, für die deutsche und internationale Schiffahrt Service an Navigations- und Kommunikationsgeräten zu geben. Über den Service hinaus befassen wir uns damit, für dieses Marktsegment den Vertrieb von Navigations- und Kommunikations- und Automationsanlagen durchzuführen.

Es ist immer eine sehr enge technische Zusammenarbeit zwischen den Firmen notwendig. Produkte, die wir aus England importieren, werden als Grundkonzept in England hergestellt und müssen gegebenenfalls nach den Vorschriften und Bedingungen der hiesigen Behörden hier bei uns modifiziert werden.

DATABASE
Es befaßte sich ... mit der Aufgabenstellung, ... zu geben *It was concerned ... with the objective of giving ...*
Über ... hinaus *In addition to ...*
Es ist immer ... notwendig *... is always necessary*
gegebenenfalls *as necessary*
Vorschriften und Bedingungen *regulations and conditions*
der hiesigen Behörden *of the German authorities*

FILASKILL
If you hit a problem which you cannot solve immediately, don't be discouraged. Carry on to the next section and come back later.

> **TIP**
> *Presence in Germany, whether through a subsidiary or agent, was singled out by Herr Schick as crucial to a foreign company looking to operate in the German market. The important factor was having personnel with experience of the market and market trends.*

Absolute Priorität

Nowhere are strict deadlines more important than in contracts which have penalty clauses.

FACTFINDER
- ****3** What is Herr Schick's main point concerning delivery?

Herr Schick: Der Liefertermin hat in Deutschland eine absolute Priorität. Wenn der Kaufvertrag mit einer Werft geschlossen wird, dann ist gleichzeitig der Fertigstellungstermin des Schiffes bekannt, und dieser Termin wird von einer deutschen Werft auch gehalten. Wenn Maschinenteile, Propeller oder Wellen innerhalb des vorgesehenen Liefertermins nicht rechtzeitig eintreffen, dann führt das ja zu einer Gesamtverzögerung, und das kann sich keine Werft erlauben, weil in solchen Verträgen jeweils sogenannte Vertragsstrafen enthalten sind.

FILAWORD
der Vertrieb *sales, distribution*
der Liefertermin *delivery date/time*
das Bauteil *component*
das Ersatzteil *spare part*

DATABASE
Wenn der Kaufvertrag ... geschlossen wird *When a contract of sale is concluded ...*
Fertigstellungstermin (*m*) *completion date*
Gesamtverzögerung (*f*) *delay to the whole project*

FILAFACT *subordinate clauses*
In clauses beginning with *wenn* (if, when) or *weil* (because), you can expect to find the verb at the end:

> *Wenn* der Kaufvertrag mit einer Werft geschlossen **wird**, ...
> ..., *weil* in solchen Verträgen Vertragsstrafen enthalten **sind**.

For other conjunctions introducing subordinate clauses with the verb at the end ➡ **P 106.**

EXECUTIVE SKILLS
- ****1** Can you put these topics in the order in which Herr Schick mentioned them?
  a Penalty clauses *b* Ship's date of completion *c* Supply of machine parts *d* Contract of sale *e* Delivery date.
- ***2** What is the German equivalent of *if/when ... then?*

Geschäftsführer Peter Schick

Service an Bord und in der Werkstatt

A large proportion of ELNA's business is concerned with service activities. Herr Frank Braun, service manager, explains what his job entails.

ELNA
Menschen mit Know-How...

FACTFINDER
***1 Herr Braun mentions four main tasks of a service manager. What are they?
*2 What are the two possible service locations?
**3 What are the two ways of rectifying a defect?

Herr Braun: Serviceleiter bedeutet: Koordination von Service, Einteilen von Service, Beaufsichtigen von Servicetechnikern und die ganze Abwicklung, die damit zusammenhängt, einen Service durchzuführen, von der Ersatzteilbeschaffung über die Manpower bis nachher zur Abrechnung.

Bei großen Anlagen findet der Service grundsätzlich an Bord statt, in Form von tatsächlicher Reparatur an Bord oder in Form von Austausch von Platinen, Komponenten, Bauteilen usw. Bei kleinen Anlagen, die man verschicken kann, machen wir die Arbeiten in der Werkstatt.

DATABASE
Beaufsichtigen (n) *supervision*
Abrechnung (f) *invoicing*
Austausch (m) *exchange, replacement*

FILAFACT *preposition + infinitive*
Notice how Herr Schick pointed out that the company is *concerned with* carry**ing** out sales:

Wir *befassen uns* **da**mit, den Vertrieb durch**zu**führen.

The verb in the first clause (*sich befassen*) goes with a preposition (*mit*); da- points forward to the second clause, which has a verb in the infinitive.

Herr Braun uses the same construction in a relative clause when he talks about the processing which *is connected with* carry**ing** out a service:

die Abwicklung, die **da**mit zusammenhängt, einen Service **durchzu**führen
➡ P 105 -106, 108

EXECUTIVE SKILLS
***1 Herr Braun enumerates three stages of carrying out a service (*einen Service durchführen*). Which prepositions introduce them?

🅱 Vom Coil zum Kunden 7
Lackiererei

Nächste Station ist die Lackiererei. Zuerst Reinigung und Entfettung, dann Zinkphosphatierung für das blanke Blech. Gurgelnd versinkt die Autokarosserie in einem Bad aus wassergelöstem Lack. Durch Kataphorese wird der Grundlack aufgetragen. Roboter spritzen einen dauerhaften Unterbodenschutz auf. Die zweite Lackschicht, den Füller, versprühen überwiegend Automaten in einem elektrostatischen Feld. Jede Lackschicht wird – weit über 100°C – in Trockentunnels dauerhaft eingebrannt.

Danach wird geschliffen: Präzise Handarbeit. Erst dann bekommen die Wagen überwiegend von Automaten ihr farbiges Gesicht aufgespritzt. Von Wagen zu Wagen kann die Farbe wechseln. Anschließend werden die Hohlräume dauerhaft konserviert. (*Zum Thema BMW*)

Die Karosserie wird lackiert.

Der Kundenwunsch ist Befehl

Herr Bareuther: Jedes Jahr werden ein oder zwei Farbtöne durch neuere ersetzt. Wir haben außerdem eine ganze Menge Farbvarianten, die wir nur spritzen, wenn der Kunde sehr darauf besteht. Der Kundenwunsch ist Befehl. Sonderlackierung stört aber unseren Normalablauf und ist sehr aufwendig, denn wir müssen dann manuell eingreifen und können keinen automatisierten Ablauf fahren.

Schadstoffreduzierung

Herr Bareuther: Modernste Technik zur Schadstoffreduzierung wird bei BMW natürlich nicht nur beim Auto selbst, sondern auch bei dessen Produktion eingesetzt. So wurde beim Lackieren durch spezielle Verfahren die Auftragswirkung erhöht. Der Feststoffanteil im Lack wurde verdoppelt und somit der Lösemittelanteil gesenkt. Die Abluft wird von Partikeln gereinigt und passiert dann Aktivkohlefilter und Nachverbrennungsanlagen. So konnte in den letzten zwei Jahrzehnten die Emission z.B. beim Trocknen um ca. 97% reduziert werden.

Die Karosserie ist fertig lackiert.

Hamburg

Mit sehr hohem Einsatz

Health care in Germany is provided through contributions made to insurance schemes under state supervision (*Krankenkassen*). Private top-up insurance is available, and high-earners and the self-employed are entitled to opt out of state schemes and take private insurance. There are three main types of hospital (*Krankenhaus/Klinik*): public, private, and non-profit making. General practitioners are thin on the ground, and patients are free to go straight to one of the large number of specialist practices using one of their health-insurance vouchers (*Krankenschein*), issued under their insurance scheme. Practices generally have substantial investment in expensive and sophisticated equipment.

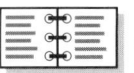

Fallstudie: Verdoppelung der Kapazität

When *Deutsches Business-Magazin* visited Medic-Eschmann GmbH in Hamburg, the company was in the middle of a lightning reorganization after the surprise expansion of their product range. With the takeover of the Eschmann Group by Smiths Industries plc in 1985, Medic-Eschmann GmbH joined Portex Ltd as a subsidiary of Smiths Industries. Portex continued to export its products to Germany using an independent importer, but when the importer jumped ship in May 1988, Medic-Eschmann quickly assumed responsibility for importing Portex products – a move which suddenly doubled Medic-Eschmann's product range. Managing director Herr Lucas Garabet outlined the steps Medic-Eschmann took to meet the challenge.

Firmenprofil

Company Profile
1 What sector does Medic-Eschmann operate in?
2 What is their traditional product range?
3 What is the relationship between Portex and Medic-Eschmann?
4 How do Portex traditionally distribute their product range abroad?

Die Firma Medic-Eschmann

Herr Garabet: Medic-Eschmann GmbH ist ursprünglich als kleine Einfuhrfirma von einer Privatperson gegründet worden und wurde in den sechziger Jahren der Hauptimporteur für die Firma Eschmann England. 1985 wurde die ganze Gruppe Eschmann durch den Konzern Smiths Industries übernommen.

Die Firma Portex

Herr Garabet: Die Firma Portex ist eine bekannte englische Firma, die Einwegprodukte der Anästhesie herstellt. Sie ist in England absoluter Marktführer und in der ganzen Welt bekannt für hochwertige Produkte. Portex hat die Produkte in allen Ländern über örtliche Einfuhrfirmen vertrieben, mit großem Erfolg vor allem in Skandinavien, Deutschland, Frankreich und Japan. Portex hat entsprechend viele *Queen's Awards* für diese außerordentlich starken exportorientierten Aktivitäten bekommen.

Die Produkte

Herr Garabet: Die Organisation der Firma Medic-Eschmann teilt sich hauptsächlich in zwei große Produktgruppen. Eine Produktgruppe sind die Produkte der Stomaversorgung, das heißt Produkte für Patienten mit künstlichem Darmausgang. Dafür gibt es einen Außendienst mit zehn Personen und einen Verkaufsleiter. Die andere Produktgruppe, die wir seit Mitte Juni neu aufgenommen haben, sind Einwegprodukte der Anästhesie, die von unserer Schwesterfirma Portex stammen.

Lucas Garabet

Filaskill
By now you should be thinking about looking at German newspapers or magazines occasionally. Of course you won't understand every word, but you should be able to get a pretty good idea of what an article is about and glean some essential facts. Concentrate on what you *can* understand and be encouraged by it! This case study gives you the opportunity to see what you can do on your own with the help of the *Glossary* and *Grammar. Database* has therefore been omitted.

Problemstellung

The Problem
1 What problem was Portex confronted with and when?
2 How did they resolve it?
3 What was the main problem this created for Medic-Eschmann?

Neue Dimensionen

Herr Garabet: Durch den Kauf der Eschmann-Gruppe 1985 wurde die Firma Medic-Eschmann eine Schwesterfirma von Portex. Durch diesen Kauf wurde der Importeur für Portex-Produkte in Deutschland gewarnt, daß irgendwann wahrscheinlich ein Wechsel stattfinden würde (obwohl das nicht der Stil der Firma Portex ist – Portex ist seinen *Distributors* gegenüber immer sehr treu gewesen). Also hat sich diese Importfirma in Deutschland dann entschieden, vom Portex-Produkt auf ein Konkurrenz-Produkt zu wechseln. Diese neuen Produkte kamen aus USA.

Im Mai 1988 erschienen auf dem deutschen Markt schon Prospekte, Literatur und Produkte des neuen amerikanischen Herstellers – durch die Importfirma vertrieben. Die Portex Geschäftsführung erfuhr zufällig auf dem Weltkongreß der Anästhesie in Washington Ende Mai von diesem Wechsel in Deutschland. Das war natürlich eine große Überraschung, und plötzlich wurde der Firma Medic-Eschmann in Hamburg der Auftrag erteilt, schnellstens die Produktaufnahme der Portex-Produkte im Vertrieb zu organisieren. Da wir bis zu diesem Zeitpunkt für solche Dimensionen gar nicht vorgesehen waren, stellte das für uns selbstverständlich ein großes organisatorisches Problem dar.

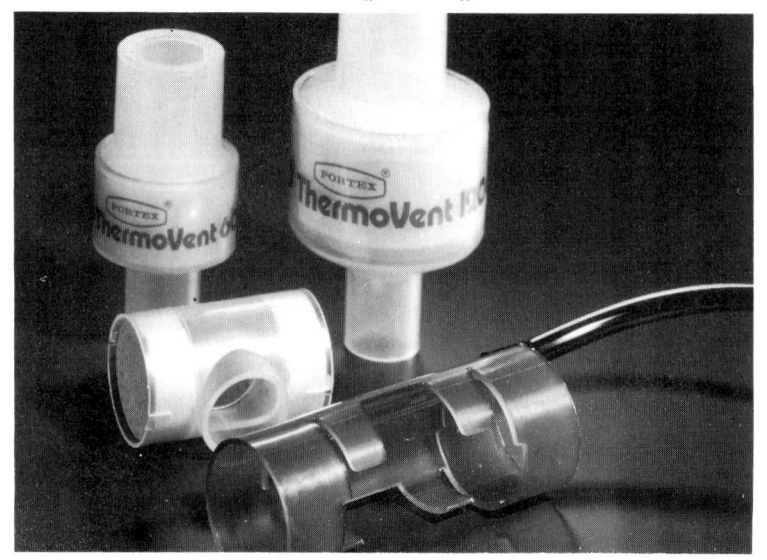

PORTEX Einwegprodukte für die Anästhesie: ThermoVent

Die Aufgabe

THE TASK
1 What was the task?
2 Breakdown in supplies was particularly unacceptable for Portex products. Why?

Schnellstmögliche Lieferung

Herr Garabet: Durch die Natur des Produktes durfte keine große Lieferverzögerung im Markt stattfinden; die Produkte sind ja Produkte für die Anästhesie. Jedes Krankenhaus hält sich einen begrenzten Bestand von Produkten als Reserve, und es gibt noch einen Bestand bei den entsprechenden Fachhändlern. Wenn diese Bestände aufgebraucht sind, muß das Krankenhaus auf ein Alternativprodukt umsteigen. Und wenn ein Wechsel im Krankenhaus stattgefunden hat, ist das Zurückgewinnen der Krankenhäuser ziemlich schwierig. Also war unsere Aufgabe, schnellstmöglich das Produkt Portex lieferfähig bei uns im Lager zu haben.

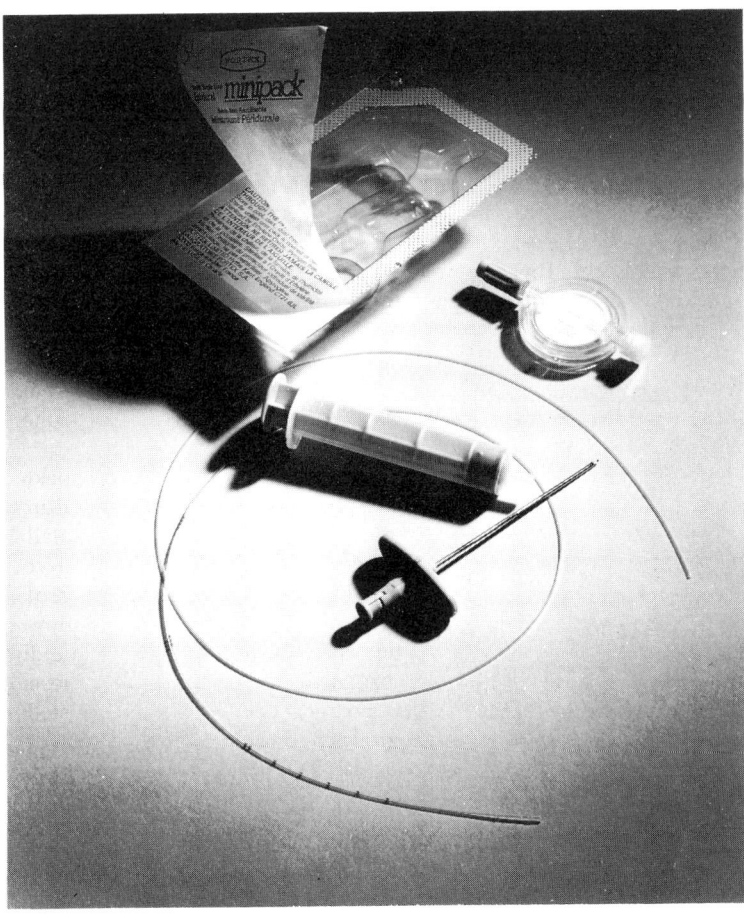

PORTEX Einwegprodukte für die Anästhesie: Epidural-Minipack

FILASKILL
Dates are a good indication of the time referred to. If you see e.g. 1985, look out for verbs referring to the past. Another signal for the past are time expressions like *damals, vor (20) Jahren, früher*.

> **T i P**
> *Salaries are referred to in terms of the amount paid per month. Many companies pay a 'thirteenth month's salary' (dreizehntes Monatsgehalt) at Christmas and a further bonus payment at holiday time. Discussion of salaries is generally taboo amongst colleagues.*

Die Lösung

THE SOLUTION
1 How many products had Medic-Eschmann carried up to 1988, and how many new ones were being added?
2 How did Medic-Eschmann solve its warehousing problems?
3 When was Medic-Eschmann in a position to deliver urgent supplies?
4 Personnel training was an essential step in the reorganization. Who carried out training and what factor expedited the training process?
5 How many new sales representatives did the company employ?
6 Breakdown in communications easily destroys confidence. What steps were taken to provide continuity for the changeover in distributors?
7 Informative documentation is an important factor in the communication equation. How long would it be before a catalogue in German was available?

Lager und EDV

Herr Garabet: Wir hatten nicht genug Lagerkapazität, also haben wir innerhalb von Tagen zirka 550 Quadratmeter zusätzlich angemietet. Dann haben wir eine Firma beauftragt, Regale für Paletten aufzubauen. Dann mußte das Lager hier organisiert werden. Es handelt sich um 1500 Produkte, die sowohl ins Lager als auch in die EDV neu aufgenommen werden mußten. Bis dahin hatten wir ein Artikelsortiment von zirka 1300 bis 1500 Produkten gehabt; die Aufnahme von Portex-Produkten bedeutete also eine Verdoppelung der EDV-Kapazität. Wir haben seit Mitte Juni erst mal dringende Waren ausgeliefert, und seit dem 1. Juli läuft das ganz normal über EDV.

Innendienst

Herr Garabet: Danach kamen zwei englische Kollegen von Portex, die unseren Innendienst und das Lagerpersonal auf die neuen Produkte geschult haben – mit sehr hohem Einsatz, dafür sind wir sehr dankbar. Beide sprachen sehr gut Deutsch, so daß wir innerhalb von zwei bis drei Wochen lieferfähig wurden.

Außendienst

Herr Garabet: Die Promotion der Produkte wird über den Außendienst in den Kliniken gemacht. Der Außendienst bestand zu dem Zeitpunkt noch nicht. Zum 1. Juli haben wir also erst mal fünf Mitarbeiter im Außendienst eingestellt, die schnellstens geschult werden mußten.

Kommunikation

Herr Garabet: Wir haben sofort Mitte Juni, als die Situation offiziell bekannt war, durch Mailings an unsere Fachhändler und an die Kliniken auf die neue Situation hingewiesen. Diese Mailings haben wir natürlich wiederholt.

Dann haben wir eine Telefonmarketingaktion durchgeführt. Wir haben eine Firma für Telefonmarketing beauftragt, in unserem Namen zirka 1400 Kliniken anzurufen und dort zu fragen, ob die Information, die wir herausgeschickt haben, auch angekommen ist und ob Bedarf ist an weiterem Informationsmaterial, Mustern oder eventuell auch an einem Außendienstbesuch. Diese Operation kostete zirka 30 000 Mark.

Wir konnten bis jetzt nur einen Prospekt in Deutsch bringen. Ein erweiterter Katalog mit zirka 140 Seiten ist jetzt in Arbeit. Die Übersetzungsarbeiten sind schon vollzogen, und wir hoffen, daß wir in maximal zwei, drei Wochen auch diesen Katalog in Deutsch auf den Markt bringen können. Es ist sehr wichtig, daß alles, was in Deutschland vertrieben wird, auch mit deutscher Literatur und deutschen Prospekten unterstützt wird.

Hamburg

Herr Preuß (links) bei der Beladung der Super Guppy

„Made in Europe"

Hamburg's involvement in aviation followed naturally from the ship-building tradition. Lufthansa's maintenance centre is located at Hamburg's Fuhlsbüttel Airport, and production facilities in Hamburg-Finkenwerder provide the German contribution to the European Airbus.

Deutsche Airbus is an 80% subsidiary of Messerschmitt-Bölkow-Blohm, now part of the giant Daimler-Benz arms to automobiles conglomerate. It is responsible for final assembly of fuselage sections and for interior furnishings and fittings in the passenger cabins for Airbus Industrie.

Die komplette Ausstattung

Herr Bernhard Preuß is responsible for assembly of interior furnishings and fittings, and for air transport between Hamburg and Toulouse.

Factfinder
**1 At what point are electrical systems installed in the cabin?

Herr Preuß: Wir bekommen ein Basisflugzeug angeliefert. Die ersten Tage – die sind variabel, das kann von drei bis zu fünf Tagen dauern – werden die Basissysteme auf den Kunden modifiziert. Nach dieser sogenannten Modifizierung der Basis wird dann die Elektrik installiert, und danach wird von den Mechanikern die Ausstattung eingebaut. Wir statten das Flugzeug mit der kompletten Ausstattung aus, das heißt mit allem, was man in so einer Kabine sieht: vom Teppich bis zu den Möbeln, Toiletten, Waschbecken, Himmelbereichen, Tapeten, Seitenverkleidungen usw.

Filaword
die Luftfahrt *aviation*
die Luft- und Raumfahrt *aerospace*
die Ausstattung *furnishings and fittings*
die Fertigung *production, manufacture*
fertigen *to produce, manufacture*

Database
Wir bekommen ... angeliefert *We get ... delivered*
auf den Kunden *to the customer's requirements*
Himmelbereiche (*m, pl*) *overhead areas*

> **Tip**
> "Every effort should be made before a trade fair to attract buyers to the stand. Invitations to potential German buyers need to be in native-speaker German." (British-German Trade, *German Chamber of Industry & Commerce*)

Flugzeugbau in Hamburg

This press release outlines the role played by Deutsche Airbus GmbH in the European Airbus project.

FACTFINDER
*1 Where are the main flight systems installed?
*2 Where does final assembly of the Airbus take place?

Im Werk Hamburg ist die Deutsche Airbus verantwortlich für die Montage der bis zu 25 Meter langen Segmente des Flugzeugrumpfes. Dazu liefern die Werke im Weserraum große Teilschalen an, die in Hamburg endmontiert werden. Wenn die Struktur komplett ist, wird der deutsche Bauanteil am Airbus-Rumpf in Finkenwerder mit allen flugwichtigen Systemen von Hydraulik über Elektrik bis hin zu Pneumatik ausgerüstet und überprüft. Bei dieser computergesteuerten Prüfung werden alle Ergebnisse dokumentiert. Dann fliegt eine Super Guppy – das ungewöhnlichste Transportflugzeug der Welt – die riesigen Großbauteile und die Prüfdokumentation nach Toulouse, an den Ort der Airbus-Endmontage in Südfrankreich. Das Zusammenfügen der fertig ausgerüsteten Großbauteile aus den Partnerländern – ein optisch eindrucksvoller Vorgang – macht bei Aérospatiale aber nur noch rund fünf Prozent der Arbeit aus. Alle übrige Arbeit ist vor Ort in den europäischen Werkstätten der Partner bereits getan worden.

Mit eigener Kraft kommt der in Toulouse montierte und außen bemalte Airbus kurz nach seinem Erstflug dann noch einmal nach Hamburg-Finkenwerder. Das Flugzeug ist jetzt fertig und technisch komplett – aber es ist innen völlig leer, „grün", wie die Flugzeugbauer sagen. 27 000 verschiedene Ausstattungselemente vom Sitz bis zur Bordküche, vom Teppichboden bis zum Flugzeughimmel müssen jetzt bei der Deutschen Airbus montiert werden, damit der künftige Passagier „seinen" Airbus behaglich findet.
(*High-Tech aus Hamburg*)

DATABASE
bis zu *up to*
Dazu liefern ... ... an *For this ... supply ...*
Weserraum (*m*) *area along the River Weser*
Bauanteil am ... *share of the work in the ...*
mit ... ausgerüstet und überprüft *equipped with ... and tested*
Zusammenfügen (*n*) *assembly*
macht ... aus *makes up ...*
nur noch *only*
ist ... bereits getan worden *has already been done ...*
vor Ort *on site* (literally *at the coalface*)
Mit eigener Kraft *Under its own power*
völlig leer *completely empty*

FILAFACT *adjectival phrases*
Notice how in German, as in English, an adjective goes before the noun, e.g. *der künftige Passagier* (the **prospective** passenger). In fact, in German you can find a whole string of details about the noun in front of it, after the article that goes with the noun:

die Montage *der bis zu 25 Meter langen Segmente* des Flugzeugrumpfes
(the assembly of *the sections, which are up to 25 metres long*)
➡ P 101

EXECUTIVE SKILLS
**1 *Flugzeugbau in Hamburg* presents a production process. The main points you need to understand are the key stages in the process. See if you can work out their order.
 a Transport der Flugzeugrumpfsegmente nach Toulouse
 b Erstflug
 c Endmontage der Flugzeugrumpfsegmente
 d Ausrüstung mit flugwichtigen Systemen
 e Außenbemalung des Flugzeugs
 f Flug nach Hamburg-Finkenwerder
 g Lieferung der Teilschalen
 h Innenausstattung
 i Computergesteuerte Überprüfung der Hydraulik, Elektrik, Pneumatik
 j Endmontage des Flugzeugs
*2 *behaglich* means *a* attractive *b* economical *c* expensive *d* comfortable *e* safe?

Zahlen und Fakten

1933 Weltweite Krise im Schiffbau – Gründung der Hamburger Flugzeugbau GmbH durch Werftchef Walther Blohm.
1955 BRD erhält Souveränität und Lufthoheit zurück.
1969 Fusion der Hamburger Flugzeugbau GmbH mit Messerschmitt-Bölkow zu MBB.
1970 Beginn der Airbus-Ära. Größtes multinationales Zivilflugzeugprogramm Europas mit den Partnern Frankreich, Deutschland, Großbritannien und Spanien.
1989 Fusion von MBB mit Daimler-Benz zu einem der größten Industrieunternehmen der Welt. Die bisherige MBB-Unternehmensgruppe Transport- und Verkehrsflugzeuge wird ein selbständiges Unternehmen: Die Deutsche Airbus GmbH.

**3 *Flugzeugbau in Hamburg* includes two lists of nouns. *a* Can you find these lists (*i* and *ii*)? *b* What is the common denominator for the nouns in list *i* and for the nouns in list *ii*? *c* Can you find the prepositions that structure list *i* and list *ii*?
***4 Which definite article goes with *a Segmente* in the first sentence of paragraph one *b Airbus* in the first sentence of paragraph two? What cases do these nouns appear in (➡ P 98)?

Hamburg ist Zentrum für Rumpfheckmontage und -ausrüstung.

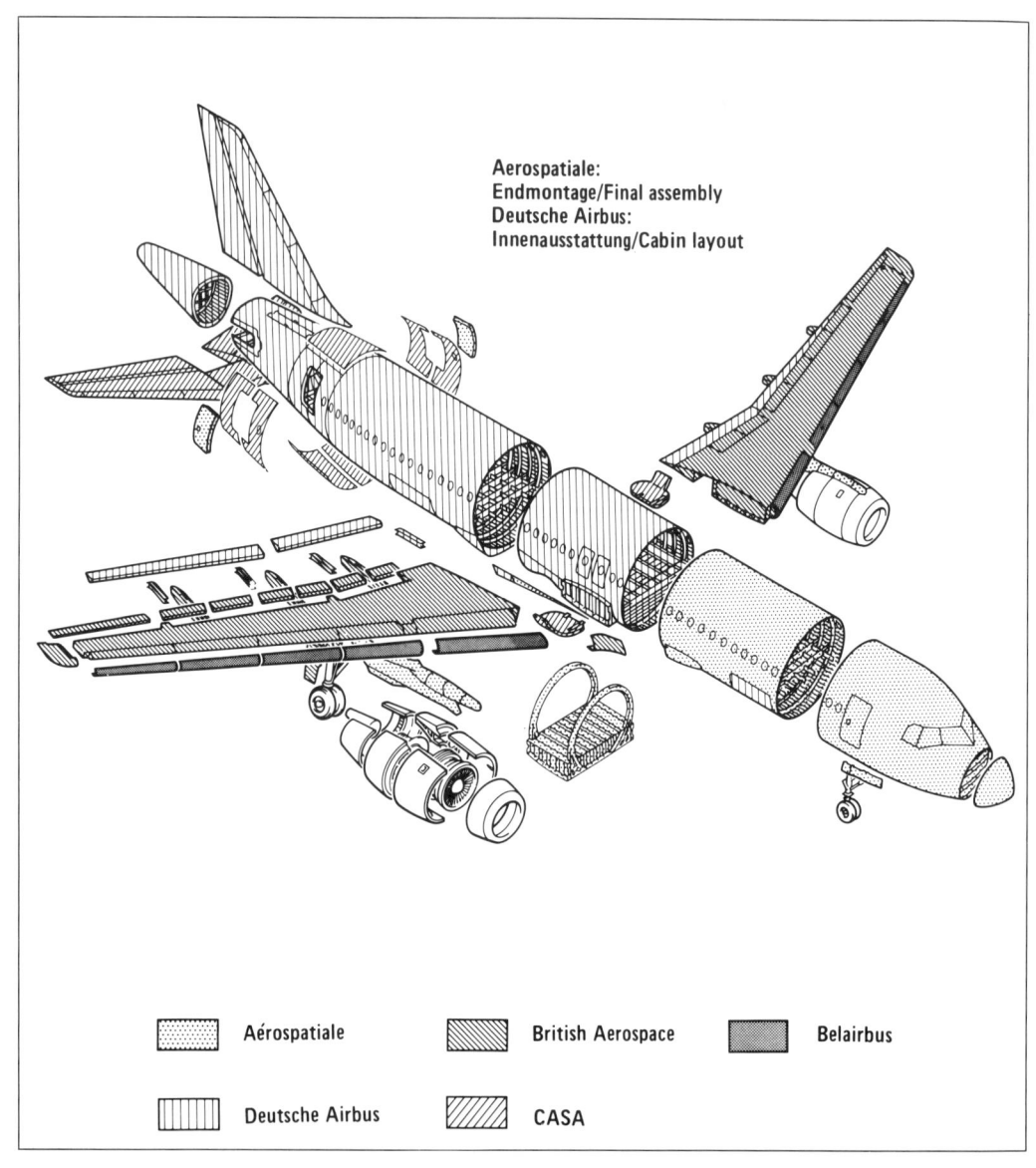

Aerospatiale: Endmontage/Final assembly
Deutsche Airbus: Innenausstattung/Cabin layout

- Aérospatiale
- British Aerospace
- Belairbus
- Deutsche Airbus
- CASA

Rund ein Drittel des europäischen Airbus wird bei der Deutschen Airbus entwickelt und produziert.

Kommunikation

Herr Preuß joined MBB in 1962 and was involved in the Airbus project from the start. We asked him about the pros and cons of having several countries working on the Airbus.

FACTFINDER
*1 What are the specialities of the British, the French and the Germans?
***2 What is an advantage?

Herr Preuß: Ich glaube, daß der Technologievorsprung gegenüber Boeing daraus resultiert, daß sich gerade beim Airbus unterschiedliche Länder gewisse technologische Vorteile geschaffen haben, wie die Engländer zum Beispiel beim Flächenbau, und im Cockpitbereich die Franzosen, und wir im Bereich der strukturellen Bearbeitung wie automatische Nietsysteme.

Die Kommunikation untereinander bringt, glaube ich, für das Projekt Vorteile, obwohl es sich immer wieder zeigt, daß der Abstimmprozeß sehr schwierig ist. Aber wenn ich so zurückblicke – ich würde sagen, in den letzten zehn, fünfzehn Jahren sind die Europäer doch enger zusammengerückt.

Deutsche Airbus

DATABASE
daraus ..., daß ... *from the fact that*
gewisse ... Vorteile *certain ... advantages*
Flächenbau (m) *wing construction*
Nietsysteme (n, pl) *riveting systems*
es sich immer wieder zeigt *it keeps emerging*
sind ... doch enger zusammengerückt *... have moved closer together*

Die Abstimmung zwischen den Partnern

Worksharing and reaching agreement on technological processes that are regulated by differing national standards are some of the problems confronting Herr Heinz Kuckuck, programme coordinator for the Airbus programmes.

FACTFINDER
**3 What example does Herr Kuckuck use to illustrate work-sharing?
**4 What example does Herr Kuckuck use to demonstrate the problems of European harmonization in manufacturing the Airbus?

Herr Kuckuck: Noch bevor überhaupt ein Strich auf irgendeiner Zeichnung oder auf irgendeinem modernen Konstruktionssystem gemacht wird, werden Arbeitsaufteilungs-, sogenannte Worksharing-Gespräche geführt. Man kann zum Beispiel sagen, die Briten bekommen den Flügel, und dafür rechnen die Deutschen ein Lastspektrum, und zwar für das ganze Flugzeug.

Dann muß eine Reihe von Dingen harmonisiert werden. Zum Beispiel hat die Fertigung von BAe ganz bestimmte Vorschriften, nach denen die Leute dort fertigen. Das heißt, wenn sie irgendein Bauteil verchromen sollen, dann bringen sie mit einem Bad das Chrom über elektrischen Strom an das Bauteil. Wir machen das hier auch, bloß haben wir ganz andere Vorschriften. Bei den Briten muß so ein Bad vielleicht 5 Grad wärmer als bei uns sein. Und nun geht natürlich das große Überlegen los: Wieso denn? Und was passiert denn dann eigentlich damit? So ist das auch mit einer ganzen Reihe anderer Dinge, die alle zwischen den Partnern harmonisiert oder doch zumindest abgestimmt werden müssen.

DATABASE
überhaupt ein Strich auf irgendeiner Zeichnung *a single stroke on any drawing*
dafür *in return*
eine Reihe von Dingen *a number of things*
nach denen *according to which*
geht ... das große Überlegen los *... the big debate begins*
Wieso denn *Why*
was passiert ... damit *what ... happens to it*
denn dann eigentlich *actually*
abgestimmt werden müssen *have to be agreed*

TiP

If you need accommodation, the local tourist office is always a good place to start. You can phone up for a recommendation or call in. If a town is booked up for a particular event, they may well know of hotels which have just opened and are less well known.

Hamburger Spezialitäten

The Free Hanseatic City of Hamburg has a long democratic tradition. Its trading history and contact with the outside world have given the city an independent spirit and cosmopolitan outlook. With an average of 203 rainy days a year it is no surprise that Hamburg's reputedly reserved citizens feel some affinity with the British.

When the sun shines, Hamburg must surely be Germany's most attractive city. Built around the *Binnenalster* and *Außenalster* lakes, its imposing warehouses and residences bear witness to Hamburg's seafaring wealth. Generations of sailors have frequented the *Reeperbahn* in St Pauli, reputedly the 'most sinful mile in the world', which now offers a seedy reputation and a wide range of entertainment. Most impressive of all is the view from the spectacular *Köhlbrandbrücke* across a vast expanse of ships and gantry cranes.

Filaword
das Wetter *weather*
der Sonnenschein *sunshine*
der Regen *rain*
der Nieselregen *drizzle*
der Schnee *snow*
der Hagel *hail*
der Nebel *fog, mist*
der Niederschlag *precipitation*

Hamburg auf einen Blick

Freie und Hansestadt Hamburg

Einwohnerzahl:	1 600 000
Flüsse:	Elbe, Alster
Postleitzahl:	D/W-2000
Telefonvorwahl:	(0)40-
Flughafen:	Hamburg-Fuhlsbüttel (11 km vom Zentrum); Airport-City-Bus zur Stadtmitte oder HVV-Airport-Express Nr. 110 nach Ohlsdorf mit U-/S-Bahn-Verbindung zur Stadtmitte.
Information:	Tourismus-Zentrale, Burchardstr. 14, Tel. 30 05 10
Postamt:	Hauptpost, Hühnerposten 12, geöffnet Mo-Fr 8-18 Uhr, Sa 8-12 Uhr; Hauptbahnhof, geöffnet täglich 6-22 Uhr.
Wichtige Messen:	**Hanseboot, InternorGa** (Hotellerie, Gastronomie), **Reisen Hamburg** (Tourismus, Caravan, Auto), **SMM** (Schiff, Maschine, Meerestechnik)
Sehenswürdigkeiten:	Hafenrundfahrt, Bürgerhäuser in der Deichstraße, Speicherstadt
Typisches Essen:	Aalsuppe, Finkenwerder Scholle, rote Grütze
Typische Getränke:	Alsterwasser, Korn
Wichtige Termine:	Drei tolle Tage im Mai (Hafengeburtstag), Alstervergnügen, DOM-Fest (März/April, August, November)

Zum Rüstzeug des hamburgischen Kaufmanns längst vergangener Tage gehörten eine gute Handschrift, ein an den Vorbildern deutscher Sprachkultur geschulter Briefstil und die Beherrschung fremder Sprachen. Die Beherrschung von zwei, drei, ja vier Fremdsprachen in den hanseatischen Kontoren war gar nichts Auffallendes. (Meyer-Marwitz, Das Hamburg Buch)

Stehimbiß

If you're pressed for time, don't turn up your nose at a *Stehimbiß* – nearly every large butcher (*Metzgerei/Fleischerei/Schlachterei*) has one.

Factfinder
*1 What city features in the list of dishes?
***2 What should you do if you aren't satisfied?

Speisekarte zum Mitnehmen

City-Schlachterei
Martin Höfner
Mohlenhofstr. 10 - 2000 Hamburg 1
Tel. (040) 33 80 86

Montag
1. Bohnen, Birnen und Speck mit Kartoffeln — 7,30
2. Frische Suppe — 4,00
Dienstag
1. Sauerbraten mit Backobst und Klößen — 7,90
2. Kartoffelsuppe — 4,00
Mittwoch
1. Burgunder Rinderbraten mit Gemüse und Kartoffeln — 7,90
2. Nudelsuppe — 4,00
Donnerstag
1. Schnitzel „Wiener Art" mit Gemüse und Kartoffeln — 7,90
2. Erbsensuppe — 4,00
Freitag
1. Gebratenes Fischfilet mit Kartoffelsalat — 7,90
2. Grüner Bohneneintopf — 4,00

Angebot der Woche:
3 Spiegeleier mit Bratkartoffeln und kl. Salat 6,90
2 Wiener mit Kartoffelsalat 5,50

Sind Sie zufrieden, sagen Sie es weiter,
sind Sie es nicht, sagen Sie es bitte mir.
Ihr Schlachtermeister Höfner

Hig

München

-Tech an der Isar

Munich is one of Germany's top-ranking industrial cities, and measured according to output of goods and services, it is top of the league, although Berlin may now catch up. The decline of heavy industry in traditional industrial areas and arrival of sunrise technology gave Munich a head-start in the popularity stakes. It is reckoned to be the centre of Germany's electronics industry, with more than 300 companies grouped around the giant Siemens. The automotive industry is number two, with car maker BMW, and MAN's production facility for commercial vehicles. Brewing, fashion and tourism are three of Munich's 'clean' industries, and the city is also a European insurance centre.

Modern industries combine with old-world charm to give the city its image of high-tech dynamism and baroque *Gemütlichkeit*. Nearby forests, lakes and mountains, and proximity to Austria and Italy add to the magnetic attraction of this *'Weltstadt mit Herz'*.

Silicon Valley

Was macht den „Silicon-Valley-Effekt" aus, den man zwischen München, Nürnberg und Stuttgart teils zu verspüren meint, teils zu erzeugen hofft? Zum Silicon-Valley-Effekt – benannt nach der jungen Industrie-Region südlich von San Francisco, wo Computerfirmen, Chip-Hersteller und Software-Designer in höchster Packungsdichte beieinandersitzen – gehören allerlei objektive Größen: gute Verkehrswege, ein funktionierendes Telefonnetz, eine reiche Palette von Betrieben, die als Zulieferer herkömmlicher Technik die Teile zu den neuen „Systemen" herstellen können, gute Facharbeiter, Hochschulen, Institute für Grundlagenforschung, eine verständige Verwaltung, die Mut macht und staatliches Geld besorgt, ein Basiswohlstand, aus dem Risikokapital herauszuholen ist, und so weiter und so Fortschritt.

Vor allem aber gehören subjektiv empfundene Reize dazu: Freizeitwert, interessante Gesellschaft, Wohnortprestige, die ganze psychologische Software, die der Kreative zur Anregung braucht. „Für mich gibt es nur einen Platz in Deutschland, wo ich leben kann ..." – München! (*Geo Special: München*)

DATABASE
Was macht ... aus *What makes up ...*
den man ... teils zu verspüren meint *which people partly think they can detect ...*
zu erzeugen hofft *hope to create*
Zum ... gehören allerlei objektive Größen *A variety of objective factors form part of the ...*
die Mut macht *which gives encouragement*
herauszuholen ist *can be obtained*
und so weiter und so Fortschritt (*play on the phrase* und so weiter und so fort *'and so on and so forth', and the word* Fortschritt *progress*)
gehören ... dazu *... play a part*

FILAWORD
zukunftsorientiert *future-oriented*
die Elektronik *electronics*
die Versicherung *insurance*
die Brauerei *brewing, brewery*
die Gemütlichkeit *geniality, cosiness, cheerfulness*

Wußten Sie schon ...?

1 München ist Deutschlands Bier- und Versicherungshauptstadt.
2 Der Freistaat Bayern ist größer als Irland.
3 Das Oktoberfest beginnt im September.
4 München ist Sitz des Europäischen und des Deutschen Patentamtes.
5 München gilt als die beliebteste Stadt Deutschlands.

T i P

If you are thinking of doing business in Germany, it is worth getting in touch with the Industrie- und Handelskammer *in your target area for details of importers and general advice. They offer their services free of charge.*

DEUTSCHES BUSINESS-MAGAZIN **67**

München

DIE FEINHEITEN DES DEUTSCHEN MARKTES

The German computer industry got off to a slow start and has had some difficulties keeping pace with American and Japanese competition. Computer culture did not find its way into schools and private homes with the same speed as in the US or Britain, which may have contributed to the hesitant response. However, German customers now know exactly what they want in terms of quality and price, making for a highly competitive market.

FILAWORD
die Textverarbeitung *word processing*
die Datei *file*
die Diskette *disk*
das Laufwerk *disk drive*
die Festplatte *hard disk*
die Grafik *graphic(s)*
pauschal *flat rate*
frei Haus *free house, franco domicile*

Westward Farbgrafik-Terminal 4420 Serie

Ein harter Markt

Herr Wilhelm Lohn is general manager of Westward Technologie GmbH, a distributing subsidiary of Telemetrix PLC.

Herr Lohn: Der deutsche Markt ist ein wesentlich härterer Markt bezüglich des Preises und bezüglich der Produktqualität als der englische Markt. Außerdem hat der deutsche Endkunde unserer Erfahrung nach einen wesentlich höheren Wissensstand über das Produkt als der englische Endkunde. Ein deutscher Endkunde schreibt zum Beispiel exakt die Konfiguration vor, die er haben will. Ein englischer Endkunde kümmert sich nicht so sehr darum – Hauptsache, sein Problem ist gelöst. Das sind so die Feinheiten des deutschen Marktes, die aber sehr typisch sind.

DATABASE
Endkunde (*m*) end user
unserer Erfahrung nach *in our experience*
kümmert sich nicht so sehr darum *doesn't bother about that so much*
Das sind so *These are*

FILAFACT *comparisons*
Check back (➡ **P 31, 52**) for comparative forms of adjectives and notice how some add an umlaut on the vowel: *hart - härter, hoch - höher* (hard - hard**er**, high - high**er**). ➡ **P 101**

FILASKILL
When you're reading, it's often only necessary to pick out certain relevant facts. The *Profiles* are designed to help you read selectively. They are in the form of short notes relating to facts in the interview or article and will enable you to locate essentials.

Wir bedanken uns ...

WESTWARD Westward Technologie GmbH — Fortschritt für Computergrafik
Joseph-Dollinger-Bogen 18
D-8000 München 40
Telefon 089/323009-0
Telex 5216406
Telefax 323009-99

Sehr geehrte/r ....,

wir bedanken uns für Ihre Anfrage und übersenden Ihnen wunschgemäß Unterlagen zu unserem umfangreichen Angebot über Computer-CAD/CAM-Produkte.

Die WESTWARD TECHNOLOGIE GMBH ist ein führendes Unternehmen in Deutschland im Bereich Entwicklung, Produktion und Distribution für Grafikkarten, -monitore, Farbdrucker, Plotter, Scanner, Grafikterminals und Hochleistungsrechner. Diese hochwertigen Produkte werden durch die Distribution von AutoCAD ergänzt und zu marktgerechten Preisen angeboten.

Unser langjähriger Service, welcher bundesweit im Einsatz ist, gibt Ihnen die Sicherheit von Responsezeiten unter 24 Stunden. Unsere langjährige Erfahrung im CAD/CAM-Markt sichert Ihnen zuverlässige und bewährte Produkte, welche mit Sicherheit auch Ihre Leistungsmöglichkeiten abdecken können.

Wir würden uns freuen, auch Sie künftig zu unserem Kundenkreis zählen zu können. Bei weiteren Fragen steht Ihnen unser Herr Lindermeier unter Telefon 089/323009-30 gerne jederzeit zur Verfügung.

Mit freundlichen Grüßen
WESTWARD TECHNOLOGIE GMBH

Wilhelm Lohn
Geschäftsführer

PROFILE *business letter*
Westward have a carefully crafted letter to accompany product literature answering enquiries. See if you can work out the order in which the following points are made:

a Product range
b Thanks for enquiry
c Invitation to become a customer
d Response times
e Contact person
f Documentation enclosed
g Service experience
h Ability to meet prospective customer's needs
i Competitive pricing
j Position of company in Germany

München

Wartung vor Ort

Westward regards itself as a service company, and as service manager it is Herr Roland Pfister's task to coordinate this side of the company's activities.

Serviceleiter Roland Pfister

Herr Pfister: Viele Kunden wollen einen sogenannten Wartungsvertrag, das heißt, sie bezahlen im Jahr eine bestimmte Summe und haben dafür die komplette Wartung des Gerätes frei. Wir bieten zwei verschiedene Typen an. Einmal haben wir eine 24-stündige Responsezeit, das heißt, maximal nach 24 Stunden ist ein Techniker vor Ort; das beläuft sich auf zirka 12% des Neupreises. Beim 48-Stunden-Wartungsvertrag sind es zirka 8% des Neupreises.

Ein Kunde, der keinen Wartungsvertrag hat, kann natürlich auch in Anspruch nehmen, daß ein Techniker zu ihm kommt. Dann wird das berechnet nach der angefallenen Fahrzeit, nach den Arbeitsstunden, die der Techniker vor Ort gebraucht hat, und nach den Teilen, die er ausgewechselt hat. Bei uns kostet die Arbeitsstunde 200 D-Mark, die Fahrtstunde 170 D-Mark, und pro Kilometer nochmal 65 Pfennige, und das ausgetauschte Teil – wir haben da einen Pauschalpreis – kostet 650 D-Mark.

DATABASE
Wartung (f) *maintenance*
das beläuft sich auf *that amounts to*
in Anspruch nehmen, daß ein Techniker zu ihm kommt *call out an engineer*
wird das berechnet nach *that's charged according to*

PROFILE *service*
Westward carries out two types of service. Try and locate the following information in the interview:
1 Number of service contracts available.
2 Alternative option and cost.

TIP
According to Herr Lohn, German customers are likely to want to go into considerable technical detail. Make sure you can discuss technicalities – preferably in German.

ⓑ VOM COIL ZUM KUNDEN 8

Vom Rohteil bis zum fertigen Motor

Aus Aluminium werden in der eigenen Gießerei Zylinderköpfe und viele andere Teile gegossen. Teile aus Eisen – den Motorblock, Nockenwellen und viele andere – liefern andere Firmen als Rohlinge zu. Sie werden in der mechanischen Fertigung fast vollautomatisch für die Montage bearbeitet. In München werden Motoren zusammengebaut, auf Prüfständen eingestellt und getestet; das Getriebe wird angeflanscht. *(Zum Thema BMW)*

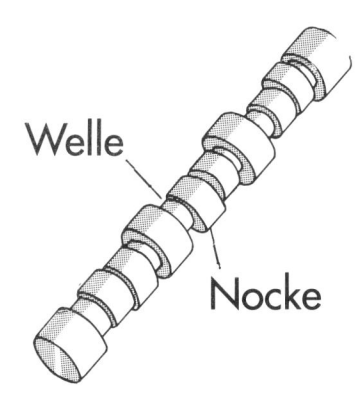

Die Nockenform ist eine Abweichung von einem Grundkreis. Mit dieser Nockenform erfolgt das Öffnen und Schließen der Ventile.

Ein wesentlicher Bestandteil des Motors

Herr Schobert: Die Nockenwelle wird durch die Wareneingangsinspektion abgenommen. In der mechanischen Fertigung durchläuft sie verschiedene Produktionsprozesse vom Rohteil bis zum Fertigteil: Ablängen, Zentrieren, Drehen, Schleifen über Finishen bis zum Bondern. Anschließend wird die Nockenwelle für den Einbau in den Motor bereitgestellt.

In der Motormontage erfolgt der Einbau der Nockenwelle in den Zylinderkopf. Die Nockenwelle dient zur Steuerung der Ventile: Ohne eine Nockenwelle kann das Ventil nicht betätigt werden, ohne Ventile läuft der Motor nicht. Somit ist die Nockenwelle ein wesentlicher Bestandteil des Motors.

BMW – Wer ist wer?
Franz Schobert, Leitung Motorenbau. Ausbildung: Lehre Maschinenschlosser; Studium Fachhochschule. Hobbys: Autoreparatur (Oldtimer), Heimwerken.

Die Nockenwelle wird in den Zylinderkopf eingeführt.

Der Funktionslauf

Herr Schobert: Jeder Motor wird im Komplettzustand auf Prüfständen funktionsgeprüft. Der Motor wird von sich aus gestartet und durchläuft einen bestimmten Funktionslauf. Getestet werden die Akustik, Dichtigkeiten, Abgaswerte und die Gesamtfunktion überhaupt. Es könnte beispielsweise sein, daß ein Ventil laut ist und somit falsch eingestellt ist. Der Funktionslauf soll gewährleisten, daß der Kunde einen einwandfrei funktionierenden Motor erhält.

Der fertige Motor

München

ELEKTRONIK IM BAUKASTENSYSTEM

The need for compatibility between European and American electronic equipment prompted the German standards authority (*Deutsches Institut für Normung*) to adopt the American 19" standard – formulated as 482.6 mm. Standardization of enclosures for electronic equipment permits modular combination of individual components. The traditional product range of Knürr AG is focused around the 19" Series, although the company has now also moved into office furniture and fittings as part of a strategy which aims to target markets closer to the consumer.

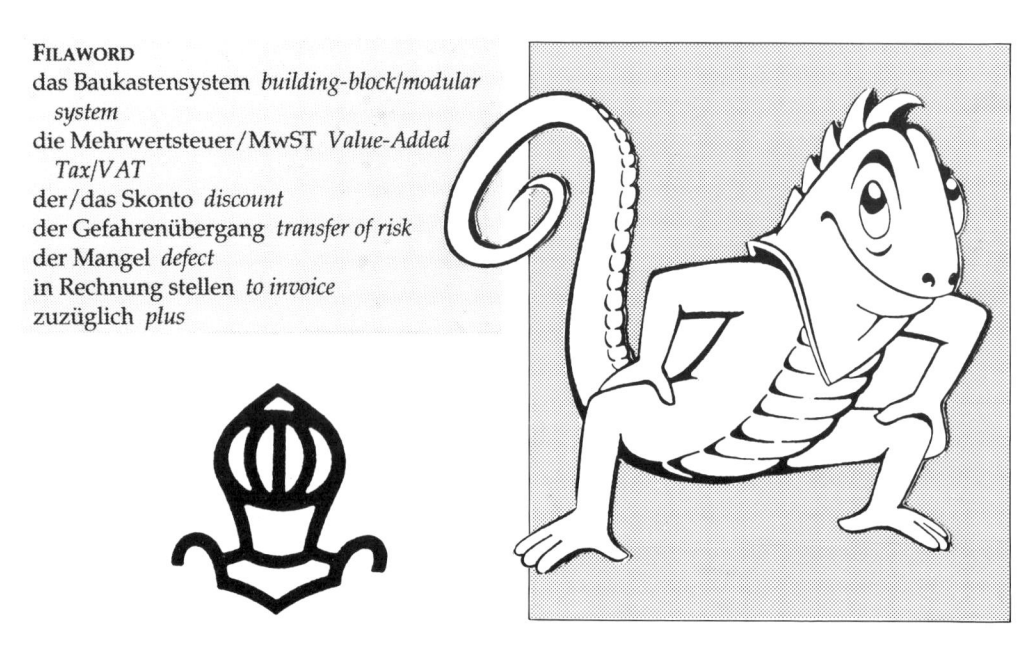

FILAWORD
das Baukastensystem *building-block/modular system*
die Mehrwertsteuer/MwST *Value-Added Tax/VAT*
der/das Skonto *discount*
der Gefahrenübergang *transfer of risk*
der Mangel *defect*
in Rechnung stellen *to invoice*
zuzüglich *plus*

Chasseleon: Ein Gehäuse muß sich der Elektronik anpassen

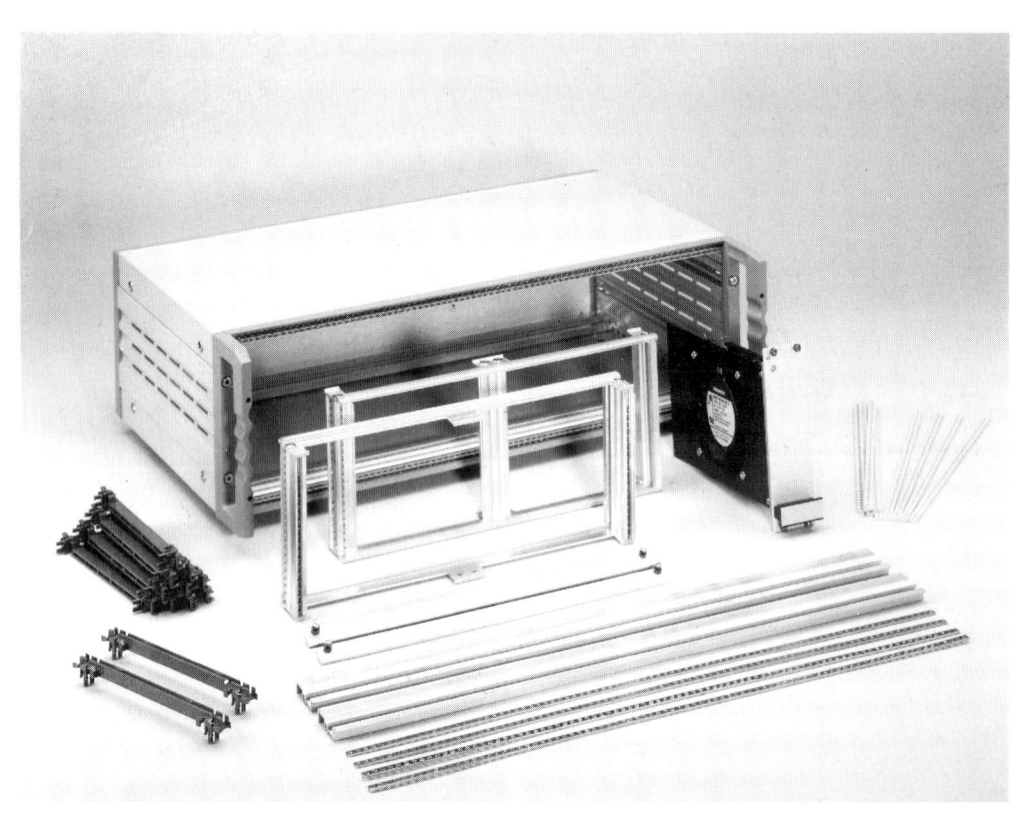

Chasseleon – eine vielversprechende Verbindung von Chassis und Chamäleon – weist auf den Grundgedanken dieses modularen Gehäusesystems hin: Das Chasseleon paßt sich der Elektronik an. Und nicht umgekehrt.

Produktentwicklung

Product development is taken particularly seriously at Knürr. Dr Dietmar Mrosek, member of the board of management, went into the company's system for identifying and realizing new products.

Dr. Mrosek: Für die Produktentwicklung haben wir sogenannte „Assessment Center" und „Taskforce". Wir haben Qualifikationsspiegel für alle Mitarbeiter des Unternehmens erstellt, in denen die Hobbys und sonstigen Neigungen enthalten sind. Daraus wählen wir dann für Assessment Center bestimmte Mitarbeiter aus, weil durchaus ein Mann zum Beispiel in der Fertigung ein hervorragender Ideenbringer für Produktentwicklungen sein kann.

Es werden dann Mitarbeiter aus sämtlichen Bereichen ausgewählt, die in einer Taskforce zusammengezogen werden, die periodisch das Produkt entwickelt. Diese Mitarbeiter tagen eine Woche in einem Hotel und gehen dann wieder zurück in die Firma. Die Entwicklungsabteilung muß das ausführen, und das Produkt wird dann wieder in der Taskforce schrittweise weiterentwickelt.

Es sind schon ganz hervorragende Ideen rausgekommen, zum Beispiel der neue Stahlschrank, dann das sogenannte „Chasseleon" – das ist ein 19-Zoll Gehäuse und Baugruppensystem – und das „Dacomobile". Das sind alles Produkte, die in so einer Taskforce entstanden sind – alle sehr erfolgreich.

FILAFACT *es*
Notice how Dr Mrosek uses *es* at the beginning of the sentence:

Es sind schon *ganz hervorragende Ideen* rausgekommen.
(*Really excellent ideas* have emerged.)
Es werden dann *Mitarbeiter* ausgewählt.
(Then *employees* are selected.)

He might have said: '*Ganz hervorragende Ideen* sind schon rausgekommen' and '*Mitarbeiter* werden dann ausgewählt'. Dr Mrosek highlights the underlined subject by postponing it and beginning the sentence with *es*. ➡ **P 100**

PROFILE *product development*
Try and work out the sequence in which the stages of product development at Knürr take place.

a First meeting of the *Taskforce*
b Design by the development department
c Compiling a qualification profile for each employee
d Selection for *Assessment Center*
e Selection for *Taskforce*

dacomobile
Der kleine PC-Wagen

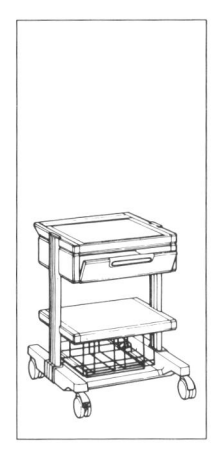

Für das kleine Büro ist vielleicht die niedrige PC-Station der unentbehrliche Helfer. Auf Wunsch mit eingebauter Steckdosenleiste.

Höhe	860 mm
Standardzusammenstellung	1 Tischplatte mit Griff 1 Tastaturauszug 1 Drucker-Auszug 1 Druckerpapierablage

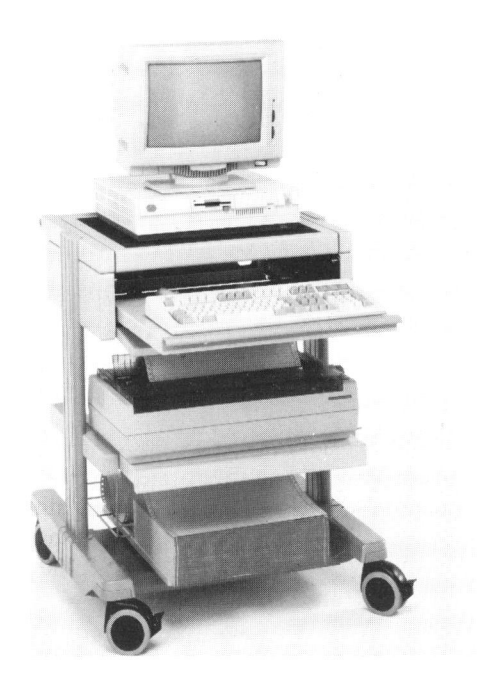

Allgemeine Geschäftsbedingungen
(Auszug)

Bestellungen:
Bestellungen können schriftlich, telefonisch oder per Telefax erfolgen.

Lieferungen:
Lagerhaltige Ware verläßt spätestens 24 Stunden nach Bestelleingang unser Haus. Bis 20 kg Paketgewicht Versand per Post. Alle anderen Lieferungen mit Spedition.

Gefahrenübergang:
Der Gefahrenübergang erfolgt bei Übergabe der Ware an den Spediteur.

Preise:
Alle Preise verstehen sich als Nettopreise ab Lager zuzüglich der gesetzlichen MwSt. Fracht- und Verpackungskosten werden zusammen mit der Ware in Rechnung gestellt. Es gelten die Preise des jeweils neuesten Kataloges.

Zahlung:
Ihre Zahlung ist innerhalb von 14 Tagen mit 2% Skonto, spätestens 30 Tage ab Rechnungsdatum ohne Abzug zu leisten.

Änderungen:
Technische Änderungen, Preisänderungen und Änderungen im Design bleiben uns im Interesse der Qualitätsverbesserung vorbehalten.

Garantie:
Sofort erkennbare Mängel sind innerhalb von 7 Tagen nach Erhalt der Ware anzuzeigen. Die 6monatige Garantiezeit beginnt mit dem Gefahrenübergang.

Gerichtsstand:
Der Gerichtsstand ist München.

T i P
"If you're selling a technical product, you have to have someone who can speak German, because the man on the shop floor who's actually going to work your machine is unlikely to be able to discuss the technicalities of the product in English." (Peter Bryant, consul general, Düsseldorf)

FILAFACT *obligation*
Notice how the reader is told that payment *is to be* made and defects *are to be* reported:

Ihre Zahlung *ist* innerhalb von 14 Tagen *zu* leisten.
Mängel *sind* innerhalb von 7 Tagen *an*zu*zeigen.

The verb *sein* is used together with *zu* and an infinitive. ➡ **P 103**

PROFILE *terms of delivery and payment*
Mistakes can be costly when it comes to the small print. See if you can get the essential information on these points:

1 Methods of ordering
2 Time of dispatch
3 Methods of delivery
4 Charges on top of catalogue price
5 Terms of payment
6 Warranty period

München

SCHNELL UND BEQUEM

Mail order has gained a strong presence in Germany, not least because it avoids problems with parking and closing times. Mail-order houses have a share of around five per cent of total retail trade, and for some goods they have extremely high market shares. Mail order is proving particularly popular in eastern Germany.

Quelle, Europe's biggest mail-order firm, is based in the north of Bavaria, at Fürth near Nuremberg. Quelle publishes 7.5 million catalogues twice yearly. It has a 33% share in the domestic market for washing machines and an even higher share for sewing machines. Herr Wolfgang Keck, head of import, explained the form of the company before going on to highlight the stringent standards Quelle sets for its suppliers.

Einkaufen per Post
Umsatz im Versandhandel je Einwohner in DM

- Schweden 215
- Schweiz 241
- Frankreich 200
- Niederlande 283
- Großbritannien 179
- USA 340
- Österreich 169
- BR Deutschland 386 DM
- Belgien 99
- Japan 81
- Italien 32

Stand 1986 © Globus 7539

Eine Personengesellschaft

In contrast to the *Kapitalgesellschaft* (incorporated company), a *Personengesellschaft* (partnership) has one or more *Komplementäre* (general partners) and at least one *Kommanditist* (limited partner). Quelle is still a family company led by Frau Grete Schickedanz.

Herr Keck: Die Großversandhaus Quelle Gustav Schickedanz KG ist ein Familienunternehmen. Eine Kommanditgesellschaft (KG) ist eine sogenannte Personengesellschaft im Gegensatz zu einer Kapitalgesellschaft, wie es eine Aktiengesellschaft oder eine GmbH wäre. Bei einer Kapitalgesellschaft haften die Einleger nur mit der Höhe des Geldes, das sie als Einlage geben, während bei der Kommanditgesellschaft der Komplementär, also der persönlich Haftende, mit seinem ganzen Vermögen haftet.

DATABASE
im Gegensatz zu *as opposed to*
wie es ... wäre *such as ...*
Bei ... während bei *In the case of ... while in the case of*
haften *are liable*

FILAWORD
der Versand *mail order*
der Marktanteil *market share*
das Angebot *offer*
die Nachfrage *demand*
das Muster *sample*
pünktlich *on time, punctual(ly)*
zuverlässig *reliable (-ly)*

Traditionell begründet

A poor reputation is easily acquired and often takes a lot of hard work to break down. Herr Keck had a rather jaundiced view of British suppliers, though he conceded that there seemed to have been a sea change.

Herr Keck: Unsere Importe aus dem Vereinigten Königreich sind relativ gering. Die britische Konsumgüterindustrie war eigentlich nie besonders exportorientiert nach Europa, sondern war viel mehr orientiert ins Commonwealth. Das drückt sich zum Beispiel in unterschiedlichen Standards in der Elektroindustrie aus: Die britischen Geräte sind auf 240 Volt ausgelegt, während man bei uns 220 Volt braucht.

Dann waren auch in der Mode bis Mary Quant eigentlich von England nur sehr konservative Dinge zu erwarten; das war eigentlich der erste Durchbruch, daß ein „swinging" London kam und nicht ein tristes London. Das sind Dinge, die eben traditionell begründet sind und die sich nur langsam abbauen. Inzwischen ist das anders, es gibt also in England zum Beispiel rund um Birmingham herum eine sehr leistungsfähige und auch hochmodische Strickwarenindustrie.

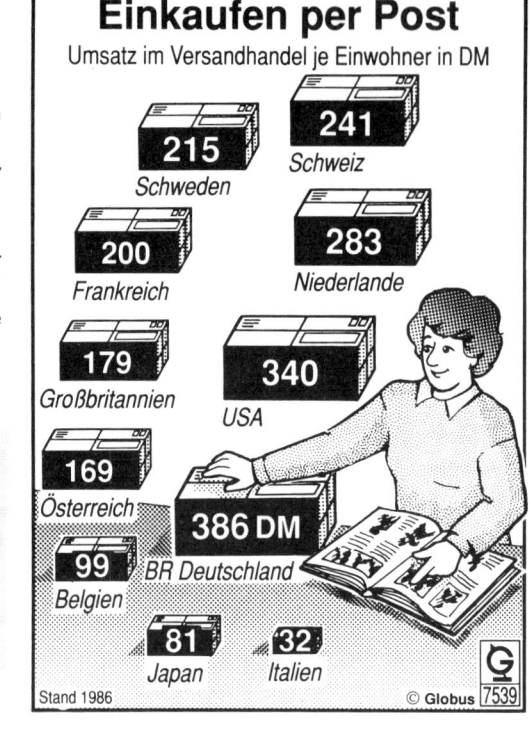

DATABASE
gering *low, restricted*
traditionell begründet *based on tradition*
die sich ... abbauen *which are broken down ...*
Inzwischen ist das anders *Now things have changed*

FILAFACT *sein + zu + infinitive*
Check back (➡ P 71) to see how *sein + zu + infinitive* was used to express obligation. Herr Keck uses the same construction (with the past tense of *sein*) to say that only conservative clothing *'was to be expected'* from Britain:

Dann *waren* von England nur konservative Dinge *zu* erwarten.

Make sure you recognize this construction – it can cause confusion. ➡ P 103

PROFILE *suppliers*
The UK is not among Quelle's big suppliers. Can you work out why, by picking out the main points made by Herr Keck (1-4)?

1 The traditional orientation of the UK consumer industry's export drive
2 An example illustrating the problem
3 The traditional image of British fashion
4 A positive example in the fashion industry

Importleiter Wolfgang Keck

München

Das Angebot

Herr Keck: Wenn ein interessantes Angebot da ist, wird zunächst mal von uns ein Muster gezogen. Entspricht dieses Muster von der Qualität, von der Aufmachung, von der Farbe, vom Stil her unseren Vorstellungen, dann kommt der Preis. Und wenn auch der Preis letztlich gefunden werden kann, dann wird ein Größensatz bestimmt. Dann macht unser Institut für Warenprüfung – das ist die größte Qualitätsprüfungsorganisation des Handels überhaupt in Europa – produktionsbegleitende Stichproben. Dann muß noch die Lieferzeit stimmen, und dann wird der Artikel irgendwann in den Katalog aufgenommen.

DATABASE

wird ... von uns ... gezogen *is ... ordered by us*
Entspricht dieses Muster ... unseren Vorstellungen *If this sample conforms to our requirements ...*
von ... her *in terms of ...*
Warenprüfung (f) *product testing, quality control*

PROFILE *selection*

See if you can find the order in which Quelle makes decisions on what to include in their catalogue.

a Festlegung des Preises
b Bestimmung der Lieferzeit
c Musterziehen
d Qualitätsprüfung
e Bestimmung des Größensatzes
f Beurteilung des Musters

T i P

"If you approach a German buyer with a printed price list, he will always feel the prices are too high. He always wants a special price and only views the printed price list as a starting point. It is a distinct advantage to have a German bank account, since customers like to use the simplest method of payment." (Heinz Leyerle, Werga Tools GmbH)

Ihr direkter Draht zur Quelle über 140 mal in Deutschland:

QUELLE TELEFON SERVICE
... meist zum Ortstarif!

Das ist der schnellste und bequemste Weg, bei Quelle zu bestellen. Auch wenn Sie irgendwelche Fragen haben oder einmal etwas reklamieren möchten, hilft Ihnen unser Telefon-Service-Büro jederzeit mit Rat und Auskunft.

Liefertreue

Herr Keck: Ein Versandunternehmen ist darauf angewiesen, daß die Waren, die es im Katalog anbietet, auch pünktlich da sind, wenn der Katalog an den Verbraucher geschickt wird. Die britische Industrie hatte immer mit Lieferzuverlässigkeit, mit Streiks und vor allem mit einem im europäischen Vergleich nicht sehr zuverlässigen Transportsystem zu kämpfen, und das waren echte Nachteile. Das ist allerdings in den letzten Jahren auch besser geworden.

Das Ideal ist natürlich, daß der Termin auf den Tag eingehalten wird – dafür macht man ihn ja. Sinn der Planung ist ja, die Kapitalströme halbwegs zu lenken, die Lagerkapazität zu steuern und die Nachfrage zu befriedigen, die der Katalog auslöst. Das setzt also voraus, daß die Liefertreue nach Möglichkeit sehr exakt ist.

DATABASE

ist darauf angewiesen, daß ... sind *is reliant on ... being*
wenn ... geschickt wird *when ... is sent*
hatte immer ... zu kämpfen *always had to contend with ...*
dafür macht man ihn ja *that's why you set it, after all*
Das setzt ... voraus *... that presupposes*

PROFILE *delivery*

The logistics of computerized warehousing and distribution make special demands on the suppliers. Try and work out these points:

1 Three problems with supply from the UK
2 Three aims of planning
3 The key to efficient distribution

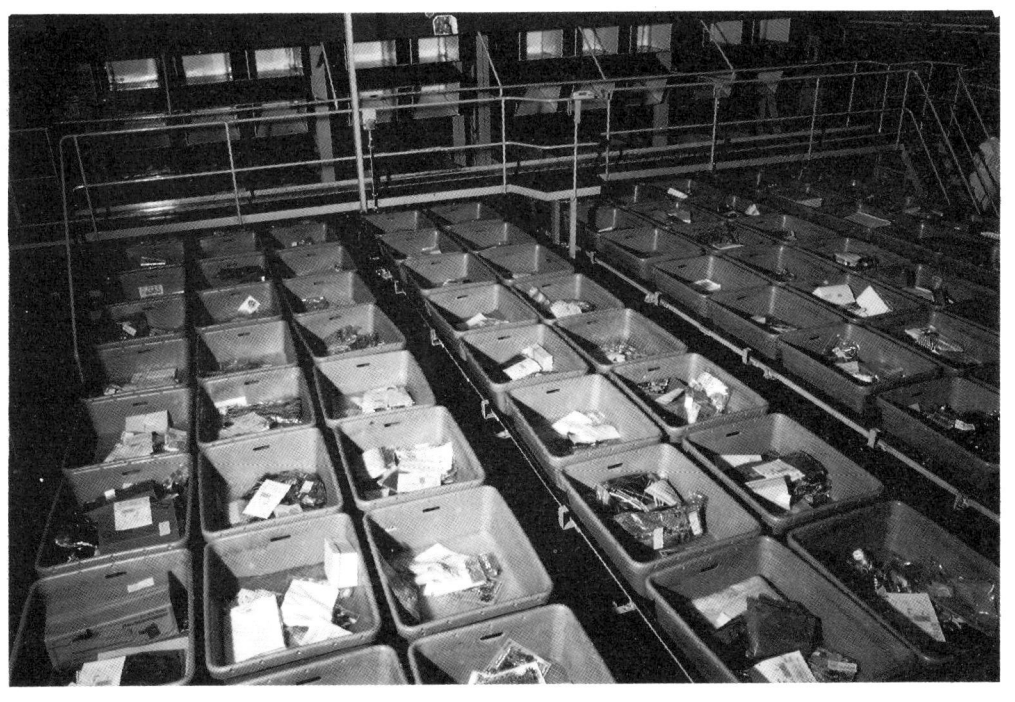

Computergesteuert werden die Kundenaufträge zusammengestellt.

München

EIN ANSPRUCHSVOLLER ENDVERBRAUCHER

Nuremberg is home to the world's biggest toy trade fair. Most toys in Germany are sold by specialist toy retailers able to offer expert advice and full customer service. The German consumer sets high standards for quality and safety, and likes toys to be educational.

Germany's big specialist retail shops are grouped together in the cooperative *Vereinigung der Spielwaren-Fachgeschäfte* (VEDES). Originally its purpose was to enable members to purchase goods at preferential rates. Today the cooperative offers members an array of services such as bookkeeping, market research and advertising.

Ausmusterung

Frau Ursula Safar is a buyer's assistant concerned with games, music and computers, and Herr Werner Schwarz is head of import. They discussed the annual process of selecting the new range of toys.

Frau Safar: Nach der Spielwarenmesse im Februar, die in Nürnberg stattfindet, wird unser Sortiment neugestaltet für ein Jahr. Wir laufen über die Messe, und dann ziehen wir die Muster, die uns interessieren. Wir haben dann im März eine Ausmusterung.

Herr Schwarz: Bei den Ausmusterungen wird das ganze Angebot herangezogen. Maßgeblich ist erst einmal die Gängigkeit der Ware, die man sich erhofft, dann Qualität, Preis usw. – aber unabhängig von der Herkunft. Und dann ist es so, daß vielleicht von 1000 Artikeln 150 im Direktimport laufen, während 850 aus der Bundesrepublik kommen. Wenn Exklusivverträge bestehen, wird auch Importware über Importeure bezogen.

FILAWORD
das Spielzeug *toy, toys*
die Spielwaren *(pl) toys*
das Fachgeschäft *specialist (shop)*
die Genossenschaft *cooperative*
die Marktforschung *market research*

DATABASE
wird ... herangezogen ... *is examined*
unabhängig von der Herkunft *independently of origin*

FILAFACT *word order*
Remember that in German you may find the subject of the sentence after the verb. When the verb consists of two or more components, the subject then comes after the first part of the verb. In the following passive sentences, the **subject** comes after the auxiliary verb *werden*:

Nach der Spielwarenmesse *wird* **unser Sortiment** neugestaltet.
Wenn Exklusivverträge bestehen, *wird* **Importware** über Importeure bezogen.
➡ P 106-107

PROFILE *purchasing*
The Nuremberg Fair is the showcase for suppliers, and VEDES buyers make their choices when they have seen the range of products on offer. Can you determine critical factors affecting the purchasing process?

1 Date of toy fair
2 Date of selection
3 Three criteria determining selection
4 Percentage of goods from domestic suppliers

Ausmusterungen auf der Nürnberger Spielwarenmesse 1991: Frau Safar (Mitte) begutachtet Neuheiten.

Qualitätsgefälle

Herr Reiner Loch, sales manager at VEDES, described a quality scale for some of Europe's consumers.

Herr Loch: Man kann von der Schweiz nach Holland oder Belgien ein Qualitätsgefälle feststellen. Die Schweizer Endverbraucher legen größten Wert auf qualitätsmäßig sehr hochstehendes Spielzeug. Es muß lehrreich sein, es muß griffsympathisch sein, es sollte aus natürlichen Produkten kommen; Holz, zum Beispiel, wird sehr stark in der Schweiz verkauft. Die deutschen Endverbraucher sind nicht ganz so anspruchsvoll, aber immer noch anspruchsvoll, wohingegen die Endverbraucher in Belgien sehr stark auf Spielzeug hin tendieren, wo der Preis die Hauptrolle spielt – das heißt preisgünstigeres, um nicht zu sagen billiges Spielzeug. Die Engländer dürften mit den belgischen und holländischen Mitgliedern irgendwo ähnlich stehen.

DATABASE
legen größten Wert auf *attach great importance to*
wohingegen *whereas*
um nicht zu sagen *not to say*
dürften ... irgendwo ähnlich stehen *probably stand roughly on the same level ...*

PROFILE *quality*
Expectations of quality are by no means equal in the countries VEDES deals with. See if you can work out:

1 Herr Loch's ranking of countries in terms of their quality requirements.
2 Determining factors for the most quality-conscious customers.

TiP
Instructions in German and conformance with safety regulations are considered absolute priorities for success in the German toy market. Instructions should be produced by a German speaker with expertise in the area. Toy food made of plastic is not permissible in Germany in case it is mistaken for the real thing.

PRIMA KLIMA IN DER FIRMA.
SCHENK-TIPS FÜR DEN ARBEITSPLATZ.

Stimmt das Arbeitsklima, macht es auch Spaß zu arbeiten. Ein Kollege aus der Marktforschung hat Geburtstag? Schenken Sie ihm doch gemeinsam eine Dartscheibe. Damit er auch weiterhin mit seinen Berechnungen ins Schwarze trifft.

VEDES Fachgeschäft

Aus dem VEDES Buch der Wünsche

Versand- und Lieferbedingungen für schriftliche Bestellungen: Die Ware aus dieser Jahresausgabe wird auf Wunsch zugeschickt, sofern der Gesamtpreis der Bestellung DM 50,- übersteigt. Der Versand im Inland erfolgt per Nachnahme. Übersteigt der Gesamtpreis der Bestellung DM 250,-, liefern wir frei Bestimmungsort bzw. bei Frachtgut frei nächstgelegenem Stückgutbahnhof (gilt nicht beim Kauf im Geschäft). Spezielle Verpackungen empfindlicher Ware sowie sperriger Güter berechnen wir zum Selbstkostenpreis. Mit Auslieferung der Ware an den Versandbeauftragten, spätestens jedoch mit Verlassen des Werkes oder des Lagers geht die Gefahr des zufälligen Unterganges und der zufälligen Verschlechterung der Ware auf den Besteller über. Auslandslieferungen erfolgen gemäß vorheriger Vereinbarung. Sämtliche Preise sind freibleibend. Änderungen und Liefermöglichkeiten bleiben vorbehalten.

Werbemittel

The advertising department headed by Herr Klaus Schwarzmann produces advertising material for VEDES members.

Herr Schwarzmann: Wir produzieren für unsere Händler nicht nur Schaufensterdekorationsmaterial, sondern wir liefern unseren Händlern auch acht verschiedene Prospekte und unser attraktivstes Werbemittel, ein Magazin im Umfang von 192 Seiten; das ist unser VEDES *Buch der Wünsche*. Dann haben wir noch Beihefter, die gleichzeitig als Zeitungsbeilage genutzt werden, und zwar drucken wir etwa 17,5 Millionen; davon werden 15 Millionen in den sechs namhaftesten deutschen Fernsehzeitschriften beigeheftet. Hier haben wir die Sicherheit, daß es kaum Streuverluste gibt, weil man davon ausgehen kann, daß jeder Endverbraucher sich nur eine Fernsehzeitschrift hält. Obenauf setzen wir noch Rundfunkwerbung, und Fernsehwerbung in Form von 24- oder 30-Sekunden-Spots.

Database
weil man davon ausgehen kann *because one can assume*
Obenauf setzen wir *On top we use*

Filafact *conditions*
In German you can make a conditional statement by starting with the verb:

> **Übersteigt** der Gesamtpreis der Bestellung DM 250,-, liefern wir frei Bestimmungsort.
> (*If* the total price of the order **exceeds**, ...)
> **Stimmt** das Arbeitsklima, macht es auch Spaß zu arbeiten.
> (*If* the atmosphere at work **is right**, ...)

The italicized conditional clauses could be rephrased using *wenn* (if): 'Wenn der Gesamtpreis der Bestellung DM 250,- **übersteigt**, ...'; 'Wenn das Arbeitsklima **stimmt**, ...'. It's important to look out for this construction so that you can interpret it correctly. ➡ P 107

Profile *conditions of dispatch and delivery*
Can you locate the main information?

1 Cost above which goods are delivered cash on delivery
2 Cost above which carriage is free
3 Exception to **2**
4 Cost of special packaging for fragile and bulky goods
5 Point at which risk is transferred
6 Destinations requiring prior agreement
7 Rights that are reserved

Factfinder
*1 How could the dartboard help a colleague with his calculations?

Executive Skills
Find German equivalents for the following in *Aus dem VEDES Buch der Wünsche:*

*1 *a* on request *b* total price *c* order *d* cash on delivery *e* to exceed *f* freight *g* cost price *h* customer *i* shop *j* dispatch *k* warehouse *l* agreement *m* packaging *n* forwarding agent.

Vom Versand bis in die Reklamation

Frau Tanja Franke is training for the qualification *Groß- und Außenhandelskauffrau*.

Frau Franke: Man durchläuft hier die Abteilungen vom Versand bis in die Reklamation, dann Einkauf, Registratur, Mitgliederberatung. In einer Abteilung ist man zwischen zwei und sechs Wochen, manchmal auch acht Wochen. Außerdem haben wir zweimal in der Woche Berufsschule. Das sind hauptsächlich kaufmännische Fächer: allgemeine Wirtschaftslehre, Handelsbetriebslehre, Rechnungswesen, Buchführung, kaufmännisches Rechnen, dann Sozialkunde, Deutsch, Sport, Religion.

Profile *training*
Check back (➡ P 53, 57) for some of the complexities of the training process in German companies, then work out these details for Frau Franke:

1 Departments mentioned
2 Vocational subjects studied at college
3 Other subjects

München

EIN STARKER KONKURRENZKAMPF

Herr Claus B. Fritz runs CBF Electronics Vertriebs GmbH, a distributor and agent for electronic components in Baldham near Munich. He coordinates development and production by British manufacturers with the requirements of German purchasers, buying the products for resale to the customer. Herr Fritz regards closeness to both manufacturer and customer as essential for success when dealing in specialist electronic components.

FILAWORD
vertreten *to represent, act as an agent for*
der Handelsvertreter *agent*
das Vertriebsbüro *sales office*
der Lieferant *supplier*
die Provision *commission*
der Vertrag *contract*

Der größte Einzelmarkt in Europa

Herr Fritz: Der deutsche Markt gilt für diese Art Produkte als der größte Einzelmarkt in Europa. Es gibt hier einen sehr starken Konkurrenzkampf. Wenn man aber einmal in einer Firma drin ist – zum Beispiel Bosch, Siemens oder AEG –, dann ist man drin. Man kann also in Deutschland nach wie vor recht gute Geschäfte machen.

Wir vertreten im Moment sechs Firmen, die alle in England zu Hause sind. Die Produkte, die wir anbieten, werden über den Entwicklungsingenieur erst in neue Gerätekonzeptionen hineinentwickelt. Wir unterhalten uns also die ersten zwei oder drei Jahre ausschließlich mit Entwicklern. Dann geht das Gerät in Serie, und dann müssen wir uns zwangsläufig auch mit dem Einkauf unterhalten, weil der Einkauf ja letztendlich den Auftrag plaziert, hinter dem wir unterm Strich auch her sind. Wir sind eigentlich ein Bindeglied zwischen dem Hersteller der Einzelbauteile und dem deutschen Entwicklungsingenieur, der das Gerät für eine zukünftige Serie entwickelt.

DATABASE
gilt ... als ... *is considered to be*
Wenn man aber einmal in ... drin ist *But once you're in ...*
nach wie vor *still*
zu Hause sind *are domiciled/based*
werden ... erst in ... hineinentwickelt *first have to be designed ... into ...*
geht ... in Serie *... goes into production*
hinter dem wir unterm Strich auch her sind *which is what we're after, as our bottom line*

FILAFACT *relative clauses*
You can't always expect to find the relative pronoun that introduces a relative clause right after the comma. It may be preceded by a *preposition:*

den **Auftrag** ..., hinter **dem** wir her sind
➡ **P 107-108**

Wenn es darauf ankommt, empfindliche Halbleiter-Schaltkreise gegen Stromstöße und Überstrom zu schützen...

...können Sie sich auf SEMITRON Überstromdioden verlassen.

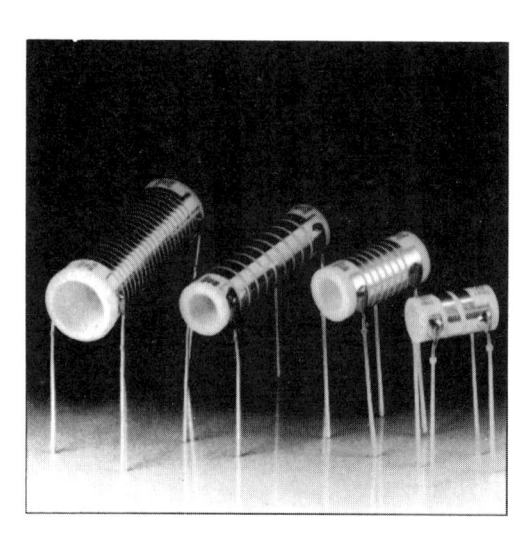

Hohe Stabilität und Güte. Induktivitätswerte von 0,045 µH bis 1,830 µH erhältlich. Temperaturbereich: -55°C bis +125°C. Oxley CERAMOX^R Al$_2$O$_3$-Keramikkörper.

PROFILE *electronic components*
1 Can you reconstruct the sequence in which Herr Fritz made the following points?
a The number of companies CBF represents
b The long-term prospects once a supplier is feeding into a German company
c Department responsible for finally awarding the contract
d The size of the German market
e CBF's contacts in the early stages of seeking to place a product
2 Now try to extract the important points in *a* to *e*.

Hochwillkommen auf dem Markt

CBF acts as the buffer between the supplier and the customer and has to ensure that strict deadlines are adhered to. Mr Bernard Rodden, a British engineer with the company, specifies essentials for success in the German market. Herr Fritz goes on to discuss CBF's handling of delivery schedules.

Herr Rodden: Die Engländer nehmen sich zu viel Zeit; im deutschen Markt können wir uns das nicht leisten. Wir müssen sehr schnell reagieren, wir können uns hier nicht diese Ruhezeiten leisten. Wir brauchen schnelle Antworten, schnelle Muster, schnelle Fertigung. Die Engländer dazu zu bringen, uns diesen Service zu geben, ist teilweise sehr schwer, denn sie sind nicht daran gewöhnt.

Herr Fritz: Wir schlagen auf jede Lieferzeit, die wir von England bekommen, zwei Wochen drauf. Es ist einfach für uns eine Sicherheit, und da liegen wir manchmal auch noch mal um zwei Wochen daneben, weil aus den sechs Wochen zehn Wochen geworden sind. Es fehlt dort die Präzision in der Produktionsplanung und wahrscheinlich auch die Motivation. Ich kann das gar nicht richtig erklären, aber mit dieser Eigenart muß man einfach leben, denn das, was sie an Produkten vorstellen, ist immer toll und hochwillkommen auf dem Markt.

DATABASE
... dazu zu bringen *To persuade ...*
liegen wir ... auch noch mal ... daneben *we're still off the mark ...*
aus den sechs Wochen ... geworden sind *the six weeks have turned into ...*

FILAFACT *relative clauses*
These can start with *was*, following *das*. *Das, was* is equivalent to the English 'that which':
Das, was sie an Produkten vorstellen, ist immer toll.
➡ **P 99**

PROFILE *delivery times*
Try to find out CBF's attitude to delivery deadlines:
1 CBF's strategy for punctual delivery
2 Mr Rodden's explanation for slow service from UK companies
3 Herr Fritz's explanation for slow response times
4 The flip side

Mit Hurrah in Deutschland

As an agent, Herr Fritz is convinced that opening a sales office is not necessarily the right answer for a company just starting up in the German market.

Herr Fritz: Ich kenne viele englische oder amerikanische Firmen, die mit Hurrah in Deutschland ein eigenes Vertriebsbüro aufgemacht haben. Das erste Problem war, jemanden zu finden, der das für sie macht. Dann haben sie den einen gefunden, aber der hat sich natürlich überhaupt nicht um den Vertrieb kümmern können. Der hat sich erst mal nur mit administrativen Dingen beschäftigen müssen: Büromöbel, Visitenkarten, Übersetzung von Geschäftsbedingungen usw. Erst braucht er eine Sekretärin. Dann braucht er einen Außendienstmitarbeiter, der natürlich erst einmal geschult werden muß. Das dauert auch noch mal ein halbes Jahr, so daß Sie, wenn Sie ein eigenes Büro aufmachen, unter Umständen schon zwei Jahre vertrödelt haben, ohne daß Sie überhaupt irgendwelche Umsätze getätigt haben. Dann kommt die Phase, in der der Außendienstmitarbeiter überhaupt nicht weiß, zu welchen Kunden er hingehen soll, es sei denn, Sie haben das Glück gehabt, irgend jemanden von der Konkurrenz anzuwerben, und dann müssen Sie schon sehr tief in die Tasche greifen.

DATABASE
den einen *the right person, somebody*
der hat sich ... überhaupt nicht um ... kümmern können ... *he wasn't able to deal with ...*
der hat sich ... nur mit ... beschäftigen müssen ... *he had to deal solely with ...*
zu welchen Kunden er hingehen soll *which customers to visit*
es sei denn *unless*
sehr tief in die Tasche greifen *dig very deep in your pocket*

PROFILE *sales office*
Can you penetrate the obstacle course outlined by Herr Fritz?

1 Administrative problems confronting the would-be manager of a sales office in Germany
2 Essential personnel to be employed
3 Length of training for the sales engineer
4 Problem initially faced by an inexperienced sales engineer
5 Problem of head-hunting from the competition

T*i*P
"Having an agent is only half the story. You have to support the agent and give him back-up. I think one of the most important aspects of back-up is to come over and visit some of your customers with him every now and then."
(Charles Pattinson, vice-consul (commercial), Munich)

VOM COIL ZUM KUNDEN 9
Endmontage und Hochzeit

In der Endmontage entsteht aus der lackierten Karosse das fertige Automobil. Es erhält Scheiben und Instrumente, Sitze und Scheinwerfer. Der Motor wird zusammen mit den Achsen montiert: Das ist die „Hochzeit". In eineinhalb Minuten ist sie vollbracht. Die Räder werden befestigt. Benzin und andere notwendige Flüssigkeiten werden eingefüllt. *(Zum Thema BMW)*

Die Trennwand von British Steel verschwindet hinter Filz.

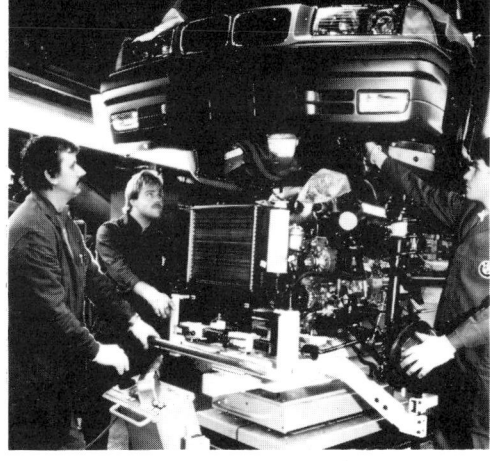

Prüfung auf Herz und Nieren

Herr Schobert: Auf dem Rollenprüfstand wird die Spur überprüft und eingestellt. Über die Spureinstellung wird auch automatisch im rollenden Prozeß der Mittenstand des Lenkrades eingestellt. Dann werden die Vorder- und Hinterachsbremsen, die Funktionen und der gesamte Antrieb überprüft.

Anschließend kommt der Wagen in den sogenannten Finish. Im Finish wird das Fahrzeug nochmal innen und außen in Augenschein genommen, um festzustellen, ob beispielsweise irgendwo noch ein Lackfehler oder ein Montagefehler ansteht. Wenn alles in Ordnung ist, geht das Fahrzeug zur Auslieferung.

Die „Hochzeit" ist der Zusammenschluß eines Fahrzeuges mit den Aggregaten. Zu den Aggregaten gehört nicht nur der Motor, sondern auch die Vorder- und Hinterachse.

Der BMW bekommt sein Emblem.

Der Wagen ist fertig; aber die Arbeit ist noch nicht zu Ende. Auf Herz und Nieren wird er – wie schon die Einzelteile – nochmals geprüft. Fertige Automobile gehen von München in alle Welt.

Der Produktkontakt zur Spitze

Small family engineering companies form the backbone of Germany's mechanical engineering industry. They have the flexibility and know-how to create and exploit niche markets, but require heavy investment to sustain the necessary research and development. Traditionally, German investors are cautious. Venture and investment capital for innovative products are relatively hard to come by.

FILAWORD
der Maschinenbau *mechanical engineering*
das Wagniskapital/Risikokapital *venture capital*
das Beteiligungskapital *investment capital*
die Selbständigkeit *independence*
der Ertrag *profit, earnings*

Visitenkarte

Herr Klaus Michaelis is head of Elfema, a family firm with 15 employees. Like many German engineers, he did an apprenticeship before going on to take a degree in engineering. He believes that practical experience is a prerequisite for managerial success.

Herr Michaelis: Mein Name ist Klaus Michaelis – Klaus Vorname, Michaelis Familienname. Ich bin ausgebildeter Ingenieur. Ich bin Geschäftsführer der Firma Elfema GmbH.

Ich habe erst eine Ausbildung als Werkzeugmacher gemacht und habe dann die Fachhochschule besucht. Es ist typisch für sehr viele deutsche Ingenieure, daß sie erst eine praktische Ausbildung machen und damit eine gewisse Erfahrung im praktischen Beruf als Voraussetzung zum Studium mitbringen. Meiner Meinung nach ist ohne praktische Erfahrung sehr wenig Erfolg im Management zu erzielen.

Nach Beendigung meines Studiums als Ingenieur war ich in der Automobilbranche bei Daimler-Benz. Ich habe anschließend zehn Jahre in Karlsruhe in der Kernforschung gearbeitet. Dann bin ich vier Jahre im Patentrecht aktiv gewesen: Ich habe Patente und Lizenzen aus dem Forschungsbereich für die Industriefirmen verkauft. Dann habe ich mich selbständig gemacht.

ACTIONPACK
Check back to earlier *Actionpacks* (➡ P 10, 37, 40) and then make a note of some key facts about your education and career with the help of Herr Michaelis' summary.
1 Introduction 2 Profession 3 Present position
4 Education 5 1st job 6 2nd job ...

FILASKILL
Why not get a feel for the German press by trying to get hold of a different newspaper or magazine each month? Concentrate on getting the gist, and if you find a particular style that suits you – stick to it.

Fallstudie: Kapitalbedarf

Elfema develops and builds sophisticated welding machines requiring a highly skilled workforce of engineers and technicians, and heavy investment in research and development. The company now stands at a crossroads where independence may have to be sacrificed in order to remain at the leading edge of technology.

Produkte für eine Marktnische

COMPANY PROFILE
1 What is Elfema's product?
2 Why did Elfema choose this product?
3 Why is there now a strong demand for such products?
4 To what end did Elfema optimize the welding process?
5 What are Elfema's products used for?
6 Which companies are among Elfema's customers?

Herr Michaelis: Wir haben als kleine Firma erst einmal vertriebsstrategisches Denken praktiziert. Wir haben also Marktnischenüberlegungen geführt, das heißt, wir versuchen mit unseren Produkten in Gebiete zu kommen, wo sehr wenig oder fast keine Konkurrenz existiert.

Wir bauen Elektronenstrahlschweißmaschinen. Dieses Gebiet wird heute wieder sehr populär, denn es werden an viele Fügetechniken sehr hohe Qualitätsanforderungen gestellt, und man verwendet heute sehr viel exotische Materialien wie zum Beispiel Titan oder Sonderlegierungen. Solche Materialien kann man nur durch ganz spezielle Umgebungsbedingungen schweißtechnisch bearbeiten. Wir bauen Anlagen, die vollautomatisch computergesteuert einsetzbar sind; wir haben also das Verfahren optimiert, um es computersteuerbar zu machen, und der Markterfolg zeigt uns, daß unsere Idee eigentlich sehr positiv war.

Wir liefern Schweißanlagen, die für Triebwerksbau oder für *Maintenance*, also Reparatur und Wartung, eingesetzt werden. Wir sind bei Porsche; wir sind bei BMW; wir versuchen jetzt mit Mercedes ins Geschäft zu kommen; wir sind in England bei Rolls Royce ins Geschäft gekommen; wir sind bei Lucas ins Geschäft gekommen; Siemens ist ein Großkunde von uns; AEG – also alle Firmen, die selbst mit ihren Labors modernste Technologie praktizieren, kaufen dann oft bei kleineren Firmen neue Anlagen.

DATABASE
es werden an viele Fügetechniken ... gestellt *many joining methods have to meet ...*
Umgebungsbedingungen (f, pl) *ambient conditions*
die vollautomatisch computergesteuert einsetzbar sind *which can be used with fully automated computer control*
Triebwerksbau (m) *power plant/engine construction*
ins Geschäft zu kommen *to get into business*

Problem: Das Überleben

THE PROBLEM
1 What problems eventually beset any small high-tech company, according to Herr Michaelis?
2 Why?

Herr Michaelis: Die kleinen Unternehmen, die sich in einem technologisch sehr vorgeschrittenen Stadium befinden – also Hi-Tech-Marken –, werden irgendwann immer mit finanziellen Problemen zu kämpfen haben. Das heißt, in den kleinen Unternehmen werden heute sehr anspruchsvolle Techniken und Entwicklungsbestrebungen, die sehr viel Geld kosten, nicht mehr über die Ertragssituation des Produktes, das sie herstellen und verkaufen, gedeckt.

DATABASE
werden ... ... zu kämpfen haben *will ... be confronted with ...*
werden ... nicht mehr ... gedeckt *can no longer be financed ...*
Ertragssituation (f) *profitability*

München

Drei mögliche Schritte

In the view of Herr Michaelis, three avenues are open to a small company which no longer has the financial muscle to invest in further research and development.

Der Schritt in die Abhängigkeit

OPTION 1
1 What is the normal source of capital in Germany?
2 What is a prerequisite for taking out credit?
3 What is an alternative way of obtaining the necessary capital?

Herr Michaelis: Es ist bei Firmen vom kleinen bis mittelständischen Bereich ein allgemeiner Trend zu sehen, daß sich der Bedarf des Kleinen entwickelt, mehr Kapital zu investieren; und das kann er nur in der Partnerschaft mit dem großen oder finanzstarken Unternehmen machen. Normalerweise ist es sehr schwierig für ein kleines Unternehmen, Kapital zu beschaffen; das passiert in Deutschland nur über Banken, über Kredite. Kredite müssen immobil oder in irgendeiner Form abgesichert werden, und daran scheitert das; so daß also nur der Schritt zur Partnerschaft des Großen in Frage kommt. Wenn der Große an dem Produkt und der Flexibilität des Kleinen interessiert ist, dann wird – nach der Erfahrung des Profit-Center-Wesens – die kleine Firma weiter selbständig existieren, aber in absoluter finanzieller und wirtschaftlicher Abhängigkeit vom Großen.

DATABASE
Es ist ... zu sehen ... *can be seen*
daran scheitert das *that's where projects founder*
nur ... in Frage kommt *the only option is ...*
Abhängigkeit vom *dependence on the*

FILAFACT *nouns from adjectives*
Notice how Herr Michaelis turns adjectives into nouns:

das *kleine* Unternehmen
der *Kleine* (the small one)
das *große* Unternehmen
der *Große* (the big one)

➡ P 101

Weiterhin Selbständigkeit

OPTION 2
1 What is the danger of continued independence?
2 Why is developing a new product not an option?
3 What could enable small innovative companies to survive?

Herr Michaelis: Die Selbständigkeit kostet einen gewissen Preis. Wenn ich im technischen Bereich nicht mehr innovativ tätig sein kann, verliere ich irgendwann den Produktkontakt zur Spitze und damit auch unter Umständen meine wirtschaftliche Selbständigkeit. Oder ich muß ein neues Produkt suchen; dann stellt sich auch wieder die Frage, wie hoch technisiert das neue Produkt ist und wie weit der finanzielle Background reicht, um wieder ein neues Produkt starten zu können. Irgendwann ist das eine Schraube, die ins Unendliche geht. Man stößt immer wieder an gewisse finanzielle Probleme. Und das ist eine typische Entwicklung im gesamten europäischen Bereich.

Deswegen versucht man auch im angelsächsischen Bereich, das *venture capital* anders zu praktizieren: Man stellt bestimmte Innovationssummen für definierte Zeitabstände zur Verfügung und trägt voll das Risiko, das Geld zu verlieren oder eine positive Produktentwicklung zu erreichen. Die Produktentwicklung wird dann vermarktet, und die Firma bekommt dann wieder eine neue Aufgabe. So wäre ein mögliches Überleben in vielen innovativen kleinen Firmen zu sehen.

DATABASE
Spitze (f) *top*
unter Umständen *potentially*
stellt sich auch wieder die Frage *the question again arises*
um ... zu können *in order to be able to ...*
Man stellt ... ... zur Verfügung *... are provided ...*
So wäre ein mögliches Überleben ... zu sehen *this might permit survival ...*

Geschäftsführer Klaus Michaelis

	T i P

The German press is essentially regional, although certain dailies have nationwide distribution: Frankfurter Allgemeine Zeitung *(conservative/liberal),* Süddeutsche Zeitung *(liberal),* Die Welt *(conservative).* Handelsblatt *covers business. The magazine* Der Spiegel *specializes in hard-hitting investigative journalism,* Stern *is renowned as the publisher of the spurious Hitler diaries, while* Capital *and* Manager *are specifically geared to executive interests.*

Elektronenstrahlschweißmaschine der Firma Elfema

Liquidation

OPTION 3
1 What is the inevitable problem in winding up a company?
2 How does this particularly affect the owner of a small family company?

Herr Michaelis: Es ist sehr schwierig, eine Liquidation durchzuführen. Man kann nicht von klassischen betriebswirtschaftlichen Regularien ausgehen. Eine Liquidation bedeutet ja auch letztendlich, daß man den Mitarbeitern, die man hier im Anstellungsverhältnis hat, ein weiteres Überleben garantieren muß. Das heißt also, man muß versuchen, ihnen Alternativjobs zu beschaffen. Man muß unter Umständen eine Überbrückungsphase finanzieren. Und meine Firma ist ein typisches Familienunternehmen: Mein Schwiegersohn ist als Ingenieur in der Firma beschäftigt, mein Sohn hat Anteile von dieser Firma mitübernommen, meine Frau macht in der Firma Buchhaltung und Sekretariat. Wenn ich liquidiere, verliert also meine ganze Familie ihren Arbeitsplatz und damit ihre Existenzgrundlage.

DATABASE
Man kann nicht von ... ausgehen *You can't proceed on the basis of ...*
ihnen ... zu beschaffen *to get them ...*

THE WAY FORWARD
What step is Herr Michaelis likely to take and how will this affect Elfema's independence?

DEUTSCHES BUSINESS-MAGAZIN

München

ZUKUNFTSORIENTIERTE TECHNOLOGIEN

The *Münchner Technologiezentrum* is designed to house small companies working on future-oriented technologies, help entrepreneurs get through the difficult start-up phase, and bridge the gap between development, commencement of production, and market launch.

Messestand des Münchner Technologiezentrums

Kornelia Huber

Münchner Technologiezentrum

Das Münchner Technologiezentrum ist eine Einrichtung zur Förderung von Innovationsvorhaben im Bereich zukunftsorientierter Technologien.

Es will die Startchancen innovativer Unternehmensgründer verbessern sowie die wirtschaftliche Umsetzung von Forschungs- und Entwicklungsergebnissen bis hin zu Produktionsaufnahme und Markteinführung unterstützen.

Das MTZ wird von der Landeshauptstadt München, der Industrie- und Handelskammer für München und Oberbayern und der Handwerkskammer für Oberbayern getragen. Die Landeshauptstadt München und der Freistaat Bayern fördern das MTZ im Rahmen eines Pilotprojektes. (*Münchner Technologiezentrum*)

DATABASE
Es will ... verbessern sowie ... unterstützen *It is intended to improve ... and support ...*
bis hin zu *right through to*
wird von ... getragen *is financed by ...*

PROFILE *the package*
Use the *Glossary* to help find out what the *Technologiezentrum* has to offer its entrepreneurs.

1 The two options for renting space
2 Facilities available in the conference room
3 Option available for shortfall in equipment
4 Available consultancy facilities
5 Benefit offered by regular meetings
6 Contacts provided

Das Angebot	
4100 m² Betriebsfläche	•Vermietung von Büro-, Labor- und Produktionsräumen in erweitertem Rohbauzustand oder mit vollständigem Innenausbau.
Zentrale Serviceleistungen	•Telefon- und Schreibdienst •Telex, Telefax, Kopiergerät •Konferenzraum mit Dia- und Overheadprojektor, Video-System etc. •Leistungsfähige CAD-Anlage für Elektronikentwicklungen •Fachbibliothek •Zentrale Geräteerfassung (Verleih zwischen den Firmen)
Beratung und Betreuung	•Gründungsberatung •Beratung über öffentliche Fördermittel •Beratung bei Produktionsaufnahme und Markteinführung

Kontaktvermittlung	•Erfahrungsaustausch zwischen den MTZ-Firmen im Rahmen regelmäßiger Meetings
	•Vermittlung von Kontakten zu
	  •Hochschulen und außeruniversitären Forschungseinrichtungen
	  •der gewerblichen Wirtschaft und den Kammern
	  •Kapitalgebern
	  •Meinungsbildnern und Fachpresse

München

Münchner Hybrid Systemtechnik GmbH

Münchner Hybrid Systemtechnik GmbH is a small company at the Münchner Technologiezentrum. The company was founded with the aid of a grant provided by the Federal Ministry of Research and Technology (*Bundesministerium für Forschung und Technik*). The maximum possible grant is DM 900,000. Frau Kornelia Huber, an electrical engineer, is one of the five founders.

Entwicklung, Herstellung, Know-how

Die Firma Münchner Hybrid Systemtechnik GmbH wurde 1985 gegründet. Schwerpunkte des Unternehmens sind die Entwicklung und Herstellung von Fertigungsgeräten für die Hybridtechnik sowie die Herstellung von Hybrid- und SMD-Schaltungen im Kundenauftrag.

Die Firma hat derzeit drei Geräte im Programm. Die Geräte sind so konzipiert, daß sie den Anforderungen moderner CAM-Techniken genügen. Grundsätzlich besteht die Möglichkeit, die Geräte speziellen Kundenwünschen anzupassen.

Neben den Geräten bietet die Firma auch ihr Know-how an. So sind die Mitarbeiter nicht nur bei der Herstellung von Hybrid- und SMD-Schaltungen, sondern auch bei der Konzeption von Laborräumen und der Auswahl von Geräten und Materialien beratend tätig.
(*Münchner Hybrid Systemtechnik*)

Der Clou

Frau Huber: Wir entwickeln Fertigungsgeräte zur Herstellung von Hybridschaltkreisen. Der Clou dabei ist, daß wir wissen, wie man solche Schaltkreise macht, daß wir die Schaltkreise selber herstellen und daß das Know-how, das wir beim Fertigen dieser Schaltungen gewinnen, auch wieder in die Geräte einfließt. Das ist relativ einmalig, denn die meisten Geräteherstellern kommen aus dem Maschinenbau und wissen nicht, wie man so eine Schaltung macht. Da gibt es kaum Kommunikation zwischen den Schaltungsherstellern und den Geräteherstellern.

Das Schwierigste

Frau Huber: Der Vertrieb ist eigentlich das Schwierigste. Wir dachten zuerst, es reicht, wenn man ein tolles Gerät baut und den Leuten sagt, „schaut euch das mal an, das ist doch super". Aber das reicht natürlich nicht. Wir versuchen jetzt, die Geräte über Vertriebsfirmen zu verkaufen.

DATABASE

SMD-Schaltungen *SMD circuits*
So sind ... ... beratend tätig ... *advise on ...*
und daß das Know-how ..., ... einfließt *and that the know-how ... is incorporated ...*
Maschinenbau (m) *mechanical engineering*
schaut euch das mal an *have a look at this*

PROFILE *start-up*

Build up a short profile of the company and its products from the literature and interview.

1 Date of foundation
2 Focus of company's activities
3 Number of machines in the company's product range
4 Consultancy work undertaken by the company
5 The company's advantage over manufacturers of similar machines
6 The company's most difficult task

BABYLONISCHES SPRACHGEWIRR?

The export motor driving the German economy has necessitated a coordinated approach to foreign languages. In multilingual markets the challenge is to provide an integrated strategy for language within corporate communication. Company administrative language, standardization of terminology, deployment of foreign-language skills, the use of translators and interpreters, awareness of foreign cultures, and advertising all form part of such a strategy.

Übersetzer auf dem Weg nach Europa

Lawinenartig entstehen in der Industrie durch die Entwicklung von neuen Technologien, Verfahren und Materialien neue Wortbildungen oder Begriffe. Manchmal existieren sogar innerhalb eines Unternehmens mehrere Ausdrücke für ein und denselben Fachbegriff. Für den Übersetzer wird seine Aufgabe immer schwieriger, zeitaufwendiger.

Abhilfe schaffen kann hierbei nur eine Datenbank, die von „Terminologiestellen" im Unternehmen gepflegt wird und die möglichst verbunden ist mit anderen Datenbanken des In- und Auslandes.

Ein nationaler oder auch internationaler Informationsaustausch und damit eine Harmonisierung zumindest der Fachsprache ist notwendig, um auch in diesem Bereich den Fortschritt für den europäischen Binnenmarkt zu schaffen.
(*MBB-Nachrichten*)

Vom Wunderheiler bis zu BMW

Frau Irmgard Nohr-Wechselberger, a conference interpreter in Munich, explains the process of preparing for a wide range of clients.

Irmgard Nohr-Wechselberger in der Kabine

Frau Nohr-Wechselberger: Ich bitte zunächst den mich anrufenden Kunden oder Vermittler, mir Unterlagen zu liefern, und zwar so breitgefächert wie möglich. Das sind dann Fachvorträge oder Protokolle aus früheren Sitzungen, so daß man sich selber Terminologielisten erarbeiten kann. Diese Listen werden dann vom Computer sortiert.

Als Konferenzdolmetscher, der freiberuflich arbeitet – und das machen in Europa alle Konferenzdolmetscher außer denen, die bei der EG, beim Europarat oder beim Europaparlament arbeiten –, kann man sich nicht spezialisieren; auf dem freien Markt muß man alles querbeet machen. Ähnlich breitgefächert ist dann in der Praxis auch die Palette der Kunden, mit denen man zu tun hat: Das reicht vom Wunderheiler aus Amerika bis zu Siemens, BMW und den großen Messen.

T i P

"Any knowledge of German will be admired and appreciated by your German opposite number. Nevertheless, do not overestimate your linguistic abilities at any important negotiation, and if in any doubt take a qualified interpreter along with you." (Features of the German Market, *German Chamber of Industry & Commerce*)

München

MASSGESCHNEIDERTER VERSICHERUNGSSCHUTZ

Munich is home to Europe's biggest insurer, Allianz Versicherungs-AG, and the world's largest re-insurer, Münchener Rückversicherungs-AG. The German insurance industry and its customers have had a rough ride this century with devaluations after both wars wiping out the benefits of life insurances. Security has therefore been of paramount importance. The industry watchdog (*Bundesaufsichtsamt*) in Berlin has protected the consumer and prevented insolvency in insurers, but the trend towards deregulation brought about by the single market is rolling back state control and giving more scope for market forces.

Traditionally a German insurer cannot sell a product until it has been approved by the *Bundesaufsichtsamt*. However, the single market now demands that a British insurer should be able to sell a product from London without establishing a branch office in Germany. For industrial clients, property and liability insurance has been deregulated, allowing companies to seek tailor-made solutions in a European insurance market. Increasingly, insurance is being sold not only by traditional insurers but also by the banks in their drive to offer *Allfinanz*, a comprehensive range of financial services under one roof.

FILAWORD
die Assekuranz *insurance industry*
der Rückversicherer *re-insurer*
die Haftpflicht *liability*
die Sachversicherung *non-life insurance*
der Makler *broker*
der Beitrag *premium*
die Police *policy*
die Allfinanzdienstleistungen (*f, pl*) *financial services*

Staatlicher Schutz

Herr Jörn Badenhoop is deputy director of the German insurers' federation, the *Gesamtverband der Deutschen Versicherungswirtschaft*, which is closely involved in negotiations to create a single market for the insurance industry.

FACTFINDER
*1 How does Herr Badenhoop refer to the individual consumer?
*2 Who does the individual consumer buy his/her insurance from?
**3 What type of customer will cease to have state protection?

Herr Badenhoop: In Deutschland gibt es eine lange Tradition der Hausversicherer. So hat zum Beispiel Siemens seit 50 Jahren seinen Hausversicherer, und Mercedes hat seinen Versicherer; da brauchen wir keine Makler, das geht direkt. Und Lieschen Müller, der Kleinkunde, geht sowieso nicht zu einem Makler, sondern versichert sich zum Beispiel über einen festangestellten Ausschließlichkeitsvertreter der Aachen-Münchener. Dieser ist also kein Makler, der viele verschiedene Versicherer vertritt, sondern ein Mann eines einzigen Unternehmens. So wird der Service des Versicherungsunternehmens zu einem wichtigen Element des Wettbewerbs.

Die deutsche Industrie wird in Zukunft – wie die britische – frei sein, sich in ganz Europa den Versicherungsschutz maßgeschneidert auszusuchen – also keine Genehmigung mehr durch das Bundesaufsichtsamt. Wir differenzieren jetzt und sagen, diese Industriekunden haben das Know-how, um ohne staatlichen Schutz selbst Verträge mit den Versicherern auszuhandeln. Aber die Masse der Kunden, also der Verbraucher Lieschen Müller, sollte weiterhin staatlichen Schutz bekommen.

DATABASE
Hausversicherer (*m, sing. and pl*) 'house insurer(s)'
Aachen-Münchener (*f*) *insurance company based in Aachen*
... wird ... frei sein, sich ... auszusuchen ... ... *will be at liberty to choose* ...

FILAFACT *sondern*
When you see *sondern*, look back for a negation earlier in the sentence:

Lieschen Müller geht *nicht* zu einem Makler, *sondern* versichert sich ...
Dieser ist *kein* Makler, *sondern* ein Mann eines einzigen Unternehmens.

➡ P 106

FILASKILL
Drawing on general (and of course specialist) knowledge will help you to get the sense of what you read. Make the most of what you *do* understand!

TiP

"German legislation on sampling, trial-purchasing or lotteries is stricter than in the UK. Obtain legal clearance for any such activity. Do not assume what was OK in the UK is OK in Germany."
(Roy Edleston, *Food from Britain*, British Business)

Irgendwann kommt jeder an den Punkt, an dem ihm der Wert von Versicherungen schlagartig klar wird.

FACTFINDER

*1 What risks are covered by social insurance?
**2 How are social-insurance contributions calculated?
***3 What is the crucial difference between social insurance and individual insurance?

STAATLICHE UND PRIVATE VORSORGE

	Sozialversicherung	Individualversicherung
Grundsatz	Pflichtversicherung	Freiwillige Versicherung
Versicherte Personen	Arbeitnehmer	Natürliche und juristische Personen
Versicherte Risiken	Krankheit (Krankenversicherung) Arbeitsunfall (Unfallversicherung) Arbeitslosigkeit (Arbeitslosenversicherung) Altersversorgung (Rentenversicherung)	Alle versicherbaren Risiken des Alltags, z.B. – Krankheit, – Unfall, – Tod, – Feuer, – Einbruchdiebstahl, – Hagel, – Haftpflicht usw.
Beitragshöhe	Richtet sich nach dem Einkommen des Versicherten	Richtet sich nach Art und Höhe des versicherten Risikos
Leistungen	Sind gesetzlich festgelegt	Werden vertraglich vereinbart
Träger	Staatliche Einrichtungen	Private und öffentlich-rechtliche Versicherungsunternehmen

FACTFINDER

*4 Which of the three 'columns' of retirement insurance is obligatory for someone in employment?

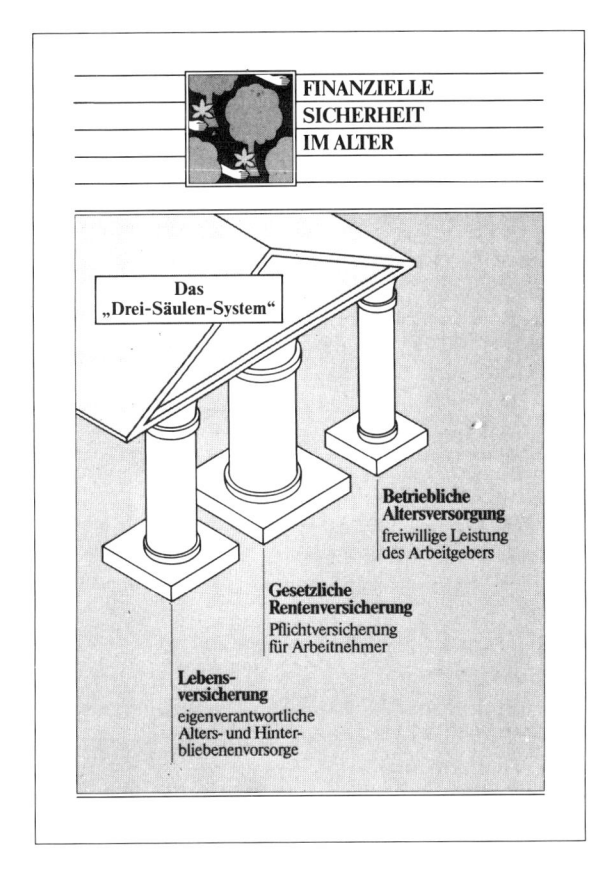

FINANZIELLE SICHERHEIT IM ALTER

Das „Drei-Säulen-System"

Betriebliche Altersversorgung
freiwillige Leistung des Arbeitgebers

Gesetzliche Rentenversicherung
Pflichtversicherung für Arbeitnehmer

Lebensversicherung
eigenverantwortliche Alters- und Hinterbliebenenvorsorge

FACTFINDER

*5 What do social-insurance contributions come to?
***6 What are the circumstances of the employee who is the basis for this calculation?
*7 How many different personal taxes are there?

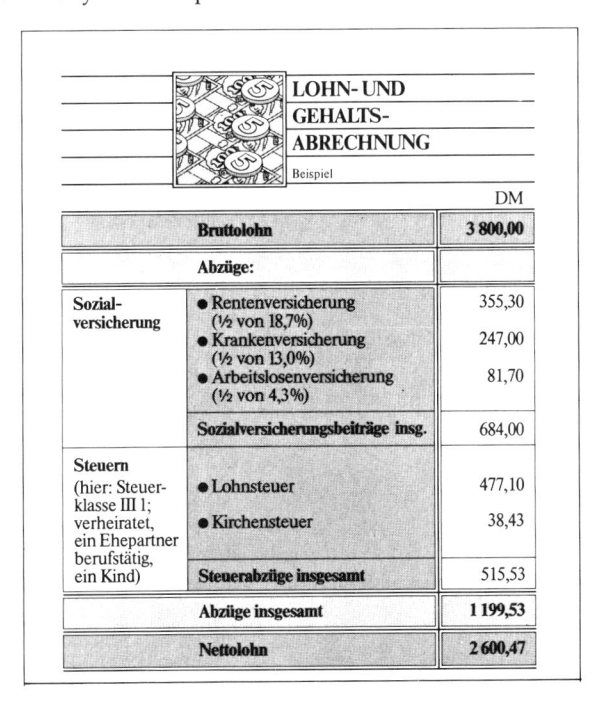

LOHN- UND GEHALTSABRECHNUNG
Beispiel

		DM
Bruttolohn		3 800,00
Abzüge:		
Sozialversicherung	• Rentenversicherung (½ von 18,7%)	355,30
	• Krankenversicherung (½ von 13,0%)	247,00
	• Arbeitslosenversicherung (½ von 4,3%)	81,70
	Sozialversicherungsbeiträge insg.	684,00
Steuern (hier: Steuerklasse III 1; verheiratet, ein Ehepartner berufstätig, ein Kind)	• Lohnsteuer	477,10
	• Kirchensteuer	38,43
	Steuerabzüge insgesamt	515,53
Abzüge insgesamt		1 199,53
Nettolohn		2 600,47

FACTFINDER

*8 What is covered under contents insurance?

Die Individualversicherung
Privater Schutz

Personenversicherung	Schadenversicherung
Lebensversicherung	Kfz-Versicherung
Private Krankenversicherung	Haftpflichtversicherung
Private Unfallversicherung	Hausratversicherung Feuer Einbruch Sturm Leitungswasser Beraubung Glasbruch
	Rechtsschutzversicherung Reisegepäckversicherung
	Verkehrs-Service-Versicherung Transportversicherung

München

ALLES AUS EINEM HAUS

Bosch and Siemens are household names as suppliers of kitchen equipment. The merger of the two companies' activities in the household-appliance sector created a unique structure – Bosch-Siemens Hausgeräte GmbH (BSHG) – which permitted economies of scale and effectively countered foreign competition. For the purpose of marketing their appliances Bosch and Siemens continue to maintain separate identities, as Robert Bosch Hausgeräte GmbH and Siemens Elektrogeräte GmbH.

FILAWORD
der Zusammenschluß *merger*
die Einbauküche *fitted kitchen*
nützlich *useful*
zweckmäßig *functional*
sinnvoll *sensible, practical*

Fallstudie: Zusammenschluß

Herr Gerd Strobel, sales director for Bosch kitchens, described events leading up to the merging of production and development.

THE PROBLEM
1 What problem confronted Bosch and Siemens in the early 1960s?
2 What was the main advantage foreign products had over German products?

THE SOLUTION
1 How did German companies react?
2 What was their aim?
3 How did Bosch and Siemens cooperate initially?
4 What form did the cooperation eventually take?
5 What three areas are controlled by BSHG?
6 What is controlled individually by Bosch and Siemens?
7 How are Bosch products perceived?
8 What reputation does Siemens have?

Starker Importdruck

Herr Strobel: Der Zusammenschluß zwischen den Häusern Siemens und Bosch auf dem Sektor der Hausgeräte hat Anfang der sechziger Jahre begonnen. Der Ausgangspunkt war eigentlich der sehr starke Importdruck von Hausgeräten vom italienischen Markt und damals auch schon vom französischen Markt. Insbesondere die Italiener haben damals den deutschen Markt mit preiswerten Geräten sehr stark dominiert – nicht vergleichbar von der Qualität, aber entschieden preiswerter. Die Reaktion der gesamten deutschen Hausgeräteindustrie war die Konzentration, um durch Zusammenlegung von Serien auf größere Baueinheiten zu kommen und kostenmäßig entsprechend günstiger zu sein. Eine dieser Reaktionen war der Zusammenschluß – zunächst auf dem Produktionssektor – zwischen Siemens und Bosch, die beide Aktivitäten auf dem Hausgerätesektor hatten.

Eine eigenständige Firma

Herr Strobel: Aus dem lockeren und losen Verbund der Produktionszusammenlegung ist dann mit der Zeit eine eigenständige Firma geworden. 1972 sind die Hausgerätezweige dieser beiden Firmen fusioniert worden in eine Firma, die heute Bosch-Siemens Hausgeräte GmbH heißt. Wir haben eine einheitliche Entwicklung, eine einheitliche Produktion und – was die Geräte betrifft – eine einheitliche Administration. Der Vertrieb, das Positionieren der Produkte nach außen und das Verkaufen in den Handel hinein und vom Handel aus an den Endverwender geschieht aber ganz getrennt.

Traditionell oder modern

Herr Strobel: Während Bosch etwas traditioneller ist, hat die Marke Siemens den Ruf und das Image, ein eher fortschrittliches Unternehmen zu sein. Es gibt Käufergruppen, die eher der konservativen Marke Bosch verhaftet sind, und es gibt Käufer, die lieber ein Siemens-Produkt haben möchten. Danach richten sich die gesamten Vertriebsaktivitäten aus, danach richtet sich das ganze Unternehmen bis hin zum Personal aus.

DATABASE
um ... auf größere Baueinheiten zu kommen *in order to get bigger assembly units ...*
die beide ... hatten *both of which had ...*
nach außen *in the market*
in den Handel hinein *to the trade*
verhaftet sind *are attached*
die lieber ... haben möchten *who prefer ...*
Danach richten sich ... aus *... are geared to that*

FILAFACT *werden*
Notice how Herr Strobel says that the two household-appliance divisions **were merged**:

1972 *sind* die Hausgerätezweige *fusioniert worden.*

Worden is the past participle of the auxiliary verb *werden*, which is used in passive and future constructions. Don't confuse this with the main verb *werden* (to become), which forms the past participle with *ge-* (➡ P 102, 104):

Aus dem Verbund *ist* eine eigenständige Firma *geworden.*
(The association *became* an independent company.)

Aus einer Hand

Bei der Bosch-Küche bekommen Sie Möbel und Geräte aus einer Hand. Exakt aufeinander abgestimmt. Beliebig variierbar. Systematisch kombinierbar. Zu einer Küchenlösung aus einem Guß – optisch wie funktionell.

Und sollten Sie besonderen Wert auf modernste, höchstkomfortable Geräte-Technik legen, sind Sie mit Bosch ohnehin bestens beraten. Schließlich: Wer hat schon diese Fülle technisch anspruchsvoller Lösungen? Diese ausgereifte, sensible Elektronik? Diese Auswahl an arbeits- und energiesparenden Modellen?

Das gilt auch für die übrige Küchentechnik. Das reichhaltige Innenleben der Schränke zum Beispiel. Die durchdachte Nischengestaltung. Überhaupt die vielen neuen, nützlichen Funktionsdetails. Kurz und gut: bei Bosch finden Sie, was Sie suchen. Alles aus einem Haus. In bester Qualität. Von Bosch.

⊕ BOSCH

Syncro
Der neue Trend: schimmernde Fronten in Metallic-Lackierung.

Der modernen, asymmetrischen Architektur des Hauses paßt sich dieses neue Bosch-Küchenmodell vollendet an. Innovativ in Form und Farbgebung: das Frontdesign und die Metallic-Lackierung. Auch die Küchentechnik wird allen aktuellen Ansprüchen gerecht. Siehe die sehr zweckmäßigen Jalousien-Schränke, das ergonomisch geformte, vorbildliche Bosch-Funktions-Spülzentrum, oder den neuen Bosch-Herd, sinnvoll und effektvoll ergänzt durch eine futuristisch anmutende Dunstabzugskonstruktion.

(Bosch Küche Collection)

DATABASE
aus einem Guß *integrated* (literally *from one casting*)
Wert auf ... legen *value ...*
wird ... gerecht *meets ...*

EXECUTIVE SKILLS

**1 Which paragraph in *Aus einer Hand* deals with *a* design details *b* appliances *c* modular design?

**2 Which word or words in the list *a - g* could you use instead of *i* neu *ii* nützlich *iii* ausgereift?
a modern *b* innovativ *c* funktionell *d* durchdacht *e* zweckmäßig *f* aktuell *g* sinnvoll

**3 Can you find the adjectives or adverbs (➡ P 100-102) in Bosch's publicity material deriving from these nouns? *a* der Effekt *b* der Anspruch *c* der Sinn *d* die Technik *e* die Optik *f* das System *g* das Vorbild *h* der Nutzen *i* die Aktualität *j* die Funktion *k* die Ergonomie *l* die Asymmetrie *m* der Zweck *n* der Komfort.

***4 See if you can find the subject (➡ P 98) in the first sentence of *Syncro*.

**5 Can you spot one or more equivalents for *a* from the same manufacturer *b* in a nutshell?

FILASKILL
You'll find that a writer often gives a general idea first, and then specifies details. It therefore makes sense to start by concentrating on the beginning of each paragraph to get the gist.

T i P

Test *is a consumer magazine produced by the German Consumer Council (Stiftung Warentest), Lützowplatz 11, 1000 Berlin 30 (Tel.: (030) 2 63 11). A positive test result published in this magazine is a great plus for sales.*

In 127 Ländern

Munich's engineering and electronics giant Siemens has undergone extensive restructuring to create smaller, more flexible units and bring decision-making closer to the market. A spending spree has countered criticisms of cash hoarding, and launched the company on a spate of acquisitions and cooperations in a move to consolidate and expand their share of the global market.

Der klassische Fertiger im Lande

Over the years Siemens has built up manufacturing bases abroad, and Herr Achim Meilenbrock, head of international advertising based in Munich, emphasized the difference between the classical exporter and the traditional Siemens approach.

FACTFINDER
**1 What proportion of Siemens' total sales is generated by plants abroad?

Herr Meilenbrock: Wir sind in 127 Ländern dieser Welt vertreten und machen über die Hälfte unseres Geschäftes – das sind etwa 55% des Gesamtumsatzes – im Ausland. Die Hälfte dieses Auslandsgeschäftes sind Exporte von Deutschland ins Ausland, und die andere Hälfte sind Eigenleistungen, die im Land erbracht werden. In diesen Ländern existieren Fabriken, wo Siemens-Produkte gebaut werden oder wo diese Produkte weiterveredelt werden, das heißt also zu kompletten Systemen zusammengebaut werden. Siemens ist also nicht der klassische Exporteur, sondern eigentlich mehr der klassische Fertiger im Lande. Wir könnten heute in sehr viele Länder überhaupt nicht mehr exportieren, hätten wir nicht vor vielen Jahren bereits unsere Fabriken dort aufgebaut.

DATABASE
Eigenleistungen, die im Land erbracht werden *products manufactured by the foreign subsidiaries*
vor vielen Jahren *many years ago*

FILAWORD
die Richtlinie *guideline*
der Wettbewerb *competition*
der Konkurrent *competitor*
die Verkaufsförderung *sales promotion*
der Binnenmarkt *single/internal market*

FILAFACT *conditions*
In German you can make a conditional statement by starting with the verb (➡ **P 75, 107**), but the conditional clause does not necessarily start the sentence:

> Wir könnten heute in viele Länder nicht exportieren, **hätten** wir nicht vor vielen Jahren bereits unsere Fabriken dort aufgebaut.
> (We would not be able to export to many countries today, **had** we not (or: *if we had not*) set up our factories there many years ago.)

Notice that Herr Meilenbrock uses **könnten** and **hätten**, special forms of the verbs *können* and *haben*, called the subjunctive. The subjunctive can be used to speculate about what *would have happened* if a given fact in the past had been different. ➡ **P 105**

Zahlen und Fakten

Gründung:	1847, Berlin
Hauptsitz:	München
Mitarbeiter:	rund 373 000 weltweit
Umsatzvolumen:	ca. DM 63 Mrd., 55% im Ausland erwirtschaftet
Fertigungsstätten:	173 in 35 Ländern

Fábrica Malaga, Spanien

Klar und deutlich

FACTFINDER
*2 Which means of presentation to the outside world does Herr Meilenbrock list for projection of corporate identity?

Herr Meilenbrock: Es muß überall die Firma Siemens klar und deutlich erkannt werden. Das heißt also, daß die Mittel der Marketingkommunikation, der Werbung oder der Verkaufsförderung, aber auch das Produktdesign, die Gebäude von Siemens bis hin zu Kraftfahrzeugen und deren Beschriftung einheitlich gestaltet werden müssen, nach Richtlinien, die wir hier in Deutschland erlassen.

DATABASE
daß ... einheitlich gestaltet werden müssen
that ... have to be designed within a uniform concept

Transport eines Motorsegments für die derzeit größten Ringmotoren der Welt in Chile

Neuer Stellenwert für Corporate Identity

This newspaper article describes the conclusions of a study on corporate identity in the context of the single market.

FACTFINDER
*1 How many organizations were involved in preparing the study?

Unternehmen, die sich Corporate-Identity-Ziele vorgeben und sie strategisch verfolgen, haben gegenüber ihren Konkurrenten Wettbewerbsvorteile. Mit Blick auf den EG-Binnenmarkt müssen selbst Großunternehmen, die bereits weltweit arbeiten, ihre CI-Politik überdenken, weil sich das Unternehmen in seiner neuen europäischen Dimension erkennen und nach außen darstellen muß. Zu diesem Fazit kommt eine Untersuchung über die strategische Bedeutung von Corporate Identity in Industrieunternehmen, welche die Dr. Höfner & Partner Management-Beratung, München, gemeinsam mit dem Institut für Unternehmensführung der Universität Innsbruck und dem Internationalen Management-Institut Franklin College Switzerland, Lugano, erarbeitet hat.

Im Zusammenhang mit dem EG-Binnenmarkt erhält der Studie zufolge das CI-Konzept einen besonderen Stellenwert. Aufgrund der Marktöffnung sei es erforderlich, „daß die Europa-Position des Unternehmens festgelegt wird". Vor allem müsse das Selbstverständnis und das Leitbild des Unternehmens bestimmt und intern gegenüber den Mitarbeitern vermittelt werden. So müßten sich vor allem Großunternehmen zum Beispiel fragen, „ob sie sich als deutsches Unternehmen mit ‚deutschen Tugenden' und zentraler Führung verstehen oder als ein internationales mit internationalen Prägungen und dezentraler Führung. Kein Management kommt um diese neue Definition herum."
(*Süddeutsche Zeitung*)

DATABASE
die sich ... vorgeben und sie ... verfolgen *which set themselves ... and pursue them ...*
Zu diesem Fazit kommt *This is the result reached by*
welche ... erarbeitet hat *which ... has carried out*
sei es erforderlich *it was necessary*
müsse ... bestimmt und ... vermittelt werden *... had to be established, and communicated ...*
So müßten sich ... fragen *Thus ... had to ask themselves*
ob sie sich ... verstehen *whether they regard themselves ...*
ein internationales *an international one*
kommt um ... herum *can avoid ...*

FILAFACT *reported speech*
Neuer Stellenwert für Corporate Identity reports the results of a study. In German, the subjunctive form of the verb is often used to show that a statement is being reported, as in English 'the study stated that companies *had to* ask themselves'. The actual words of the study would have been 'companies *must/have to* ask themselves'.

  Aufgrund der Marktöffnung *sei* es erforderlich ... (reported speech)
  „Aufgrund der Marktöffnung *ist* es erforderlich ..." (direct speech)
  So *müßten* sich vor allem Großunternehmen fragen ... (reported speech)
  „So *müssen* sich vor allem Großunternehmen fragen ..." (direct speech)

The context, and signals such as *der Studie zufolge* (according to the study) also indicate that you're reading a reported opinion rather than the author's own. ➡ P 105

PROFILE *corporate identity*
Picking out the main points of an article is a useful skill. Can you work out the order in which these points are mentioned?

a Definition as German or international company
b Definition of identity and image for employees
c Single market – corporate identity concept special status
d Single market – review of corporate identity policies
e Corporate identity – competitive advantage
f Single market – positioning within Europe

TiP
When you deal with Germany, remember that there are more public holidays than in the UK and that they vary from Land *to* Land. *If a public holiday falls on a Thursday, many people will take the Friday off.*

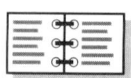

Fallstudie: Italienisch

Dr Klaus Möller, executive director with international operations at Siemens, spent four years in Milan at a subsidiary. He learnt Italian in the course of his work as a commercial manager.

Dr. Möller: Ich war vier Jahre in Mailand kaufmännischer Leiter in einer von unseren Tochtergesellschaften, über die wir Datenverarbeitungsgeräte vertreiben.

Ich habe ein paar Brocken Italienisch gekonnt, weil wir oft in den Urlaub nach Italien fahren, und ich konnte schon Französisch – das hat sehr geholfen.

In der Anfangsphase habe ich immer einen halben Tag in einer Sprachenschule verbracht und die zweite Hälfte des Tages im Unternehmen. Da es in diesem Unternehmen erhebliche Probleme gab, hat sich dann nach einiger Zeit herausgestellt, daß ich das Sprachstudium an der Schule abbrechen mußte, weil es mich einfach zu viel Zeit kostete. Es war eigentlich auch nur nötig, um eine sichere Basis in der Grammatik zu bekommen. Der übrige Teil, die Ausweitung des Wortschatzes, war viel effektiver in der Firma im Gespräch mit Kollegen.

Sprechen lernen ist dort vielleicht das Einfachste gewesen, weil man gegenüber Fehlern in der Sprache sehr tolerant war. Verstehen lernen ist etwas schwieriger; jeder spricht anders, und man muß sich auf die verschiedenen Leute einhören. Das braucht Zeit.

Lesen lernen mußte ich von Anfang an, denn es kam ja sehr viel Geschäftspost auf den Tisch. Schreiben lernen auch, aber da hat mir meine Sekretärin geholfen. Obwohl ich nach sehr kurzer Zeit in Italienisch diktiert habe mit allen Fehlern, hat sie dann natürlich den Brief fehlerfrei runtergeschrieben, und ich habe hinterher nur noch mal geschaut, ob der Sinn stimmte.

Das Lesen zum Vergnügen oder zur Allgemeininformation ging sehr schnell. Eine Zeitung oder eine Zeitschrift oder ein italienisches Buch verstehen ging relativ schnell, weil man sich auch immer das ausgesucht hat, was man leicht verstand. Schwieriger ist es, geschäftliche Vorgänge zu lesen, vor allen Dingen, wenn man sie zu bearbeiten hat, weil es einem am Anfang nicht gelingt zu unterscheiden, welche Dinge wichtig sind und welche nicht.

Database

hat sich ... herausgestellt ... *it turned out*
man muß sich ... einhören *you have to become attuned ...*
weil man sich auch immer das ausgesucht hat, was *because you always chose what*
vor allen Dingen *especially*
wenn man sie zu bearbeiten hat *if you have to process them*
weil es einem ... nicht gelingt zu unterscheiden *because ... you can't distinguish*

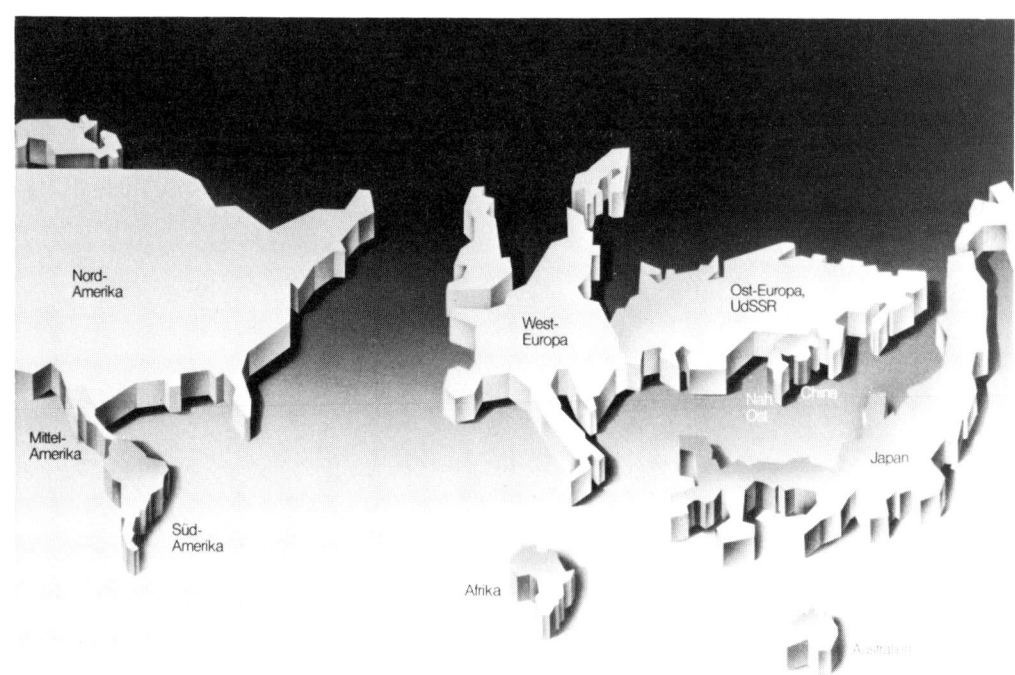

Weltkarte der Elektromärkte
(Fläche entspricht der Bedeutung des Elektromarktes)

Filafact *languages*

Notice how Dr Möller talks about the *languages* he **knew** before he went to Italy:

   Ich **habe** ein paar Brocken *Italienisch* **gekonnt**.
   Ich **konnte** schon *Französisch*.

and how he talks about **learning** *to speak/understand/read/write*:

   sprechen **lernen**   lesen **lernen**
   verstehen **lernen**   schreiben **lernen**

Filaskill

Have you invested in a dictionary yet? If not, now is a good time. Make sure you study its introduction, so you know how to look up words efficiently. Remember that a dictionary can often only serve as a general guide to the meaning of a word.

Profile *the Italian case*

Outline how Dr Möller came to grips with Italian.

1. How much Italian he knew before he went to Milan
2. Other languages he knew
3. The language training he had in a language school
4. The best way he found of extending his vocabulary
5. The attitude of the Italians to his mistakes
6. What he found difficult about understanding spoken Italian
7. What he learnt to read quite quickly
8. What he found difficult about reading business documents

Klaus Möller

Sachbearbeiterin - Sekretärin - Schreibkraft

Frau Doris Lasch originally did a commercial training as a *Kauffrau* but then entered employment as a secretary at Siemens where she now works in international sales. In her view, the main difference between the work of clerical staff, secretaries and copy typists is the degree of independence.

FILAFACT *doch, ja, eigentlich*
Notice how Frau Lasch uses *ja, eigentlich, doch, nun wirklich* to express and emphasize her personal opinions.

Sachbearbeiterin - Sekretärin

Frau Lasch: Ich bin an und für sich Kaufmann – oder Kauffrau, wie man sagt –, bin aber dann auf Sekretärin umgestiegen. Als Sachbearbeiterin hat man ein Sachgebiet, was man selbständig bearbeitet. Ich bekomme ja von meinem Chef alles delegiert und kann eigentlich nicht selbständig arbeiten.

Sekretärin - Schreibkraft

Frau Lasch: Eine Sekretärin muß doch ein bißchen selbständiger arbeiten als eine Schreibkraft; sie muß die ganzen Termine machen usw. Eine Schreibkraft sitzt nun wirklich nur an ihrer Maschine und schreibt permanent ihre Sachen. Ich habe doch noch mehr Abwechslung. Man muß auch ein bißchen den Überblick haben über das Ganze.

DATABASE
an und für sich *actually, really*
Man muß auch ein bißchen den Überblick haben *You've also got to have a bit of an overview*

> **T i P**
> "In general, German buyers will only give serious consideration to quotes submitted in German and - perhaps even more important - based on DM prices including all freight/customs clearance to the customers' warehouse. Calculate the price carefully. An increase after listing is virtually impossible to obtain." (Roy Edleston, Food from Britain, British Business)

VOM COIL ZUM KUNDEN 10

Export nach England

Herr Woiwod: Unsere Fahrzeuge kommen zunächst zu einem *Preparation Centre* nach Doncaster. Dort werden alle Fahrzeuge überprüft und entwachst. Teilweise werden Radios, Telefone oder andere Zubehörteile eingebaut. Danach erfolgt die Verteilung direkt an unsere Händler.

Grundausstattung und Sonderausstattung

Herr Woiwod: Prinzipiell bieten wir in Großbritannien die gleichen Fahrzeugtypen an wie in Deutschland. Die Ausstattung variiert allerdings, denn jede Vertriebsgesellschaft hat natürlich einen Einfluß darauf, welche Grundausstattung ein Fahrzeug haben soll und welche Sonderausstattungen angeboten werden sollen. In England ist die Grundausstattung der Fahrzeuge in der Regel auf einem höheren Niveau als in Deutschland.

Jeder Kunde hat die Möglichkeit, Sonderausstattungen nach seiner Wahl zu spezifizieren. Die meisten Fahrzeuge werden nach Kundenauftrag gebaut, und die Anzahl möglicher Varianten ist nahezu unbegrenzt. Die logistische Steuerung in der Fertigung ist entsprechend komplex.

Qualität und Image

Herr Woiwod: Qualität und Image sind zwei Hauptfaktoren für den Erfolg von BMW in Großbritannien. Die Qualität der Produkte wird entscheidend durch die Auswahl der am besten geeigneten Lieferanten bestimmt. Sollten dennoch Probleme auftreten, muß der Kundendienst perfekt funktionieren. Dazu gehört auch ein 24-Stunden-Pannendienst für liegengebliebene Fahrzeuge. Das hohe Image von BMW in Großbritannien ist auf ausgezeichnete Marketingaktivitäten zurückzuführen. Ohne entsprechend hohe Produktqualität wäre dieses allerdings nicht haltbar. Insgesamt wird sehr viel getan, um den Kunden zufriedenzustellen, und wir versuchen, auf diesem Trend weiterzufahren.

München

MÜNCHNER SPEZIALITÄTEN

The Wittelsbach family reigned in Munich for over 600 years from 1255 to 1918. Perhaps the most intriguing Wittelsbach was Ludwig II, the dream king, who devoted himself to constructing fairy-tale castles until his untimely death in the *Starnberger See*. More than any other German *Land*, Bavaria has cultivated a notional independence as the Free State of Bavaria, *Freistaat Bayern*. Bavarians are fiercely proud of their heritage and traditions, and Munich still retains much of the character of a provincial *Residenzstadt*, for all its metropolitan aspirations and jet-setting 'Schickeria' in the city's fashionable district of Schwabing.

The 1972 Olympics launched the city on a programme of infrastructure expansion which produced a sparkling new underground and suburban rail network and a futuristic sports and leisure complex. Since then, the *Kulturzentrum Gasteig* – an ambitious arts centre – has been added to Munich's wide range of cultural facilities.

The German work ethic is softened here by a southern capacity for enjoyment, evident in the beer gardens, at the *Oktoberfest*, on the nearby lakes and ski slopes, and at boisterous parties and balls in the carnival period.

FILAWORD

die Residenzstadt *seat of a royal court*
die U-Bahn *underground, subway*
die S-Bahn *suburban railway*
der Feierabend *knocking-off time, evening*
der Biergarten *beer garden*
der Fasching *carnival*

Ein Fest voll bayerisch-barocker Lebensfreude

Mindestens sechs Dutzend am Spieß gebratene Ochsen, 30 000 Stück Steckerlfisch, 400 000 Paar Schweinswürstel und 750 000 Brathendl werden bei jedem Oktoberfest verzehrt – und etwa 6 Millionen Maß Bier dazu getrunken.

München auf einen Blick
Landeshauptstadt Freistaat Bayern

Einwohnerzahl:	1 300 000
Fluß:	Isar
Postleitzahl:	D/W-8000
Telefonvorwahl:	(0)89-
Flughafen:	Ab 1992 Flughafen München II im Erdinger Moos (40 km vom Zentrum); S3 zur Stadtmitte.
Information:	Fremdenverkehrsamt, Ruffinihaus, Eingang Pettenbeckstraße, Tel. 2 39 12 73.
Post:	Bahnhofplatz 1 (durchgehend geöffnet)
Wichtige Messen:	**Elektronica, Mode-Woche, ISPO** (Sportartikelmesse)
Sehenswürdigkeiten:	Alte Pinakothek (Do bis 21 Uhr), Hofbräuhaus, Asamkirche, Deutsches Museum, Olympiaturm, Englischer Garten
Typisches Essen:	Schweinshaxe, Weißwurst
Typische Getränke:	Helles (Bier), Weißbier
Wichtige Termine:	Oktoberfest (September/Oktober), Fasching (Januar-Februar/März)

TiP

Tourist offices in Germany come with a variety of names, which can cause confusion if you are trying to get hold of the phone number: in Munich it is the Fremdenverkehrsamt, *in Frankfurt and Berlin the* Verkehrsamt, *in Düsseldorf the* Verkehrsverein, *and in Hamburg the* Touristen-Zentrale. *But you may just find plain old* Tourist Information!

FEEDBACK

The German given in brackets is intended to help locate the necessary information. Occasional rephrasing and/or omission of words should help to isolate the main facts. Bear in mind that the English answers the question, and is not necessarily a translation of the German in brackets.

Key

Factfinder = **Ff**
Executive skills = **Es**
Executive puzzle = **Ep**
Actionpack = **Ap**
Profile = **Pr**
Fallstudie = **Fs**

Frankfurt

P 7 Ff1 An international reputation. **Es 1** *a* centre; *b* finance/financial; *c* metropolis; *d* imposing, impressive; *e* skyline; *f* hard; *g* big business; *h* is; *i* international; *j* hundred; *k* credit; *l* institute (*Kreditinstitut* bank); *m* and; *n* bank; *o* here. **2** *a + ii* (or *iii*); *b + i*; *c + iv*; *d + iii* (or *ii*). **3** Handelszentrum. **4** It's on the River Main, and the word's a pun on Manhattan.

P 8 Es 1 *a* Stunde; *b* Tag; *c* Woche. **2** *a* False, one day (from the first to the seventh day) costs DM 20,- (*1.-7. Tag (pro Tag) DM 20,-*); *b* True, one week costs DM 140,- (*1 Woche DM 140,-*); *c* True, one week costs DM 140,-, and from the 8th day, the price is DM 10,- per day (*1 Woche DM 140,-, ab 8. Tag (pro Tag) DM 10,-*). **Ff1** About 95 (*Etwa 95 Fluggesellschaften im Linienverkehr*). **Ff2** About 900 (*Rund 900 Starts und Landungen täglich*). **Ff3** Four (*Harrods, Kindergarten, Zahnklinik, Tierstationen*). **Ep 1** *a iii*; *b i*; *c iv*; *d ii*; **2** *a vii*; *b v*; *c viii*; *d vi*.

P 9 Ff1 Four (*Tagungen, Seminare, Konferenzen, Meetings*). **Ap** Only you know! **Ff2** Leiter. **Ap** Ich heiße ... . **Ff3** Five days, from 25 to 29 July (*vom 25. bis 29. Juli*). **Ff4** How you can motivate your personnel (*wie man Mitarbeiter motiviert*). **Ff5** reinfliegen, rausfliegen.

P 10 Ff1 Herr Dodt: 18 years (*seit 18 Jahren*); Herr Goldbach: 30 years (*30 Jahre*). **Es 1** Mein Name ist ...; Ich heiße ... . **2** Ich bin ... Jahre alt. **3** Unternehmen, Betrieb, Firma (*Haus* is also possible). **4** Ich bin seit X Jahren in diesem Unternehmen, ich bin X Jahre hier im Betrieb. **Ap 1** Ich heiße (*or* Mein Name ist) ... . Ich bin X Jahre alt. **2** Ich bin ... . Ich bin verantwortlich für ... . **Ep 1 + 2** = Kunden/beratung; **5 + 3 + 8** = Ersatz/teil/lager; **6 + 4+ 7** = Kunden/dienst/werkstatt.

P 11 Ff1 A smooth-running customer service (*Ein einwandfrei funktionierender Kundendienst ist essentiell für einen Markenhersteller*). **Es 1** *a* ist; *b* haben; *c* haben. **Ff2** For the problems of the employees (*Der Betriebsrat ist zuständig für die Probleme der Mitarbeiter*). **Ff3** He says *zum Beispiel* (for example).

P 12 Ff1 Germany, France, England (*Deutschland, Frankreich, England*). **Ff2** The kettle (= *der Wasserkessel*). **Es 1** 'Dustsucker', or as we know it 'hoover'. **2** The general statement (*Man muß das Vertriebsprogramm immer auf das einzelne Land ausrichten*). **3** Hauptmärkte (*principal markets*), Töchter (*subsidiaries*), Märkte (*markets*), Netz (*network*), Distributoren (*distributors*), Deutschland (*Germany*), Bereich (*area*), Stammhaus (*parent company*), Nummer (*number*), Frankreich (*France*), Fabrikation (*production (facilities)*), England, Nummer, Vertriebsgesellschaft (*sales company, distributor*), Vertriebsprogramm (*sales/product range*), Land (*country*), England, Zeit (*time, zur Zeit at the moment*), Bügeleisen (*irons*), Toaster (*toasters*), Kaffeemaschinen (*coffee machines*), Staubsauger (*vacuum cleaners*), Produkt (*product*), Wasserkessel (*kettle*), 'Kettle', England, Tradition (*tradition*) (Don't worry about the endings at this stage, or if you didn't recognize the plural. If you do want to find out ➡ P 97-98). **4** *a* wir; *b* der 'Kettle'. **Ff3** A full glass (against some background or other) (*eine Flasche mit einem gefüllten Glas vor irgendeinem Hintergrund*).

P 14 Ff1 Issuing banknotes (*Banknoten ausgeben*) - only the central bank is allowed to issue these (*Banknoten darf nur die Notenbank ausgeben*); mortgages (*Hypotheken*) - most banks have a subsidiary for this activity (*Die meisten Institute haben für das Hypothekengeschäft Tochtergesellschaften*).

P 15 Ff1 The marketing side and risk assessment (*Wir haben klar getrennt zwischen der Marketing-Seite und der Risikobetrachtung*). **Ff2** To do as much business as possible (*so viel Geschäft wie nur möglich zu machen*) and to avoid risk as far as possible (*möglichst das Risiko zu verhindern*). **Ep 1** The amount (*Betrag*). **2** Currency (*Währung*) and place (*Ort*). **3** *a* Bankleitzahl *b* Konto-Nummer *c* Scheck-Nummer. **Ff3** The weather (*Wetter*) and holidays (*Urlaub*).

P 16 Ff1 No - they can't expect always to do the same thing in all countries (*Wir können nicht erwarten, daß wir in allen Ländern immer das gleiche machen*). **Ff2** Influence (*Wir haben Einfluß*). **Ff3** Deutsche Bank, with 28% (*wir sind mit über 28% der größte Aktionär*). **Ep 1** Schweiz. **2** Frankreich. **3** Niederlande. **4** Österreich. **5** Großbritannien. **6** Spanien.

P 17 Ff1 More than 20,000 (*Der deutsche Durchschnittsverdiener braucht über 20 000 Stunden*). **2** The average British person only needs 9000-10,000 hours (*der durchschnittliche Brite braucht nur 9000 bis 10 000 Stunden*). **Es 1** *a* durchschnittlich (adjective) / Durchschnitt (noun: the average); *b* der europäische Binnenmarkt; *c* die europäische Gemeinschaft (➡P 100-101 if you want an explanation of the varying endings). **2** fest*stellen* - *die Nationwide Anglia* stellte *Unterschiede* fest (the Nationwide Anglia discovered **differences**). **3** *b* and *d*. **Ep 1** *e*. **2** *a*. **3** *b*. **4** *d*. **5** *c*.

P18 Ff1 *e* (*Welche Stellung ...?*); *d* (*Wie viele Messeplätze ...?*); *b* (*Was bietet eine Messe ...?*); *f* (*Was für Firmen ...?*); *a* (*Kommen viele britische Firmen?*); *c* (*Wie hoch sind die Kosten ...?*)*:*

P 19 Es 1 *a* Messe, Platz; *b* Konkurrenz, Kampf; *c* Fach, Besucher; *d* Welt, Markt; *e* Dienst, Leistung; *f* Stand, Kosten. **2** *a* Dienstleistungen; *b* Messen; *c* Firmen; *d* Plätze; *e* Produkte; **3** sondern auch. **4** eins, fünf. **Ep 1** *c*; **2** *e*; **3** *b*; **4** *d*; **5** *f*; **6** *a*.

P 20 Ff1 *a* 200 km (*200 Kilometer Eisenbahnschienen*); *b* over 2000 km (*über 2000 Kilometer Rohrleitungen*); *c* 100 km (*100 Kilometer Straßen*). **Ff2** Around a third (*Rund ein Drittel des Sortiments der BASF wurde in den letzten zehn Jahren entwickelt*). **Ff3** Of being employees of BASF (*Die Leute sind richtig stolz darauf, „Aniliner" zu sein*). **Ff4** In production (*Je besser wir unsere jungen Leute ausbilden, desto besser sind sie in der Produktion*).

P 21 Es 1 A sensitive area. **2** Umwelt, Schutz, Überwachung, Zentrale. **Ff1** Sie sind gefallen (They have decreased). **Ff2** shareholders = *Aktionäre*; supervisory board = *Aufsichtsrat*; board of management = *Vorstand*.

P 22 Ff1 Polyester, and Polyamid ('Perlon' in Germany, and 'Nylon 66' in the US). **Es 1** *b* ('synthetic fibre' is the generic term). **2** *a*, *c*. **3** *a* basiert, (*inf.*) basieren; *c* hergestellt, (*inf.*) herstellen (the syllable **ge** is added in the past participle ➡P 103). **Ff2** In Germany and England (*Wir kaufen zum Teil die Ausrüstung hier in Deutschland oder in England*). **Ff3** A product; quality and quantity (*Wir garantieren ein Produkt. Wir garantieren Qualität und Quantität*). **Ff4** They train the customer's personnel (*Das Kundenpersonal wird geschult*). **Es 1** *a* ausliefern (liefern ... aus); *b* rausgehen (gehen ... raus); *c* zurückkommen (kommen ... zurück). **2** *d*, *g*, *b*, *f*, *a*, *e*, *c*.

P 23 Es 1 forschen; entwickeln; planen; beraten; finanzieren; beschaffen; liefern; errichten; schulen; warten; modernisieren. **Ap** Only you know! **Ff1** The existence of nitrates in the drinking water (*Das Vorhandensein von Nitraten im Trinkwasser*). **Ff2** They used to be able to get into the ground unchecked (*Viele Schadstoffe konnten früher unkontrolliert in den Boden gelangen*). **Es 1** *a* Probleme; *b* Stoffe; *c* Verfahren (For a list of plural forms ➡P 97).

P 25 Ff1 Summer (*Sommer*). **Ff2** No (It's a 'day of rest', *Ruhetag*). **Ff3** With a group (*Reservierung für Gruppen nötig*). **Ep 1** *n*; **2** *g*; **3** *c*; **4** *k*; **5** *m*; **6** *f*; **7** *e*; **8** *i*; **9** *l*; **10** *a*; **11** *h*; **12** *j*; **13** *d*; **14** *b*; **15** *p*; **16** *o*.

Düsseldorf

P 27 Ff1 Partly as a result of its own growth and partly due to the decline of industry (*teils infolge eigenen Wachstums, teils infolge des Rückgangs der Industrie*). **Ff2** Metal-processing sectors such as tubing production, steel, machinery and plant construction (*Dieser Strukturwandel hat vor allem die metallverarbeitenden Bereiche wie Röhrenproduktion, Stahl-, Maschinen- und Anlagenbau erfaßt*).

P 29 Ff1 Four (*vier Arten von Ständen*). **Ff2** DM 140 per m² for the duration of the event, including erection and dismantling (*Der Durchschnittspreis liegt bei DM 140 pro Quadratmeter für die Gesamtzeit der Veranstaltung, also für Aufbau, Laufzeit der Messe und Abbau*). **Ff3** A maximum of 20%, i.e. a fifth (*Die Miete beträgt maximal 20 Prozent der Gesamtkosten einer Messebeteiligung, also ein Fünftel*). **Es 1** *a*, *q*. **2** *b*, *f*, *g*, *h*, *k*, *l*, *n*. **3** *o*. **4** *i*, *j*, *m*, *p*, (*f* is arguably also part of publicity). **5** *c*, *d*, *e*.

P 30 Ep 1 GARDENEX. **2** 96 Church Street. **3** Great Bedwyn, Marlborough (Wilts.) SN8 3PF. **4** Großbritannien. **5** 0672 870392. **6** 0672 870788. **7** 13.2. **8** C. **9** 10. **10** 886 534.

P 31 Ff1 Green (*grün, Gartengrün*). **Ep 1** *f*; **2** *h*; **3** *g*; **4** *e*; **5** *b*; **6** *a*; **7** *d*; **8** *c*. **Ff2** The south (*Wir haben im Norden wesentlich weniger Großstädte als im Süden*). **Ff3** In the south (*Das Amateurgärtnern ist in Deutschland mit einem Süd-Nord-Gefälle versehen*). **Ff4** Because it is much easier to find an innovation there (*weil da eine Innovation viel leichter zu finden ist als in den herkömmlichen Dingen*). **Es 1** *i f*; *ii a*; *iii b*; *iv c*; *v e*; *vi d*. **2** *a* leichter; *b* weniger; *c* stärker.

P 33 Ff1 With the individual unions (*Die einzelnen Gewerkschaften müssen ihre Machtposition behalten*). **Ff2** The amount of the subscription, the benefits offered to the members, and policy for pay and working conditions (*Beitrag, Leistung für die Mitglieder, Tarifpolitik*). **Ep 1** *f*; **2** *g*; **3** *j*; **4** *i*; **5** *c*; **6** *e*; **7** *a*; **8** *b*; **9** *h*; **10** *d*.

P 34 Ff1 Six (*Die IGEDO ist der Veranstalter von 6 Modemessen im Jahr*). **Ff2** High fashion (*der gehobene Fachhandel, anspruchsvolle Mode*). **Es 1** die Mode; die IGEDO; die IGEDO; die IGEDO. **2** *a* der Stadt; *b* des Fachhandels; *c* der Mode. **3** *a* aus (compare: *mit Einkäufern aus der ganzen Welt*); *b* von (compare: *die Abwicklung von Information*); *c* seit (compare: *seit 1945*); *d* im (compare: *Ordermöglichkeiten im Bereich*); *e* nach (compare: *aus dem Marktbedürfnis nach Informationsmöglichkeiten*).

P 35 Ff1 Three: Coats, knitwear, accessories (*Mäntel, Strickwaren, Accessoires*). **Ff2** Neuer Jungfernstieg, Perusastraße. **Ff3** The south (*Im Süden gibt es viel mehr kleine Damen als im Norden*). **Ff4** Munich (*Olive Töne gehen besser im süddeutschen Raum*). **Ff5** Gentlemen (*Die Herren bevorzugen generell Baumwolle*).

P 36 Ff1 Give advice on minimizing it or at any rate spreading it over time (*Beratung, wie man seine Steuerlast minimieren oder zeitlich verlagern kann*). **Es 1** *a* Ihr Schreiben vom, Fotokopie anbei, Kenntnisnahme; *b* Ihr Anruf vom, Anlage, Stellungnahme; *c* Fotokopie anbei, unser Gespräch am, Rückruf; *d* Ihr Anruf vom, Anlage, Erledigung *e* Irrläufer. **2** *a* vom; *b* am; *c* Unser Zeichen; *d* Ihr Zeichen. **3** *b*.

F e e d b a c k

P 37 **Ff1** Two years (*Ich bin für ein Jahr nach Milwaukee gegangen. Ich bin dann nochmal ein gutes Jahr in New York gewesen*). **Ff2** After 10 years (*Nach zehn Jahren bin ich Partner geworden*). **Ap** One example might be: **1** Ich bin Exportkaufmann. **2** Ich habe 1980 „0 Levels" gemacht. Ich habe in Leeds Exportkaufmann gelernt. **3** Ich habe als Sachbearbeiter bei Boby Ltd angefangen. **4** Ich bin dann Kaufmann geworden. Ich bin nach 3 Jahren zu Allparts Ltd gegangen. **5** Ich bin jetzt Exportkaufmann. Ich bin verantwortlich für den Export nach Frankreich. **Ff3** No - it's a 'small' company; all incorporated companies **except** small companies have to submit a full annual financial statement (***Außer*** *kleinen Gesellschaften müssen alle Kapitalgesellschaften ihre Jahresabschlußunterlagen einreichen*). **Ff4** Yes - it's a medium-sized company and therefore not exempt from the statutory audit (*Außer kleinen Gesellschaften sind alle GmbHs abschlußprüfungspflichtig*).

P 38 **Ff1** Tourism, home and garden (*Die Aktivitäten im Zusammenhang mit der hauswirtschaftlichen Freizeit sind neben dem Tourismus der größte Freizeitbereich*). **Es** **1** den. **2** *a* auf ... ansteigen; *b* um ... zunehmen, um ... wachsen. **3** *b* (wird) wachsen; *c* (werden) ansteigen. **4** prognostizieren (wird prognostiziert). **Ff2** Five - his job (*mein Beruf*), his family (*ich habe eine große Familie*), sports (*ich treibe relativ viel Sport*), academic work (*ich beschäftige mich unheimlich gerne mit wissenschaftlichen Dingen*), DIY (*Heimwerken*). **Ap** One example might be: Ich habe drei Hobbys. Ich spiele unheimlich gerne Tennis. Dann beschäftige ich mich viel mit Fotografie, und ich arbeite gerne im Garten.

P 39 **Ff1** Market leader (*Wir können uns Marktführer nennen*). **Ff2** 20,000-25,000 (*In einem OBI-Markt werden durchschnittlich 20 000 bis 25 000 Artikel geführt*). **Ff3** Under 10% (*Unter zehn Prozent wird importiert*). **Es** **1** *a* sealing (*Abdichten*), insulating (*Isolieren*), filling in (*Ausfüllen*), gluing (*Kleben*), mounting (*Montieren*); *b* inserting rawlplugs (*Verdübeln*), pouring/casting (*Gießen*), anchoring (*Verankern*), fixing (*Befestigen*); *c* filling (*Schließen*), smoothing (*Glätten*); these are all infinitive forms of verbs (➡**P 102,103**) used as nouns (➡**P 97**). **2** zum (= zu + dem). **3** neuter.

P 40 **Ap** One example might be: **1** Ich bin Einkäufer bei der Firma Glassware Ltd. **2** Die tägliche Arbeit besteht darin, Lieferanten zu besuchen. **3** Zu meinen Aufgaben gehört es auch, Messen zu besuchen. **4** Ich bin verantwortlich für den Einkauf von Kristallglas. **Ff1** Head of the offshore department (*Leiter der Abteilung Offshore*). **Ff2** Head of the controlling department and organization department (*Ich leite die Controlling-Abteilung dieses Hauses und die Organisationsabteilung*).

P 41 **Ff1** Because each day's delay when extracting oil and gas costs money (*Jeder Tag Verspätung bei der Förderung von Öl und Gas kostet Geld*). **Es** **1** *b; d; c; g; a; f; e.* **Ff2** The company (*Er kann für das Unternehmen handeln*). **Ff3** No (*Sachbearbeiter haben keinerlei Führungsfunktionen*).

P 43 **Pr** ***operation Ekofisk*** **1** Phillips Petroleum Company Norway (*Mannesmann Rexroth erhielt von der Phillips Petroleum den Auftrag, sechs Gasbohrplattformen anzuheben; sechs Plattformen der Phillips Petroleum Company Norway*). **2** Mannesmann Rexroth (*Mannesmann Rexroth hob sechs Nordsee-Bohrinseln in die Höhe; Mannesmann Rexroth erhielt von der Phillips Petroleum den Auftrag, sechs Gasbohrplattformen anzuheben; Mannesmann Rexroth hat diese Plattformen angehoben; mit der Durchführung der Aktion wurde die Mannesmann Rexroth-Gruppe beauftragt*). **3** 1987 (*Mannesmann Illustrierte*, 1988: *im vergangenen Jahr; Mannesmann Post*, November 1987: *vor einigen Wochen*). **4** Germany, Holland and France (*Hydraulik-Spezialisten aus Deutschland, Holland und Frankreich*). **5** Subsidence of the sea bed (*das Absinken des Meeresbodens; diese Plattformen hatten sich abgesenkt; ein stetiges Absinken des Meeresbodens*). **6** Four (*um den Komplex zum Teil gleichzeitig anheben zu können ...; vier der sechs Inseln mußten gleichzeitig angehoben werden;* Dr Graf Plettenberg's statements that *Mannesmann Rexroth hat gleichzeitig diese Plattformen angehoben* and *Das ganze Unternehmen mußte gleichzeitig erfolgen* are not precise as they suggest that all six were lifted simultaneously). **7** By computer (*Ein Computer steuerte die ganzen Vorgänge*). **8** 122 (*122 Hydraulikzylinder*). **9** The hydraulic cylinders were bolted on (*An die Plattformbeine wurden Hydraulikzylinder angeschraubt*). **10** (More than) 40,000 t (*ein Gesamtgewicht von 40 000 t; ein Gesamtgewicht von über 40 000 t*). **11** Steel (*neue Stahlstücke*). **12** More than $ 350 million (*mehr als 350 Mill. Dollar*). **13** A few hours (*Es geschah innerhalb weniger Stunden*). **Es** **1** *a* hat ... angehoben; *b* ist gelungen. **2** *a* hob; *b* setzte ... ein; *c* erhielt; *d* bestand x2; *e* geschah x2; *f* mußte x3, mußten; *g* blieben; *h* steuerte; *i* sorgte; *j* entschloß sich; *k* verfügte; *l* wog; *m* kostete. **3** *a* sich ... verringert hatte; *b* hatten sich ... abgesenkt; *c* hatten ... festgestellt. **4** *a* wurde ... wiederhergestellt; *b* wurden ... angeschraubt; *c* wurden ... durchgetrennt; *d* wurden ... angehoben x2; *e* (wurden) ... eingesetzt; *f* (wurden) ... verschraubt; *g* wurde erreicht; *h* wurde ... beauftragt; *i* wurde ... verlangt (the verbs *hieven* and *anheben* also appear in the passive, together with the past form of *müssen*: 'mußte ... gehievt werden' and 'mußten ... angehoben werden').

P 45 **Ff1** Four (*Norwegischer Lachs und Jakobsmuscheln, Suppe von Steinbutt, Garnelen und Jakobsmuscheln, Lachs und Petersfisch, Seezungenfilet mit Shrimps*). **Ff2** *Medaillons vom Schweinefilet*; and you might also want to steer clear of *Spargelcrème mit Parmaschinken, Seezungenfilet mit Speck* and *Rinderroulade mit Speck*. **Ff3** *Seezungenfilet, gebraten*.

Hamburg

P 47 **Ff1** Industries connected with ship-building, and industries involving bulk transport of goods, e.g. oil refining and the chemicals industry (*Industriezweige, die mit Schiffbau verbunden waren, und Industriezweige, die Massengüter transportierten, wie zum Beispiel die Mineralölverarbeitung und die chemische Industrie*). **Ff2** Future-oriented industries, especially everything connected with electronics (*zukunftsträchtige Industriezweige; insbesondere alle Bereiche, die mit Elektronik zu tun haben*).

P 48 **Fs** ***Containerdienst*** DATA PROCESSING AND COMMUNICATION **1** The sack (*der Sack*). **2** EDP (*Die elektronische Datenverarbeitung ist Voraussetzung für jeden Containertransport; der Computer war Grundvoraussetzung für den gesamten Containerverkehr*). **3** As a means of planning, deploying, monitoring and optimizing shipments (*Wir nutzen die EDV und moderne Kommunikations-systeme als Instrument der Planung, Disposition, Kontrolle und Optimierung der Transporte*). **4** Reliability and punctuality (*Zuverlässigkeit und Pünktlichkeit*).

P 49 **Fs** ***Containerdienst*** SHIPMENT **1** Hapag-Lloyd's agent (*Der Ladungseigentümer wendet sich an unsere Vertretung in München*). **2** When the owner of the shipment makes his booking (*... es entsteht eine Buchung. In dem Moment bucht unser Verkauf den Schiffsraum für diesen Container für das Schiff X nach Dubai*). **3** To the loading bay at the customer's factory (*Diesem Kunden soll ein 20-Fuß Container auf den Hof der Fabrik gestellt werden*). **4** 24 hours before arrival of the ship (*Container müssen 24 Stunden vor Ankunft des Schiffes hier sein*). **5** At the terminal gate (*Der Containertruck fährt an das Gate des Terminals. Dort wird ein Interchange gemacht*). **Es** **1** *d, f, c, b, a, e.* **2** No, he uses a container truck, the diagram shows a freight train. **3** Paragraph 1: *Kundenkontakt*; Paragraph 2: *Sofortbuchung, Containergestellung, Inlandtransport*; Paragraph 3: *Ladehafen, Schiffsreise, Bestimmungshafen/Empfänger*. **4** *b, c, e, f*; they all start with a relative pronoun (➡**P 99**) and have a verb at the end of the clause (➡**P 107**). **Fs** ***Containerdienst*** THE CONTAINER **1** *a* Kühl-Container; *b* Standard-Container; *c* Tank-Container; *d* Standard-Container; *e* Bulk-Container; *f* Platform; *g* Tank-Container.

P 50 **Ff1** Fast delivery (*Der deutsche Handel ist gewohnt, relativ schnell beliefert zu werden*). **Ff2** They are their main customers (*Hauptabnehmer sind traditionell die Kaufhäuser*). **Es** **1** *a* auf eigene Rechnung; *b* auf Lager; *c* von heute auf morgen. **Ff3** When the machine is running (*laufend*).

P 52 **Ff1** Because it is necessary to compensate for a declining population (*Heute ist die Bevölkerung rückläufig, und es geht jetzt für uns darum, das durch qualitatives Wachstum auszugleichen*). **Ff2** Bread, sausage and beer (*Deutschland ist das Land mit den meisten Brotsorten, mit den meisten Wurstsorten, mit den meisten Biersorten*). **Ff3** That they sell bread by the slice, so you have more choice (*In Brotshops verkaufen sie Brot scheibenweise. Es ist doch viel schöner, wenn man vier verschiedene Sorten hat*). **Ff4** Money (*Der Preis wird nicht mehr unbedingt entscheidend sein. Geld hat er [der Verbraucher] ja*).

P 53 **Ff1** *b* (*monatliche Ausbildungsvergütung*). **Ff2** *c* (*Versicherungskaufmann*).

P 54 **Ff1** Bayer (*Der Name ist mit Bayer verwechselbar*). **Ff2** BDF, an abbreviation of the name Beiersdorf, and four dots (*BDF - eine Abkürzung aus Beiersdorf - mit vier Punkten*). **Pr** *e* (*Wir haben erkannt, daß es notwendig ist, ein Firmenprofil aufzubauen,* also *Wir haben beschlossen, daß wir ein Firmenprofil aufbauen müssen*, i.e. after point *a*); *h* (*Der Firmenname Beiersdorf stand eigentlich nie im Vordergrund, sondern immer seine Marken*); *f* (*Heute sind die Märkte eng. Die Produkte sind ähnlich*); *d* (*Wir haben durch viele Untersuchungen festgestellt, daß man unsere Marken kennt, aber eigentlich nicht weiß, wer dahinter steht*); *a* (*Der Name ist mit der Firma Bayer verwechselbar, und er wird auch manchmal mit einem Dorf in Bayern in Verbindung gebracht*); *i* (*ein Firmenprofil ..., um den Goodwill aller Bereiche zu einer Kraft zu bündeln*); *g* (*Es entstanden Sparten: cosmed, medipharm, tesa*); *c* (*Dann haben wir unser Symbol entwickelt*); *b* (*Wir brauchten einen Slogan. ... Dieser Slogan ...*).

P 55 **Ff1** Two (*2 Vertreter der Gewerkschaften*). **Ff2** 12 (*Aufsichtsrat* (= 12 people) *wählt seinen Vorsitzenden*). **Ff3** The supervisory board (*Aufsichtsrat beaufsichtigt den Vorstand*).

P 56 **Ff1** To ensure that each product is environmentally sound (*..., daß die Produkte völlig unbedenklich für die Umwelt sind*). **Ff2** They have changed the bottle from PVC to polyethylene as well as the box, labels etc. (*Wir haben die Flasche umgestellt von der PVC-Verpackung auf eine Polyäthylenverpackung. Das geht konsequent bis in die Kartonnagen, Etiketten usw*). **Ff3** Very little apart from the marketing (*Die Rezepturen ähneln sich. Das ist der Grund, warum für uns Marketing so wichtig ist*). **Ff4** Specialist trade, food trade (*Fachhandel, Lebensmittelhandel*). **Es** **1** All nine belong to category 3). **2** *a* sich ähneln, sich interessieren; *b* rauskriegen, aussehen. **3** unterstützt werden. **4** *a iii; b i.*

P 57 **Ff1** Nine (*Personalabteilung, Personalentwicklung, Lohn- und Gehaltsbüro, Einkauf, Vertriebsinnendienst, Öffentlichkeitsarbeit, Abrechnung, Marketing, Zentrale; Kundenbuchhaltung* and *Finanzbuchhaltung* could be regarded as separate, in which case she mentions 10). **Ff2** Arranged in blocks (*Wir haben fast alle Vierteljahre sieben Wochen Berufsschule*). **Es** **1** sich richten nach (➡**P 105-106**). **2** *b, d.*

P 58 **Ff1** Age: 38 years (*Das Unternehmen ist 38 Jahre alt*); Activities: service and sales (*Service und Vertrieb*); Product areas: navigation, communication and automation systems/equipment (*Navigations- und Kommunikations- und Automationsanlagen/-geräte*). **Ff2** German regulations and conditions (*Vorschriften und Bedingungen der hiesigen Behörden*). **Ff3** The delivery date has top priority in Germany (*der Liefertermin hat in Deutschland eine absolute Priorität*). **Es** **1** *e, d, b, c, a.* **2** wenn ..., dann.

P 59 **Ff1** Coordinating service; planning service; supervising service engineers; administering the whole process of carrying out a service, including spare-parts procurement, manpower and invoicing (*Koordination von Service, Einteilen von Service, Beaufsichtigen von Servicetechnikern, die Abwicklung, die damit zusammenhängt, einen Service durchzuführen, von der Ersatzteilbeschaffung über die Manpower bis zur Abrechnung*). **Ff2** On board ship and in the workshop (*an Bord, in der Werkstatt*). **Ff3** Repair, replacement (*Reparatur, Austausch*). **Es** **1** von, über, bis.

P 60 **Fs** ***Verdoppelung der Kapazität*** COMPANY PROFILE **1** Medical sector (Name Medic-Eschmann, product range) **2** Products for stoma care (*Produkte der Stomaversorgung, das heißt Produkte für Patienten mit künstlichem Darmausgang*). **3** Sister companies (*unsere Schwesterfirma Portex*). **4** Local import companies (*Portex hat die Produkte in allen Ländern über örtliche Einfuhrfirmen vertrieben*). **Fs** ***Verdoppelung der Kapazität*** THE PROBLEM **1** Portex's import company in Germany switched allegiance to a rival product range from the US (because they assumed that Portex would change to their new sister company Medic-Eschmann) (*Diese Importfirma in Deutschland hat sich entschieden, vom Portex-Produkt auf ein Konkurrenz-Produkt zu wechseln (durch den Kauf wurde der Importeur für Portex-Produkte in Deutschland gewarnt, daß irgendwann wahrscheinlich ein Wechsel stattfinden würde)*; at the end of May 1988 (*Im Mai 1988 erschienen auf dem deutschen Markt schon Prospekte ....; Die Portex Geschäftsführung erfuhr Ende Mai von diesem Wechsel in Deutschland*). **2** Portex transferred distribution to Medic-Eschmann (*Der Firma Medic-Eschmann wurde der Auftrag erteilt, schnellstens die Produktaufnahme der Portex-Produkte im Vertrieb zu organisieren*). **3** An organizational problem, since the company had not been conceived on such a scale (*Da wir*

Feedback

für solche Dimensionen gar nicht vorgesehen waren, stellte das für uns ein großes organisatorisches Problem dar).

P 61 Fs ***Verdoppelung der Kapazität*** THE TASK **1** To have the Portex product range available for delivery as soon as possible (*Unsere Aufgabe war, schnellstmöglich das Produkt Portex lieferfähig bei uns im Lager zu haben*). **2** Because the products are used in anaesthesia (*Durch die Natur des Produktes durfte keine große Lieferverzögerung im Markt stattfinden; die Produkte sind ja Produkte für die Anästhesie*). **Fs** ***Verdoppelung der Kapazität*** THE SOLUTION **1** Medic-Eschmann had carried 1300 to 1500 products (*Bis dahin hatten wir ein Artikelsortiment von zirka 1300 bis 1500 Produkten gehabt*); 1500 products were being added (*1500 Produkte mußten neu aufgenommen werden*). **2** They rented 550 m^2 extra warehousing capacity (*Wir hatten nicht genug Lagerkapazität, also haben wir zirka 550 Quadratmeter zusätzlich angemietet*). **3** Mid-June 1988 (*Wir haben seit Mitte Juni erst mal dringende Waren ausgeliefert*). **4** Two colleagues from Portex carried out training, and the fact that they spoke very good German expedited the training process (*Zwei englische Kollegen von Portex haben unseren Innendienst und das Lagerpersonal geschult. Beide sprachen sehr gut Deutsch, so daß wir innerhalb von zwei bis drei Wochen lieferfähig wurden*). **5** Five (*Wir haben fünf Mitarbeiter im Außendienst eingestellt*). **6** Mailing to trade suppliers and hospitals, which was then repeated (*Wir haben durch Mailings an unsere Fachhändler und an die Kliniken auf die neue Situation hingewiesen. Diese Mailings haben wir wiederholt*); Telephone marketing campaign to 1400 hospitals (*Wir haben eine Telefonmarketingaktion durchgeführt. Wir haben eine Firma für Telefonmarketing beauftragt, zirka 1400 Kliniken anzurufen*); Production of a brochure in German (*Wir konnten bis jetzt nur einen Prospekt in Deutsch bringen*). **7** Two to three weeks (*Wir hoffen, daß wir in maximal zwei, drei Wochen diesen Katalog in Deutsch auf den Markt bringen können*).

P 62 Ff1 After the basic systems have been modified for the customer and before the furnishings and fittings are installed (*Nach der Modifizierung der Basis wird die Elektrik installiert, und danach wird die Ausstattung eingebaut*).

P 63 Ff1 The flight systems for the German contribution to the fuselage are installed in Hamburg-Finkenwerder (*Der deutsche Bauanteil am Airbus-Rumpf wird in Finkenwerder mit allen flugwichtigen Systemen ausgerüstet*). **Ff2** Toulouse (*Toulouse, der Ort der Airbus-Endmontage*). **Es 1** *g, c, d, i, a, j, e, b, f, h.* **2** *d.* **3** *a i* Hydraulik, Elektrik, Pneumatik; *ii* Sitz, Bordküche, Teppichboden, Flugzeughimmel. *b i* flugwichtige Systeme; *ii* Ausstattungselemente. *c i* von ... über ... bis hin zu; *ii* von ... bis zu, von ... bis zu. **4** *a* der; *b* der; *a* genitive (*Segmente* here is neuter plural); *b* nominative (*Airbus* here is masculine singular).

P 64 Ff1 British: wing construction (*Flächenbau*); French: Cockpit (*Cockpitbereich*); Germans: structural craftsmanship e.g. automatic riveting systems (*Bereich der strukturellen Bearbeitung wie automatische Nietsysteme*). **Ff2** Communication (*Die Kommunikation untereinander bringt für das Projekt Vorteile*). **Ff3** The wings and the load spectrum (*Die Briten bekommen den Flügel, und dafür rechnen die Deutschen ein Lastspektrum für das ganze Flugzeug*). **Ff4** Chrome-plating - national regulations for the temperature of the bath (*Zum Beispiel ... wenn die Leute von BAe irgendein Bauteil verchromen sollen, bringen sie mit einem Bad das Chrom an das Bauteil. Wir haben ganz andere Vorschriften*).

P 65 Ff1 Vienna (*Schnitzel „Wiener Art", Wiener (Würstchen)*). **2** Tell Herr Höfner, the butcher (*Sind Sie nicht zufrieden, sagen Sie es bitte mir*).

München

P 68 Pr ***business letter*** *b* (*Wir bedanken uns für Ihre Anfrage*; *f* (*wir übersenden Ihnen Unterlagen*); *j* (*ein führendes Unternehmen in Deutschland*); *a* (*... Grafikkarten, -monitore, Farbdrucker, Plotter, Scanner, Grafikterminals und Hochleistungsrechner*); *i* (*marktgerechte Preise*); *g* (*Unser langjähriger Service*); *d* (*Responsezeiten unter 24 Stunden*); *h* (*Produkte, welche mit Sicherheit Ihre Leistungsmöglichkeiten abdecken können*); *c* (*Wir würden uns freuen, Sie zu unserem Kundenkreis zählen zu können*); *e Herr Lindermeier steht Ihnen jederzeit zur Verfügung*).

P 69 Pr ***service*** **1** Two (*Wartungsvertrag ... Wir bieten zwei verschiedene Typen an*). **2** Calling out the engineer without a service contract (*Ein Kunde, der keinen Wartungsvertrag hat, kann in Anspruch nehmen, daß ein Techniker zu ihm kommt*); Labour per hour DM 200 (*die Arbeitsstunde 200 D-Mark*), Travel time per hour DM 170 (*die Fahrtstunde 170 D-Mark*), Cost per kilometre 65 Pfennigs (*pro Kilometer 65 Pfennige*), Flat-rate for a part DM 650 (*das ausgetauschte Teil - wir haben einen Pauschalpreis - kostet 650 D-Mark*).

P 70 Pr ***product development*** *c* (*Qualifikationsspiegel für alle Mitarbeiter des Unternehmens*); *d* (*wir wählen dann für Assessment Center bestimmte Mitarbeiter aus*); *e* (*Mitarbeiter werden in einer Taskforce zusammengezogen*); *a* (*Diese Mitarbeiter tagen eine Woche*); *b* (*die Entwicklungsabteilung muß die Entwicklung des Produktes ausführen*).

P 71 Pr ***terms of delivery and payment*** **1** In writing (*schriftlich*), by phone (*telefonisch*) or by fax (*per Telefax*). **2** For ex-stock products maximum of 24 hours after receipt of order (*Lagerhaltige Ware verläßt spätestens 24 Stunden nach Bestelleingang unser Haus*); **3** Up to 20 kg by post, otherwise by freight forwarder (*Bis 20 kg Paketgewicht Versand per Post. Alle anderen Lieferungen mit Spedition*); **4** VAT (*zuzüglich der gesetzlichen Mehrwertsteuer*), freight and packaging charges (*Fracht- und Verpackungskosten werden zusammen mit der Ware in Rechnung gestellt*); **5** 2% Discount within 14 days, and without any deductions within 30 days of the invoice date at the latest (*innerhalb von 14 Tagen mit 2% Skonto, spätestens 30 Tage ab Rechnungsdatum ohne Abzug*); **6** Six months (*6monatige Garantiezeit*).

P 72 Pr ***suppliers*** **1** The Commonwealth (*Die britische Konsumgüterindustrie war orientiert ins Commonwealth*). **2** Differing standards in the electrical industry (*Das drückt sich zum Beispiel in unterschiedlichen Standards in der Elektroindustrie aus*). **3** Very conservative (*In der Mode waren bis Mary Quant von England nur sehr konservative Dinge zu erwarten*). **4** The knitwear industry around Birmingham (*Es gibt in England zum Beispiel rund um Birmingham herum eine sehr leistungsfähige und auch hochmodische Strickwarenindustrie*).

P 73 Pr ***selection*** *c* Ordering a sample (*Zunächst wird von uns ein Muster gezogen*); *f* Judging the sample (*Entspricht dieses Muster von der Qualität, von der Aufmachung, von der Farbe, vom Stil her unseren Vorstellungen ...*); *a* Fixing a price (*Dann kommt der Preis*); *e* Fixing the quantity to be supplied (*Dann wird ein Größensatz bestimmt*); *d* Quality control (*Dann macht unser Institut für Warenprüfung produktionsbegleitende Stichproben*); *b* Fixing a delivery date (*Dann muß noch die Lieferzeit stimmen*). **Pr** ***delivery*** **1** Reliability of delivery (*Lieferzuverlässigkeit*), strikes (*Streiks*), unreliable transport system (*ein nicht sehr zuverlässiges Transportsystem*). **2** Directing the flow of capital as much as possible (*die Kapitalströme halbwegs zu lenken*), controlling warehouse capacity (*die Lagerkapazität zu steuern*), satisfying the demand triggered by the catalogue (*die Nachfrage zu befriedigen, die der Katalog auslöst*). **3** Reliable delivery (*Liefertreue*).

P 74 Pr ***purchasing*** **1** February (*die Spielwarenmesse im Februar*). **2** March (*Wir haben im März eine Ausmusterung*). **3** Assumed sales potential (*die Gängigkeit der Ware, die man sich erhofft*), quality (*Qualität*), price (*Preis*). **4** 85% (*von 1000 Artikeln kommen 850 aus der Bundesrepublik*). **Pr** ***quality*** **1** Top to bottom: Switzerland, Germany, and finally Holland, Belgium and Britain on roughly the same level (*Man kann von der Schweiz nach Holland oder Belgien ein Qualitätsgefälle feststellen. Die Schweizer Endverbraucher legen größten Wert auf qualitätsmäßig sehr hochstehendes Spielzeug. Die deutschen Endverbraucher sind nicht ganz so anspruchsvoll (wie die Schweizer Endverbraucher), aber immer noch anspruchsvoll. Die Endverbraucher in Belgien tendieren auf Spielzeug hin, wo der Preis die Hauptrolle spielt. Die Engländer dürften mit den belgischen und holländischen Mitgliedern irgendwo ähnlich stehen*). **2** It should be educational (*lehrreich*), pleasant to the touch (*griffsympathisch*), and made of natural materials (*Es sollte aus natürlichen Produkten kommen*).

P 75 Pr ***conditions of dispatch and delivery*** **1** DM 50 (*Die Ware wird zugeschickt, sofern der Gesamtpreis der Bestellung DM 50,- übersteigt. Der Versand im Inland erfolgt per Nachnahme*). **2** DM 250 (*Übersteigt der Gesamtpreis der Bestellung DM 250,-, liefern wir frei Bestimmungsort bzw. frei nächstgelegenem Stückgutbahnhof*). **3** When goods have been purchased in the shop (*gilt nicht beim Kauf im Geschäft*). **4** Cost price (*Spezielle Verpackungen empfindlicher Güter berechnen wir zum Selbstkostenpreis*). **5** When goods are accepted by the forwarding agent and at the latest when they leave the factory or warehouse (*Mit Auslieferung der Ware an den Versandbeauftragten, spätestens jedoch mit Verlassen des Werkes oder des Lagers geht die Gefahr des zufälligen Unterganges und der zufälligen Verschlechterung der Ware auf den Besteller über*). **6** Foreign destinations (*Auslandslieferungen erfolgen gemäß vorheriger Vereinbarung*). **7** Changes to prices, products and delivery conditions (*Sämtliche Preise sind freibleibend. Änderungen und Liefermöglichkeiten bleiben vorbehalten*). **Ff1** It helps him continue to hit the bull's eye with his calculations (*Damit er auch weiterhin mit seinen Berechnungen ins Schwarze trifft*). **Es 1** *a auf Wunsch; b Gesamtpreis; c Bestellung; d per Nachnahme; e übersteigen; f Fracht(gut); g Selbstkostenpreis; h Besteller; i Geschäft; j Versand; k Lager; l Vereinbarung; m Verpackung; n Versandbeauftragter.* **Pr** ***training*** **1** Dispatch (*Versand*), Customer service (*Reklamation*), Purchasing (*Einkauf*), Filing department (*Registratur*), Members' advisory department (*Mitgliederberatung*). **2** General economics and business studies (*allgemeine Wirtschaftslehre*), business administration (*Handelsbetriebslehre*), accountancy (*Rechnungswesen*), book-keeping (*Buchführung*), maths for business purposes (*kaufmännisches Rechnen*). **3** Social studies (*Sozialkunde*), German (*Deutsch*), sport (*Sport*), religion (*Religion*).

P 76 Pr ***electronic components*** **1** *d* (*Der deutsche Markt gilt für diese Art Produkte als der größte Einzelmarkt in Europa*); *b* (*Wenn man aber einmal in einer Firma drin ist, dann ist man drin. Man kann also recht gute Geschäfte machen*); *a* (*Wir vertreten im Moment sechs Firmen*); *e* (*Wir unterhalten uns die ersten zwei oder drei Jahre ausschließlich mit Entwicklern*); *c* (*der Einkauf plaziert den Auftrag*). **2** *a* Six; *b* Good - Once you're in, you're in, and you can do good business in Germany! *c* Purchasing department; *d* It's considered the biggest in Europe for this type of product; *e* Development engineers. **Pr** ***delivery times*** **1** They add on two weeks to the delivery date given by the UK company (*Wir schlagen auf jede Lieferzeit, die wir von England bekommen, zwei Wochen drauf*). **2** They're not used to reacting fast (*Sie sind nicht daran gewöhnt*). **3** Precision in production planning is lacking and probably also motivation (*Es fehlt dort die Präzision in der Produktionsplanung und wahrscheinlich auch die Motivation*). **4** The products are fantastic and very welcome on the market (*Das, was sie an Produkten vorstellen, ist immer toll und hochwillkommen auf dem Markt*).

P 77 Pr ***sales office*** **1** Office furniture, business cards, translation of terms and conditions of business etc. (*Büromöbel, Visitenkarten, Übersetzung von Geschäftsbedingungen usw.*). **2** A secretary and a sales engineer/representative (*Erst braucht er eine Sekretärin. Dann braucht er einen Außendienstmitarbeiter*). **3** Six months (*Der Außendienstmitarbeiter muß geschult werden. Das dauert ein halbes Jahr*). **4** Not knowing which customers to approach (*Dann kommt die Phase, in der der Außendienstmitarbeiter überhaupt nicht weiß, zu welchen Kunden er hingehen soll*). **5** It's very expensive (*Um jemanden von der Konkurrenz anzuwerben, müssen Sie schon sehr tief in die Tasche greifen*).

P 78 Ap For some suggestions on how to give a profile of yourself see the answers to **Ap** on ➡**P 10,37,40.** **Fs** ***Kapitalbedarf*** COMPANY PROFILE **1** Electron beam welding machines (*Wir bauen Elektronenstrahlschweißmaschinen*). **2** Because it was a market niche with virtually no competition (*Wir haben Marktnischenüberlegungen geführt, das heißt, wir versuchen mit unseren Produkten in Gebiete zu kommen, wo sehr wenig oder fast keine Konkurrenz existiert*). **3** Because many joining methods have to meet high-quality demands and because of the extensive use of exotic materials like titanium or special alloys where special ambient conditions are necessary for welding (*Dieses Gebiet wird heute wieder sehr populär, denn es werden an viele Fügetechniken sehr hohe Qualitätsanforderungen gestellt, und man verwendet heute sehr viel exotische Materialien wie zum Beispiel Titan oder Sonderlegierungen. Solche Materialien kann man nur durch ganz spezielle Umgebungsbedingungen schweißtechnisch bearbeiten*). **4** To allow it to be used with fully-automated computer control (*Wir haben das Verfahren optimiert, um es computersteuerbar zu machen*). **5** Engine construction and maintenance (*Wir liefern Schweißanlagen, die für Triebwerksbau oder für „Maintenance" eingesetzt werden*). **6** Porsche, BMW, Rolls Royce, Lucas, Siemens, AEG, and they're trying to get into business with Mercedes (*Wir sind bei Porsche und BMW, wir sind bei Rolls Royce und Lucas ins Geschäft gekommen, Siemens ist ein Großkunde, AEG; wir versuchen jetzt mit Mercedes ins Geschäft zu kommen*). **Fs** ***Kapitalbedarf*** THE PROBLEM **1** Financial problems (*Hi-Tech-Marken werden irgendwann immer mit finanziellen Problemen zu kämpfen haben*). **2** Because in small companies, highly sophisticated technologies and development programmes, which are

Feedback

extremely expensive, can no longer be financed by the profits from the product which they manufacture and sell (*In den kleinen Unternehmen werden heute sehr anspruchsvolle Techniken und Entwicklungsbestrebungen, die sehr viel Geld kosten, nicht mehr über die Ertragssituation des Produktes, das sie herstellen und verkaufen, gedeckt*).

P 79 **Fs** *Kapitalbedarf* OPTION 1 **1** Credit from the banks (*Normalerweise kann ein kleines Unternehmen nur über Banken, über Kredite Kapital beschaffen*). **2** Loans have to be secured with immovable property or in some other way (*Kredite müssen immobil oder in irgendeiner Form abgesichert werden*). **3** Partnership with a large company (*Es kommt nur der Schritt zur Partnerschaft des Großen in Frage*). **Fs** *Kapitalbedarf* OPTION 2 **1** That you can no longer afford to be innovative and can therefore no longer have leading-edge products. That way you again potentially lose your economic independence (*Wenn ich im technischen Bereich nicht mehr innovativ tätig sein kann, verliere ich irgendwann den Produktkontakt zur Spitze und damit auch unter Umständen meine wirtschaftliche Selbständigkeit*). **2** Because you'll again face unlimited expenditure and again hit financial problems (*Irgendwann ist das eine Schraube, die ins Unendliche geht* (literally: A screw which turns and turns to infinity). *Man stößt immer wieder an gewisse finanzielle Probleme*). **3** Venture capital as available in the UK and US (*Im angelsächsischen Bereich versucht man, das* venture capital *anders zu praktizieren: ... So wäre ein mögliches Überleben in vielen innovativen kleinen Firmen zu sehen*). **Fs** *Kapitalbedarf* OPTION 3 **1** You have to guarantee survival for your employees (*Eine Liquidation bedeutet letztendlich, daß man den Mitarbeitern, die man im Anstellungsverhältnis hat, ein weiteres Überleben garantieren muß*). **2** It means that the members of his family employed in the company lose their jobs and consequently their livelihood (*Wenn ich liquidiere, verliert meine ganze Familie ihren Arbeitsplatz und damit ihre Existenzgrundlage*). **Fs** *Kapitalbedarf* THE WAY FORWARD All his arguments point towards seeking partnership with a large company at some point and relinquishing the company's independence.

P 80 **Pr** *the package* **1** Structural shell with utilities connected (*in erweitertem Rohbauzustand*); with complete interior fittings (*mit vollständigem Innenausbau*). **2** Slide projector (*Diaprojektor*), OHP (*Overheadprojektor*), video system (*Video-System*) etc. **3** Borrowing from other companies, using the central register of equipment (*Zentrale Geräteerfassung (Verleih zwischen den Firmen)*). **4** Advice on founding a company (*Gründungsberatung*); Advice on public sources of funding (*Beratung über öffentliche Fördermittel*); Advice on starting up production and market launch (*Beratung bei Produktionsaufnahme und Markteinführung*). **5** Exchange of experiences (*Erfahrungsaustausch*). **6** Institutes of higher education and research institutes (*Hochschulen und außeruniversitäre Forschungseinrichtungen*); Industry and chambers of commerce (*gewerbliche Wirtschaft und Kammern*); Investors (*Kapitalgeber*); Opinion leaders and trade press (*Meinungsbildner und Fachpresse*).

P 81 **Pr** *start-up* **1** 1985 (*Die Firma Münchner Hybrid Systemtechnik GmbH wurde 1985 gegründet*). **2** Development and manufacture of production equipment for hybrid technology, and custom manufacture of hybrid and SMD circuits (*Schwerpunkte des Unternehmens sind die Entwicklung und Herstellung von Fertigungsgeräten für die Hybridtechnik sowie die Herstellung von Hybrid- und SMD-Schaltungen im Kundenauftrag*). **3** Three (*Die Firma hat derzeit drei Geräte im Programm*). **4** Consultancy on manufacturing hybrid and SMD circuits, designing labs and selecting equipment and materials (*Die Firma bietet ihr Know-how an. Die Mitarbeiter sind bei der Herstellung von Hybrid- und SMD-Schaltungen, bei der Konzeption von Laborräumen und bei der Auswahl von Geräten und Materialien beratend tätig*). **5** The know-how gained from manufacturing the circuits flows back into the machines (*Das Know-how, das wir beim Fertigen dieser Schaltungen gewinnen, fließt wieder in die Geräte ein*). **6** Selling their products (*Der Vertrieb ist eigentlich das Schwierigste*).

P 82 **Ff1** As Lieschen Müller (*Lieschen Müller, der Kleinkunde; die Masse der Kunden, also der Verbraucher Lieschen Müller*). **Ff2** From an employee of the insurance company (*Lieschen Müller versichert sich zum Beispiel über einen festangestellten Ausschließlichkeitsvertreter der Aachen-Münchener*). **Ff3** Industry (*Die deutsche Industrie wird in Zukunft frei sein, sich in ganz Europa den Versicherungsschutz maßgeschneidert auszusuchen - also keine Genehmigung mehr durch das Bundesaufsichtsamt. Wir sagen, diese Industriekunden haben das Know-how, um ohne staatlichen Schutz Verträge auszuhandeln*).

P 83 **Ff1** Illness, industrial accident, unemployment, retirement (*Sozialversicherung: Krankheit, Arbeitsunfall, Arbeitslosigkeit, Altersversorgung*). **Ff2** According to the income of the insured (*Beitragshöhe: Richtet sich nach dem Einkommen des Versicherten*). **Ff3** Social insurance is obligatory (*Pflichtversicherung*) while individual insurance is voluntary (*Freiwillige Versicherung*). **Ff4** The middle column (*Gesetzliche Rentenversicherung, Pflichtversicherung für Arbeitnehmer*). **Ff5** DM 684,00 in this example. **Ff6** Tax schedule III 1 - married, one spouse gainfully employed, one child (*Steuerklasse III 1, verheiratet, ein Ehepartner berufstätig, ein Kind*). **Ff7** Two (*Lohnsteuer, Kirchensteuer*). **Ff8** Fire (*Feuer*), water from apparatus and pipes (*Leitungswasser*), burglary (*Einbruch*), robbery (*Beraubung*), storm (*Sturm*), breakage of glass (*Glasbruch*).

P 84 **Fs** *Zusammenschluß* THE PROBLEM **1** The strong pressure of domestic-appliance imports from Italy and also France (*der sehr starke Importdruck von Hausgeräten vom italienischen Markt und damals auch schon vom französischen Markt*). **2** They were cheaper (Herr Strobel actually said 'better value for money' but probably meant '*billiger*', 'cheaper'!) (*Insbesondere die Italiener haben damals den deutschen Markt mit preiswerten Geräten sehr stark dominiert - nicht vergleichbar von der Qualität, aber entschieden preiswerter*). **Fs** *Zusammenschluß* THE SOLUTION **1** By concentration (*Die Reaktion der gesamten deutschen Hausgeräteindustrie war die Konzentration*). **2** Their aim was to combine series and create larger production units, thereby reducing costs (*... um durch Zusammenlegung von Serien auf größere Baueinheiten zu kommen und kostenmäßig entsprechend günstiger zu sein*). **3** By merging their production (*der Zusammenschluß*). **4** That of an independent company (*Aus dem Verbund der Produktionszusammenlegung ist eine eigenständige Firma geworden*). **5** Development, production and administration relating to the actual appliances (*Wir haben eine einheitliche Entwicklung, eine einheitliche Produktion und - was die Geräte betrifft - eine einheitliche Administration*). **6** Marketing, product positioning, wholesale, and retail to the consumer (*Der Vertrieb, das Positionieren der Produkte nach außen und das Verkaufen in den Handel hinein und vom Handel aus an den Endverwender geschieht ganz getrennt*). **7** As traditional and conservative (*Bosch ist etwas traditioneller. Es gibt Käufergruppen, die eher der konservativen Marke Bosch verhaftet sind*). **8** That of being progressive (*Siemens hat den Ruf, ein fortschrittliches Unternehmen zu sein*).

P 85 **Es 1** *a* paragraph 3; *b* paragraph 2; *c* paragraph 1. **2** i *a, b, f*; ii *c, e, g*. iii *d*. **3** *a* effektvoll; *b* anspruchsvoll; *c* sinnvoll; *d* technisch; *e* optisch; *f* systematisch; *g* vorbildlich; *h* nützlich; *i* aktuell; *j* funktionell; *k* ergonomisch; *l* asymmetrisch; *m* zweckmäßig; *n* komfortabel (In a dictionary you'd find adjectives in the basic form without endings, as they're given here (➡ **P 100-101**)). 4 Dieses neue Bosch-Küchenmodell ('*Der ... Architektur*' is in the dative case - Architektur is feminine. If it were in the nominative case it would be '*die moderne, asymmetrische Architektur*' ➡ **P 98,101**). 5 *a* aus einer Hand, aus einem Haus; *b* kurz und gut.

P 86 **Ff1** Roughly 27% (*Wir machen über die Hälfte unseres Geschäftes - etwa 55% des Gesamtumsatzes - im Ausland. Die Hälfte dieses Auslandsgeschäftes sind Eigenleistungen, die im Land erbracht werden*). **Ff2** Marketing communication (*Marketingkommunikation*), advertising (*Werbung*), sales promotion (*Verkaufsförderung*), product design (*Produktdesign*), buildings (*Gebäude*), vehicles and their livery (*Kraftfahrzeuge und deren Beschriftung*).

P 87 **Ff1** Three (*Dr Höfner & Partner Management-Beratung, Institut für Unternehmensführung der Universität Innsbruck, Internationales Management-Institut Franklin College Switzerland*). **Pr** *corporate identity* e (*Unternehmen, die sich Corporate-Identity-Ziele vorgeben und die konsequent verfolgen, haben gegenüber ihren Konkurrenten Wettbewerbsvorteile*); d (*Mit Blick auf den EG-Binnenmarkt müssen selbst Großunternehmen ihre CI-Politik überdenken*); c (*Im Zusammenhang mit dem EG-Binnenmarkt erhält das CI-Konzept einen besonderen Stellenwert*); f (*Aufgrund der Marktöffnung sei es erforderlich, „daß die Europa-Position des Unternehmens festgelegt wird"*); b (*Vor allem müsse das Selbstverständnis und das Leitbild des Unternehmens bestimmt und intern gegenüber den Mitarbeitern vermittelt werden*); a (*So müßten sich vor allem Großunternehmen fragen, ob sie sich als deutsches Unternehmen verstehen oder als ein internationales*).

P 88 **Fs** *Italienisch* **Pr** *the Italian case* **1** A smattering of Italian (*Ich habe ein paar Brocken Italienisch gekonnt*). **2** French (*Ich konnte Französisch*). **3** Mornings during the early stages (*In der Anfangsphase habe ich immer einen halben Tag in einer Sprachschule verbracht (und die zweite Hälfte des Tages im Unternehmen)*). **4** Talking to colleagues in the company (*Die Ausweitung des Wortschatzes war viel effektiver in der Firma im Gespräch mit Kollegen*). **5** They were very tolerant (*Man war gegenüber Fehlern in der Sprache sehr tolerant*). **6** That everybody speaks differently (*Jeder spricht anders*). **7** Reading for enjoyment or general information, a newspaper, magazine or Italian book (*Das Lesen zum Vergnügen oder zur Allgemeininformation ging sehr schnell. Eine Zeitung oder eine Zeitschrift oder ein italienisches Buch verstehen ging relativ schnell*). **8** At first he was unable to distinguish whether things were important or not (*Schwieriger ist es, geschäftliche Vorgänge zu lesen, weil es einem am Anfang nicht gelingt zu unterscheiden, welche Dinge wichtig sind und welche nicht*).

Spelling and Pronunciation

The following pronunciation guide will give you an idea of how the words you read are pronounced, to help you remember them. German words of more than one syllable tend to have the main stress on the first syllable. Exceptions are words beginning with the prefixes *be-*, *emp-*, *ent-*, *er-*, *ge-*, *ver-*, *zer-*, which have the stress on the second syllable (*Geschäft*, *verantwortlich*), and words of Greek or Latin origin, where it generally falls on the last (*Symbol*, *Psychologie*). Words of English or French origin are usually pronounced approximately as in the original language (*Know-how*, *Branche*).

Vowels

As in English, German vowels can be pronounced long or short. The long vowels sound more like Scottish or northern English vowels than southern ones. You can't always tell whether a vowel is pronounced long or short, but here are some hints: vowels are pronounced long if they're doubled (e.g. *Saal*, *Boot*) or if they're followed by h (e.g. *Stahl*, *Lohn*). They're pronounced short if they're followed by a double consonant (e.g. *Messe*, *sollen*).

Letter	Usual Pronunciation	Examples
a	short: as in southern English 'c*u*t'	B**a**nk, St**a**dt
	long: as in English 'sp*a*'	T**a**g, H**a**fen
ai	like ei	M**ai**n, K**ai**ser
au	as in 'h*ou*se'	H**au**s, Fr**au**
ä	short: like short e	Gesch**ä**ft, B**ä**cker
	long: like long e	**ä**hnlich, Qualit**ä**t
äu	like eu	Fr**äu**lein, Geb**äu**de
e	short stressed: as in 'r*e*d'	Z**e**ntrum, d**e**nn
	short unstressed: as in unstressed 'th*e*'	Ger**ä**t, imposant**e**
	long: as in Scottish 'gr*ea*t'	d**e**n, Probl**e**m
ei	as in '*i*ce'	**ei**n, L**ei**ter
eu	as in '*oi*l'	n**eu**, d**eu**tsch
i	short: as in 'b*i*g'	m**i**t, F**i**lm
	long: as in 'f*ee*'	w**i**r, Tar**i**f
ie	like long i	d**ie**, fl**ie**gen
o	short: as in 'b*o*x'	s**o**llen, v**o**n
	long: as in Scottish 's*o*'	**o**der, Telef**o**n
ö	short: like short German e, but with lips rounded as for o	ge**ö**ffnet, B**ö**rse
	long: like short ö, but with lips more rounded and pushed forward, as if giving someone a kiss	L**ö**sung, m**ö**glich
u	short: as in 'f*oo*t'	z**u**m, h**u**ndert
	long: as in 'f*oo*d'	z**u**, R**u**f
ü	short: like short German i, but with lips rounded as for u	gr**ü**nden, f**ü**llen
	long: like short ü, but with lips more rounded and pushed forward, as if giving someone a kiss	f**ü**r, f**ü**hren
y	short: like short ü	S**y**mbol, S**y**stem
	long: like long ü	Anal**y**se, t**y**pisch

Consonants

These are basically pronounced as in English, with the following main exceptions:

Letter	Usual Pronunciation	Examples
c	Before a, l, o, r, u: like English *k*	**c**irca, **C**lou
	Otherwise like English *ts*	**c**irca
ch	After a, o, u (but not äu/eu): as in Scottish 'Lo*ch*'	Wo**ch**e, au**ch**
	At the beginning of most German proper names and Greek words, and usually before s: like English *k*	**Ch**lor, we**ch**seln
	Otherwise like the *h* in '*h*uman', but exaggerated	si**ch**, wel**ch**e
h	At the beginning of words and parts of compounds: as in English	**h**aben, Flug**h**afen
	Otherwise not pronounced	Verke**h**r, fü**h**ren
j	Like *y* in *y*es	**j**a, Pro**j**ektor
l	Like *l* as in '*l*eft', i.e. always with tongue flat against roof of mouth, not rounded as in 'fo*l*d' or 'a*ll*'	Fi**l**m, Ge**l**d
p	As in English. Also pronounced before n and s	**P**neumatik, **p**sychologisch
qu	Like English *kv*	**Qu**elle, **Qu**alität
r	Pronounced at the back of the throat like *ch* in Scottish 'Lo*ch*', but with less force	**R**uf, P**r**eis
	Exceptions: the endings -er and -r on words and parts of compounds sound like a very short unstressed German a	Frankfurt**er**, ein**er** hi**er**, wi**r**
s	As in English	i**s**t, Me**ss**e
	Exceptions: pronounced like English *z* before a vowel (if single s)	**s**o, impo**s**ant
	Pronounced like English *sh* before p or t at the beginning of a word or part of a compound	**S**port, **S**tunde
sch	Like English *sh*	**sch**ön, techni**sch**
ß	Equivalent to, and pronounced like ss. Used before consonants, at the end of a word or part of a compound, and between vowels if the preceding vowel is long	grö**ß**te, Einflu**ß**, Stra**ß**e, hei**ß**en
v	Like English *f* in indigenous German words and at the end of a word	**V**ertrieb, akti**v**
	Otherwise like English *v*	**V**ideo, nervö**s**
w	Like English *v*	**W**elt, z**w**ei
z	Like English *ts*	**Z**entrum, Konfer**z**

Grammar

This section presents the main grammar points you'll need in order to find your way through *Deutsches Business-Magazin*. It's specifically designed for understanding written German. For a comprehensive explanation of German grammar you'll need to refer to one of the standard grammars available. Page numbers refer to *Filafacts* in the main part of the book or to other parts of the grammar section.

It helps to spend some time at regular intervals coming to grips with the structure of the German language, as this can save you a lot of time and frustration in the long run! But don't attempt to read through the grammar section in one go. It's intended for reference when you come to a *Filafact*, or whenever you feel you want a particular point explained. If you get bogged down in the detail - leave it and come back later, when you've read some more of *Deutsches Business-Magazin*.

ABBREVIATIONS

m	masculine	*sing.*	singular	*nom.*	nominative	*lit.*	literally
f	feminine	*pl*	plural	*acc.*	accusative		
n	neuter			*gen.*	genitive		
				dat.	dative		

SUMMARY OF PARTS OF SPEECH

The following sentence gives examples of various 'parts of speech':

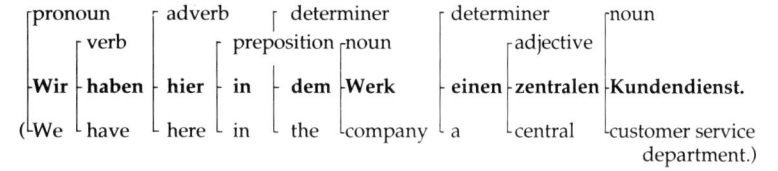

```
 pronoun    adverb    determiner        determiner     noun
   verb        preposition  noun           adjective
 Wir  haben   hier  in    dem  Werk    einen zentralen Kundendienst.
(We   have    here  in    the  company a     central   customer service
                                                              department.)
```

NOUN

Nouns identify people/animate creatures (e.g. 'child'), objects (e.g. 'computer') and concepts (e.g. 'democracy'). They can be preceded in English by 'the'. In German, they're easily recognizable because they're always written with a capital letter: *Kind, Computer, Demokratie*.

DETERMINER

A noun is usually preceded by a determiner, and this helps to show the noun's role in the sentence. Most often you'll find the definite article 'the' (*der/die/das/...*) or indefinite article 'a' (*ein/eine/ein/...*).

PRONOUN

A pronoun can be used instead of a noun, e.g. *sie* (she, they), *es* (it), *wir* (we).

ADJECTIVE

Adjectives describe or modify nouns or pronouns, e.g. *ein typisches Produkt* (a **typical** product), *es ist typisch* (it is **typical**).

ADVERB

Adverbs modify verbs, adjectives, other adverbs or whole word-groups, and usually give information about time, place, manner, or degree, e.g. *jetzt* (now), *hier* (here), *schnell* (fast), *sehr* (very).

VERB

Verbs indicate an action or state and often specify past, present or future time, e.g. *wir arbeiten* (we work), *wir arbeiteten* (we worked), *wir werden arbeiten* (we shall work).

PREPOSITION

Prepositions are words like *in* (in), *für* (for), *mit* (with). They affect the case of a following noun or pronoun.

CONJUNCTION

Conjunctions are words like *und* (and), *aber* (but), *weil* (because). They connect words, phrases or clauses.

OTHER GRAMMATICAL CONCEPTS

PREFIX - STEM - SUFFIX

German has many words that are closely 'related'. Recognizing how a word is formed can help when you're trying to remember it, and you can expand your vocabulary by learning related words.

Nouns: Arbeit (work)   Arbeiter (worker)   Mitarbeiter (colleague)
Verbs: arbeiten (to work)   verarbeiten (to process)
Adjective: arbeitsam (industrious)

By removing any **prefix** (e.g. **ver-**) and **suffix** (e.g. **-en**) you're left with the **stem** of a word (e.g. -arbeit-).

COMPOUND WORDS

These are a typical feature of German. Two or more words can be joined to form one word, e.g. *Kaffee + Maschine = Kaffeemaschine* (coffee machine), *mit + Arbeiter = Mitarbeiter* (colleague). When you read German, it helps to recognize the components that make up words.

NUMBER

Nouns, pronouns and verbs may be **singular**, when there's only one (e.g. *Maschine*), or **plural**, when there's more than one (e.g. *Maschinen*). The number of a noun affects the form of any accompanying determiner and adjective. When you're trying to work out which noun goes with a verb, it's important to recognize that they 'agree' in number: a verb in the singular goes with a singular noun, a plural verb with a plural noun.

GENDER

Each German noun has a particular gender:
masculine (*m*)   feminine (*f*)   neuter (*n*)

CASE

In German, the relationship between a noun or pronoun and other words in the sentence is partly indicated by its case. Case affects the form of nouns and any accompanying determiners and adjectives, as well as the form of pronouns. German has four cases: nominative (*nom.*), accusative (*acc.*), genitive (*gen.*) and dative (*dat.*). When a noun is given out of context, as in *Filaword*, in the *Glossary*, or in a dictionary, it's in the nominative case. The form and use of cases is explained below (➡ **P 97-98**).

CLAUSE

A sentence may consist of one or more clauses. A sentence like the following consists of a main clause (in bold), which contains the principal information, and a subordinate clause, which is dependent on the main clause. They're separated by a comma.

Wir haben Vertragswerkstätten, mit denen wir das Bundesgebiet abdecken.
(We have authorized service centres, with which we cover the Federal Republic.)

Nouns and Articles

Nouns

You can recognize nouns easily in written German, because they always begin with a capital letter. They make a good starting-point when you're trying to work out what a piece of German is about.

Compound Nouns

These may consist of two or more nouns, or a noun and some other type of word:

noun + noun:	Messe + Turm	= Messeturm
verb + noun:	pressen + Werk	= Preßwerk
adjective + noun:	fein + Blech	= Feinblech

Sometimes an element is inserted in the joining process:

- **-(e)s-** Kommunikations**z**entrum, Bund**es**republik
- **-(e)n-** Aktie**n**gesellschaft, Hypothek**en**bank

If two compound words have an element in common, this may be replaced by a hyphen in one of them (➡ P 9):

das Büro- und Kommunikations*zentrum* = das Büro*zentrum* und Kommunikations*zentrum*

*Grafik*karten, -monitore = *Grafik*karten, *Grafik*monitore

Plurals

In German it's not always easy to recognize whether a noun is singular or plural, since a plural can be formed in several different ways. The *Glossary* and dictionaries list the plural form after each noun. Here's a list of the main ways in which plurals are formed from the nominative form of singular nouns:

No change:	–	Partner, Unternehmen, Mitarbeiter
Added umlaut on vowel:	¨	Garten/Gärten, Mantel/Mäntel
Added ending:	– e	Kredit/e, Preis/e, Produkt/e
	– (e)n	(Most feminine nouns:) Zahl/en, Leistung/en, Gesellschaft/en Maschine/n, Messe/n ('Weak masculines' ➡ P 98:) Kollege/n, Franzose/n
	– s	(Especially words of English and French origin:) Büro/s, Meeting/s
	– er	Kind/er
Added ending and umlaut:	¨ e	Markt/Märkte, Platz/Plätze
	¨ er	Land/Länder, Mann/Männer

Nouns ending on **-in** or **-nis** double the final consonant in the plural.

Kundin/nen, Verhältnis/se

Some words of Latin origin have special ways of forming the plural, which usually involve modifying the ending.

Firma/Firmen, Konto/Konten

-n is added to the above plural forms in the **dative case**, except where the plural form ends in **-n** or **-s**. (➡ P 98)

Gender

Gender may be 'natural', e.g. Mann (*m*), Frau (*f*), Büro (*n*). You'll often find that a woman is distinguished from a man by the ending **-in**.

Verkäufer/Verkäufer**in**, Lehrer/Lehrer**in**, Kunde/Kund**in**

Usually, though, there's no rational reason for a noun having a particular gender. It therefore makes sense to learn each noun with the appropriate definite article *der* (*m*), *die* (*f*) or *das* (*n*). A few rules to help are:

Masculine

Days, Months, Seasons (➡ P 108)

Nouns with the ending	-er	(if denoting a person:) Gründer, Arbeiter
	-eur	Ingenieur, Exporteur
	-or	Motor, Projektor

Feminine

Nouns with the ending	-ei	Lackiererei, Gießerei
	-enz	Konferenz, Konkurrenz
	-heit, -keit	Sicherheit, Krankheit, Festigkeit
	-ie	Karosserie, Drogerie
	-ik	Technik, Fabrik
	-in	Sekretärin, Mitarbeiterin
	-schaft	Gesellschaft, Belegschaft
	-sion, -tion	Dimension, Information, Kommunikation
	-tät	Kapazität, Qualität
	-ung	Gründung, Werbung (➡ P 23)
	-ur	Reparatur, Kultur

Neuter

Other parts of speech used as nouns, e.g. infinitives (➡ P 102) — Tagen, Parken

Fractions except *die Hälfte* — Viertel, Zehntel

Nouns with the ending **-ment** — Sortiment, Instrument

Compound nouns have the gender of the last noun element:

das Heim + der Werker + der Markt + die Branche = die Heimwerkermarktbranche

Articles

A noun is usually preceded by an article or some other determiner (➡ P 99) which helps to show the role that noun is playing in the sentence. Articles vary according to gender, number and case. The **definite article** *der/die/das* corresponds to the English 'the', and the **indefinite article** *ein/eine/ein* to the English 'a'. As in English, there's no plural form of the indefinite article.

Masculine	Feminine	Neuter	Plural
der Mann **ein** Betrieb	**die** Frau **eine** Firma	**das** Mitglied **ein** Unternehmen	**die** Männer/Frauen/Mitglieder Betriebe/Firmen/Unternehmen

Note that *ein/eine/ein* can also mean 'one', e.g. *ein Mitglied* (one member). *Ein/eine/ein* has a negative form in German, with the same endings: *kein/keine/kein* (not a) (➡ P 16).

Cases

In the previous sections, nouns and determiners have been given in the **nominative case**, with gender variations. In sentences, the endings also vary according to the role of the noun in the sentence. The case of a noun is often the only indication as to the noun's role. It's also sometimes necessary to recognize case in order to find out which determiner goes with which noun. (➡ P 34)

Grammar

Forms

	Singular		
	Masculine	Feminine	Neuter
Nom.	der Mann ein Betrieb	die Frau eine Firma	das Mitglied ein Unternehmen
Acc.	den Mann einen Betrieb	die Frau eine Firma	das Mitglied ein Unternehmen
Gen.	des Mann(e)s eines Betrieb(e)s	der Frau einer Firma	des Mitglied(e)s eines Unternehmens
Dat.	dem Mann(e) einem Betrieb(e)	der Frau einer Firma	dem Mitglied(e) einem Unternehmen

	Plural
Nom.	die Männer/Frauen/Mitglieder Betriebe/Firmen/Unternehmen
Acc.	die Männer/Frauen/Mitglieder Betriebe/Firmen/Unternehmen
Gen.	der Männer/Frauen/Mitglieder Betriebe/Firmen/Unternehmen
Dat.	den Männern/Frauen/Mitgliedern Betrieben/Firmen/Unternehmen

The **accusative case** can be distinguished from the nominative in the **masculine singular** by the form of the determiner. In the feminine and neuter singular, the accusative and nominative forms are identical.

The **genitive case** is recognizable in the **masculine singular** and the **neuter singular** by the endings -es on the determiner and -(e)s on the noun.

The **dative case** is recognizable in the **masculine singular** and **neuter singular** by the ending -em on the determiner. Sometimes you may find an additional -e on the noun.

The **plural** of the determiners is the same for all genders. The **dative case** is recognizable by the noun ending -n, unless the nominative plural form ends in -n, as with most feminine nouns, or in -s, e.g. die Büros, den Büros.

Exceptions:

'**Weak masculine nouns**' have the ending -(e)n in all cases except the nominative singular. This group includes (masculine) nouns ending in -e in the nominative singular, and many (masculine) nouns of foreign origin, e.g. *Kollege, Franzose*. In the *Glossary*, these nouns are followed by: (wk m).

Adjectives and participles used as nouns always keep the adjectival case endings (➡ P 101). In the *Glossary* these are listed as follows:

Things/people: der, die, das Kleine (-n) *(the) little thing/one*
People: der/die Angestellte (-n), ein Angestellter *(the) employed person, employee*

When working out the case of a noun in the context of a sentence, you'll often need to check

1) the gender of the noun (see *Glossary*)
2) the plural form of the noun (see *Glossary*)
3) the case endings (check *Glossary* for 'weak masculines' and nouns formed from adjectives and past participles)
4) the overall sense of the sentence in context.

Common sense plays an important part! In the following sentence, the subject (*nominative*) is indistinguishable from the direct object (*accusative*) in terms of form alone. But it isn't hard to guess who/what produces who/what:

Rund die Hälfte (*f sing. acc.*) des Fahrzeugwertes stellt die Belegschaft (*f sing. nom.*) von BMW her.
(The workforce of BMW produces about half the value of a car.)

Main Uses

Nominative

- This is the case you'll find when nouns or pronouns are used in isolation, e.g. in a dictionary.
- In a sentence it usually marks the **subject** of the **finite verb** (➡ P 102), i.e. who or what does the action indicated by the verb. It agrees with that verb in number. (➡ P 34, 41)

    Banknoten (*f pl acc.*) darf (*3rd person sing.*) heutzutage nur **die Notenbank** (*f sing. nom.*) ausgeben.
    (Nowadays, only **the central bank** may issue banknotes.)

- It's used after the verbs *sein, werden, scheinen, bleiben, heißen*.

    Der Flughafen (*m sing. nom.*) ist **eine Stadt** (*f sing. nom.*).
    (The airport is **a town**.)

Accusative

- This marks the **direct object** of a verb, i.e. the person or thing receiving the 'direct action' of the verb. (➡ P 41)

    Die Firma Mannesmann Rexroth (*f sing. nom.*) erhielt von der Firma Phillips Petroleum (*preposition + f sing. dat.*) **den Auftrag** (*m sing. acc.*).
    (The company Mannesmann Rexroth received **the commission** from the company Phillips Petroleum.)

- It's used to indicate a length of time or point in time.

    82.000 Passagiere *jeden Tag*   (82,000 passengers *each day*)

- It's used after many prepositions. (➡ P 106)

Genitive

- Links nouns or noun phrases, usually corresponding to the English 'of'. (➡ P 17)

    Der Ruf (*m sing. nom.*) **der Stadt** (*f sing. gen.*) ist international.
    (The reputation **of the city** is international.)
    Die Fusion von MBB mit Daimler-Benz zu einem **der größten Industrieunternehmen** (*n pl gen.*) der Welt (*f sing. gen.*)
    (The merger of MBB with Daimler-Benz to form one **of the biggest conglomerates in the world**)

- It's used after a few prepositions. (➡ P 106)

Dative

- This is used to mark the **indirect object** of a transitive verb, i.e. the person 'to whom' (*dat.*) something (*acc.*) is given, shown etc. (➡ P 41)

    Düsseldorf Fashion House 2 (*n sing. nom.*) bietet **Mietern** (*m pl dat.*) und **Kunden** (*m pl dat.*) die technische Voraussetzung (*f sing. acc.*).
    (Düsseldorf Fashion House 2 offers **tenants** and **customers** the technical prerequisite.)

- Occasionally you'll find it used as an equivalent to the English '*for* someone'.

    ..., daß *diesem Kunden* ein Container auf den Hof der Fabrik gestellt werden soll.
    (... that a container should be delivered to the loading bay of the factory *for this customer*.)

- It's used after many prepositions. (➡ P 106)

Grammar

DETERMINERS AND PRONOUNS

A determiner – such as the definite and indefinite articles (➡ **P 97**) – precedes a noun and helps to show its role in the sentence. A number of determiners can be used as pronouns. Whereas a determiner is followed (immediately, or at the end of the 'noun phrase') by a noun, a pronoun stands in place of a noun which is obvious from the context.

DEMONSTRATIVES

DER/DIE/DAS

The German equivalent of 'this' and 'that' is very often *der/die/das*. The demonstrative pronoun usually denotes something that has already been mentioned. The pronoun *das* may refer back to a whole idea. The form of the demonstrative pronoun differs from the definite article in the genitive singular and plural and in the dative plural.

Pronoun	Singular			Plural
	Masc.	Fem.	Neut.	
Nom.	der	die	das	die
Acc.	den	die	das	die
Gen.	dessen	deren	dessen	deren/derer
Dat.	dem	der	dem	denen

Kurze Meetings (pl), **das** ist: ...
(*Short meetings*, **that** is: ...)
*Wir haben in Deutschland eine nüchterne Mentalität. **Das** wirkt sich in der Werbung aus.*
(*We have a sober mentality in Germany. **That** affects advertising.*)

DIESER/DIESE/DIES(ES)

This demonstrative, equivalent to 'this', can be used as a determiner or pronoun. The forms are the same for both.

Determiner/Pronoun	Singular			Plural
	Masc.	Fem.	Neut.	
Nom.	dieser	diese	dies(es)	diese
Acc.	diesen	diese	dies(es)	diese
Gen.	dieses	dieser	dieses	dieser
Dat.	diesem	dieser	diesem	diesen

Determiner: *Ich bin seit 18 Jahren in **diesem** Unternehmen* (n sing. dat.).
(*I've been in **this** company for 18 years.*)
Pronoun: *Wir brechen die Nocken* (pl), *um zu sehen, wie weit **diese** (pl) weißerstarrt sind.*
(*We break the cams in order to see how far **these** are chilled.*)

SOME OTHER DETERMINERS

These determiners have the same endings as *dieser/diese/dieses*:

jener/jene/jenes (that, pl those; in contrast to *dieser/diese/dieses*)
jeder/jede/jedes (every)
welcher/welche/welches (which)
solcher/solche/solches (such)

RELATIVE PRONOUNS

These have the same form as the demonstrative pronouns *der/die/das*. They introduce **relative clauses** (➡ **P 107**) and are equivalent to the English 'who' or 'which'. (➡ **P 41, 56**)

*Man redet über **den** Urlaub, **der** vielleicht gerade bevorsteht.*
(*You talk about the holiday **which** may be coming up.*)

Sometimes you may find the alternative relative pronouns *welcher/welche/welches*, which have the same endings as *dieser/diese/dieses*.

*Unser langjähriger Service, **welcher** bundesweit im Einsatz ist, ...*
(*Our well-established service network, **which** covers the whole of the Federal Republic ...*)

A relative clause may also be introduced by *was*, following a demonstrative pronoun in the previous clause (equivalent to the English 'that which'). (➡ **P 76**)

*... den Kernteil **dessen, was** wir unsere 'Corporate Culture' nennen*
(*... the core of **what** we call our corporate culture*)

PERSONAL PRONOUNS

Their form varies according to person, number, and case. Notice that the German equivalent of the English second-person pronoun 'you' has two forms: the familiar *du* (*sing.*) and *ihr* (*pl*), and the polite *Sie* (*sing.* and *pl*). The polite *Sie* has the same pronoun forms and verb forms as the 3rd person plural *sie* (they).

	Person	Nom.	Acc.	Dat.
Sing.	I	ich	mich	mir
	you (familiar)	du	dich	dir
	you (polite)	Sie	Sie	Ihnen
	he/it	er	ihn	ihm
	she/it	sie	sie	ihr
	it	es	es	ihm
Plural	we	wir	uns	uns
	you (familiar)	ihr	euch	euch
	you (polite)	Sie	Sie	Ihnen
	they	sie	sie	ihnen

The genitive forms are hardly ever used.

The polite *Sie* is always spelt with a capital, and the familiar *du* and *ihr* are spelt with a capital in letters. Other pronouns (including *ich*) are written small.

A pronoun is the same gender as the noun it refers to, so the pronoun referring to *der Computer* will be *er*, the pronoun referring to *die Maschine* will be *sie*.

*Der Wagen ist fertig. Auf Herz und Nieren wird **er** nochmals geprüft.*
(*The car is finished. **It** is tested again down to the last detail.*)

When referring to things, a pronoun used with a preposition is generally replaced by the prefix *da-* or *dar-* before the preposition: *dafür* (for it/them), *damit* (with it/them) *daran* (on it/them), *darin* (in it/them), etc. (➡ **P 50, 106**)

SPECIAL USES OF ES

When you see the pronoun *es*, you can't always assume that it refers to a thing (or person) mentioned earlier:

Es may refer back to a whole idea, like the demonstrative pronoun *das*.

*Sind Sie zufrieden, sagen Sie **es** weiter.*
(*If you're satisfied, pass **it** on.*)

Grammar

Es gibt (past tense: *es gab*) is generally equivalent to 'there is/are' (there was/were). (➡ **P 15**)

Wie viele Messeplätze *gibt es*?
(How many trade-fair centres *are there*?)
Da *es* in diesem Unternehmen erhebliche Probleme *gab*, ...
(Since *there were* considerable problems in this company, ...)

Es may be used as a stopgap subject at the beginning of the sentence, so that the 'real' subject can be postponed for emphasis. (➡ **P 70**)

Es vergeht manchmal *ein Jahr*, bis der Kunde den Auftrag plaziert.
(*A year* sometimes goes by before the customer places the order.)
Es wird nicht mehr unbedingt *der Preis* entscheidend sein.
(*The price* will no longer necessarily be decisive. OR *It* will no longer necessarily be *the price* which is decisive.)

Es may be used as a stopgap subject in the main clause of a sentence in which the 'real' subject is a following *daß* clause or infinitive clause. (➡ **P 108**)

Es war nötig, *Profit Centers zu schaffen*.
(*It* was necessary *to create profit centres*.)

Es may be used as the subject in some impersonal constructions.

Es geht jetzt für uns *darum, das auszugleichen*.
(For us *the issue* now *is* to make up for that.)
Es handelt sich um 1500 Produkte.
(*We're talking about* 1500 products.)

Man

This pronoun is used to refer to people in general. It's equivalent to the English 'one' or 'you' in the sense of 'people in general', or sometimes to 'we'. *Man* is only used in the nominative case. The accusative form is *einen*, and the dative *einem* – not to be confused with the forms of the far more frequent indefinite article.

Es gelingt *einem* am Anfang nicht zu unterscheiden, ...
(Initially *one* does not succeed in distinguishing ...)

Reflexive Pronouns

Some verbs need a **reflexive pronoun**, which refers to the subject of the clause, as in the English 'I wash myself', 'you wash yourself' etc. German has more reflexive verbs than English. In the *Glossary* **reflexive verbs** are given in the infinitive form preceded by the pronoun *sich*. The pronoun can be accusative or dative, and it changes according to the person. Notice that the pronouns are the same as for the personal pronoun, except with *er/sie/es/man* and *sie/Sie*. (➡ **P 38**)

Infinitive	*sich konzentrieren*/acc.		*sich erlauben*/dat.	
ich	konzentriere	**mich**	erlaube	**mir**
du	konzentrierst	**dich**	erlaubst	**dir**
er/sie/es/man	konzentriert	**sich**	erlaubt	**sich**
wir	konzentrieren	**uns**	erlauben	**uns**
ihr	konzentriert	**euch**	erlaubt	**euch**
sie/Sie	konzentrieren	**sich**	erlauben	**sich**

In England *konzentrieren* **wir uns** auf Bügeleisen. (sich konzentrieren)
(In the UK **we** *are concentrating* on irons.)
Wir *bedanken* **uns** für Ihre Anfrage. (sich bedanken)
(**We** *thank you/are grateful* for your enquiry.)
Das kann *sich* keine Werft *erlauben*. (sich erlauben)
(**No shipyard** can *permit* that.)

Note that the pronoun may be a long way away from the verb in subordinate clauses (➡ **P 107**).

Englands Bausparkassen blicken auf die Chancen, **die *sich*** für sie in dem Binnenmarkt *bieten*. (sich bieten)
(Britain's building societies are looking to the opportunities **which** present ***themselves*** for them in the internal market.)

Possessives

These express 'possession', i.e. they indicate who or what somebody or something belongs to. The basic forms are:

Person	Singular	Person	Plural
my	mein	our	unser
your (familiar)	dein	your (familiar)	euer
your (polite)	Ihr	your (polite)	Ihr
his/its	sein	their	ihr
her/its	ihr		
its	sein		

Possessive determiners add the same endings as the indefinite article *ein/eine/ein*, and agree with the following noun in gender, number and case. For *sein*, the endings are:

	Singular		
	m	f	n
Nom.	sein Betrieb	seine Firma	sein Unternehmen
Acc.	seinen Betrieb	seine Firma	sein Unternehmen
Gen.	seines Betrieb(e)s	seiner Firma	seines Unternehmens
Dat.	seinem Betrieb(e)	seiner Firma	seinem Unternehmen

	Plural
Nom.	seine Betriebe/Firmen/Unternehmen
Acc.	seine Betriebe/Firmen/Unternehmen
Gen.	seiner Betriebe/Firmen/Unternehmen
Dat.	seinen Betrieben/Firmen/Unternehmen

Hamburg mit *seinem* über 800 Jahre alten *Hafen* (*m sing. dat.*)
(Hamburg with *its* port, which is over 800 years old)
99 Prozent *unserer* Aussteller (*m pl gen.*)
(99 per cent *of our* exhibitors)

Adjectives and Adverbs

Adjectives

The form of adjectives varies depending on the role of the noun they describe. Luckily, when you're reading German it's usually clear which adjective goes with which noun without looking at its ending. However, sometimes the ending of the adjective helps to show what role the noun is fulfilling, so it's a good idea to familiarize yourself with the following tables. The underlying principle is, that a noun should be preceded by an indicator of its case, a role which has to be fulfilled by the adjective if there's no determiner or if the determiner has no case ending (e.g. *ein*). (➡ **P 31**)

No Ending

An adjective has its basic form when it doesn't appear in front of a noun.

Der Ruf der Stadt *ist international*.
(*The reputation* of the city *is international*.)

Endings

When an adjective precedes the noun it qualifies, it has one of the following endings: *-e, -em, -en, -er, -es*. The endings vary depending on whether there's a determiner, and if so, which determiner:

1) Determiner + Adjective + Noun

a) After the following determiners there are only two possible adjective endings:

der/die/das
dieser/diese/dieses
jener/jene/jenes
jeder/jede/jedes
welcher/welche/welches

	Sing.			Pl
	m	f	n	
Nom.	-e	-e	-e	-en
Acc.	-en	-e	-e	-en
Gen.	-en	-en	-en	-en
Dat.	-en	-en	-en	-en

	Singular		
	m	f	n
Nom.	der lange Kongreß	die lange Tagung	das lange Seminar
Acc.	den langen Kongreß	die lange Tagung	das lange Seminar
Gen.	des langen Kongresses	der langen Tagung	des langen Seminars
Dat.	dem langen Kongreß	der langen Tagung	dem langen Seminar

	Plural
Nom.	die langen Kongresse/Tagungen/Seminare
Acc.	die langen Kongresse/Tagungen/Seminare
Gen.	der langen Kongresse/Tagungen/Seminare
Dat.	den langen Kongressen/Tagungen/Seminaren

b) After the following determiners, there are three deviations from the endings given under (a):

ein/eine/ein
kein/keine/kein
possessive determiners
(mein/meine/mein etc.)

	Sing.			Pl
	m	f	n	
Nom.	-er	-e	-es	-en
Acc.	-en	-e	-es	-en
Gen.	-en	-en	-en	-en
Dat.	-en	-en	-en	-en

m sing. nom. ein lang**er** Kongreß
n sing. nom. ein lang**es** Seminar
n sing. acc. ein lang**es** Seminar

2) Adjective + Noun

The adjective here fulfils a role equivalent to that of a determiner, and adds the same endings as *dieser/diese/dieses*, except that the **genitive singular masculine and neuter** add *-en* instead of *-es*.

	Sing.			Pl
	m	f	n	
Nom.	-er	-e	-es	-e
Acc.	-en	-e	-es	-e
Gen.	-en	-er	-en	-er
Dat.	-em	-er	-em	-en

	Singular		
	m	f	n
Nom.	langer Kongreß	lange Tagung	langes Seminar
Acc.	langen Kongreß	lange Tagung	langes Seminar
Gen.	langen Kongresses	langer Tagung	langen Seminar(e)s
Dat.	langem Kongreß	langer Tagung	langem Seminar

	Plural
Nom.	lange Kongresse/Tagungen/Seminare
Acc.	lange Kongresse/Tagungen/Seminare
Gen.	langer Kongresse/Tagungen/Seminare
Dat.	langen Kongressen/Tagungen/Seminaren

Compare: das *Deutsche* Business-Magazin (*n sing. nom./acc.*)
Deutsches Business-Magazin (*n sing. nom./acc.*)
mit d**er** modernst**en** Konferenztechnik (*f sing. dat.*)
mit modernst**er** Konferenztechnik (*f sing. dat.*)

Adjectives used as Nouns

Adjectives (and also present and past participles ➡ **P 103**) may be used as nouns, e.g. *der Kleine* (the small one). The endings of adjectival nouns are like those an adjective would have if it were followed by a noun. The gender depends on the noun implicitly referred to. (➡ **P 79**)

der Kleine (Mann, Computer etc.)
die Kleine (Frau, Schreibmaschine etc.)
das Kleine (Kind, Unternehmen etc.)
die Kleinen (Kinder, Computer etc.)

A neuter adjectival noun may indicate an abstract quality, e.g. *das Schwierigste* (the most difficult thing).

Adjectival Phrases

Descriptive details about a noun may appear between the determiner and the noun itself, where English would use a relative clause. (➡ **P 63**)

mit *einem* im europäischen Vergleich nicht sehr zuverlässigen *Transportsystem*
(with *a transport system* that is **not very reliable in comparison with the rest of Europe**)

Adverbs

The form of adverbs doesn't change. Most adjectives can be used as adverbs, in which case they have no added ending.

Adjective: ein *typisches* Produkt (a *typical* product)
Adverb: ein *typisch* englisches Produkt (a *typically* English product)

Comparatives and Superlatives

Many adjectives and adverbs can be graded, as in the adjectives 'good - better - best' and the adverbs 'well - better - best'. The **comparative** form adds *-er*, and the superlative form *-(e)st* to the basic form of the adjective/adverb. The main vowel of the basic form often adds an umlaut, and a few forms are irregular. (➡ **P 31, 68**)

Adjectives

	Comparative		Superlative
schnell (fast)	schneller		schnellste
wichtig (important)	wichtiger		wichtigste
lang (long)	länger		längste
neu (new)	neuer		neu(e)ste
groß (big)	größer	der/die/das	größte
hoch (high)	höher		höchste
nah (near)	näher		nächste
gut (good)	besser		beste
viel (much/many)	**mehr**		meiste

The comparative and superlative forms have the usual adjective endings. The equivalent to the comparative word 'than' is *als*. (➡ **P 31, 52**)

ein wesentlich *härterer* Markt (*m sing. nom.*) als ...
(a much *tougher* market than ...)
in den *namhaftesten* deutschen Fernsehzeitschriften (*f pl dat.*)
(in the *best*-known German TV-guides)
Ein Konferenzzentrum mit *modernster* Konferenztechnik
(A conference centre with *extremely modern* conference technology)

In a comparison expressing equality, you'll find *so ... wie* (as ... as).

Hamburg ist etwa *so* groß *wie* München, Frankfurt und Düsseldorf zusammen.
(Hamburg is about *as* big *as* Munich, Frankfurt and Düsseldorf put together.)

Adverbs

The comparative form of adverbs is the same as the basic comparative form of adjectives. The superlative form is preceded by *am* and has the ending *-en*: *am längsten, am ältesten* etc.

> Das ist hier sehr viel *besser* präsentiert als auf einem Messestand.
> (It's presented far *better* here than at a fair stand.)
> die Auswahl der *am besten* geeigneten Lieferanten
> (the choice of the suppliers which are *best* suited)

Note the irregular adverb *gern, lieber, am liebsten* (like doing, *prefer* doing, *like* doing *most of all*) (➡ **P 35**):

> Die Hanseatinnen tragen *lieber* Mischware.
> (Women in the north *prefer* to wear mixed fabrics.)

Verbs

In the *Glossary* and in dictionaries you'll usually find a verb listed in its **infinitive** form. This consists of a **stem** and the ending *-en* or, in a few cases, *-n*, e.g. *arbeiten, schreiben, entwickeln*.

The main verb of a sentence varies according to:
- the person and number of the **subject** of the verb
- the **tense** of the verb, i.e. the time of the action or process indicated by the verb (past, present, future)
- whether it's **active** or **passive**
- the **mood**, i.e. whether it indicates a fact (**indicative**), a possibility or reported action (**subjunctive**), or a command (**imperative**)

The part of the verb which agrees with the subject of the sentence in person and number is called **finite**. Verbs may also appear in **non-finite** forms:
- the **infinitive**, equivalent to '(to) work' '(to) write' '(to) develop': *arbeiten, schreiben, entwickeln*
- the **present participle**, equivalent to 'work*ing*', 'writ*ing*', 'develop*ing*': *arbeitend, schreibend, entwickelnd*
- the **past participle**, equivalent to 'work*ed*', 'writt*en*', 'develop*ed*': *gearbeitet, geschrieben, entwickelt*

Weak, Strong, and Irregular Verbs

Most German verbs follow a **regular** pattern. These '**weak**' verbs simply add certain endings to the stem to create the various finite forms, and they add the prefix *ge-* and the ending *-et* to form the past participle.

> *arbeiten* (infinitive)
> *er arbeitet* (3rd person sing., present tense)
> *er arbeitete* (3rd person sing., past tense)
> *gearbeitet* (past participle)

'**Strong**' verbs (including many of the most common verbs) change the vowel of the stem in some forms, much like English verbs such as 'write' - 'wrote' - 'written' (➡ **P 16**). Their past participles have the prefix *ge-* and the ending *-en*, and usually a vowel change:

> *schreiben* (infinitive)
> *er schreibt* (3rd person sing., present tense)
> *er schrieb* (3rd person sing., past tense)
> *geschrieben* (past participle)

The *Glossary* lists any vowel change in the 2nd and 3rd person singular of the present tense in brackets, then the vowel of the simple past tense, and finally that of the past participle (➡ **P 43**):

> helfen (i), a, o = helfen (infinitive), hilft (present), half (past), geholfen (past participle)
> schreiben, ie, ie = schreiben (infinitive), schrieb (past), geschrieben (past participle)

A few verbs follow neither pattern, e.g. *gehen - ging - gegangen, bringen - brachte - gebracht*. Their main forms are listed in the *Glossary*. The most important are the following two special groups of verbs:
- the verbs *haben* (to have), *sein* (to be), *werden* (to become), which exist as ordinary verbs (➡ **P 8**) and which also act as **auxiliary verbs** combining with other verbs to form compound tenses.
- the six **modal auxiliary verbs**, which generally need a second verb to complete their meaning: *dürfen* (to be allowed to), *können* (to be able to), *mögen* (to like to), *müssen* (to have to), *sollen* (to be supposed to), *wollen* (to want to).

Separable and Inseparable Verbs

In German it's possible to combine verbs with a variety of different prefixes. These prefixes may consist of syllables which remain attached to the stem in all forms (**inseparable verbs**) or they may consist of prepositions or other types of word which separate off in some contexts (**separable verbs**) (➡ **P 14**). A few prefixes (e.g. *um-, unter-*) may be inseparable or separable.

Inseparable prefixes: *be-, emp-, ent-, er-, ge-, ver-, zer-*.
> *be*festigen, *emp*finden, *ent*wickeln, *er*finden, *ge*lingen, *ver*kaufen, *zer*stören

Separable prefixes: e.g. *ab-, an-, auf-, aus-, bei-, ein-, los-, mit-, nach-, vor-, weg-, zu-* . Other prepositions, as well as nouns, adjectives, adverbs, participles and infinitives can also act as separable prefixes.
> *an*kommen, *ein*kaufen, *zu*schicken, *fertig*stellen, *ski*fahren

The *Glossary* indicates all verbs that are separable (*sep.*). The prefix remains attached to the stem when the verb is in the participle or infinitive forms. The syllable *-ge-* is inserted between the prefix and the stem in the past participle (e.g. *angekommen*). If there is only one verb in a main clause, the prefix separates and appears at the end.

> Die Hälfte des Fahrzeugwertes *stellt* die Belegschaft von BMW *her*.
> (The workforce of BMW *produces* half the value of a car.)

When a separable verb appears with an auxiliary or modal verb, or in a subordinate clause (➡ **P 107**), the prefix is attached to the stem.

> Die Pressen werden in Pressenstraßen *aufgestellt*.
> (The presses are *set up* in press lines.)
> Portex ist eine Firma, die Einwegprodukte *herstellt*.
> (Portex is a company which *produces* single-use products.)

Reflexive Verbs (➡ P 100)

Haben, Sein, Werden

Infinitive		haben	sein	werden
Present tense	ich	habe	bin	werde
	du	hast	bist	wirst
	er/sie/es/man	hat	ist	wird
	wir	haben	sind	werden
	ihr	habt	seid	werdet
	sie/Sie	haben	sind	werden
Past tense	ich	hatte	war	wurde
	du	hattest	warst	wurdest
	er/sie/es/man	hatte	war	wurde
	wir	hatten	waren	wurden
	ihr	hattet	wart	wurdet
	sie/Sie	hatten	waren	wurden
Past participle		gehabt	gewesen	geworden worden (*for passive*)

Haben helps to form the perfect and pluperfect of the majority of verbs.
Sein helps to form the perfect and pluperfect of some verbs (➡ **P 104**), and is used to form the perfect and pluperfect passive forms.
Werden helps to form the future (present tense of *werden* and infinitive of another verb) and the passive (*werden* and past participle of another verb).

Modal Verbs

Infinitive	*dürfen*	*können*	*mögen*	*müssen*	*sollen*	*wollen*
Present tense						
ich	darf	kann	mag	muß	soll	will
du	darfst	kannst	magst	mußt	sollst	willst
er/sie/es/man	darf	kann	mag	muß	soll	will
wir	dürfen	können	mögen	müssen	sollen	wollen
ihr	dürft	könnt	mögt	müßt	sollt	wollt
sie/Sie	dürfen	können	mögen	müssen	sollen	wollen
Past tense						
ich	durfte	konnte	mochte	mußte	sollte	wollte
du	durftest	konntest	mochtest	mußtest	solltest	wolltest
er/sie/es/man	durfte	konnte	mochte	mußte	sollte	wollte
wir	durften	konnten	mochten	mußten	sollten	wollten
ihr	durftet	konntet	mochtet	mußtet	solltet	wolltet
sie/Sie	durften	konnten	mochten	mußten	sollten	wollten

The modal verbs are generally completed by the infinitive of another verb, which normally comes at the end of a main clause, or just before the modal verb in a subordinate clause. (➡ **P 33, 107**)

Man **muß** das Vertriebsprogramm auf das einzelne Land *ausrichten*.
(You **have to** *gear* your sales range to the individual country.)
Viele Schadstoffe, die früher in den Boden *gelangen* **konnten**, **müssen** heute *entfernt werden*.
(Many pollutants which **could** in the past *get* into the ground, now **have to** *be removed*.)

The perfect tense of a modal verb is usually formed with its infinitive rather than the past participle:

Der *hat* sich nicht um den Vertrieb kümmern **können**.
(He *was* not **able** to deal with sales.)

Note that *müssen* with a negation is usually not equivalent to 'must not', which would be *darf nicht*, but to 'need not'.

Das *muß nicht* sein.
(That is *not necessary*.)

Infinitives

Infinitives (➡ **P 102**) may be used to form the future tenses (➡ **P 104**) and to complete the meaning of modal verbs. They also often appear in infinitive clauses (➡ **P 108**). Together with the verb *sein* and *zu*, an infinitive can be used to express obligation (equivalent to 'must' or 'should') and possibility (equivalent to 'can') (➡ **P 71, 72**).

Ihre Zahlung *ist* innerhalb von 14 Tagen *zu leisten*.
(Your payment *is to be made* within 14 days.)
Dann *waren* von England nur konservative Dinge *zu erwarten*.
(Only conservative things *were to be expected* from the UK.)

Present Participles

These are recognizable by the ending *-(e)nd*. They're used far less in German than in English, as there's no equivalent to the 'continuous tenses' (e.g. 'I am work**ing**') and they're rarely used as verbs elsewhere.

Gurgelnd versinkt die Autokarosserie in einem Bad aus Lack.
(*Gurgling*, the chassis disappears in a bath of paint.)

You'll mainly find present participles used as adjectives.

Über den Tee das *sprudelnde, kochende* Wasser gießen.
(Pour the *bubbling, boiling* water over the tea.)

Past Participles

You can recognize most past participles by the syllable *ge-* in front of the verb stem, and the ending *-(e)t* (weak verbs) or *-en* (strong verbs). Strong verbs may have a vowel change compared with the infinitive. If the verb has a separable prefix, *-ge-* goes between the prefix and the stem.

gefüll**t**, **ge**trenn**t**, ab**ge**bilde**t**, her**ge**stell**t**, an**ge**schraub**t**, ein**ge**setz**t**
gefall**en**, **ge**geb**en**, **ge**stieg**en**, ab**ge**lad**en**, zu**ge**nomm**en**, an**ge**hob**en**

There's no *ge-* added to verbs that have an inseparable prefix.

*ent*wickel**t**, *er*zeug**t**, *ge*hör**t**, *ver*arbeite**t**, *zer*stör**t**
*be*rat**en**, *emp*fang**en**, *ge*scheh**en**, *ver*lor**en**

With strong verbs that have an inseparable prefix and no vowel change, the past participle can't be distinguished from the infinitive (e.g. *beraten, empfangen, geschehen*).

Verbs ending on *-ieren* – all of which are weak – also have no *ge-*.

exportier**t**, kritisier**t**, integrier**t**, passier**t**

As in English, past participles are used in compound forms of verbs such as the perfect and the passive (➡ **P 104**). They're also used as adjectives (with the usual adjective endings) to describe things or people. (➡ **P 21**)

eine komplett *ausgestattete* Stadt (a completely *equipped* town)

Tenses

German has six tenses in the indicative mood (active):

present and **past** (simple tenses)
perfect and **pluperfect** (compound tenses, i.e. using an auxiliary verb)
future and **future perfect** (compound tenses)

German has no 'continuous' tenses like English (e.g. 'he **is** buy**ing**', 'he has **been** buy**ing**').

Present

Weak verbs only add personal endings to the stem. **Strong verbs** have personal endings added to the stem, and often a vowel change in the 2nd and 3rd person singular.

	Weak verbs		Strong verbs	
	kaufen	*arbeiten*	*fahren*	*sehen*
ich	kaufe	arbeite	fahre	sehe
du	kaufst	arbeitest	fährst	siehst
er/sie/es/man	kauft	arbeitet	fährt	sieht
wir	kaufen	arbeiten	fahren	sehen
ihr	kauft	arbeitet	fahrt	seht
sie/Sie	kaufen	arbeiten	fahren	sehen

When reading German, the main endings you need to recognize are the 3rd person singular *-(e)t* and the 3rd person plural *-(e)n*. (➡ **P 19**)

Use of the present tense is similar to its use in English (e.g. 'he buys'): it describes states, present actions or events, and habitual or timeless occurrences. It may, however, sometimes be equivalent to

– the English 'continuous' present tense (e.g. 'he is buying')

In England *konzentrieren* wir uns auf Bügeleisen.
(In the UK we *are concentrating* on irons.)

- the English perfect tense, when it refers to a past state, event or action that continues into the present

> Ich *bin* seit 18 Jahren in diesem Unternehmen.
> (I *have been* in this company for 18 years.)

- the English future tense

> Wenn Sie etwas reklamieren möchten, *hilft* Ihnen unser Telefon-Service-Büro.
> (If you would like to query something, our telephone service office *will help* you.)

Past

The form of the past tense (e.g. 'he bought') depends on the type of verb. **Weak verbs** add *-(e)t* to the stem, followed by personal endings. **Strong verbs** have a vowel change and add personal endings.

	Weak verbs		Strong verbs	
	kaufen	*arbeiten*	*fahren*	*sehen*
ich	kauf*te*	arbeit*ete*	fuhr	sah
du	kauf*test*	arbeit*etest*	fuhr*st*	sah*st*
er/sie/es/man	kauf*te*	arbeit*ete*	fuhr	sah
wir	kauf*ten*	arbeit*eten*	fuhr*en*	sah*en*
ihr	kauf*tet*	arbeit*etet*	fuhr*t*	sah*t*
sie/Sie	kauf*ten*	arbeit*eten*	fuhr*en*	sah*en*

The main use of the past tense in German is to relate events, states or facts that were completed in the past. (➡ **P 43**)

> Wir *brauchten* einen Slogan.
> (We *needed* a slogan.)
> Im Mai 1988 *erschienen* schon Prospekte.
> (Already in May 1988 brochures *appeared*.)

Perfect

The perfect tense (e.g. 'he has bought') is formed with the present tense of *haben* or *sein* and the past participle of another verb.

> er/sie/es/man **hat ge**kauft   er/sie/es/ man **ist ge**gangen
> sie/Sie **haben ge**sehen   sie/Sie **sind ge**wesen

Most verbs form the perfect with *haben*. Some verbs that cannot take an accusative object ('intransitive verbs') form the perfect with *sein*:

- *sein, werden, bleiben*
- verbs of movement, e.g. *gehen, fahren, ankommen*
- verbs indicating a change of state, e.g. *vergehen, verschwinden*
- some impersonal verbs, e.g. *einfallen, gelingen, geschehen, passieren*

In the *Glossary* you'll find an asterisk against verbs which form the perfect tense with *sein*.

The perfect tense is often used in German to describe a past action, event or state that is directly relevant to the present, similar to its use in English. But it's also used where English demands the past tense. It may be interchangeable with the past tense, and sometimes both are used with no difference in meaning. (➡ **P 37, 43**)

> Nach 1945 *gab* es die Vorstellung, das Dach muß sehr stark werden. Da *haben* jedoch die Briten *eingegriffen* und *haben gesagt*, „No".
> (After 1945 there *was* the idea that the umbrella organization must become very strong. But at that point the British *intervened* and *said* "No".)

Pluperfect

The pluperfect tense (e.g. 'he had bought') is formed with the past tense of *haben* or *sein* (see **Perfect** for verbs with *sein*) and the past participle of another verb. (➡ **P 43**)

> er/sie/es/man **hatte ge**kauft   er/sie/es/man **war ge**gangen
> sie/Sie **hatten ge**sehen   sie/Sie **waren ge**wesen

> Diese Plattformen *hatten* sich *abgesenkt*, und es bestand die Gefahr ...
> (These platforms *had subsided* and there was the danger ...)

Future

The **future tense** (e.g. 'he will buy') is formed with the present tense of *werden* plus the infinitive of another verb. It's used to refer to an event or action in the future, or for a prediction.

> Ich glaube, daß die Nachfrage nach dem Deutschen *wachsen wird*.
> (I think that the demand for German *will grow*.)

Don't confuse the future with the passive, which you're likely to find more often in general business contexts. (➡ **P 38**)

The **future perfect tense** (e.g. 'he **will have** bought', *er wird gekauft haben*) is formed with the present tense of *werden*, a past participle, and the infinitive of *haben/sein*). It's roughly equivalent to English, though less frequent.

Passive

The **passive**, indicating that 'something is (being) done' (e.g. 'the goods are being bought'), is formed with the auxiliary verb *werden* – in any of the six tenses – and the past participle of another verb. The past participle of *werden* when it's used in the compound tenses of the passive is *worden*.

The passive is used frequently in written German, especially when the agent ('doer' of the action) is left unspecified, as in the description of (e.g. industrial) processes. (➡ **P 12, 22**)

> Das Material *wird* bei Eingang auf Fehler *begutachtet*.
> (The material *is inspected* for defects on arrival.)
> Anschließend *wurden* die Plattformen hydraulisch *angehoben*.
> (Then the platforms *were raised* hydraulically.)
> ... damit das Material einwandfrei *verarbeitet werden* kann.
> (... so that the material *can be processed* smoothly.)

The **perfect passive** is formed with the perfect tense of *werden* (consisting of the present tense of *sein* and the past participle *worden*) and the past participle of another verb. (➡ **P 84**)

> Die Firma Lydmet *ist* von unserem Außendienst *besichtigt worden*.
> (Lydmet *was inspected* by our field staff.)
> Ich *bin* hier schnell *befördert worden*.
> (I *was promoted* quickly here.)

Distinguish this from the perfect tense of *werden* (to become).

> Nach zehn Jahren *bin* ich Partner *geworden*.
> (After ten years I *became* a partner.)

Note that if an agent is specified (e.g. **by** our field staff), that agent is introduced with *von* (*von unserem Außendienst*).

Sometimes you may find the passive used without a subject, where this is obvious or unimportant, or the clause may begin with an impersonal *es*.

> Danach *wird geschliffen*.
> (After that the surface *is rubbed* down.)
> Man hat sich davon überzeugt, daß dort richtig *gegossen werden* kann.
> (We ascertained that *casting can be done* properly there.)
> Es *wird* auf dem deutschen Markt *eingekauft*.
> (We buy in the German market.)

SUBJUNCTIVE

Most written and spoken German (like English) is in the **indicative mood**. The **subjunctive mood** (e.g. 'If he were to buy') is used in some contexts to express **possibility** or to indicate that the writer or speaker is **reporting** something stated or written by someone else. The subjunctive tends to be confined to formal written German, except for some common uses with modal verbs.

FORMS

The **subjunctive I** (often called 'present subjunctive') is formed from the stem of the verb (without vowel changes) and the same personal endings as the past indicative of weak verbs, e.g. *er habe/könne/fahre*). The sole exception is *sein*.

The **subjunctive II** (often called 'past subjunctive') varies depending on the type of verb. With **weak verbs** it's identical to the past indicative, e.g. *er kaufte/arbeitete*. With most **strong verbs**, the subjunctive II has the same stem as the past indicative, with an added umlaut on **a**, **o**, **u**, and the same personal endings as the past indicative of weak verbs, e.g. *er führe/sähe*. The subjunctives I and II of the auxiliary verbs *sein*, *haben* and *werden* are used to form compound tenses of other verbs.

The subjunctive II form of *werden* is equivalent to the English 'would' (e.g. 'I would buy').

	Subjunctive I	Subj. II		Subjunctive with *werden*
	other verbs	strong verbs		all verbs
	sein	müssen	fahren	arbeiten
ich	sei	müsse	führe	würde arbeiten
du	seist	müssest	führest	würdest arbeiten
er/sie/es/man	sei	müsse	führe	würde arbeiten
wir	seien	müssen	führen	würden arbeiten
ihr	seiet	müsset	führet	würdet arbeiten
sie/Sie	seien	müssen	führen	würden arbeiten

The main verbs you need to be able to recognize in their subjunctive forms are the auxiliary verbs *haben*, *sein* and *werden* and the modal verbs.

MODAL VERBS

These are often used in the subjunctive form. Notice the special role often played by the subjunctive II form of *dürfen*.

Es *könnte* beispielsweise sein, daß ein Ventil laut ist.
(For instance, it *could* be that a valve is noisy.)
Den Einfluß *möchten* wir ausnutzen.
(We *would like to* take advantage of that influence.)
Der Tee *sollte* zwischen 4 und 5 Minuten ziehen.
(The tea *ought to* brew for 4 to 5 minutes.)
Die Engländer *dürften* mit den belgischen und holländischen Mitgliedern irgendwo ähnlich stehen.
(The British *probably* stand roughly on the same level as the Belgian and Dutch members.)

CONDITIONAL STATEMENTS

The subjunctive can be used to speculate about what **would** be, or **would have** been if ... . (➡ P 86)

Wir *könnten* heute in viele Länder nicht exportieren, *hätten* wir nicht vor vielen Jahren bereits unsere Fabriken dort aufgebaut.
(We *would not* be able to export to many countries today, *had* we not set up our factories there many years ago.)
Sollten Sie besonderen Wert auf modernste Geräte-Technik legen, sind Sie mit Bosch bestens beraten.
(*Should* you set special store by the latest in appliance technology, your ideal partner is Bosch.)

REPORTED SPEECH

The subjunctive can be used to show that someone else's statement is being reported. In the following sentence, the study that is being reported would have used the indicative forms *muß* and *müssen* respectively. Notice that the subjunctive I form *müsse* is used for the 3rd person singular, but the subjunctive II form *müßten* is used for the 3rd person plural in order to distinguish it from the present indicative. There's no difference in meaning. (➡ P 87)

Vor allem *müsse* das Leitbild des Unternehmens bestimmt werden. So *müßten* sich Großunternehmen fragen, „ob ...
(First and foremost the image of the company *had to* be established. Thus large companies *had to* ask themselves "whether ...)

IMPERATIVE

In commands, the verb usually comes at the beginning of the clause. Weak verbs have the following forms: stem+(e) (*you (familiar) sing.*), stem+**t** (*you (familiar) pl*), stem+**en** + Sie (*you (polite) sing./pl*). Notice the vowel change in the strong verb *sehen*.

Siehe die Jalousien-Schränke. (*See* the units with roller shutters.)
Schaut euch das mal an! (*Have a look* at this!)
Delegieren Sie! (*Delegate!*)

VERBS AND THEIR COMPLEMENTS

Verbs vary in the types of 'complement' they require to complete their meaning. Here are the main basic patterns:

SUBJECT + VERB

Some verbs are used without a direct object (accusative case), and can form a sentence consisting just of subject and verb.

Die Emissionen (*f pl nom.*) **fallen**. (The emissions **are falling**.)

SUBJECT + VERB + ACCUSATIVE OBJECT

Many verbs require a direct object, which is in the accusative case. (➡ P 98)

Die Messe Frankfurt (*f sing. nom.*) **verkauft** keine Hallen (*f pl acc.*).
(The Frankfurt Fair does not **sell** exhibition halls.)

SUBJECT + VERB + DATIVE OBJECT + ACCUSATIVE OBJECT

A few verbs in addition take an indirect object (in the dative case), which is usually a person. (➡ P 98)

Wir (*pl nom.*) **bieten** unseren Kunden (*m pl dat.*) eine breite Service-Palette (*f sing. acc.*).
(We **offer** our customers a wide range of services.)

SUBJECT + VERB + PREPOSITIONAL OBJECT

Some German verbs require a particular preposition which introduces an object. The object may be in the accusative, dative or (rarely) genitive case, depending on the case required by the preposition (➡ P 106).

Der Jahresabschluß (*m sing. nom.*) **besteht** *aus* Bilanz (*f sing. dat.*) und Gewinn- und Verlustrechnung (*f sing. dat.*).
(The annual financial statement **consists** *of* a balance sheet and a profit and loss account.)
Der Ladungseigentümer (*m sing. nom.*) **wendet** sich *an* unsere Vertretung (*f sing. acc.*).
(The owner of the shipment **contacts** (*lit.* **turns** *to*) our agent.)

Often the object does not consist of a noun or noun phrase, but of an infinitive clause (➡ **P 108**). In that case, the clause is completed by the stopgap object ***da(r)-***, which is attached to the preposition that goes with the verb. The following clause ends with a verb in the infinitive, with *zu*. (➡ **P 59**)

...die Abwicklung, die *mit* dem Service **zusammenhängt**
(*zusammenhängen mit* + dative noun)
(the processing which **is connected** *with* service)
... die Abwicklung, die ***damit* zusammenhängt**, einen Service durch***zu***führen (*zusammenhängen mit* + infinitive clause)
(... the processing which **is connected** *with* carry***ing*** out a service)

If a verb requires a particular preposition, this is given in the *Glossary*.

PREPOSITIONS

Prepositions determine whether the following noun or pronoun is in the accusative, dative, or (rarely) genitive case (➡ **P 48, 97-98**). The form of prepositions does not vary, except that some may be fused with a following definite article (➡ **P 20**):

am, beim, im, unterm, vom, zum = **an/bei/in/unter/von/zu** + **dem**
(*m/n sing. dat.*)

ans, fürs, ins, übers, ums = **an/für/in/über/um** + **das** (*n sing. acc.*)
zur = **zu** + **der** (*f sing. dat.*)

PREPOSITIONS USED WITH THE ACCUSATIVE

bis, durch, für, gegen, ohne, um

durch einen Computer, *für* den Bereich, *um* den Vertrieb

Note that *bis*, *ohne* and *um* are also used as **conjunctions**.

PREPOSITIONS USED WITH THE DATIVE

aus, außer, bei, gegenüber, mit, nach, seit, von, zu

aus dem Ausland, *mit* denen, *zu* kompletten Systemen

Note that *zu* is also used to introduce an infinitive.

PREPOSITIONS USED WITH THE GENITIVE

Those in *Deutsches Business-Magazin* are: *während, wegen, innerhalb*

während der Abpressung, *wegen* diverser Brücken, *innerhalb* Deutschlands

Note that *während* is also used as a **conjunction**. *Innerhalb* is often used with *von* + dative, e.g. *innerhalb von 7 Tagen*.

PREPOSITIONS USED WITH THE ACCUSATIVE OR THE DATIVE

an, auf, hinter, in, neben, über, unter, vor, zwischen

The **accusative** indicates directional movement from one place to another, answering the question 'where to', while the **dative** indicates a state of rest or non-directional movement and answers the question 'where' (➡ **P 48**):

Accusative (*where to?*)	Dative (*where?*)
auf den Hof (*into the* loading bay)	*auf dem* Hof (*in the* loading bay)
an die Presse (*onto the* press)	*an der* Spitze (*at the* top)
in die Werbung (*into* advertising)	*in der* Firma (*in the* company)

DA + PREPOSITION

You'll often find a preposition attached to the syllable *da(r)-*. This syllable is usually equivalent to 'this' or 'that', e.g. *dazu, danach, dafür, daran, darauf* (➡ **P 50**). It may go with the preposition demanded by a verb (➡ **P 59, 105-106**).

Danach kamen zwei englische Kollegen.
(*After that* two English colleagues came.)

Wir haben Einfluß und sind auch stolz *darauf*.
(We have influence and are proud *of it*.)
Die Leute sind stolz *darauf*, „Aniliner" zu sein.
(People are proud *of* be*ing* „Aniliner"– employees of BASF.)

CONJUNCTIONS

COORDINATING CONJUNCTIONS

The following conjunctions may link words, phrases or clauses. If they link main clauses, the finite verb (➡ **P 102**) stays in its normal 'second' place (➡ **P 107**).

und (and)
oder (or)
aber, doch, jedoch (but, however)
denn (as, because, for)
sondern (but) (used after negations in which an idea is excluded) (➡ **P 82**)

Note that the conjunctions *aber* and *jedoch* may come in the middle of the clause.

Wir können *aber* nicht erwarten, daß ...
(We can't, *however*, expect that ...)

Look out for conjunctions which occur in pairs:

entweder ... oder (either ... or)
nicht nur ... sondern auch (not only ... but also)
sowohl ... als auch (both ... and)
teils ... teils (partly ... partly)
weder ... noch (neither ... nor)

... *entweder* durch Roboter *oder* durch automatisierte Anlagen
(... *either* with robots *or* with automated systems)
Wir bauen *nicht nur* Ihren Ausstellungsstand, *sondern* nehmen Ihnen *auch* alle mit der Messe zusammenhängenden Arbeiten ab.
(We *not only* build your exhibition stand, *but also* relieve you of all tasks connected with the trade fair.)

SUBORDINATING CONJUNCTIONS

The following conjunctions introduce subordinate clauses (➡ **P 107**), in which you can expect to find the finite verb at the end:

Time: *als* (when), *bis* (until), *nachdem* (after), *seit(dem)* (since), *während* (while), *wenn* (when)

Cause: *da* (since), *weil* (because)

Consequence: *damit, so daß* (so that)

Concession: *obwohl* (although)

Comparison: *als* (than), *wie* (as)

Contrast: *während* (whereas, while)

Condition: *falls* (in case, if), *wenn* (if), *sofern* (provided that)

Other: *daß* (that)

CLAUSES AND WORD ORDER

In order to understand a German sentence, it's important to recognize the clause structure. A sentence may consist of only one clause, but often German sentences have several clauses. You can use punctuation as a guide: each clause will be separated off from other clauses by a comma or other punctuation mark. Each clause has a verb, which you need to identify.

In English, the subject is at or near the beginning of a sentence, before the verb. In German, the nominative case helps to identify the subject, allowing it to come after the verb, or after the object. Word order varies depending on the type of clause.

Word Order in Main Clauses

A sentence consists of at least one main clause, which expresses the principal idea. In a main clause the **finite verb** (➡ **P 102**) is the '**second**' **element**. The 'first' element may be the subject, or an object, time expression, subordinate clause etc., often for the sake of emphasis (➡ P 12, 34, 74). In the following examples, the subject is in italics:

BMW **produziert** 550 000 Autos im Jahr.
(*BMW* **produces** 550,000 cars a year.)
Zu diesem Ergebnis **kommt** *das Institut für Freizeitwirtschaft*.
(*The Institute for the Leisure Industry* **has arrived** at this conclusion.)
Die zweite Lackschicht **versprühen** überwiegend *Automaten*.
(*Robots* generally **spray on** the second coating of paint.)

Two or more parallel main clauses may be linked up by a coordinating conjunction such as *und* (and), *oder* (or), *aber* (but), or *denn* (for) (➡ **P 106**). Each of the following clauses could stand on its own and form a complete sentence, and in each, the verb is the second element (discounting the conjunction):

In Hauptmärkten **haben** *wir* eigene Töchter, *und* in kleineren und mittleren Märkten **haben** *wir* ein Netz von Distributoren.
(In principal markets *we* **have** our own subsidiaries, *and* in smaller and medium-sized markets *we* **have** a network of distributors.)

If the verb consists of two or more parts, the part with the personal ending (finite verb) comes in second place, and the remainder at the end of the clause, forming a frame for the other elements:

Compound verb forms: the appropriate finite form of *haben*, *sein* or *werden* comes in second place, and the past participle and/or any infinitives come at the end of the clause.

Dieser Strukturwandel **hat** vor allem die metallverarbeitenden Bereiche *erfaßt*.
(This restructuring **has** particularly *affected* the metal-processing industries.)
Viele Schadstoffe **werden** heute mit modernen Meßgeräten *festgestellt*.
(Nowadays many pollutants **are** *detected* with modern measuring instruments.)
Alle übrige Arbeit **ist** in den europäischen Werkstätten der Partner bereits *getan worden*.
(All the other work **has** already *been done* in the European workshops of our partners.)

Modal verbs: You can normally expect the modal verb in second place, and the infinitive at the end of the clause. (➡ **P 33**)

Ein Automobilwerk **kann** nicht alles allein *herstellen*.
(A car maker **can**not *produce* everything itself.)
27 000 Ausstattungselemente **müssen** bei der Deutschen Airbus *montiert werden*.
(27,000 fittings and furnishings **have to** *be installed* at Deutsche Airbus.)

Separable verbs: In simple tenses, the finite part of the verb comes in second place, and the separable prefix goes to the end of the clause (➡ **P 14**). In compound tenses, the prefix is joined to the other part of the verb at the end of the clause.

Der modernen, asymmetrischen Architektur des Hauses **paßt sich** dieses neue Bosch-Küchenmodell vollendet **an**. (verb: sich anpassen)
(This new Bosch kitchen **adapts itself** perfectly to the modern, asymmetrical architecture of your home.)
Experten **hatten** ein Absinken des Meeresbodens *festgestellt*. (verb: feststellen)
(Experts **had** *established* the subsidence of the sea bed.)

'**Telegraph-style**': Especially in advertising language, you may of course find sentences which have neither subject nor verb.

Kurz und gut: bei Bosch finden Sie, was Sie suchen. Alles aus einem Haus. In bester Qualität. Von Bosch.
(In a nutshell: with Bosch you'll find what you're looking for. Everything from the same source. Top quality. From Bosch.)

Word Order in Subordinate Clauses

In addition to one or more main clauses, a sentence may include subordinate clauses. A subordinate clause depends on another clause and doesn't make sense on its own. Subordinate clauses are normally linked to the main clause (or to another subordinate clause) by a **subordinating conjunction** (➡ **P 106**) or a **relative pronoun** (➡ **P 99**). In a subordinate clause, you'll usually find the **finite verb at the end** (➡ **P 102**). The following sentence has a main clause and three subordinate clauses: 1) a *daß* clause 2) a relative clause with the relative pronoun *die* (*pl*), which elaborates on the noun *Probleme* (*pl*) 3) a *daß* clause. (➡ P 23, 49, 58)

Heute **stellt** man *fest*,
    daß es sehr viele Probleme **gibt**,
        die in früheren Jahren dazu *geführt* **haben**,
            daß das Grundwasser *verschmutzt* **wurde**.
(Today people **are realizing** *that* there **are** a lot of problems *which* in the past **led** to the groundwater *being* polluted.)

Auxiliary verbs *sein*, *haben*, *werden* and **modal verbs**: The finite form comes at the end of a subordinate clause, immediately following the past participle or infinitive it's used with.

... Industriezweige, *die* mit Schiffbau *verbunden* **waren**.
(Sectors *which* **were** *connected* with ship-building.)
Wenn der Kaufvertrag mit einer Werft *geschlossen* **wird**, ...
(*When* the contract of sale **is** *concluded* with a shipyard, ...)
..., *so daß* mögliche Fehler von vornherein *ausgeschaltet werden* **können**.
(..., *so that* possible defects **can** *be excluded* from the start.)

Separable verbs: The prefix is attached to the main part of the verb at the end of a subordinate clause. (➡ **P 14**)

..., *daß* sie die Abwicklung von Aufträgen richtig *durch***führen**.
(..., *that* they **are carrying** *out* the processing of orders correctly.)

Conditional clauses without *wenn*: These form an exception to the rule that the verb comes at the end of a subordinate clause. (➡ **P 75, 86**)

Übersteigt der Gesamtpreis der Bestellung DM 250,-, ...
(**If** the total price of the order **exceeds**, ...)
Sollten dennoch Probleme *auftreten*, ...
(**Should** problems still *arise*, ...)

Relative Clauses

A relative clause is recognizable by the **relative pronoun** (➡ **P 99**) after the comma that indicates the beginning of the clause. Look out for these forms: *der, die, das, den, dem, dessen, deren*. The pronoun agrees in **number** and in **gender** with the noun about which it gives extra information. The case of the pronoun depends on its role in the relative clause (e.g. nominative case indicates subject of relative clause). (➡ **P 41, 49**)

Dieser Strukturwandel (*m sing*), **der** (*m sing*) sich auch gegenwärtig noch fortsetzt, ...
(This restructuring, **which** is still continuing, ...)
... alle Arbeiten (*pl*) ..., **die** (*pl*) Sie gerne loswerden wollen.
(... all the tasks **which** you want to get rid of.)

Occasionally, the relative pronoun is preceded by a *preposition* (➡ P 76):

> An die Plattformbeine (*pl*), *mit* **denen** (*pl*) die Plattformen auf dem Meeresboden stehen, ...
> (Onto the platform legs, *with* **which** the platforms stand on the sea bed, ...)

INFINITIVE CLAUSES

An **infinitive** (➡ P 102) with *zu* may be used to form a clause that elaborates on part of another clause. In an infinitive clause, the infinitive comes at the end, following *zu*. If the verb has a separable prefix, *zu* goes after the prefix, e.g. *festzustellen*. (➡ P 40)

The infinitive clause may give added information about a noun. (➡ P 15)

> Plötzlich wurde der Firma *der Auftrag* erteilt, die Produktaufnahme im Vertrieb *zu organisieren*.
> (Suddenly the company was given *the task of organizing* the integration of the products in the sales organization.)

The infinitive clause may be needed to complete the meaning of a verb.

> Wir *versuchen* jetzt, die Geräte über Vertriebsfirmen *zu verkaufen*.
> (We're now *trying to sell* the appliances through distributors.)

Often, the syntax of a clause will be completed by the pronoun *es*, which acts as a stopgap subject. In the following sentence, *es* in the main clause stands for a whole string of infinitive clauses (➡ P 40):

> Zu meinen Aufgaben gehört *es*, Werbeaktionen *zu starten*, Messen *zu besuchen*, die Mitarbeiter *zu kontrollieren*.
> (*It's* part of my job *to launch* advertising campaigns, *to visit* fairs, *to supervise* staff.)

UM ... ZU

This is equivalent to 'in order to'. (➡ P 56)

> ..., *um* den Materialfluß weiter *zu optimieren* und die Flexibilität noch mehr *zu erhöhen*.
> (..., *in order to optimize* the flow of materials and further increase the flexibility.)
> *Um* den Komplex gleichzeitig anheben *zu können*, ...
> (*In order to be able* to raise the complex simultaneously, ...)

PREPOSITION + INFINITIVE

Some verbs need to be followed by a preposition that introduces an object (➡ P 105-106). The object may be an infinitive clause, with **da(r)-** + preposition pointing forward to the infinitive clause. (➡ P 59)

> Die Leute sind stolz *darauf*, „Aniliner" *zu sein*.
> (People are proud *of being* "Aniliner" – employees of BASF.)

QUESTIONS AND COMMANDS

Questions may start with a W question word (e.g. *was, wie, wo,* ➡ P 18), or they may start with a verb and invite a 'yes/no' answer.

> **Macht** Sie der Gedanke an Ihre nächste Messebeteiligung nervös?
> (**Does** the thought of your next trade-fair exhibition **make** you apprehensive?)

Commands also begin with a verb.

> **Schaut** euch das mal an!
> (**Have** a look at this!)

NUMBERS

0-9	10-19	20-29	30, 40 ...	100, 200 ...
null	zehn	**zwanzig**		
eins	elf	ein*und***zwanzig**		(ein)**hundert**
zwei	zwölf	zwei*und***zwanzig**		zwei**hundert**
drei	dreizehn	drei*und***zwanzig**	drei**ßig**	drei**hundert**
vier	vierzehn	vier*und***zwanzig**	vier**zig**	vier**hundert**
fünf	fünfzehn	fünf*und***zwanzig**	fünf**zig**	fünf**hundert**
sechs	sechzehn	sechs*und***zwanzig**	sech**zig**	sechs**hundert**
sieben	siebzehn	sieben*und***zwanzig**	sieb**zig**	sieben**hundert**
acht	achtzehn	acht*und***zwanzig**	acht**zig**	acht**hundert**
neun	neunzehn	neun*und***zwanzig**	neun**zig**	neun**hundert**

Notice that in e.g. fünf*und*zwanzig, the unit (*fünf*) comes before *zwanzig*, as in 'five *and* **twenty** to four' and 'four *and* **twenty** blackbirds'.

1000, 2000: (ein)**tausend**, zwei**tausend**
1 000 000, 2 000 000: eine **Million**, zwei **Millionen**
1 000 000 000: eine **Milliarde**
1 000 000 000 000: eine **Billion**
101, 2022: (ein)hunderteins, zweitausend(und)zweiundzwanzig
3 333 000: drei Millionen dreihundertdreiunddreißigtausend

die **achtziger**/**80er** Jahre (the eighties)
die **neunziger**/**90er** Jahre (the nineties)

The first, second, third	Firstly, secondly	Half, third, quarter (➡ P 20)
der/die/das ers**te**	ers**tens**	
der/die/das zwei**te**	zwei**tens**	die/eine Hälfte
der/die/das drit**te**	drit**tens**	das/ein Drit**tel**
der/die/das vier**te**	vier**tens**	das/ein Vier**tel**
der/die/das fünf**te**	fünf**tens**	das/ein Fünf**tel**
der/die/das sechs**te**	sechs**tens**	das/ein Sechs**tel**
der/die/das sieb**te**	sieb**tens**	das/ein Sieb**tel**
der/die/das ach**te**	ach**tens**	das/ein Ach**tel**
der/die/das neun**te**	neun**tens**	das/ein Neun**tel**
der/die/das zehn**te**	zehn**tens**	das/ein Zehn**tel**
der/die/das zwanzig**ste**	zwanzig**stens**	das/ein Zwanzig**stel**
der/die/das dreißig**ste**	dreißig**stens**	das/ein Dreißig**stel**

Stops and Commas

1. = erster/erste/erstes (first); erstens (firstly)
2. = zweiter/zweite/zweites (second); zweitens (secondly)
12.345 = zwölftausenddreihundert(und)fünfundvierzig (12,345)
12,3   = zwölf Komma drei (twelve point three) (12.3)

In German figures, the thousands are separated by a **stop** or a **space**, not a comma. (➡ P 8)

DAYS, MONTHS, SEASONS

Tage	Monate	Jahreszeiten
der Montag	der Januar	der Frühling/das Frühjahr
der Dienstag	der Februar	der Sommer
der Mittwoch	der März	der Herbst
der Donnerstag	der April	der Winter
der Freitag	der Mai	
der Samstag/Sonnabend	der Juni	
der Sonntag	der Juli	
	der August	
am Montag/Dienstag	der September	
(on Monday/Tuesday)	der Oktober	
montags/dienstags	der November	im Januar/Februar
(on Mondays/Tuesdays)	der Dezember	(in January/February)

GLOSSARY

The *Glossary* gives translations of words and phrases in the context in which they appear in *Deutsches Business-Magazin*, to help you get the most out of your reading.

Abbreviations used in the *Glossary*:

coll.	colloquial
f	female
lit.	literally
m	male
pl	plural
sep.	separable verb ➡ P 102
wk m	weak masculine ➡ P 98
sth.	something

Nouns
Plurals of nouns are given in brackets after the noun. For a list of possible plural forms ➡ P 97.

Verbs
Any changes to the verb in the present tense, past tense or past participle are indicated after the infinitive form. For an explanation ➡ P 102. Reflexive verbs (➡ P 100) are preceded by *sich*. Verbs which take the auxiliary *sein* are indicated by an asterisk *.

A

à see Carte
A: das A und O *the be-all and end-all*
die Aachen-Münchener *insurance company based in Aachen*
die Aalsuppe (– n) *eel soup*
ab *from*; ab und zu (mal) *now and then*
der Abbau *dismantling*
abbaubar *biodegradable*
sich abbauen (sep.) *to be broken down*
abbilden (sep.) *to depict*
abbrechen (sep.) (bricht ab), brach ab, abgebrochen *to break (sth.) off*
abbrechen (sep.) (bricht ab), brach ab, abgebrochen * *to break off*
der Abbruch: Abbruch *Cancel*
abdecken (sep.) *to cover*
das Abdichten *sealing*
der Abend (– e) *evening*
das Abendbrot (– e) *supper*
die Abendsperre (– n) *evening curfew*
der Abendverkauf *late opening (times), late shopping*
aber *but, however*; oder aber *or alternatively*
der Abfall (:e) *waste (material), scrap*
der Abflug (:e) *departure*
der Abgaswert (– e) *exhaust emission value*
abgebildet *depicted (see abbilden)*
abgeblockt *(from abblocken) cut short*
abgeladen *unloaded (see abladen)*
abgenommen *inspected (see abnehmen)*
abgesenkt *subsided (see absenken)*
abgesichert *secured (see absichern)*
abgestimmt *agreed, matched (see abstimmen)*
abhängen (sep.) (von) *to depend (on)*
die Abhängigkeit (– en) *independence*; Abhängigkeit von *dependence on*
die Abhilfe (– n) *remedy*; hierbei Abhilfe schaffen *to ease/remedy the situation, provide a solution*
die Abkürzung (– en) *abbreviation*
abladen (sep.) (ä), lud, geladen *to unload*
das Ablängen *cutting to length, trimming*
der Ablauf (:e) *process, operation*; automatisierter Ablauf *automated operation*
ablaufen (sep.) (äu), ie, au * *to proceed*
die Abluft *used air, emission(s)*
abnehmen (sep.) (nimmt ab), nahm ab, abgenommen *to relieve of, inspect*
der Abnehmer (–) *purchaser*
abpressen (sep.) *to press, stamp*
die Abpressung (– en) *pressing*
die Abrechnung (– en) *invoicing, accounts department*
absatzpolitisch *marketing*; absatzpolitisches Instrumentarium *marketing mix*
abschließen (sep.), o, o *to close off, finish*
das Abschlußgespräch (– e) *final discussion/meeting*
die Abschlußprüfung (– en) *statutory audit, audit of annual accounts*
abschlußprüfungspflichtig *subject to a statutory audit (annually)*
die Abschottung (– en) *partition*
sich absenken (sep.) *to subside*
abschichern (sep.) *to secure*
das Absinken *subsidence*
absolut *absolute(ly), complete(ly), definite(ly)*; absolute Priorität *top priority*
der Abstand (:e) *distance, interval*; mit Abstand *by a long chalk*; immer im Abstand von *at intervals of*
abstimmen (sep.) *to agree*
der Abstimmprozeß (–prozesse) *process of agreement (harmonization)*
die Abstimmung (– en) *agreement, harmonization*
die Abteilung (– en) *department, division*; Abteilung Offshore *offshore department*
das Abwasser (:) *wastewater*
die Abwechslung (– en) *change, variety*
die Abweichung (– en) *deviation*
die Abwicklung (– en) *administering, administration, processing*; Abwicklung von etwas *administration of sth.*
der Abzug (:e) *deduction*; ohne Abzug *without deduction, net(t)*; 30 Tage ohne Abzug *30 days nett*
das Accessoire (– s) *accessory*
die Achse (– n) *axle*
der Achsschenkel (–) *stub axle*
acht *eight*
der, die, das achte *(the) eighth*
achtzehn *eighteen*
achtzig *eighty*
die Actien (pl) see HAPAG
Adenauer, Konrad *first post-war chancellor of West Germany*
die Administration (– en) *administration*
administrativ *administrative*
adressiert *(from adressieren) addressed*
die AEG = Allgemeine Elektricitäts-Gesellschaft *(note Elektricität is now spelt Elektrizität)*
Afrika *Africa*
die AG (– s) = Aktiengesellschaft *comparable with Plc (see Aktiengesellschaft)*
die Agentur (– en) *agency*
das Aggregat (– e) *major assembly/system, unit*
Ägypten *Egypt*
sich ähneln *resemble each other*
ähnlich *similar(ly)*; ähnlich stehen *to be on the same level*
der Airbus (– se) *Airbus*
der Airport (– s) *airport*
die Aktie (– n) *share*
die Aktiengesellschaft (– en) *(public) limited company, public corporation (see AG)*
die Aktion (– en) *campaign, action, operation*
der Aktionär (– e) *shareholder*
aktiv *active(ly)*; aktiv sein *to work*; ich bin vier Jahre im Patentrecht aktiv gewesen *I worked in patent law for four years*
die Aktivität (– en) *activity*
der Aktivkohlefilter (–) *activated-carbon filter*
die Aktualität *topicality*
aktuell *current(ly)*
die Akustik *acoustics*
der Akzent (– e) *accent, emphasis*
all, alle, allem, allen, aller, alles *(to/from/for/of) all, every*; alle everybody; alles *everything*; in aller Regel *generally*; alle Vierteljahre *every quarter/three months*; vor allem *above all, mainly, first and foremost*;

particularly; aus aller Welt *from all over the world*
allein(e) *alone, only, itself*
allerdings *of course, (al)though, admittedly, however*
allerlei *a variety of, all kinds of*
alles *everything, all*
die Allfinanz *comprehensive range of financial services under one roof*
die Allfinanzdienstleistungen (f, pl) *financial services*
allgemein *general(ly), in general*; allgemeine Dienstleistungen *general services*
die Allgemeininformation (– en) *general information*
der Alltag *everyday life*
als *when, as, than*; sowohl ... als auch *both ... and*; nicht nur ... sondern auch *not only ... but also*
also *so, therefore, that is, well, i.e.*
die Alster *Alster River, Alster Lake*
das Alstervergnügen *Alster festival*
das Alsterwasser (–) *Alster schnapps*
alt *old*; alt, älter als der/die/das älteste *old, older than, the oldest*
das Altbier (– e) *dark beer (lit. old beer)*
Alte: Alte Pinakothek *Alte Pinakothek (art gallery)*
das Alter (–) *age*; im Alter *in old-age/retirement*
älter (als) *older (than)*
der Alternativjob (– s) *alternative job/employment*
das Alternativprodukt (– e) *alternative product*
die Altersstruktur (– en) *age structure*
die Altersversorgung (– en) *(provision for) retirement, superannuation*; betriebliche Altersversorgung *company pension scheme*
die Altersvorsorge (– n) *provision for retirement, superannuation, retirement pension*
der, die, das älteste *(the) oldest (one)*
am ältesten *oldest*
die Altstadt *old city/town*
das Aluminium *aluminium*
am = an dem
der Amateurgärtner (–) *amateur gardener*
das Amateurgärtnern *amateur gardening*
Amerika *America*
amerikanisch *American*
das Amt (:er) *office, authority (see Bundesaufsichtsamt)*
an *at, on, onto, to, of, by, in*; an die 9000 Fachbesucher *close on/around 9000 trade visitors*; am Rhein *on the Rhine*; an die Presse *to the press*; an der Spitze *at the top*; an und für sich *really, actually*; Bauanteil am *share of the work in the*; am Montag *on Monday*; am liebsten (noch) *best of all, ideally*
die Analyse (– n) *analysis*
die Anästhesie *anaesthesia*
anbei *enclosed*; Fotokopie anbei *photocopy enclosed*
anbieten (sep.), o, o *to offer, sell*
der Anbieter (–) *supplier*
andere, anderem, anderen, anderer, anderes *(to/from/for/of) other(s), another*; unter anderem *amongst other things*
anders *different(ly)*; inzwischen ist das anders *now things have changed*
die Änderung (– en) *change*
anfahren (sep.) (fährt an), fuhr an, angefahren *to start up, commission*
der Anfang (:e) *beginning, start*; am Anfang *initially, at the beginning*; Anfang der siebziger Jahre *at the beginning of the seventies*; von Anfang an *from the start*
anfangen (sep.) (ä), i, a *to begin*
die Anfangsphase (– n) *start-up phase, beginning*; in der Anfangsphase *at the beginning*
die Anfertigung (– en) *manufacture*
die Anforderung (– en) *demand, requirement*; hohe Anforderungen *high standards*
die Anfrage (– n) *enquiry*
die Angabe (– n) *specification*; die Angabe einer Zahlungsfrist *specifying a term of payment*

das Angebot (– e) *offer, (product) range, proposal*
angeboten *offered (see anbieten)*
angefahren *started up, commissioned (see anfahren)*
angefallen: die angefallene Fahrzeit *the amount of travel time*
angefangen *begun (see anfangen)*
angeflanscht *(from anflanschen) flange-mounted*
angehoben *lifted, raised (see anheben)*
angekommen *arrived (see ankommen)*
angeliefert *delivered (see anliefern)*
das Angeln *angling, fishing*
angelsächsisch *Anglo-Saxon, in the UK and US*
angemietet *rented (see anmieten)*
angenehm *comfortable, convenient*
angenehmer (als) *more comfortable/convenient (than)*
angeräuchert *smoked*
angerechnet *credited (see anrechnen)*
angeschraubt *bolted (on) (see anschrauben)*
der/die Angestellte (– n), ein Angestellter *(the) employed person, (salaried) employee, white-collar worker*; leitender Angestellter *member of the middle management*
angewiesen (auf) *reliant (on)*
der Anhang (:e) *appendix, notes (to accounts/financial statements)*
anheben (sep.), o, o *to raise, lift*
das Anilin *aniline (see BASF)*
der Aniliner (–) *employee of BASF*
ankommen (sep.), a, o * *to arrive*; darauf ankommen *to depend on*; wenn es darauf ankommt *when it's important*
die Ankunft (:e) *arrival*
die Anlage (– n) *plant (see Polyester), enclosure(s)*; Anlage *enclosure(s)*
die Anlagen (pl) *plants*
der Anlagenbau *plant construction*
der Anlagenbauer (–) *plant builder/manufacturer, plant-construction company*
die Anlagenmodernisierung (– en) *plant modernization*
anlegen (sep.) *to build up, compile, accumulate*
die Anleitung (– en) *instruction*; nach Anleitung *according to instructions*
anliefern (sep.) *to supply*
anmieten (sep.) *to rent*
anmutend *seeming, looking*
annehmen (sep.) (nimmt an), nahm an, angenommen *to assume*; nehmen wir an *let's assume*
anonym *anonymous*
anpassen (sep.) *to adapt, tailor*; speziellen Kundenwünschen anpassen *to customize*
sich anpassen (sep.) (paßt) *to adapt (itself)*; paßt sich vollendet an *perfectly matches*
anrechnen (sep.) *to credit (with)*
die Anregung (– en) *stimulation*; zur Anregung *for stimulation*
die Anreise (– n) *journey*; Anreise-Information *travel information*
der Anruf (– e) *(phone) call*; Ihr Anruf vom *your phone call of*
anrufen (sep.), ie, u *to call, phone*
anrufend *phoning, calling*; den mich anrufenden Kunden *the customer who has called me*
ans = an das
anschauen (sep.) *to look*
sich anschauen (sep.) *to inspect*; schaut euch das mal an! *have a look at this!*
anschließend *later, finally*
anschrauben (sep.) *to bolt/screw on*
ansiedeln (sep.) *to establish*
der Anspruch (:e) *claim, approach*; dieser rationale Anspruch *this rational approach*; in Anspruch nehmen *to use, take advantage of*; in Anspruch nehmen, daß ein Techniker zu ihm kommt *to call out an engineer*
anspruchsvoll *sophisticated, demanding, quality-conscious, superior*; anspruchsvolle Mode *high fashion, haute couture*; anspruchsvolle Techniken *sophisticated technologies*
anstehen (sep.), stand an, angestanden

Glossary

to be imminent, be present; ob ein Lackfehler ansteht *if there is a paint defect*
ansteht *is imminent (see* anstehen*)*
ansteigen (*sep.*), ie, ie * *to increase*
das Anstellungsverhältnis (– se) *employment*
der Anteil (– e) *proportion, share, holding, stake;* Anteil an *share/proportion of*
der Antrieb (– e) *drive*
die Antwort (– en) *answer*
die Anwendung (– en) *application, use*
anwerben (*sep.*) (i), a, o *to recruit*
die Anzahl (– en) *number*
anzeigen (*sep.*) *to notify*
anzuheben *see* anheben
anzupassen *see* anpassen
anzurufen *see* anrufen
anzusiedeln *see* ansiedeln
anzuwerben *see* anwerben
anzuzeigen *see* anzeigen
der Apfelwein (– e) *cider* (lit. *apple wine*)
die Apfelweinwirtschaft (– en) *cider tavern*
die Apotheke (– n) *chemist, pharmacy*
der April *April;* im April *in April*
die Ära *era*
die Arbeit (– en) *work, job, task*
arbeiten *to work;* an etwas arbeiten *to work on sth.*
das Arbeiten *work(ing)*
arbeitend *working*
der Arbeiter (–) *worker, wage earner*
der Arbeitgeber (–) *employer*
der Arbeitgeberverband (⸚e) *employers' association*
der Arbeitnehmer (–) *employee, worker, number of employees*
arbeitsam *industrious*
die Arbeitsaufteilung (– en) *work sharing*
die Arbeitsaufteilungsgespräche (*pl*) *work-sharing talks, discussions*
der Arbeitsdirektor (*wk m*) (– en) *worker director*
das Arbeitsfeld (– er) *area of responsibility*
die Arbeitsfolge (– n) *sequence of operations*
das Arbeitsklima (– s) *(working) atmosphere*
die Arbeitslosenversicherung (– en) *unemployment insurance*
die Arbeitslosigkeit (– en) *unemployment*
der Arbeitsplatz (⸚e) *job, workplace*
die Arbeitssicherheit *job security*
arbeitssparend *labour-saving*
die Arbeitsstätte (– n) *workplace*
die Arbeitsstunde (– n) *labour (per hour)*
der Arbeitsunfall (⸚e) *industrial accident*
die Arbeitszeit (– en) *working hours*
die Architektur (– en) *architecture*
das Aroma (– s) *aroma*
die Art (– en) *kind, way, sort, type;* jede Art von *every kind of*
der Artikel (–) *item, article, product*
das Artikelsortiment (– e) *product range*
die Arzthelferin (–nen) *medical-practice assistant*
die Assekuranz *insurance industry*
das Assessment (– s) *assessment*
die Asymmetrie (– n) *asymmetry*
asymmetrisch *asymmetrical(ly)*
der, die, das attraktivste *(the) most attractive (one)*
auch *also, as well, either, again;* nicht nur ... sondern auch *not only ... but also;* sowohl ... als auch *both ... and*
der *or* das Audit (– s) *audit*
auf *on (to), in (to), to, for, at;* auf den Hof *into the loading bay;* auf dem Hof *in the loading bay;* auf 300 Mrd. ansteigen *to increase to 300 billion;* auf ... hin *towards*
der Aufbau *setting up, erection*
aufbauen (*sep.*) *to set up, build up*
aufeinander *to each other;* aufeinander abgestimmt *matched*
der, die, das Auffallende *(the) striking thing/one*
die Aufgabe (– n) *task, function, job, duty;* die Kollegen haben die Aufgabe *it's the job of my colleagues;* zu meinen Aufgaben gehört es *it's part of my job*
die Aufgabenstellung (– en) *problem formulation, objective, task*
aufgebaut *set up (see* aufbauen*)*
aufgebracht (*from* aufbringen) *applied, attached*
aufgebraucht (*from* aufbrauchen) *used up, exhausted*
aufgemacht *opened (up) (see* aufmachen*)*
aufgenommen *added, taken up, accepted (see* aufnehmen*)*
aufgespritzt *sprayed on (see* aufspritzen*)*
aufgestellt *set up (see* aufstellen*)*
aufgetragen (*from* auftragen) *applied*
aufgrund *on account of, due to*
aufmachen (*sep.*) *to open*
die Aufmachung (– en) *presentation, layout, packaging*
die Aufnahme *acceptance, accommodation*
aufnehmen (*sep.*) (nimmt auf), nahm auf, aufgenommen *to accept, accommodate, record, take on, employ, add, take up;* kurzfristig aufnehmen *accept for short-term stays*
aufschneiden (*sep.*), schnitt auf, aufgeschnitten *to cut up*
das Aufsehen *sensation;* sorgte für Aufsehen *caused a sensation*
das Aufsichtsgremium (–gremien) *supervisory authority/body*
der Aufsichtsrat (⸚e) *supervisory board*
der/die Aufsichtsratsvorsitzende (– n), ein Aufsichtsratsvorsitzender *chairman/chairperson of the supervisory board*
aufspritzen (*sep.*) *to spray on, apply*
aufstellen (*sep.*) *to set up*
der Auftrag (⸚e) *order, commission;* einen Auftrag plazieren *to place an order;* einen Auftrag erteilen *to give a task, place an order, to commission*
die Aufträge (*pl*) *orders*
die Auftragswirkung (– en) *deposition effect*
auftreten (*sep.*) (tritt auf), a, e * *to appear, arise, occur*
aufwendig *expensive, complex*
aufzubauen *see* aufbauen
aufzuschneiden *see* aufschneiden
der Augenblick (– e) *moment;* im Augenblick *at the moment;* im Augenblick versuche ich *at the moment I am trying*
der Augenoptiker (–) *optician*
der Augenschein *visual inspection;* in Augenschein nehmen *to give a visual inspection*
der August *August;* im August *in August*
aus *from, out of;* aus verschiedenen Gründen *for a number of reasons;* ein Bad aus wassergelöstem Lack *a bath of paint in aqueous solution;* Teile aus Eisen *parts made of iron;* aus aller Welt *from all over the world;* aus der ganzen Welt *from all over the world;* aus einer Hand *from the same source/manufacturer;* aus einem Haus *from the same source/manufacturer*
ausbilden (*sep.*) *to train, educate*
das Ausbilden *education*
die Ausbildung (– en) *education, training*
der Ausbildungsablauf (- e) *training course*
die Ausbildungsvergütung (– en) *trainee pay*
die Ausbildungswerkstätte (– n) *training workshop*
der Ausdruck (⸚e) *expression*
ausdrücken (*sep.*) *to express*
sich ausdrücken (*sep.*) *to express oneself/itself*
die Ausfahrt (– en) *exit*
ausführen (*sep.*) *to carry out, design*
ausführlich *comprehensive, extensive, detailed*
das Ausfüllen *filling in*
die Ausgaben (*f, pl*) *expenditure*
der Ausgangspunkt (– e) *starting point*
ausgeben (*sep.*) (i), a, e *to pay out, spend, issue*
ausgebildet *educated, trained, qualified (see* ausbilden*);* ich bin ausgebildeter Ingenieur *I am a qualified engineer*
ausgegeben *issued (see* ausgeben*);* ausgegebene Kreditkarten *credit cards issued*
ausgehen (*sep.*), ging aus, ausgegangen * (von) *to go out, depart, start out (from), assume, proceed on the basis of;* man kann davon ausgehen *you can assume;* man kann nicht davon ausgehen *you can't proceed on the basis*
ausgehend *departing*
ausgelegt (*from* auslegen) *designed*
ausgeliefert *dispatched (see* ausliefern*)*
ausgereift (*from* ausreifen) *refined*
ausgerüstet *equipped, installed (see* ausrüsten*)*
ausgeschaltet (*from* ausschalten) *excluded*
ausgestattet *equipped (see* ausstatten*)*
ausgesucht (*see* aussuchen) *chosen, selected*
ausgetauscht *exchanged (see* austauschen*)*
ausgeübt (*from* ausüben) *done, carried out, practised*
ausgewählt *selected (see* auswählen*)*
der, die, das Ausgewählte *(the) selected thing/one*
ausgewechselt (*from* auswechseln) *exchanged, replaced*
ausgezeichnet (*from* auszeichnen) *excellent, superior*
ausgleichen (*sep.*), i, i *to make up for, compensate for*
aushandeln (*sep.*) *to negotiate*
das Aushilfspersonal *temporary staff, casual labour*
die Auskunft (⸚e) *information*
ausladen (*sep.*) (lädt aus), lud aus, ausgeladen *to unload, discharge*
das Ausland *abroad;* im Ausland *in other/foreign countries;* aus dem Ausland *from other countries*
ausländisch *foreign*
das Auslandsgeschäft (– e) *foreign/international business*
die Auslandslieferung (– en) *international delivery, foreign destinations, export sales*
ausliefern (*sep.*) (an) *to deliver/supply (to)*
die Auslieferung (– en) *delivery, acceptance;* mit Auslieferung der Ware *when goods are delivered/accepted*
auslösen (*sep.*) *to release, trigger (off)*
ausmachen (*sep.*) *to make up, constitute, matter, distinguish, make up;* macht fünf Prozent der Arbeit aus *makes up five percent of the work;* während das nichts ausmacht *while that doesn't matter*
die Ausmusterung (– en) *sampling, selection*
die Ausnahme (– n) *exception;* mit Ausnahme von *except for, with the exception of*
der Ausnahmefall (⸚e) *exception*
ausnutzen (*sep.*) *to exercise, exploit, make use of, take advantage of*
ausrichten (*sep.*) (auf) *to gear to*
sich ausrichten (*sep.*) (auf, nach) *to be geared/tailored to;* richten sich danach aus *are geared to*
ausrüsten (*sep.*) *to equip, install*
die Ausrüstung (– en) *equipment*
ausschauen (*sep.*) *to look like*
ausschließlich *exclusive(ly)*
der Ausschließlichkeitsvertreter (–) *sole/exclusive representative*
der Ausschnitt (– e) *cutout, knock-out*
der Ausschuß (⸚sse) *reject(s)*
aussehen (*sep.*) (ie), a, e *to look (like), appear*
außen *outside, exterior, externally;* nach außen *in the market;* das Positionieren nach außen *market positioning*
die Außenalster *Outer Alster*
die Außenbemalung (– en) *external painting*
der Außendienst (– e) *field staff, technical/field salesmen, field engineers, technical representatives, sales force*
der Außendienstbesuch (– e) *field-staff/sales visit*
der Außendienstmitarbeiter (–) *sales engineer/representative, field engineer, technical/field salesman*
die Außenhandelskauffrau (– en) *export clerk/trader (f)*
der Außenhandelsplatz (⸚e) *centre for import/export trade* (lit. *foreign trade*)
außer *except (for)*
außerdem *besides, in addition, also*
äußerlich *on the outside*
außerordentlich *extraordinary (-ily)*
außeruniversitär *extramural*
ausstatten (*sep.*) *to equip*
die Ausstattung (– en) *(interior) furnishings and fittings, equipment*
die Ausstattungselemente (*pl*) *furnishings and fittings*
ausstellen (*sep.*) *to exhibit*
der Aussteller (–) *exhibitor*
die Aussteller-Befragung (– en) *exhibitor (opinion) poll*
die Ausstellerberatung (– en) *exhibitor consultancy*
der Ausstellerservice *exhibitor service*
das Aussteller-Verzeichnis (– se) *register of exhibitors*
die Ausstellung (– en) *exhibition*
der Ausstellungsstand (⸚e) *exhibition stand*
sich aussuchen (*sep.*) *to choose, select, seek out*
der Austausch *exchange, replacement*
austauschen (*sep.*) *to exchange*
Australien *Australia*
die Auswahl (– en) *choice, selection*
auswählen (*sep.*) *to select*
die Ausweitung (– en) *expansion*
sich auswirken (*sep.*) (auf) *to affect, have an effect (on)*
die Auszahlung (– en) *payment;* „Auszahlung" *Payment*
der Auszahlungsbetrag (⸚e) *amount*
der/die Auszubildende (– n), ein Auszubildender *trainee, apprentice*
der Auszug (⸚e) *extract, shelf*
auszugleichen *see* ausgleichen
auszuhandeln *see* aushandeln
auszusuchen *see* aussuchen
das Auto (– s) *car*
AutoCAD = AutoCAD *(software programme)*
die Auto-Ersatzteile (*pl*) *spare car parts*
die Autokarosserie (– n) *car body*
der Automat (*wk m*)(– en) *automatic cash dispenser, automatic teller, robot, automat, automated machine*
die Automation *automation*
die Automationsanlage (– n) *automation system*
das Automationsgerät (– e) *automation instrument*
automatisch *automatic(ally), automated*
automatisiert *automated;* automatisierte Anlagen *automated systems;* automatisierter Ablauf *automated operation*
der Automatisierungsgrad (– e) *level of automation*
die Automatisierungstechnik *automation (engineering) (see* Meßtechnik*)*
das Automobil (– e) *automobile, car, auto*
die Automobil-Ausstellung (– en) *motor show/exhibition*
die Automobilbranche (– n) *automobile sector, car industry*
das Automobilwerk (– e) *car/motor factory, car company, car maker*
autonom *autonomous(ly)*
die Autoreparatur (– en) *car repair*
das Auto-Zubehör *car accessories*
die Avocado (– s) *avocado*

B

babylonisch *Babylonian;* babylonisches Sprachgewirr *confused babble of tongues, babel*
der Bach (⸚e) *stream*
der Bäcker (–) *baker*
der Background (– s) *background*
das Backobst *dried fruit*
das Bad (⸚er) *bath, bathroom*
badisch *(of/from) Baden (see* BASF*)*
BAe = British Aerospace
die Bahn (– en) *rail, railway*
der Bahnhof (⸚e) *station*
der Bahnhofplatz (⸚e) *station square*
die Bandfertigung (– en) *assembly line, flow production*
die Bank (– en) *bank*
der Bankenplatz (⸚e) *banking centre;* Banken- und Börsenplatz *financial centre* (lit. *banking and stock-exchange centre*)
das Bankgeschäft (– e) *banking transaction*
die Bankleitzahl (– en) *bank sort code*
die Banknote (– n) *banknote*
die Bar (– s) *bar*
das Bargeld *cash*
barock *baroque*
die BASF = Badische Anilin– und Sodafabrik
basieren (auf) *to be based (on), founded (on)*

Glossary

basiert (is) based (see basieren)
das Basilikum basil
die Basis base, basis, basic systems, basic aeroplane
das Basisflugzeug (– e) basic aeroplane
das Basissystem (– e) basic system
der Basiswohlstand basic/fundamental level of prosperity
das Basteln making things as a hobby, craftsmanship, modelmaking
die Bastlerzentrale (– n) model-making centre
der Bau (–ten) construction, building; Bau– und Heimwerkermarkt DIY centre/superstore, home-improvement centre; Bau– und Heimwerkermarktbranche DIY sector
der Bauanteil (– e) share/part (of the work), contribution
die Baueinheit (– en) assembly unit, production unit
bauen to build, construct, produce
die Baugruppe (– n) module
das Baugruppensystem (– e) modular system
das Baukastensystem (– e) building-block/modular system
der Baum (¨e) tree
der Baumarkt (¨e) DIY centre/superstore; Bau– und Heimwerkermarkt DIY centre/superstore, home-improvement centre
die Baumwolle cotton
die Bausparkasse (– n) building society
der Bausparvertrag (¨e) home-loan agreement/contract
der Baustein (– e) building block, unit, module
das Bauteil (– e) component, sub-assembly, assembly
die Bauweise (– n) format, construction, structure
bayerisch Bavarian
Bayern Bavaria
BDF = Beiersdorf
der Beamte (– n), ein Beamter government employee, public official with special legal status
bearbeiten to process, work, machine; schweißtechnisch bearbeiten to weld (see schweißen)
die Bearbeitung (– en) processing, handling, craftsmanship
das Beaufsichtigen supervision, monitoring
beaufsichtigen to supervise
beauftragen to commission
sich bedanken to thank, be grateful
der Bedarf need, demand; Bedarf an demand for
bedeuten to mean
die Bedeutung (– en) meaning, importance, significance; haben an Bedeutung verloren have diminished in importance
die Bedingung (– en) condition
das Bedürfnis (– se) need, requirement; Bedürfnis nach etwas need for sth.
die Beendigung (– en) ending, termination
sich befassen (mit) to be concerned (with)
der Befehl (– e) order, command
das Befestigen fixing
befestigen to fix
befestigt fixed (see befestigen)
der Befestigungspunkt (– e) fixing/mounting point
sich befinden, a, u to be (located), operate; die sich in einem technologisch sehr vorgeschrittenen Stadium befinden which are operating at the leading edge of technology
befindlich in the process of; im Rückgang befindlich declining
befördern to transport, carry, promote
die Befragung (– en) opinion poll
befriedigen to satisfy
der Beginn beginning
beginnen, a, o to begin
begonnen begun (see beginnen)
begreifen, i, i to understand, realize
begrenzt (from begrenzen) limited
die Begrenzung (– en) limit, restriction; keine Begrenzung no restrictions
der Begriff (– e) idea, concept, term
begriffen (from begreifen): im Wachsen begriffen sein to be growing
begründen to found, start
die Begründung (– en) reason, foundation

sich begrüßen to greet one another; man begrüßt sich you greet each other
begutachten to inspect
behaglich comfortable
behalten (ä), ie, a to keep
die Beherrschung mastery
der/die Behinderte (– n), ein Behinderter (the) disabled person
der Behinderten-Service facilities for the disabled
die Behörde (– n) authority
bei at, near, with, for, when, in the case of, on the point of; bei uns in our/the company/country; bei der BASF at/with BASF; bei Bosch at/with Bosch; liegt bei 140 DM is DM 140; bei der Anfertigung von Steuererklärungen in filling out tax returns; bei der Förderung von Öl when extracting oil; bei Eingang on arrival
beide(s) both
beieinander together
beieinandersitzen (sep.) to congregate, sit together
das Beige beige
beigeheftet (from beiheften) inserted, included
der Beihefter (–) insert
die Beilage (– e) insert
beim = bei dem
das Bein (– e) leg
das Beispiel (– e) example; zum Beispiel/z.B. for example/e.g.
beispiellos unparalleled
beispielsweise for example, for instance
der Beitrag (¨e) contribution, subscription, sub, due, fee, premium
die Beitragshöhe (amount of) contribution/premium
bekannt well-known, familiar
die Bekanntheit reputation
der Bekanntheitsgrad (– e) level of awareness; ungestützte Bekanntheit unprompted level of awareness
die Bekleidung (– en) clothing, garment(s), clothing/garment industry
bekommen, a, o to get, receive; wir bekommen angeliefert we get delivered
die Beladung (– en) loading
die Belastung (– en) load, burden, pollution
sich belaufen (äu), ie, au (auf) to amount to; das beläuft sich auf that amounts to
die Belegschaft (– en) workforce, employees, manpower
Belgien Belgium
belgisch Belgian
beliebig any, to your requirements, unlimited
beliebt popular
der, die, das beliebteste (the) most popular (one)
beliefern to deliver, supply, source; schnell beliefert zu werden fast delivery
die Belieferung (– en) delivery
bemalt painted; außen bemalt externally painted
benannt appointed, named (see benennen); benannt nach named after
benennen, a, a to appoint, name
benutzen to use
benützen to use
das Benzin (– e) petrol
die Beobachtung (– en) observation
bequem convenient, comfortable, relaxing
der, die, das bequemste (the) most comfortable (one)
beraten (ä), ie, a to advise, give advice; er wird durch unseren Verkauf beraten über he is advised by our sales office about
beraten advised (see beraten)
beratend advising, advisory; beratend tätig sein to advise on, give advice, provide consultancy services
die Beratung (– en) consultancy, advice, service, care; Management-Beratung management consultancy; Gründungsberatung advice on founding a company, start-up advice
die Beraubung (– en) robbery
berechnen (nach) to charge (according to)
die Berechnung (– en) calculation, costing
der Bereich (– e) area, sphere, sector, industry
der Bereichsleiter (–) section manager
bereitgestellt supplied, provided, prepared
bereits already; die bereits vorhandenen the existing ones
die Bereitstellung (– en) supply, provision, allocation
der Bergbau mining
der Bergmechaniker (–) mining mechanic/technician
das Bergsteigen mountaineering
der Bericht (– e) report
die Berichterstattung (– en) reporting
der Beruf (– e) job, occupation, trade, profession
beruflich professional(ly); berufliche Tätigkeit job, occupation
das Berufsbild (– e) professional profile
die Berufsschule (– n) vocational (training) college
berufstätig in employment, (gainfully) employed
beschädigen to damage
beschaffen to procure, get, obtain; Kapital beschaffen to obtain capital
die Beschaffung (– en) procurement
beschäftigen to employ, occupy
sich beschäftigen (mit) to deal with, occupy oneself, to do; dann beschäftige ich mich gern mit wissenschaftlichen Dingen I like doing academic things
der/die Beschäftigte (– n), ein Beschäftigter (the) employed person, employee; die Beschäftigten workforce
der Bescheid (– e) notice of assessment (tax)
beschließen, o, o to decide, approve
beschlossen decided (see beschließen)
beschränkt (from beschränken) limited; beschränkte Haftung limited liability (see Gesellschaft)
beschriften to write, label; Bitte dieses Feld nicht beschriften und nicht bestempeln No writing or stamping in this space
die Beschriftung (– en) labelling, livery
besetzt (from besetzen) occupied, full
besichtigen to inspect
der, die, das besondere (the) special (one)
die Besonderheit (– en) (special) feature
besonders particularly, especially
besorgen to obtain
die Besprechung (– en) meeting
besprochen (from besprechen) discussed
besser (als) better (than)
der Bestand (¨e) stock
bestand (from bestehen): es bestand die Gefahr there was the danger
der Bestandteil (– e) component, part, element
die Bestätigung (– en) confirmation; Bestätigung confirm
der, die, das beste (the) best (one); in bester Qualität top quality
bestehen, bestand, bestanden to exist, be; (es) besteht die Möglichkeit it is possible; bestehen aus to consist of, comprise; besteht darin festzustellen consists in ascertaining
besteht (see bestehen)
der Bestelleingang (¨e) order entry, receipt of order, incoming order
bestellen to order, appoint
der Besteller (–) customer, purchaser, person ordering
bestellt ordered, appointed (see bestellen)
die Bestellung (– en) order
bestempeln to stamp; Bitte dieses Feld nicht beschriften und nicht bestempeln No writing or stamping in this space
am besten best
bestens: Sie sind mit Bosch bestens beraten your ideal/perfect partner is Bosch
bestimmen to fix, determine, establish
bestimmt definite(ly), certain(ly), fixed, specific, predetermined
bestimmt established (see bestimmen)
die Bestimmung (– en) fixing, determining, regulation, rule
der Bestimmungshafen (¨) port of destination
der Bestimmungsort (– e) destination; frei Bestimmungsort free/franco domicile

die Bestrebung (– en) programme, drive
der Besuch (– e) visit
besuchen to visit
der Besucher (–) visitor
die Besucher-Analyse (– n) visitor analysis
sich betätigen to operate, move
sich beteiligen (an) to be part (of), take part (in); die an der Transportkette beteiligt sind which are part of the transport chain
das Beteiligungskapital investment capital
betonen to emphasize
betont marked(ly), emphatical(ly), emphasized
beträchtlich considerable, substantial(ly)
der Betrag (¨e) amount, payment, sum (of money); Betrag in Buchstaben amount in words
betragen (ä), u, a to be, amount to
betreffen (betrifft), betraf, betroffen to concern, affect; was die Geräte betrifft as far as the appliances are concerned
betreiben, ie, ie to pursue, carry out, operate with, be engaged in
betreuen to support, look after, be in charge of
die Betreuung (– en) (customer) support, back-up; Presse-Betreuung press relations
der Betrieb (– e) company, business, firm, operation, service
betrieblich company; betriebliche Altersversorgung company pension scheme
betriebsbereit operational
die Betriebsdatenerfassung production/company data acquisition
die Betriebsferien (pl) works holiday, annual holiday/shutdown
die Betriebsfläche (– n) works/site area, space
die Betriebsmittel (pl) resources, production facilities
die Betriebsprüfung (– en) tax audit, external audit
der Betriebsrat (¨e) works council, employees' elected representative (member of the works council)
der/die Betriebsratsvorsitzende (– n), ein Betriebsratsvorsitzender chairman/chairperson of the works council
das Betriebsverfassungsgesetz (– e) Industrial Constitution Act
die Betriebswirtschaft business studies, business administration
betriebswirtschaftlich business, economic, budgeting; das betriebswirtschaftliche Gewissen the budgeting conscience; betriebswirtschaftliche Regularien principles of business administration
betrifft: concerns (see betreffen); Betrifft: re:
die Beurteilung (– en) judging
die Bevölkerung (– en) population, public
bevor before
bevorstehen (sep.), stand bevor, bevorgestanden to come up
bevorsteht come up (see bevorstehen); gerade bevorsteht is coming up
bevorzugen to prefer
bewährt (from bewähren) proven, established, tried and tested
bewerben (i), bewarb, beworben to target (by advertising)
das Bewertungsgutachten (–) valuation appraisal
die Bewirtung (– en) entertainment
beworben targetted (see bewerben)
bezahlen to pay
bezahlt (from bezahlen) paid
die Beziehung (– en) relation(ship); internationale Beziehungen international relations
beziehungsweise or, and/or, i.e.
bezogen (from beziehen) purchased
bezüglich regarding
bezugsfertig turnkey, ready-to-use
das Bier (– e) beer
der Biergarten (¨) beer garden
der Biermarkt (¨e) beer market
die Biersorte (– n) type/make of beer
sich bieten, o, o to offer, present
das Big Business big business (großes Geschäft)

Glossary

die Bilanz (– en) *balance sheet, annual accounts*
das Bilanzrecht *accounting legislation*
die Bilanzsumme (– n) *balance-sheet total*
bilden *to form*
billig *cheap, cost-effective, low-cost*
die Billion (– en) *1,000,000,000,000, billion*
bin *am;* bin befördert worden *was promoted (see sein);* ich bin Ingenieur *I am an engineer*
das Bindeglied (– er) *link*
die Binnenalster *Inner Alster*
der Binnenmarkt (ːe) *internal/single market;* europäischer Binnenmarkt *single European market*
biologisch *biological(ly)*
die Birne (– n) *pear*
bis *to, until, through, before, by;* von etwas bis zu *from sth. through to;* bis zu *up to;* bis hin zu *right through to;* 9000 bis 10 000 Stunden *9000 to/or 10 000 hours;* bis 1995 wird die Freizeit zunehmen *by 1995 leisure will have increased;* bis nachher *until finally*
bisherig *previous*
Bismarck, Otto von *first chancellor of the German Reich*
bißchen: ein bißchen *a little/bit, a bit (of)*
bitte *please*
die Bitte (– n) *request;* mit der Bitte um *please;* Mit der Bitte um Kenntnisnahme/Stellungnahme *for information/comment*
blank *plain, pure, bright, shiny*
das Blatt (ːer) *sheet, page*
blättern* *to peel off*
das Blech (– e) *sheet (metal/steel), strip, plate*
die Blechrolle (– n) *(metal/steel) coil*
das Blechteil (– e) *panel*
der Blechwender (–) *plate turner*
die Bleibe (– n) *dwelling;* für den Kauf einer Bleibe *for purchasing a home*
bleiben, ie, ie * *to stay, remain;* bleiben uns vorbehalten *we reserve the right to*
der Blick (– e) *view, glance;* auf einen Blick *at a glance;* auf den ersten Blick *at a first glance*
blicken (auf) *to look (to)*
blieben *remained (see bleiben)*
das Blinklicht (– er) *indicator*
der Blitz (– e) *lightning*
der Blitzzement *quick-setting cement (lit. lightning cement)*
der Blockstand (ːe) *block stand (four sides open)*
bloß *only, but*
die Blume (– n) *flower*
BMW = Bayerische Motorenwerke
der BMW (– s) *BMW (car)*
der Boden (ː) *floor, ground*
das Bodenblech (– e) *floor panel, floor pan*
der Bogen (– or ː) *curve, ring, crescent, sheet*
die Bohne (– n) *bean*
der Bohneneintopf (ːe) *bean soup/stew;* grüner Bohneneintopf *stew/soup made with green beans*
das Bohrfeld (– er) *drilling field*
die Bohrinsel (– n) *drilling platform;* Bohr– und Förderinsel *drilling and production platform*
das Bolzensetzen *placing bolts*
das Bondern *bonderizing*
das Boot (– e) *boat*
die Bootsausstellung (– en) *boat exhibition/show*
das Bord (– e) *board;* an Bord *on board (ship)*
die Bordküche (– n) *galley*
die Börse (– n) *stock exchange*
der Börsenplatz *see Bankenplatz*
brach *broke (see brechen)*
brachte *brought (see bringen)*
die Branche (– n) *sector*
branchenmäßig *by sector, sector*
das Brathendl (–) *roast/barbecued chicken*
die Bratkartoffel (– n) *fried potatoes*
brauchen *to need*
die Brauerei (– en) *brewing, brewery*
die BRD (= Bundesrepublik Deutschland) *FRG*
die BR Deutschland *(FR) Germany*
brechen (bricht), brach, gebrochen *to break*
breit *wide*
die Breite (– n) *width*

breitgefächert *broadly-based, comprehensive*
das Bremsteil (– e) *brake component*
brennbar *flammable*
der Brief (– e) *letter*
der Briefstil (– e) *art of letter writing*
bringen, brachte, gebracht *to bring, have;* in Verbindung bringen mit *to associate with;* dazu zu bringen *to persuade;* sie bringen das Chrom an das Bauteil *they deposit the chrome on the component*
der Brite (wk m) (– n) *British person*
britisch *British*
der Brocken: ein paar Brocken Italienisch *a smattering of Italian*
die Brokkoli (pl) *broccoli*
das Brot (– e) *bread, loaf*
der Brotshop (– s) *bread shop*
die Brotsorte (– n) *kind/type of bread*
die Brücke (– n) *bridge*
brückenreich *abundant in bridges (lit. rich in bridges);* die brückenreichste Stadt *the city with the most bridges*
der Bruttolohn (ːe) *gross pay, total pay*
das Bruttosozialprodukt (– e) *gross domestic product*
die BSE = Industriegewerkschaft Bau-Steine-Erden *(see Gewerkschaft)*
die BSHG = Bosch-Siemens Hausgeräte GmbH
das Buch (ːer) *book*
buchen *to book*
die Buchführung *book-keeping, accounting*
die Buchhaltung *accounts (department)*
die Buchmesse (– n) *book fair*
der Buchprüfer: vereidigter Buchprüfer *certified accountant*
die Buchprüfung (– en) *audit*
der Buchstabe (wk m)(– n) *letter (of the alphabet);* Betrag in Buchstaben *amount in words*
die Buchung (– en) *booking*
die Buchungsvoranmeldung (– en) *advance booking*
das Bügeleisen (–) *iron(s)*
Bulgarien *Bulgaria*
der Bulk-Container (–) *bulk container*
der Bund *federation*
bündeln *to bundle, combine*
das Bundesaufsichtsamt (ːer) *federal supervisory office/authority, industry watchdog;* Bundesaufsichtsamt für das Kreditwesen *Federal Banking Supervisory Office*
die Bundesbahn *(German lit. Federal) railway, rail*
die Bundesbank *central bank;* (lit. federal bank)
der Bundesdurchschnitt (– e) *federal average*
das Bundesgebiet *Federal Republic*
das Bundesministerium (–ministerien) *federal ministry;* Bundesministerium für Forschung und Technik *Federal Ministry of Research and Technology*
die Bundespost *Federal Post Office*
die Bundesrepublik *Federal Republic;* Bundesrepublik Deutschland *Federal Republic of Germany*
der Bundesverband (ːe) *federal association;* Bundesverband deutscher Banken *Federal Association of German Banks*
bundesweit *nation-wide, the whole of the Federal Republic*
das Bürgerhaus (ːer) *patrician house*
Burgunder *Burgundian, of Burgundy*
das Büro (– s) *office*
die Büroarbeit (– en) *office/clerical work*
die Bürokauffrau (– en) *office clerk/clerical worker (f)*
die Büromöbel (–) *office furniture*
der Büroraum (ːe) *office space/area*
das Bürozentrum (–zentren) *office facilities (lit. centre)*
der Bus (– se) *bus, coach*
das Business *business;* Big Business *big business (großes Geschäft)*
die Butter *butter*
bzw. = beziehungsweise *or*

C

ca. (= circa) *approximately, around, about*
CAD = Computer Aided Design (rechnergestütztes Konstruieren)
die CAD-Anlage (– n) *CAD system*

der CAD/CAM-Markt (ːe) *CAD/CAM market*
das CAD/CAM-Produkt (– e) *CAD/CAM product*
CAM = Computer Aided Manufacturing (rechnergestützte Fertigungssteuerung)
die CAM-Technik *CAM technology/engineering*
der Caravan (– s) *caravan*
Carte: à la Carte *à la Carte*
das Center (–) *centre*
der Chamäleon (– s) *chameleon*
der Champignon (– s) *mushroom*
die Chance (– n) *chance, opportunity*
die Chartergesellschaft (– en) *charter company*
das Chassis (–) *chassis*
die Checklist (– s) *check list*
der Chef (– s) *boss, manager, head (m), company bosses*
die Chemie *chemistry, chemicals, chemicals industry*
das Chemieareal (– e) *chemical complex*
die Chemikalie (– n) *chemical*
die Chemikalien (f, pl) *chemicals*
chemisch *chemical;* chemische Industrie *chemicals industry*
Chile *Chile*
China *China*
der Chip (– s) *chip*
das Chlor *chlorine*
das Chrom *chrome, chromium*
die CI = Corporate-Identity
das CI-Konzept (– e) *corporate identity concept*
CIM = Computer Integrated Manufacturing (Fertigungssteuerung im Datenverbund)
die CI-Politik *corporate identity policy*
circa *about, approximately, roughly*
die City (– s) *city*
der Clou (– s) *secret, trick*
der Cockpitbereich (– e) *cockpit (area)*
das Coil (– s) *coil*
die Coilbreite (– n) *coil width*
das College (– s) *college*
der Computer (–) *computer*
die Computerfirma (–firmen) *computer company*
computergesteuert *computer controlled, by computer, computerized*
die Computergrafik (– en) *(computer) graphics*
computersteuerbar *with computer(ized) control, computer-controlled, computerized, fully automated*
das Conference-Center (–) *conference centre*
der Container (–) *container*
der Containerdienst (– e) *container service*
die Containergestellung (– en) *container delivery*
containerisierbar *containerizable, suitable for transport by container*
die Containerpalette (– n) *(container) pallet*
der Containertransport (– e) *container transport*
der Containertruck (– s) *container truck*
der Containerverkehr *container traffic*
das Controlling *controlling*
die Corporate-Identity *corporate identity*
die Creme (– s) *cream*
die Culture *culture*

D

D = Deutschland
da *here, there, since, because, at that point;* ist ... da *there is ...*
dabei *now, during this process;* wir sind dabei ... zu *we are in the process of*
das Dach (ːer) *roof, umbrella organization (lit. roof);* unter eigenem Dach *under your own roof;* unter einem Dach *under one roof*
dachte *thought (see denken)*
dadurch *that way*
dafür *for it/them, to make up for it, instead of that, in return, that's why;* dafür, daß *because;* dafür macht man ihn *that's why you set it*
dagegen *by contrast*
daher *therefore, hence*
dahinter *behind it/them*
damals *at that time, then*
die Dame (– n) *lady, woman*
die Damenoberbekleidung *ladies' wear,*

ladies' outerwear
damit *with it/them/this, so (that), i.e., consequently*
danach *by that, after that, according to this;* danach richtet sich *is determined by that;* danach richten sich ... aus *... are geared to that*
daneben *off the mark*
Dänemark *Denmark*
dankbar *thankful*
dann *then, also;* hinzu kommen dann *then there are also*
daran *at, on, about in (it/them), that's*
darauf *on it/them, of it/them;* stolz darauf *proud of it*
daraus *out of it/them, from it/them;* daraus, daß *from the fact that*
darf *may (see dürfen)*
darin *in it/them*
Darmausgang: künstlicher Darmausgang *stoma, artificial opening from the gastro-intestinal tract to the outside*
darstellen (sep.) *to present, give a presentation, to be, represent*
sich darstellen (sep.) *to present/project itself*
die Dartscheibe (– n) *dartboard*
darum *therefore, around, about it/them/that*
das *the, this, that, these, who;* das sind so *these are;* das ist *that's;* das heißt *that is (i.e.)*
daß *that;* so daß *so that*
dasselbe *the same*
die Datei *file*
die Daten (n, pl) *data*
die Datenbank (– en) *database, data bank*
die Datenerfassung (– en) *data acquisition*
die Datenverarbeitung (– en) *data processing*
das Datenverarbeitungsgerät (– e) *data-processing unit/terminal*
das Datum *date;* Daten (pl) *data*
dauerhaft *permanent(ly)*
dauern *to last, take*
davon *of it/them, away from it, with it/them*
dazu *for it, to do it, about it, in addition, for this/that;* dazu zu bringen *to persuade*
die DDR = Deutsche Demokratische Republik
decken *to cover, finance*
definiert *(from definieren) defines, defined*
die Definition (– en) *definition*
der Deich (– e) *dyke*
delegieren *to delegate;* delegieren Sie! *delegate!*
delegiert *delegated (see delegieren)*
die Delikatesse (– n) *delicacy*
dem *the/to/whom; which*
die Demokratie (– n) *democracy*
die Demokratisierung (– en) *democratization*
den *the, which, whom*
denen *(to) which/whom;* nach denen *according to which*
das Denken *thought, thinking;* vertriebsstrategisches Denken praktizieren *to apply marketing principles*
denken, dachte, gedacht *to think;* an etwas denken *to think about sth.;* denke ich insbesondere an *I'm particularly thinking of*
denn *as, because, for, then;* denn dann eigentlich *actually;* wieso denn *why*
dennoch *still*
denselben *see dasselbe*
der *the, this, who, which, it, that, he*
deren *their, whose, of which*
derjenige *the person who;* derjenige, der *the person who*
derzeit *at present*
des *of the, which, whom*
das Design (– s) *design*
der Designer (–) *designer*
dessen *his, its, whose, of which, that, what;* dessen, was ... *of what*
desto *the;* je ... desto *the ... the;* je besser ... desto besser *the better ... the better*
deswegen *therefore, for that reason*
detailliert *detailed*
deutlich *clear, obvious*
deutsch *German;* die deutsche Mark,

die D-Mark *Deutschmark, German mark, D-Mark*
das Deutsch *German*
das Deutsche *German (language)*
Deutsches: Deutsches Museum *Deutsches Museum (science museum)*
Deutschland *Germany;* Bundesrepublik Deutschland *Federal Republic of Germany*
die Devisen *(f, pl) foreign exchange/currency*
der Dezember *December;* im Dezember *in December*
dezentral *decentralized*
der DGB = Deutscher Gewerkschaftsbund
d.h. (= das heißt) *i.e.*
der Diaprojektor (– en) *slide projector*
die Dichte *density*
die Dichtigkeit *seal*
die *the, this, those, who, which, it, that, she, they*
der Diebstahl (¨e) *theft*
dienen *to serve;* die Nockenwelle dient zur Steuerung *the camshaft controls/operates*
der Dienst (– e) *service;* öffentliche Dienste *public services*
der Dienstag (– e) *Tuesday;* am Dienstag *on Tuesday*
dienstags *on Tuesdays*
die Dienstleistung (– en) *service;* allgemeine Dienstleistungen *general services*
der Dienstleistungssektor (– en) *service sector*
dies *this*
diese, diesem, diesen, dieser, dieses *(to/from/for/of) this/these*
differenzieren *to differentiate, draw a distinction*
diktieren *to dictate*
die Dimension (– en) *dimension;* für solche Dimensionen *on such a scale*
DIN = Deutsche Industrie Normen, Deutsches Institut für Normung
das Ding (– e) *thing, function;* vor allen Dingen *especially;* wissenschaftliche Dinge *academic work*
Dipl. = Diplom
das Diplom (– e) *degree*
der Diplomvolkswirt (– e) *graduate in economics*
direkt *direct(ly);* direkter Draht *direct line, hot line*
direkter (als) *more direct(ly) (than)*
der Direktimport (– e) *direct import;* laufen im Direktimport *are imported directly*
dirigieren *to conduct, direct, deploy*
die Diskette (– n) *disk(ette)*
disponieren *to distribute, deploy*
die Disposition (– en) *deploying*
die Distribution (– en) *distribution*
der Distributor (– en) *distributor*
die Distributoren *(pl) distributors*
divers *different, various*
die DM = Deutsche Mark
die D-Mark (–) *Deutschmark, German mark, D-Mark*
Do = Donnerstag
D/O = Deutschland/Ost
doch *yet, but, nevertheless, certainly, surely;* doch schon hier *yet already/even here*
die Dokumentation (– en) *documentation*
dokumentieren *to document, record*
der Dollar (– s) *dollar*
der Dolmetscher (–) *interpreter*
die Dolmetscherin (–nen) *interpreter (f)*
dominieren *to dominate;* den Markt sehr stark dominieren *to flood the market*
der Donnerstag (– e) *Thursday;* am Donnerstag *on Thursday*
donnerstags *on Thursdays*
das Dorf (¨er) *village*
dort *there*
dortig *there*
das Döschen (–) *tin, pot*
die DPG = Deutsche Postgewerkschaft (see Gewerkschaft)
Dr. (= Doktor) *Dr*
der Draht (¨e) *wire, line*
drauf = darauf
draufschlagen (sep.) (ä), u, a (auf) *to add on*
das Drehen *turning*
drei *three*

dreieinhalb *three and a half*
das Drei-Säulen-System (– e) *three-column system*
dreißig *thirty*
der, die, das dreißigste *(the) thirtieth (one)*
dreizehn *thirteen*
der, die, das dreizehnte *(the) thirteenth (one);* dreizehntes Monatsgehalt *thirteenth month's salary, annual bonus*
drin (= darin) *in;* wenn man einmal drin ist, dann ist man drin *once you're in, you're in;* besteht darin festzustellen *consists in ascertaining*
dringend *urgent(ly)*
der, die, das dritte *(the) third (one)*
das/ein Drittel (–) *(a) third*
drittens *thirdly*
die Drogerie (– n) *chemist's/drugstore (non-dispensing)*
der Drogeriemarkt (¨e) *self-service drugstore*
der Druck *pressure, printing*
drucken *to print*
drücken *to press, reduce*
der Drucker (–) *printer*
der Drucker-Auszug (¨e) *printer shelf*
die Druckerpapierablage (– n) *printer paper rack*
die Druckindustrie (– n) *printing industry*
die Druckrohrleitung (– en) *high-pressure pipeline*
drückt: drückt ... aus *see* ausdrücken
die DRUPA = Druck und Papier
du *you (familiar, singular)*
das Dunkelblau *dark blue*
die Dunstabzugskonstruktion (– en) *cooker hood*
durch *by, through, on the basis of*
durchaus *thoroughly, definitely*
der Durchbruch (¨e) *knockout, breakthrough*
durchdacht *well-thought-out, refined*
durchführen (sep.) *to carry out*
die Durchführung (– en) *execution*
durchgeführt *carried out (see* durchführen)
durchgehend *continuous(ly);* durchgehend geöffnet *open 24 hours*
durchgeschnitten *(from* durchschneiden) *cut out*
durchgetrennt *separated, cut through (see* durchtrennen)
durchlaufen (äu), ie, au *to go through*
der Durchmesser (–) *diameter*
durchschaubar *transparent*
der Durchschnitt (– e) *average*
durchschnittlich *average, on average, an average of*
der Durchschnittspreis (– e) *average price*
der Durchschnittsverdiener (–) *average earner/wage-earner*
sich durchsetzen (sep.) *to become commonplace*
durchtrennen (sep.) *to separate, cut through*
durchziehen (sep.), zog durch, durchgezogen *to carry out*
durchzuführen *see* durchführen
dürfen (a), u, u *to be allowed;* darf *may;* darf nicht *must not;* dürften *might*
dürften *might, probably are (see* dürfen); dürften ... irgendwo ähnlich stehen *probably stand roughly on the same level*
die Dusche (– n) *shower*
die Düssel *River Düssel*
Düsseldorfer *of Düsseldorf, Düsseldorf*
der Düsseldorfer(–) *person from Düsseldorf*
das Dutzend (– e) *dozen*
D/W = Deutschland/West

E

der Ebbelwei *(coll.) cider (lit. apple wine)*
eben *just, after all, precisely;* das ist es eben *it's that*
echt *genuine, traditional, really*
der Eckstand (¨e) *corner stand (two sides open)*
der Edamer (–) *Edam (cheese)*
die EDV = Elektronische Datenverarbeitung *EDP (Electronic Data Processing)*
der Effekt (– e) *effect*
effektiv *effective(ly)*
effektiver (als) *more effective (than)*
effektvoll *effective(ly), elegant(ly)*
die EG = Europäische Gemeinschaft *EC (European Community)*

die EG-Richtlinie (– n) *EC directive*
ehe *before*
ehemalig *former*
der Ehepartner (–) *spouse*
eher *rather, more*
eigen, eigene, eigenem, eigenen, eigener, eigenes *(its, his, her, their) own;* mit eigener Kraft *under its own power/steam*
die Eigenart (– en) *idiosyncrasy, quirk*
die Eigenentwicklung (– en) *in-house development/innovation*
das Eigenheim (– e) *own home; house of your own; owner-occupied house*
die Eigenleistung (– en) *in-house product*
die Eigenleistungen *(pl) products manufactured by a foreign subsidiary, in-house products*
eigenständig *independent(ly)*
eigentlich *actually, really, rather;* denn dann eigentlich *actually*
die Eigentumswohnung (– en) *owner-occupied flat*
eigenverantwortlich *voluntary*
ein, eine, einem, einen, einer, eines *(to/from/of/of) a, one, (the) right person, somebody*
der Einbau (–ten) *installation*
einbauen (sep.) *to build in, install*
die Einbauküche (– n) *fitted kitchen*
der Einbruch (¨e) *burglary*
der Einbruchdiebstahl (¨e) *burglary*
eindrucksvoll *impressive;* optisch eindrucksvoll *spectacular*
eineinhalb *one and a half*
einfach *simple (–ly), easy (-ily)*
einfacher (als) *simpler, easier (than)*
der, die, das einfachste *(the) simplest (one)*
der, die, das Einfachste *(the) easiest thing/one*
einfallen (sep.) (ä), ie, a * *to occur, think of;* was fällt Ihnen ein? *what do you think of?*
einfließen (sep.), o, o * *to become incorporated, flow into*
einführen (sep.) *to introduce*
die Einfuhrfirma (–firmen) *import company*
die Einführung (– en) *import, introduction*
der Eingang (¨e) *arrival, entrance*
eingebaut *built in, installed (see* einbauen)
eingeben (sep.) (i), a, e *to enter;* neu eingeben *to re-enter, enter again*
eingebrannt *(from* einbrennen) *burnt in, hardened*
eingeführt *introduced, inserted (see* einführen)
eingefüllt *(from* einfüllen) *poured in*
eingegriffen *intervened (see* eingreifen)
eingehalten *kept to (see* einhalten)
eingekauft *bought (see* einkaufen); es wird auf dem deutschen Markt eingekauft *we buy in the German market*
eingesetzt *used (see* einsetzen)
eingestellt *adjusted, aligned (see* einstellen)
eingetragen *(from* eintragen) *entered*
eingreifen (sep.), griff ein, eingegriffen *to intervene*
einhalten (sep.) (ä), ie, a *to keep (to)*
einheitlich *uniform(ly), within a uniform concept, joint, common*
sich einhören (auf) *to become attuned (to)*
einige, einigem, einigen, einiger, einiges *(to/from/for/of) some, several;* nach einiger Zeit *after some time*
der Einkauf (¨e) *purchase, purchasing (department)*
das Einkaufen *purchasing, shopping*
einkaufen (sep.) *to buy (in), purchase*
der Einkäufer (–) *buyer*
das Einkaufsvolumen (–) *purchasing volume, amount purchased*
das Einkommen (–) *income*
einladen (ä), (lädt ein), lud ein, eingeladen *to load*
die Einlage (– n) *investment, deposit*
der Einleger (–) *investor*
das Einlesen *reading/scanning in*
einmal *once, one of, for once, really, once in a while, sometimes, first of all;* zunächst einmal *initial(ly), first(ly)*
einmalig *unique*
einreichen (sep.) *to submit, file*
die Einrichtung (– en) *installation,*

equipment, facility, establishment, authority; staatliche Einrichtungen *state authorities, the state*
eins *one*
der Einsatz (¨e) *effort, use, commitment;* im Einsatz sein *to be in use, deployed, cover;* mit sehr hohem Einsatz *with great commitment*
einschließlich *including*
einsetzbar *can be used;* universell einsetzbar *universal;* vollautomatisch computergesteuert einsetzbar *can be used with fully-automated computer(ized) control*
einsetzen (sep.) *to use, deploy*
einstecken (sep.) *to insert*
einstellen (sep.) *to adapt, adjust, set, employ*
das Einteilen *planning*
(sich) einteilen (sep.) *to organize, divide*
eintippen (sep.) *to enter (lit. to type in)*
das Eintippen *entering, typing in*
eintreffen (ä) *(trifft ein), traf ein, eingetroffen * to arrive*
einwandfrei *smooth(ly), without any problems;* einwandfrei funktionierend *smooth-running, perfectly functioning*
das Einwegprodukt (– e) *single-use product*
der Einwohner (–) *inhabitant, member of the public*
die Einwohnerzahl (– en) *population (lit. number of inhabitants)*
das Einzelbauteil (– e) *individual component*
die Einzelbestimmung (– en) *individual/local regulation*
der Einzelhandel *retail trade*
das Einzelhandelsgeschäft (– e) *retail shop/outlet*
der Einzelhandelskaufmann (¨er) *retail salesman*
der Einzelhändler (–) *retailer*
der Einzelmarkt (¨e) *single market*
einzeln *individual(ly), single*
die Einzelperson (– en) *individual*
das Einzelteil (– e) *individual part, component*
der, die, das einzige *(the) only (one)*
das Eisen *iron*
die Eisenbahn (– en) *rail, railway*
der Eisenbahner (–) *railwayman*
die Eisenbahnschiene (– n) *rail, rail track*
die Elbe *River Elbe*
der Elefant *(wk m)*(– en) *elephant*
die Elektrik *electrical systems*
das Elektrikteil (– e) *electrical component*
elektrisch *electrical(ly)*
das Elektrogerät (– e) *electrical appliance*
die Elektroindustrie (– n) *electrical industry*
der Elektroinstallateur (– e) *electrician, electrical fitter*
der Elektromarkt (¨e) *electrical markets*
die Elektronenstrahlschweißmaschine (– n) *electron beam welding machine*
die Elektronik *electronics, electronic equipment*
die Elektronikentwicklung (– en) *electronics development, development in electronics*
das Elektronikteil (– e) *electronic component*
elektronisch *electronic(ally);* elektronische Datenverarbeitung *electronic data processing*
elektrostatisch *electrostatic(ally)*
das Element (– e) *element*
elf *eleven*
das Emblem (– e) *emblem*
die Emission (– en) *emission*
emotional *emotional(ly)*
empfangen (ä), i, a *to receive*
empfangen *received (see* empfangen)
der Empfänger (–) *recipient, receiver*
empfinden, a, a *to feel*
empfindlich *sensitive, fragile*
empfindlicher (als) *more sensitive(ly) (than)*
empfunden *felt (see* empfinden)
das Ende (– n) *end;* Ende Mai *at the end of May*
der Endkunde *(wk m)* (– n) *end user/customer*
die Endmontage (– n) *final assembly*
endmontieren *to assemble, carry out final assembly*
der Endverbraucher (–) *end user/consumer*
der Endverwender (–) *end user, consumer*
die Energie (– n) *energy*

Glossary

der Energieelektroniker (–) *electronics fitter*
energiesparend *energy-saving*
eng *close(ly), tight(ly), narrow*
enger (als) *closer (than), more closely (than)*; die Märkte sind viel enger geworden *the markets have become much more competitive*
England *England, Britain, UK*
die Engländer (pl) *(the) English, British*
englisch *English, British*
das Englisch *English*
Englischer: Englischer Garten *English Garden*
die Entenbrust (¨e) *breast of duck*
sich entfalten *to unfold, develop*
entfernen *to remove*
entfernt *removed, distant (see* entfernen*)*
die Entfettung (– en) *degreasing*
das Entgelt *pay*
enthalten (ä), ie, a *to contain*
entnehmen (entnimmt), entnahm, entnommen *to remove;* Eurocheque-Karte entnehmen *remove Eurocheque card*
sich entscheiden, ie, ie *to decide*
entscheidend *decisive(ly), important, deciding*
die Entscheidung (– en) *decision*
entschieden *considerable (-ly), substantial(ly)*
entschieden *decided (see* entscheiden*)*
sich entschließen, o, o *to decide;* man entschloß sich ... zu *it was decided to carry out*
entschloß *decided (see* entschließen*)*
entsprechen (i), a, o *to conform to, correspond to*
entsprechend *in accordance with, correspondingly, accordingly*
entspricht *conforms to, corresponds to (see* entsprechen*)*
entstanden *arisen, emerged (see* entstehen*)*
entstehen, entstand, entstanden * *to arise, form, come out, emerge, develop*; es entsteht eine Buchung *someone makes a booking*
entstehend *arising, created*
entwachst *(from* entwachsen*) dewaxed*
entweder: entweder ... oder *either ... or*
(sich) entwickeln *to develop*; das Tagesgeschäft entwickeln *to carry out the day-to-day business*
entwickelnd *developing*
entwickelt *developed (see* entwickeln*)*
der Entwickler (–) *development engineer, inventor*
die Entwicklung (– en) *development*; Forschung und Entwicklung *research and development, R & D*
die Entwicklungsabteilung (– en) *development department*
die Entwicklungsbestrebung (– en) *development drive/programme*
das Entwicklungsergebnis (– se) *development result*
der Entwicklungsingenieur (– e) *development engineer*
die Entwicklungstechnologie (– n) *development technology*
der Entwurf (¨e) *design*
er *he, it*
(sich) erarbeiten *to carry out, produce, compile*
erarbeitet *carried out, produced (see* erarbeiten*)*
erbracht *manufactured (see* erbringen*)*
erbringen, erbrachte, erbracht *to manufacture*
die Erbse (– n) *pea*
die Erbsensuppe (– n) *pea soup*
die Erde (– n) *earth*
das Erdgas *natural gas*; Erdgas-Bohrfeld *natural-gas (drilling) field*
Erdinger *of Erding, Erding*
das Ereignis (– se) *event*
erfahren (ä), u, a *to experience*
die Erfahrung (– en) *experience*; aus Erfahrung *from experience*
der Erfahrungsaustausch (– e) *exchange of experience/views, information exchange*
erfand *see* erfinden
erfassen *to affect, acquire*
erfaßt *affects, affected, acquires, acquired (see* erfassen*)*
die Erfassung *acquisition*

erfinden, a, u *to invent*
der Erfolg (– e) *success*
erfolgen * *to be made, carried out, effect, take place, occur*; Dann erfolgt die Geldausgabe *Payment is then made*; erfolgt der Einbau der Nockenwelle *the camshaft is installed*
erfolgreich *successful*
erforderlich *necessary*
erfordern *to demand*
erfuhr *see* erfahren
erfüllen *to fulfil*
ergänzt *(from* ergänzen*) complements, complemented*
das Ergebnis (– se) *result, conclusion, performance, earnings*; zu einem Ergebnis kommen *to come to a conclusion*
der Ergebnisvergleich (– e) *comparison of results*
ergiebig *productive*
ergiebiger (als) *more productive (than)*
die Ergonomie *ergonomics*
ergonomisch *ergonomic*
der Erhalt *contents, receipt*
erhält *see* erhalten
erhält: erhält ... zurück *see* zurückerhalten
erhalten (ä), ie, a *to receive, keep, gain*
erhältlich *available*
erheblich *considerable (-ly), serious*
erhielt *received (see* erhalten*)*
(sich) erhoffen *to assume, hope for*
erhofft *assumed, hoped for (see* erhoffen*)*
(sich) erhöhen *to increase*
erhöht *increased (see* erhöhen*)*
erinnern (an) *to remind (of)*
erkannt *well-known, familiar*
erkennbar *recognizable, detectable*
erkennen, a, a *to recognize*
sich erkennen, a, a (als) *to recognize/become aware of oneself (as)*
das Erkennungssymbol (– e) *symbol (of recognition)*
erklären *to explain*
erlassen (erläßt), erließ, erlassen *to issue, establish*
(sich) erlauben *to allow, permit*
der Erlebniseinkauf (¨e) *shopping as an experience*
die Erledigung (– en) *attention*; Mit der Bitte um: Erledigung *for attention*
ernst *serious(ly)*; ernst nehmen *to take seriously*
erreichen *to achieve, reach, do, ensure*
erreicht *achieves, achieved (see* erreichen*)*
errichten *to erect, build*
die Errichtung (– en) *erection, installation*
der Ersatz *substitute*
das Ersatzteil (– e) *spare/replacement part*
die Ersatzteilbeschaffung (– en) *spare-parts procurement*
das Ersatzteillager (–) *spare-parts warehouse, stock of spare parts*
erscheinen, ie, ie * *to appear*
erschienen *appeared (see* erscheinen*)*
ersetzen *to substitute, replace*
ersetzt *replaced (see* ersetzen*)*
erst *only, not until, first*
der, die, das erste *(the) first (one)*; als erstes *first of all*
erstellen *to draw up, compile*; wir erstellen Ihre Dokumentation *we draw up your documentation*
erstellt *see* erstellen
erstens *first(ly)*
der Erstflug (¨e) *maiden flight*
erstmal *first(ly), first of all, initially*
erteilen *to commission*; einen Auftrag erteilen *to give a task, place an order, to commission*
der Ertrag (¨e) *profit, earnings, yield*
die Ertragssituation (– en) *profitability, profits*
erwarb *see* erwerben
die Erwärmung (– en) *temperature increase*
erwarten *to expect*
erweitern *to expand*
erweitert *expanded, enlarged (see* erweitern*)*
erwerben (i), a, o *to purchase, buy, gain*
der/die Erwerbstätige (– n), ein Erwerbstätiger *(the) (gainfully) employed person, wage/salary earner*
erwirtschaften *to generate*
erwirtschaftet *generated (see* erwirtschaften*)*
erzählen *to tell, relate, talk about*
erzeugen *to produce, create, generate*
erzeugt *generated (see* erzeugen*)*
die Erziehung (– en) *education*
erzielen *to achieve, attain*
es *it*; es wird nicht mehr der Preis entscheidend sein *the price will no longer be decisive/a limiting factor*; es vergeht manchmal ein Jahr *a year sometimes goes by*
essen (ißt), aß, gegessen *to eat*
das Essen *food, meal*
essentiell *essential*
der Estragon *tarragon*
etc. *etc.*
das Etikett (– e, – en) *label*
etwa *approximately, around, about*
etwas *something, anything, somewhat, rather, a little, roughly*
euch *(to) you*
der Eurocheque (– s) *Eurocheque*
die Eurocheque-Karte (– n) *Eurocheque card*
Europa *Europe*
die Europa-Position (– en) *European position, positioning within Europe*
der Europäer (–) *European*
europäisch *European*; europäische Gemeinschaft *European Community*; europäischer Binnenmarkt *single European market*
das Europaparlament *European Parliament*
der Europarat *Council of Europe*
eventuell *possible (-ly), any*
exakt *exact(ly), precise(ly), perfect(ly)*
die Existenzgrundlage (– n) *livelihood*
existieren *to exist*; in diesen Ländern existieren Fabriken *there are factories in these countries*
der Exklusivvertrag (¨e) *exclusive contract/agreement*
exotisch *exotic(ally)*
der Experte (wk m) (– n) *expert*
der Export (– e) *export*
der Exporteur (– e) *exporter*
exportieren *to export*
exportiert *exports, exported (see* exportieren*)*
der Exportkaufmann (¨er) *export trader/salesman/clerk*
der Exportleiter (–) *head of exports, export manager/director*
der Exportmarkt (¨e) *export market*
exportorientiert *export-oriented*

F

Fábrica *(Spanish) factory*
die Fabrik (– en) *factory, manufacturing facility, shop floor*
die Fabrikation (– en) *production/manufacturing (facilities), fabrication, manufacture*
das Fach (¨er) *subject, trade, specialist*; kaufmännische Fächer *commercial subjects, vocational subjects*
der Facharbeiter (–) *skilled worker/craftsman/technician*
der Fachbegriff (– e) *technical/specialist term*
der Fachbesucher (–) *trade visitor*
die Fachbibliothek (– en) *technical/specialist library*
das Fachgeschäft (– e) *specialist, specialist retailer/shop*
der Fachhandel *specialist trade*; gehobener Fachhandel *exclusive fashion trade, high fashion*
der Fachhändler (–) *trade supplier, specialist dealer*
die Fachhochschule (– n) *college for higher professional training*
die Fachleute (pl) *specialists, experts*
die Fachmesse (– n) *(specialist) trade fair*
die Fachpresse (– n) *technical/specialist trade press*
die Fachsprache (– n) *technical/specialist language*
die Fachterminologie (– n) *technical/specialist terminology*
der Fachvortrag (¨e) *technical/specialist lecture*
die Fachwelt *professional/specialist world, experts*
fahrbar *mobile*
fahren (ä), u, a * *to drive, travel, go (using transport), run*; der Containertruck fährt an das Gate *the container truck drives to the gate*
der Fahrgastraum (¨e) *passenger compartment, saloon*
die Fahrt (– en) *journey*
die Fahrtstunde (– n) *travel time (lit. hour)*
die Fahrzeit (– en) *travel time*
das Fahrzeug (– e) *vehicle*
der Fahrzeugtyp (– en) *car model*
der Fahrzeugwert (– e) *value of a car*; Hälfte des Fahrzeugwertes *half the value of a car*
die Fakten *facts*; Zahlen und Fakten *facts and figures*
der Faktor (– en) *factor*
der Fall (¨e) *case*; im Falle *in the case (of)*
fallen (ä), ie, a * *to fall, decrease*
falls *in case, if*
die Fallstudie (– n) *case study*
fällt: fällt ein *(see* einfallen*)*
falsch *wrong, incorrectly*
die Familie (– n) *family*
der Familienname (wk m; genitive –ns) (– n) *family name, surname*
das Familienunternehmen (–) *family company*
fangen (ä), i, a *to catch*
fängt: fängt ... an *see* anfangen
der Farbdrucker (–) *colour printer*
die Farbe (– n) *paint, dye(stuff), colour*; von den Farben her *where colours are concerned*
die Farbgebung (– en) *decor*
die Farbgrafik (– en) *colour graphics*
farbig *coloured*; farbiges Gesicht *coloured livery (lit. face)*
der Farbton (¨e) *colour*
die Farbvariante (– n) *colour*; eine ganze Menge Farbvarianten *a wide range of colours*
der Fasching *carnival*
die Faser (– n) *fibre*
die Fashion *fashion*
fast *almost, practically*; fast keine *virtually no/none*
das Fazit (– s) *result, conclusion*; zu einem Fazit kommen *to reach a result/conclusion*
FCKW = CFC; ohne FCKW *ozone friendly (lit. without CFC)*
FCKW-frei *ozone friendly*
das FCKW-Treibgas (– e) *CFC propellant*
der Februar *February*; im Februar *in February*
fehlen *to lack, be missing*; es fehlt (an) *there is a lack of*; es fehlt die Präzision *precision is lacking*
der Fehler (–) *mistake, error, defect, fault*
fehlerfrei *error-free, without errors*
der Feierabend (– e) *knocking-off time, evening*
der Feiertag (– e) *public/bank holiday*
fein *fine*
das Feinblech (– e) *sheet (metal/steel), strip (product)*
das Feinbrot *bread made from finely-ground (brown) flour*
die Feinheit (– en) *subtlety*
das Feld (– er) *field, space, area, sphere*; elektrostatisches Feld *electrostatic field*
das Fenster (–) *window*
der Fernmeldeturm (¨e) *television/telecommunications tower*
das Fernsehen *television*
das Fernsehstudio (– s) *television studio*
die Fernsehwerbung *television advertising*
die Fernsehzeitschrift (– en) *TV-guide*
fertig *finished, ready, completed*; fertig ausgerüstet *fully equipped*
das Fertigen *manufacture, manufacturing*
fertigen *to produce, manufacture*
der Fertiger (–) *manufacturer*; Fertiger im Lande *manufacturer abroad*
fertiggestellt *completed (see* fertigstellen*)*
fertigstellen (sep.) *to complete*
der Fertigstellungstermin (– e) *date of completion*
das Fertigteil (– e) *finished part*
die Fertigung (– en) *production, manufacture*; industrielle Fertigung *industrial/mass production*
die Fertigungsgeräte (pl) *production equipment*
die Fertigungsstätte (– n) *production workshop/facility/plant*

die Fertigungssteuerung (– en) *production control*
die Fertigungstechnik *production engineering*
die Fertigungstechnologie (– n) *production technology*
das Fest (– e) *fair*
fest *firm, fixed*
festangestellt *in a permanent job, employed;* festangestellter Vertreter *employee*
festgelegt *laid down, established (see* festlegen*);* gesetzlich festgelegt *laid down by law*
festgestellt *see* feststellen
die Festigkeit (– en) *strength*
festlegen (sep.) *to lay down, establish, standardize*
die Festlegung (– en) *fixing, standard*
die Festplatte (– n) *hard disk*
feststellen (sep.) *to establish, identify, discover, lay down, realize, decide on, ascertain, detect;* stellt man fest *people are realizing;* Schadstoffe werden festgestellt *pollutants are detected*
der Feststoffanteil (– e) *solids content*
festzustellen *see* feststellen
das Feuer *fire*
die Filiale (– n) *branch (office)*
der Film (– e) *film*
der Filmprojektor (– en) *(slide) projector*
der Filz *felt*
die Finanzbuchhaltung (– en) *financial accounts (department)*
finanziell *financial(ly)*
finanzieren *to finance*
die Finanzierung (– en) *financing*
die Finanzmetropole (– n) *financial centre (lit. metropolis)*
finanzstark *financially strong, with financial muscle*
das Finanzzentrum (–zentren) *financial centre*
finden, a, u *to find*
findet: findet ... statt *see* stattfinden
das Finish *finish(ing)*
das Finishen *finishing*
die Firma (Firmen) *firm, company*
die Firmenleitung (– en) *(company) management*
der Firmenname (wk m; genitive –ns) (– n) *company name*
das Firmenprofil (– e) *company profile, corporate image*
der Fisch (– e) *fish*
das Fischfilet (– s) *fillet (of fish)*
fit *fit (see* halten*)*
der Fitnessraum (¨e) *gym (lit. fitness room)*
die Fläche (– n) *surface, land, area, site*
der Flächenbau *wing construction*
die Flasche (– n) *bottle*
das Fleisch *meat*
die Fleischerei (– en) *butcher*
die Flexibilität (– en) *flexibility*
fließt: fließt ... ein *see* einfließen
fliegen, o, o* *to fly*
der or das Flip-Chart (– s) *flip chart*
die Flöte (– n) *flute*
der Flug (– e) *flight*
der Flügel (–) *wing*
die Fluggesellschaft (– en) *airline company*
der Flughafen (¨) *airport;* Flughafen Frankfurt *Frankfurt Airport*
flugwichtig: flugwichtige Systeme *flight systems*
das Flugzeug (– e) *aeroplane, aircraft*
der Flugzeugbau *aircraft construction*
der Flugzeugbauer (–) *aircraft maker, production staff*
der Flugzeughimmel (–) *overhead area, ceiling*
der Flugzeugrumpf (¨e) *aircraft fuselage*
das Flugzeugrumpfsegment (– e) *section of the aircraft fuselage*
der Fluorchlorkohlenwasserstoff (– e) *chloro-fluorocarbon;* ohne Fluorchlorkohlenwasserstoff *ozone friendly (lit. without chloro-fluorocarbon)*
der Fluß (Flüsse) *river*
flüssig *liquid, fluid*
die Flüssigkeit (– en) *liquid, fluid*
die Folge (– n) *succession, sequence, episode, result;* in schneller Folge *in rapid succession*

das Folgejahr (– e) *following/next/coming year*
folgend *following*
folgendermaßen *as follows*
die Förderinsel (– n) *production platform (see* Bohrinsel*)*
das Fördermittel (–) *funding, grant*
fordern *to demand*
fördern *to promote*
die Förderung (– en) *extraction, promotion, subsidy;* bei der Förderung von Öl *when extracting oil*
die Form (– en) *shape, form, design;* in irgendeiner Form *in some (other) way;* in Form von *in the form of*
das Forschen *research*
forschen *to research*
die Forschung (– en) *research;* Forschung und Entwicklung *research and development, R & D*
der Forschungsbereich (– e) *research area*
die Forschungseinrichtung (– en) *research establishment/institute*
das Forschungsergebnis (– se) *research result*
die Forstwirtschaft *forestry*
fortlaufend *steadily*
der Fortschritt (– e) *progress;* und so weiter und so Fortschritt *(play on the phrase* und so weiter und so fort *'and so on and so forth', and the word* Fortschritt *'progress')*
fortschrittlich *progressive, advanced*
(sich) fortsetzen (sep.) *to continue*
der Fotograf (wk m)(– en) *photographer*
die Fotografie (– n) *photography*
die Fotokopie (– n) *photocopy;* Fotokopie anbei *photocopy enclosed*
Fr = Freitag
die Fracht (– en) *freight, load*
die Frachtabteilung (– en) *freight department*
das Frachtgut (¨er) *freight*
die Frachtkosten (pl) *freight/carriage costs*
die Frage (– n) *question, issue, matter;* in Frage kommen *to be an option;* stellt sich die Frage *the question arises*
der Fragebogen (– or ¨) *questionnaire*
fragen *to ask*
sich fragen *to ask oneself*
franca *see* Lingua
das Franchise *franchise*
das Franchising *franchising*
Frankfurter *of Frankfurt, Frankfurt*
Frankreich *France*
der Franzose (wk m)(– n) *Frenchman*
französisch *French*
das Französisch *French (language)*
die Frau (– en) *woman, wife, Mrs, Ms*
das Fräulein (– or –s) *young woman, girl, Miss*
frei *free, vacant;* frei sein *at liberty;* frei von *free from;* frei Haus *free house, franco domicile;* auf dem freien Markt *in the free/open market;* die Freie und Hansestadt Hamburg *the Free Hanseatic City of Hamburg*
freiberuflich *free-lance, independent*
freibleibend *subject to change;* Preise sind freibleibend *changes to prices*
der Freistaat (– en) *free state;* Freistaat Bayern *Free State of Bavaria*
der Freitag (– e) *Friday;* am Freitag *on Friday*
freitags *on Fridays*
freiwillig *voluntary (–ily)*
die Freizeit *spare time, leisure*
der Freizeitbereich (– e) *leisure sector*
der Freizeitkonsum *leisure consumption*
der Freizeitmarkt (¨e) *leisure market*
der Freizeitwert (– e) *leisure value/premium*
die Freizeitwirtschaft *leisure industry*
fremd *foreign, strange*
das Fremdenverkehrsamt (¨er) *tourist office*
die Fremdsprache (– n) *foreign language*
sich freuen (über) *to be pleased (about), to enjoy;* sich freuen auf *to look forward to*
freundlich *friendly;* Mit freundlichen Grüßen *Yours sincerely*
frisch *fresh*
die Friseurin (–nen) *hairdresser*
die Front (– en) *front*
das Frontdesign (– s) *front design*
früh *early*

früher *earlier, in the past, used to;* in früheren Jahren *in the past*
der, die, das frühere *(the) earlier (one)*
das Frühjahr *spring*
der Frühling *spring*
das Frühstück (– e) *breakfast*
die Fuge (– n) *joint, crack*
die Fügetechnik (– en) *joining method*
fuhr *went (see* fahren*)*
führen *to lead, guide, drive, go, hold, carry, carry out, cause, result in, have;* führen zu *to lead to;* die dazu geführt haben, daß *which led to/caused;* ein Gespräch führen *to have a discussion/hold talks;* werden nur 20 000 bis 25 000 geführt *only 20,000 to 25,000 are carried;* wir haben Marktnischenüberlegungen geführt *we considered the market niches available*
führen: führen ... durch *see* durchführen
führend *leading, major*
führte: führte ... ein *see* einführen
die Führung (– en) *management*
die Führungsfunktion (– en) *management function*
die Führungskraft (¨e) *manager, executive, management*
die Fülle *quantity, range*
füllen *to fill*
der Füller (–) *filler*
der Füllschaum *filling foam*
fünf *five*
die Fünf (pl) *five (ones);* unter diesen Fünfen *amongst these five (ones)*
der, die, das fünfte *(the) fifth (one)*
das/ein Fünftel (–) *(a) fifth*
fünftens *fifthly*
fünfzehn *fifteen*
fünfzig *fifty*
der Funk *radio*
das Funkstudio (– s) *radio studio*
die Funktion (– en) *function;* Funktions-Spülzentrum *multifunction sink unit*
funktionell *functional(ly)*
funktionieren *to function*
funktionierend *functioning*
das Funktionsdetail (– s) *functional detail, practical feature*
funktionsgeprüft: wird funktions-geprüft *has a functional/operational test*
der Funktionslauf (¨e) *functional/operational test/cycle*
die Funktionstaste (– n) *function key*
für *for*
fürs = für das
die Fusion (– en) *merger*
fusionieren *to merge*
fusioniere *see* fusionieren
Fuß (¨e) *foot*
futuristisch *futuristic*

G

gab: es gab *there was/were (see* geben*)*
die GAFA = Internationale Gartenfachmesse
die Galleria *galleria, gallery*
der Gang (¨e) *aisle;* in Gang zu halten *to keep ... going*
die Gängigkeit *sales potential*
ganz *quite, whole, all of, entire(ly), really, very, the whole of, all over;* ganz nach *in accordance with*
der, die, das Ganze *(the) whole thing/one, everything*
gar *even, at all, indeed, anyway;* das können wir gar nicht *we can't do that anyway*
die Garage (– n) *garage*
die Garantie (– n) *guarantee/warranty*
garantieren *to guarantee*
die Garantiezeit (– en) *guarantee/warranty period*
GARDENEX = The Federation of Garden & Leisure Equipment Exporters Ltd (*now* Garden & Leisure Manufacturers)
die Garnele (– n) *shrimp*
der Garten (¨) *garden*
die Gartenarbeit *gardening*
die Gartenausstattung (– en) *garden fittings/equipment*
der Gartenbau *horticulture;* Industrieverband Gartenbau *Industrial Association for Horticulture*

die Gartenfachmesse (– n) *garden (trade) fair, garden show*
das Gartengerät (– e) *garden implement/tool;* Gartengeräte *garden equipment*
das Gartengrün *(garden) green*
das Gartenhaus (¨er) *shed, summer-house, (lit. garden house)*
der Gartenschmuck *garden accessories/ornaments*
der Gärtner (–) *gardener (m)*
die Gärtnerei (– en) *nursery*
die Gärtnerin (–nen) *gardener (f)*
gärtnerisch *horticultural*
gärtnern *to garden*
das Gas (– e) *gas*
der Gasanschluß (– sse) *gas supply*
die Gasbohrplattform (– en) *gas drilling platform*
der Gasinstallateur (– e) *gas fitter*
der Gast (¨e) *guest*
die Gastronomie *gastronomy, catering trade*
die Gaststätte (– n) *public house, restaurant;* Gaststätten *catering (industry)*
das Gate (– s) *gate*
die GdED = Gewerkschaft der Eisenbahner Deutschlands (see Gewerkschaft)
die GdP = Gewerkschaft der Polizei (see Gewerkschaft)
geändert *(from* ändern*) changed, altered*
gearbeitet *worked (see* arbeiten*)*
das Gebäude (–) *building(s)*
gebaut *built, constructed, produced (see* bauen*)*
geben (i), a, e *to give, supply;* mit der Aufgabenstellung, ... zu geben *with the task of giving ...;* das wichtigste ..., das es überhaupt gibt *the most important ... there is*
das Gebiet (– e) *area, region, territory*
gebogen *(from* biegen*) bent*
gebracht *brought (see* bringen*)*
gebraten *(from* braten*) fried*
gebraucht *used*
gebrochen *broken (see* brechen*)*
der Geburtstag (– e) *birthday*
der Gedanke (wk m) (– n) *thought, idea;* der Gedanke an *the thought of*
gedeckt *covered, financed (see* decken*)*
geehrte/r *dear*
geeignet *suitable, suited*
die Gefahr (– en) *danger, risk*
der Gefahrenübergang (¨e) *passing/transfer of risk*
das Gefälle (–) *divide ('falling off') (see* Süd-Nord-Gefälle*)*
gefallen (ä), ie, a *to please;* es gefällt einem *one likes*
gefallen *decreased (see* fallen*)*
geformt *(from* formen*) formed, shaped, contoured*
geführt *led, carried (see* führen*);* dies hat dazu geführt *this meant*
gefüllt *filled, full, stuffed (see* füllen*)*
gefunden *found (see* finden*)*
gegangen *gone (see* gehen*)*
gegeben *given, supplied (see* geben*);* zu gegebener Zeit *in due course*
gegebenenfalls *as necessary*
gegen *against*
der Gegensatz (¨e) *contrast;* im Gegensatz zu *as opposed to, in contrast to*
gegenseitig *each other*
gegenüber *opposite, to, towards, for, over, compared to;* tolerant gegenüber Fehlern *tolerant towards mistakes;* seinen Distributors gegenüber *towards its distributors*
gegenwärtig *present(ly), current(ly), still, modern*
gegossen *cast (metal) (see* gießen*);* daß richtig gegossen werden kann *that casting can be done properly*
gegründet *founded*
gehabt *had;* haben ... gehabt *had, have had (see* haben*)*
das Gehalt (¨er) *salary, pay;* Lohn– und Gehaltsabrechnung *wage and salary statement, pay statement/advice;* Lohn– und Gehaltsbüro *wages and salaries office, pay office/department*
gehalten *maintained, kept to, met (see* halten*);* konstant gehalten *constantly maintained*
das Gehäuse (–) *housing, case, enclosure*
das Gehäusesystem (– e) *enclosure system*
die Geheimzahl (– en) *PIN number (lit.*

secret number)
gehen, ging, gegangen * *to go, walk, sell;* es geht darum *the issue is, it is necessary;* das geht los bei *it starts/begins with;* gehen besser *sell better;* in Richtung Gartenschmuck gehen *to move towards/in the direction of garden accessories;* geht in Serie *goes into production*
gehen: gehen ... raus *see* rausgehen
gehievt *lifted (see* hieven*)*
gehoben *lifted (see* heben*)*
gehoben *exclusive;* gehobener Fachhandel *exclusive fashion trade, high fashion*
geholfen *helped (see* helfen*)*
gehören (zu) *to belong (to), be/form part of, play a part*
gehört *heard (see* hören*)*
geht *from* gehen
geht: geht ... zurück *see* zurückgehen; geht ... hinein *see* hineingehen; geht ... über *see* übergehen
geht's (= geht es) *it's*
gekauft *sold (see* kaufen*)*
geklebt *bonded, glued (see* kleben*)*
gekommen *came (see* kommen*)*
gekonnt *could (see* können*)*
gelangen * (in) *to get (into)*
das Geld (– er) *money, payment*
die Geldausgabe (– n) *payment*
der Geldautomat (*wk m*)(– en) *cash dispenser, automatic teller*
der Geldwechsel *bureau de change, exchange*
das Gelee *garnish* (lit. *jelly*)
gelegentlich *sometimes, from time to time*
gelernt *trained, qualified (see* lernen*)*
gelingen, a, u * *to succeed;* es gelingt einem nicht *one does not succeed in, you can't;* es gelingt uns *we succeed*
gelöst *solved (see* lösen*)*
gelten (i), a, o *to apply, be regarded as, taken as;* es gelten die Preise *the prices shall be applicable*
gelungen *succeeded (see* gelingen*)*
gemacht *transacted, done (see* machen*)*
gemäß *in accordance with, by;* gemäß vorheriger Vereinbarung *by prior agreement*
die Gemeinde (– n) *local authority*
gemeinsam *together, communal*
die Gemeinschaft (– en) *community, association, society;* europäische Gemeinschaft *European Community;* auf den Wohnungsmärkten der europäischen Gemeinschaft *in the housing markets of the European Community*
das Gemüse (–) *vegetable(s)*
die Gemüsestreifen (*pl*) *strips of vegetable*
die Gemütlichkeit *geniality, cosiness, conviviality, cosy atmosphere*
genau *exact(ly), particular(ly), in detail;* genau das ist der Grund *that's precisely the reason*
die Genehmigung (– en) *authorization, approval, licence*
generell *general(ly)*
genommen *taken (see* nehmen*)*
die Genossenschaft (– en) *cooperative*
genossenschaftlich *cooperative(ly);* genossenschaftliche Kreditinstitute *cooperative banks*
genug *enough*
genügen *to be sufficient, meet, satisfy*
der Genuß (Genüsse) *enjoyment, drinks/beverages and tobacco*
die Genußmittel (*pl*) *drinks and tobacco;* Nahrungs- und Genußmittelindustrie *(see* Nahrung*)*
genutzt *used (see* nutzen*)*
geöffnet *opened (see* öffnen*);* geöffnet täglich *open daily/every day*
die Gepäckausgabe (– n) *baggage reclaim*
der Gepäckraum (¨e) *luggage compartment, boot*
der Gepäckraumbereich (– e) *luggage compartment (area)*
gepflegt (*from* pflegen) *well looked after, updated*
geprüft *tested, inspected (see* prüfen*);* geprüfte Sicherheit *safety-tested*
gerade *just, exactly, precisely;* gerade bevorsteht *may be coming up*
das Gerät (– e) *machine, unit, instrument, appliance, device, piece of equipment;*
die Geräte (*pl*) *machinery, machines, equipment*
die Geräte-Technik *appliance technology*
die Geräteerfassung (– en) *register of equipment*
der Gerätehersteller (–) *machinery/equipment manufacturer*
die Gerätekonzeption (– en) *equipment design*
gerecht: wird gerecht *meets;* gerecht machen *to make appropriate*
geregelt (*from* regeln) *regulated*
gereinigt (*from* reinigen) *cleaned*
gerelauncht (*from* relaunchen) *relaunched*
der Gerichtshof (¨e) *court*
der Gerichtsstand (¨e) *place of jurisdiction*
gering *low, restricted*
gern(e) *like (to);* gern, lieber, am liebsten *like, prefer, like most/best of all*
die Ges.m.b.H = Gesellschaft mit beschränkter Haftung *(see* Gesellschaft, GmbH*)*
gesagt *said (see* sagen*)*
gesamt *whole, entire*
der Gesamtdurchmesser (–) *overall diameter*
die Gesamtfunktion (– en) *overall function*
das Gesamtgewicht (– e) *total weight*
die Gesamtkosten (*pl*) *total cost*
die Gesamtphilosophie *(overall) philosophy*
der Gesamtpreis (– e) *total price*
das Gesamtsortiment (– e) *total range, listing*
der Gesamtumsatz (¨e) *total turnover/sales*
der Gesamtverband (¨e) *association, federation;* Gesamtverband der Deutschen Versicherungswirtschaft *German Insurance Association (association of the German insurance industry)*
die Gesamtverzögerung (– en) *delay to the whole project*
das Gesamtwohl *(overall) welfare/well-being*
die Gesamtzeit (– en) *duration*
geschaffen *created, developed (see* schaffen*)*
das Geschäft (– e) *shop, business, function, transaction;* ein Geschäft zu machen *to do business;* Geschäfte (*pl*) *shops;* gute Geschäfte *good business/deals;* ein großes Geschäft *big business*
geschäftlich *business;* geschäftliche Vorgänge *business documents/files*
die Geschäftsbank (– en) *commercial bank;* private Geschäftsbank *private commercial bank*
die Geschäftsbedingungen (*pl*) *terms and conditions of business;* allgemeine Geschäftsbedingungen *general terms and conditions*
der Geschäftsbericht (– e) *annual report, report of the board of management*
der Geschäftsbetrieb (– e) *business*
der Geschäftsführer (–) *managing director, general manager*
die Geschäftsführung (– en) *(board of) management, management*
die Geschäftsleitung (– en) *management*
der Geschäftspartner (–) *business partner*
die Geschäftspost *business post/mail*
die Geschäftswelt *business world, world of business*
geschah *happened (see* geschehen*)*
geschaut *looked (see* schauen*)*
geschehen (ie), a, e * *to happen*
geschehen *happened (see* geschehen*)*
die Geschichte *history*
geschickt *skilful(ly), skilled; sent (see* schicken*);* geschickte Hände *nimble fingers* (lit. *hands*)
geschieht *see* geschehen
geschliffen *rubbed down, ground (see* schleifen*);* danach wird geschliffen *after that (the surface) is rubbed down*
geschlossen *closed, concluded (see* schließen*)*
der Geschmack (¨e *or* ¨er) *taste;* je nach Geschmack *(according) to taste*
das Geschmackserlebnis (– se) *experience for the palate*
geschmackvoll *tasteful*
geschmort (*from* schmoren) *braised*
geschnitten (*from* schneiden) *cut*
geschrieben *written (see* schreiben*)*
geschult *trained (see* schulen*)*
geschweißt *welded (see* schweißen*)*
die Gesellschaft (– en) *company, corporation, association, society;* Gesellschaft mit beschränkter Haftung *(private) limited company*
der Gesellschafter (–) *shareholder*
die Gesellschaftsform (– en) *legal form of a company*
gesenkt *sunk (see* senken*)*
das Gesetz (– e) *law*
gesetzlich *legal(ly), obligatory, statutory;* gesetzlich festgelegt *laid down by law*
gesetzt *see* setzen
das Gesicht (– er) *face*
das Gespräch (– e) *talk, conversation, discussion, meeting;* Unser Gespräch am *Our conversation/meeting on;* im Gespräch mit Kollegen *in (the course of) talking to/conversation with colleagues*
gestaltet (*from* gestalten) *designed*
gestanzt (*from* stanzen) *stamped, pressed*
gestartet *started (see* starten*)*
gestellt *delivered (see* stellen*)*
die Gestellung (– en) *delivery*
das Gestellungsdatum (–daten) *delivery date*
gestiegen *increased, enhanced (see* steigen*)*
gestrichen (*from* streichen) *crossed out*
gesund *healthy*
getan *done (see* tun*)*
getätigt (*from* tätigen) *generated*
getestet (*from* testen) *tested*
getragen: getragen von *financed by*
das Getränk (– e) *drink, beverage*
getrennt *separate, separated (see* trennen*);* wir haben ... klar getrennt *there's a clear division*
das Getriebe (–) *gearbox*
getrost *confident(ly)*
getrunken (*from* trinken) *drunk*
die GEW = Gewerkschaft Erziehung und Wissenschaft *(see* Gewerkschaft*)*
das Gewächshaus (¨er) *greenhouse*
gewählt *elected (see* wählen*)*
gewährleisten *to ensure, guarantee*
gewarnt *alerted* (lit. *warned) (see* warnen*)*
gewerblich *industrial, technical;* gewerbliche Arbeitnehmer *blue-collar workers, manual workers;* gewerbliche Wirtschaft *industry*
die Gewerkschaft (– en) *(trade) union;* Industriegewerkschaft *industrial union;* Deutscher Gewerkschaftsbund *German Trade Union Federation;* 16 unions make up the *Deutsche Gewerkschaftsbund* as follows: Industriegewerkschaft Bau-Steine-Erden *building and construction;* Industriegewerkschaft Bergbau und Energie *mining and energy;* Industriegewerkschaft Chemie-Papier-Keramik *chemicals, paper and ceramics;* Gewerkschaft der Eisenbahner Deutschlands *railwaymen;* Gewerkschaft Erziehung und Wissenschaft *education and sciences;* Gewerkschaft Gartenbau, Land– und Forstwirtschaft *horticulture, agriculture and forestry;* Gewerkschaft Handel, Banken und Versicherungen *commerce, banks and insurance;* Gewerkschaft Holz und Kunststoff *wood and plastics;* Gewerkschaft Leder *leather;* Industriegewerkschaft Medien *media;* Industriegewerkschaft Metall *metal-working;* Gewerkschaft Nahrung-Genuß-Gaststätten *food, drink, tobacco and catering;* Gewerkschaft Öffentliche Dienste, Transport und Verkehr *public services and transport;* Gewerkschaft der Polizei *police;* Deutsche Postgewerkschaft *postal workers;* Gewerkschaft Textil-Bekleidung *textiles and clothing*
der Gewerkschaftsbund *trade union federation*
gewesen *been, gone (see* sein*)*
das Gewicht (– e) *weight*
der Gewinn (– e) *profit;* Gewinn– und Verlustrechnung *profit and loss account*
gewinnen, a, o *to win, gain*
gewiß *certain(ly)*
das Gewissen (–) *conscience*
gewohnt *used to;* der deutsche Handel ist gewohnt *the German retail trade is used to*
gewöhnt: daran gewöhnt *accustomed/used to (it)*
geworden *become, turned into (see* werden*)*
gewünscht (*from* wünschen) *desired, required, in demand*
gezogen *ordered (see* ziehen*)*
die GGLF = Gewerkschaft Gartenbau, Land und Forstwirtschaft *(see* Gewerkschaft*)*
die GHK = Gewerkschaft Holz und Kunststoff *(see* Gewerkschaft*)*
gibt (*from* geben): es gibt *there is*
das Gießen *pouring, casting*
gießen, o, o *to pour, cast (metal)*
die Gießerei (– en) *foundry*
das Gift (– e) *poison*
gilt (*from* gelten): gilt als *is considered as/to be;* gilt nicht *does not apply*
ging *went (see* gehen*)*
das Gitter (–) *bars, grid*
das Glas (¨er) *glass*
der Glasbruch (¨e) *breakage of glass*
das Glätten *smoothing*
glauben *to believe, think*
gleich *immediately, (the) same*
der, die, das gleiche *(the) same (one), (the) same thing;* das gleiche machen *to have an identical approach*
gleichmäßig *uniform(ly), even(ly)*
gleichzeitig *at the same time, simultaneous(ly)*
die Gleichzeitigkeit *simultaneity, simultaneous action*
das Gleis (– e) *platform*
gleitend: gleitende Arbeitszeit *flexitime* (lit. *gliding work time)*
die Gleitzeit (– en) *flexitime*
global *global*
der Globus (– se) *globe*
das Glück *luck;* das Glück gehabt *been lucky enough*
die GmbH (– s) = Gesellschaft mit beschränkter Haftung *comparable with Ltd (see* Gesellschaft*)*
das Gold *gold*
der Goodwill *goodwill*
der Gott (¨er) *god, God*
der Gouda *gouda*
der Grad (– e) *degree, level*
der Graf (*wk m*)(– en) *count*
die Grafik (– en) *graphic(s)*
die Grafikkarte (– n) *graphics card*
der Grafikmonitor (– e *or* – en) *graphics monitor*
das Grafikterminal (– s) *graphics terminal*
die Grammatik *grammar*
das Graubrot *bread made from rye and wheat flour*
gravierend *substantial*
greifen, griff, gegriffen *to reach;* Sie müssen sehr tief in die Tasche greifen *you have to dig deep in your pocket (i.e.* it's very expensive*)*
Grelette: Sauce Grelette *sauce grelette*
der Griff (– e) *handle, grip*
griffsympathisch *pleasant to the touch*
der Grill (– s) *grill, barbecue;* vom Grill *grilled*
das Grobblech (– e) *plate*
groß *big, large, much, tall;* groß, größer als, der/die/das größte *big, bigger than, the biggest*
das Großbauteil (– e) *large/major component*
Großbritannien *Great Britain*
der, die, das Große (– n) *(the) big thing/one;* Partnerschaft mit dem Großen *partnership with a big company*
die Größe (– n) *factor, parameter, size*
die Größenklasse (– n) *size classification*
der Größensatz (¨e) *quantity (to be supplied)*
größer (als) *bigger/greater (than)*
großgeschrieben *see* großschreiben
der Großhandel *wholesale (trade)*
die Großhandelskauffrau (– en) *wholesale clerk/trader (f)*
der Großhändler (–) *wholesaler*
der Großkunde (*wk m*) (– n) *major customer/client*
großschreiben (*sep.*), ie, ie *to attach*

great importance to
die Großstadt (¨e) *city, conurbation*
der, die, das größte *(the) biggest/greatest (one)*
das Großunternehmen (–) *large company, corporation, conglomerate, combine*
das Großversandhaus (¨er) *mail-order company*
grün *green*
der Grund (¨e) *reason, basis, bottom;* aus verschiedenen Gründen *for a number of reasons*
die Grundausstattung (– en) *standard equipment*
gründen *to found, establish*
das Gründen *founding, foundation, establishment*
der Gründer (–) *founder*
der Grundgedanke (*wk m*) (– n) *basic concept*
das Grundkonzept (– e) *basic concept*
der Grundkreis (– e) *base circle*
der Grundlack (– e) *primer*
die Grundlagenforschung (– en) *basic/pure research*
der Grundsatz (¨e) *basis*
grundsätzlich *fundamental(ly), in/on principle, always*
die Gründung (– en) *foundation, establishment*
die Gründungsberatung (– en) *advice on founding a company/start-up*
die Grundvoraussetzung (– en) *basic prerequisite, basis*
das Grundwasser *groundwater*
die Grünpflanze (– n) *plant*
die Gruppe (– n) *group*
der Gruppenleiter (–) *foreman, supervisor*
grüßen *to greet*
Grütze: rote Grütze *soft fruits boiled and set in a jelly*
GS = geprüfte Sicherheit *(see* Sicherheit*)*
die GTB = Gewerkschaft Textil-Bekleidung (*see* Gewerkschaft)
gucken *to look, watch*
günstig *cheap(ly), value for money, at a good price, at preferential rates*
günstiger (als) *cheaper, better value for money (than)*
der Guppy (– s) *guppy (fish);* die Super Guppy *Super Guppy transport aircraft*
gurgelnd *gurgling, bubbling*
der Guß (Güsse) *casting;* aus einem Guß *integrated* (lit. *from one casting*)
das Gußteil (– e) *casting, cast component*
gut *good, well, fine;* gut, besser als, der/die/das beste *good/well, better than, the best;* das ging so lange gut, wie *that was fine while;* kurz und gut *in a nutshell;* in bester Qualität *top quality*
das Gutachten (–) *expert opinion/report, certification, appraisal*
die Gutachtenerstellung (– en) *drawing up expert reports*
die Güte *quality*
die Güter (*pl*) *goods*
der Güterfernverkehr *long-distance freight (road)*
der Gutschein (– e) *voucher*

H

H = Henry *(unit of inductance)*
haben (hat), hatte, gehabt *to have;* wir hatten ein Artikelsortiment gehabt *we had carried a product range*
das Haben *credit;* Soll und Haben *debit and credit*
sich habilitieren *to habilitate (i.e. write a thesis that qualifies a person for university teaching)*
der Hafen (¨) *harbour, port, docks*
der Hafengeburtstag (– e) *port birthday/ anniversary*
die Hafenrundfahrt (– en) *port/harbour tour*
haften *to be liable*
der/die Haftende (– n), ein Haftender *(the) person liable*
die Haftpflicht *(third-party) liability*
die Haftpflichtversicherung (– en) *liability insurance*
die Haftung (– en) *liability;* beschränkte Haftung *limited liability (see* Gesellschaft*)*
der Hagel *hail*

halb *half;* halb neun *half past eight* (lit. *half to nine)*
der Halbleiter (–) *semiconductor;* Halbleiter-Schaltkreis *semiconductor circuit*
halbwegs *more or less, as much as possible*
half *helped (see* helfen*)*
die Hälfte (– n) *(the) half;* die Hälfte des Fahrzeugwertes *half the value of a car*
die Halle (– n) *exhibition hall*
hält *see* (sich) halten
halt *just*
haltbar *sustainable;* mindestens haltbar bis *best before;* haltbar sein *to keep*
die Haltbarkeit *durability*
halten (ä), ie, a *to keep;* um mich fit zu halten *to keep (myself) fit*
halten: halten ... zusammen *see* zusammenhalten
sich halten (ä), ie, a *to hold, take;* sich eine Fernsehzeitschrift halten *to take a TV guide*
Hamburger *of Hamburg, Hamburg*
hamburgisch *of Hamburg*
die Hand (¨e) *hand;* geschickte Hände *nimble fingers* (lit. *hands);* aus einer Hand *from the same source/ manufacturer*
die Handarbeit (– en) *handwork, craftsmanship*
der Handel *trade, commerce, retail trade;* in den Handel hinein *to the trade;* Handel treiben *trade and commerce*
handeln *to act;* für jemanden handeln *to act for*
sich handeln (um) *to concern;* es handelt sich um *we're talking about*
die Handelsbetriebslehre (– n) *business administration*
das Handelsblatt *Handelsblatt (newspaper for finance and business)*
die Handelskammer (– n) *chamber of commerce; (see* Industrie*)*
das Handelsregister (–) *commercial register (register of companies and authorized signatories)*
der Handelstag *see* Industrie
der Handelsvertreter (–) *agent*
das Handelszentrum (–zentren) *trade centre, centre for trade and commerce*
die Handhabungstätigkeit (– en) *manipulative operation, material-handling operation*
der Handkäse *handmade curd cheese;* Handkäse mit Musik *marinated handmade curd cheese (renowned for producing wind!)*
der Händler (–) *trader, merchant*
die Handschrift (– en) *handwriting*
die Handwerkskammer (– n) *chamber of craft trades*
hängen, i, a *to hang*
hängt: hängt ... ab *see* abhängen
Hannover *Hanover*
die Hanse *Hansa*
die Hanseatin: Hanseatinnen *women in the north, Hanseatic women* (lit. *women in the Hanseatic cities of Hamburg, Bremen and Lübeck)*
hanseatisch *Hanseatic*
die Hanseboot *International Boat Show Hamburg*
die Hansestadt (¨e) *Hanseatic city*
die HAPAG = Hamburg-Amerikanische Packetfahrt-Actien-Gesellschaft
harmonisieren *to harmonize*
die Harmonisierung (– en) *harmonization*
hart *hard, tough;* hart, härter als, der/die/das härteste *hard, harder than, the hardest*
die Härtemessung (– en) *hardness measurement, hardness test*
härter (als) *harder/tougher (than)*
hat *has (see* haben*)*
hatte *had (see* haben*)*
hätte *had, would have (see* haben*)*
hatten (*pl*) *had (see* haben*)*
hätten (*from* haben): hätten wir nicht Fabriken aufgebaut *had we not/if we had not set up factories*
der Hauptabnehmer (–) *main customer/purchaser*
der Hauptabnehmerkreis (– e) *main group of customers*

der Hauptabteilungsleiter (–) *main department manager;* Hauptabteilungsleiter Preßwerk *manager of the press works*
der Hauptbahnhof (¨e) *main/central station*
der Hauptfaktor (– en) *main factor*
der Hauptimporteur (– e) *main importer*
der Hauptmarkt (¨e) *principal market*
die Hauptmärkte (*pl*) *principal markets*
die Hauptpost *main post office*
das Hauptpostamt (¨er) *main post office*
das Hauptproblem (– e) *main problem*
das Hauptprodukt (– e) *main product*
die Hauptrolle (– n) *main role*
die Hauptsache (– n) *main thing*
hauptsächlich *main(ly)*
der Hauptsitz (– e) *headquarters, head office*
die Hauptversammlung (– en) *(annual) general meeting*
das Haus (¨er) *house, home, company, source;* im Hause *in the company;* bei uns im Hause *in our company, at e.g. Barclays;* aus einem Haus *from the same source/manufacturer;* zu Hause *at home, domiciled/based*
das Hausgerät (– e) *domestic/household appliance*
die Hausgeräteindustrie *domestic-appliance/white-goods industry*
der Hausgerätesektor (– en) *domestic-appliance/white-goods sector*
der Hausgerätezweig (– e) *domestic-appliance/white-goods sector*
der Haushalt (– e) *household;* im Haushalt *in the home*
haushoch *as high as a house*
haushohe *see* haushoch
die Hauskatze (– n) *domestic cat*
die Hausratversicherung (– en) *contents insurance*
der Hausversicherer (–) *'house insurer'*
die Hauswirtschafterin (–nen) *housekeeper*
hauswirtschaftlich *(relating to) home and garden*
die HBV = Gewerkschaft Handel, Banken und Versicherungen (*see* Gewerkschaft)
die Hebe-Aktion (– en) *jacking operation*
heben, o, o *to lift, jack*
der Hebeversuch (– e) *jacking attempt*
das Heim (– e) *home*
der Heimtierbedarf *pet supplies*
das Heimwerken *do-it-yourself, DIY*
der Heimwerker (–) *DIY enthusiast*
der Heimwerkermarkt (¨e) *DIY centre/superstore;* Bau- und Heimwerkermarkt *DIY centre/ superstore, home-improvement centre*
die Heimwerkermarktbranche (– n) *DIY sector*
heiße: ich heiße *My name is, I'm called*
heißen, ie, ei *to be called, to mean;* heißt ... bringen *means offering...;* heißt, daß *means that;* das heißt *that is, i.e.*
heißt *see* heißen
die Heizung (– en) *heating*
helfen (i), a, o *to help*
der Helfer (–) *helper (m)*
hell *light, bright*
heller (als) *lighter (than)*
das Helle, ein Helles *lager*
her *here;* vom Preis her *regarding price;* von den Farben her *where colours are concerned;* von der Ausbildung her *by training*
herangezogen (*from* heranziehen) *examined, considered*
herausgeschickt (*from* herausschicken) *sent out*
herausgestellt *turned out (see* herausstellen*)*
herausgetrennt (*from* heraustrennen) *knocked out*
herausholen (*sep.*) *to extract;* herauszuholen ist *can be extracted/ obtained*
herausnehmen (*sep.*) (nimmt heraus), nahm heraus, herausgenommen *to take out*
sich herausstellen (*sep.*) *to turn out*
herauszuholen *see* herausholen
der Herbst *autumn*
der Herd (– e) *cooker*
hergestellt *produced, manufactured (see* herstellen*)*
herkömmlich *traditional, conventional*

die Herkunft *origin*
der Herr (*wk m*) (– en) *Mr, man, gentleman*
die Herrenschneiderin (–nen) *tailor (f)*
herrschen *to reign, be;* (es) herrscht ein gesunder Konkurrenzkampf *there exists/is healthy competition*
herrscht *there's, exists* (lit. *reigns) (see* herrschen*)*
herstellen (*sep.*) *to produce, manufacture*
das Herstellen *manufacturing, production*
der Hersteller (–) *manufacturer*
die Herstellung (– en) *manufacturing, production*
herum *around, about;* rund um ... herum *around*
herumkommen (*sep.*), a, o * (um) *to avoid, get round*
hervorragend *outstanding, first-class, excellent*
das Herz (– en) *heart;* auf Herz und Nieren *down to the last detail*
heute *today, now, nowadays;* von heute auf morgen *from one day to the next;* wir können von heute auf morgen liefern *we can provide next-day delivery*
heutzutage *nowadays, currently*
das *or* die Hi-Tech *high-tech*
hier *here*
hierbei *in this connection*
hiesig *local* (i.e. *German)*
hieven *to lift*
das/die High-Tech *high-tech*
die Hilfe (– n) *help*
die Hilfestellung (– en) *assistance, support*
hilft *see* helfen
die Himmelbereiche (*pl*) *overhead areas*
hin *to, there;* bis hin zu *right through to;* hin und wieder *now and again;* auf ... hin *towards*
hinaus *out;* über etwas hinaus *in addition to sth.*
hinauskommen (*sep.*), a, o * (über) *to get away from*
hinauszukommen *see* hinauskommen
hinein *in, into*
hineinentwickeln (*sep.*) (in) *to be designed into*
hineingehen, ging hinein, hineingegangen (*sep.*) * *to go in(to)*
hineinkommen (*sep.*), a, o * *to get/come in*
hineinzukommen *see* hineinkommen
hingehen (*sep.*), ging hin, hingegangen * *to go there, visit, approach*
hingewiesen (auf) (*from* hinweisen) *informed (of)*
hinsichtlich *regarding, with respect to*
hinter *behind;* hinter ... her *after*
die Hinterachsbremse (– n) *rear brake*
die Hinterachse (– n) *rear axle*
die Hinterbliebenenvorsorge (– n) *provision for dependants, dependant's pension*
der, die, das hintere *(the) rear (one)*
hintereinander *one after another*
der Hintergrund (¨e) *background*
hinterher *afterwards, retrospective(ly)*
hinterlegen *to submit, file*
hinweg: übers Jahr hinweg *in the course of the year*
hinweisen (auf) *to point (to), inform (of)*
hinzu *also, in addition;* hinzu kommen dann *then there are also*
hob *raised, lifted (see* heben*);* hob in die Höhe *raised*
das Hobby (– s) *hobby*
hoch *high(ly), senior;* hoch, höher als, der/die/das höchste *high, higher than, the highest*
hochgehoben (*from* hochheben) *raised, jacked up*
der Hochleistungsrechner (–) *high-performance computer*
hochmodisch *highly fashionable, fashion conscious*
die Hochschule (– n) *university, college, institute (of higher education)*
höchst *highly*
der, die, das höchste *(the) highest (one), (the) maximum*
hochstehend *of high standing;* qualitätsmäßig sehr hochstehend *high quality*
höchstkomfortabel *highly convenient, maximum-convenience*
hochwertig *exclusive, high-quality*

Glossary

der, die, das hochwertigste (the) most exclusive (one)
hochwillkommen very welcome
die Hochzeit (– en) marriage, union
der Hof (⸚e) loading bay (lit. court (yard))
das Hofbräuhaus court brewery, Hofbräuhaus (beer hall in Munich)
hoffen to hope; zu erzeugen hofft hopes to create
hofft hopes (see hoffen)
die Höhe (– n) altitude, height, amount, extent, level; die Höhe des Geldes the amount of money; Höhe des Risikos level of risk
hohe see hoch
höher (als) higher (than)
der Hohlraum (⸚e) cavity
Holland Holland
holländisch Dutch
der Hollandkäse Dutch cheese
das Holz wood
hören to hear
das Hotel (– s) hotel
die Hotellerie hotel trade
die Hotelplattform (– en) hotel/accommodation platform
das Huhn (⸚er) chicken, hen
humorvoll humorous(ly)
der Hund (– e) dog; von Hunden of dogs
hundert hundred
hundertprozentig hundred percent
das Hurrah hurrah
der Hut (⸚e) hat
die Hutablage (– n) parcel shelf
der HVV = Hamburger Verkehrsverbund
hybrid hybrid
der Hybridschaltkreis (– e) hybrid circuit
die Hybridschaltung (– en) hybrid circuit/circuitry
die Hybridtechnik hybrid (semiconductor) technology
die Hydraulik hydraulics, hydraulic systems; Hydraulik-Anwendung application of hydraulics
das Hydraulikaggregat (– e) hydraulic unit
der Hydraulikzylinder (–) hydraulic cylinder
hydraulisch hydraulic(ally)
die Hypothek (– en) mortgage
die Hypothekenbank (– en) mortgage bank
das Hypothekengeschäft (– e) mortgage business

I

die IAA = Internationale Automobil-Ausstellung
ich I
das Ideal (– e) ideal (situation)
die Idee (– n) idea
der Ideenbringer (–) provider of ideas
identifizieren to identify
die Identity identity
die IG = Industriegewerkschaft, Interessengemeinschaft
die IGEDO = Interessengemeinschaft Damenoberbekleidungs-Industrie
die IGM = Industriegewerkschaft Metall (see Gewerkschaft)
ihm (to) him/it
ihn him, it
ihnen, Ihnen (to/from) them/you; nehmen Ihnen ... ab relieve you of ...
ihr(e) her, its, their
Ihr(e) your (polite)
ihrem (to/from) it/her
Ihren your (polite)
ihrer of her/your/its/their
ihres of his/its
illustriert illustrated
im = in dem
das Image (– s) image
die Imagesache (– n) (matter of) image
immer always; immer stärker more and more; immer da, wo always where; es zeigt sich immer wieder it keeps emerging; immer noch, noch immer still; immer im Abstand von at intervals of; auch immer always; immer stärker more and more, increasingly; immer wieder again and again
immerhin after all
immobil with immovable property
der Import (– e) import
der Importdruck import pressure, pressure of imports

der Importeur (– e) importer
die Importfirma (–firmen) import company
importieren to import
der Importleiter (–) head of import, import manager
die Importware (– n) imported goods
imposant imposing, impressive
der Impuls (– e) impulse, impetus
in in, into; in die Werbung into advertising; in der Firma in the company; in allen Ländern in/for every country; im Jahr a year; im Januar in January; im Herbst in autumn; in Rechnung stellen to invoice
die Inbetriebnahme (– n) start-up, commissioning
incl. (= inclusive) incl. (inclusive)
die Individualversicherung (– en) individual/private insurance
individuell individual
der Induktivitätswert (– e) inductance (value)
die Industrie (– n) industry; Industrie– und Handelskammer Chamber of Industry and Commerce; Industrie– und Handelstag Association of German Chambers of Industry and Commerce; metallverarbeitende Industrie metal-processing industry
die Industriebeteiligung (– en) industrial holding(s)
die Industriefirma (–firmen) industrial company
die Industriegewerkschaft (– en) industrial union; IG Chemie union for the chemicals, paper and ceramics industry; IG Metall union for the metalworking industry; IG Medien union for the media industry
der Industriekaufmann (⸚er) industrial clerk (trained in business administration), industrial salesman, businessman
der Industriekunde (wk m) (– n) industrial customer/client
industriell industrial
der Industriemechaniker (–) industrial mechanic/machinist
der Industriestandort (– e) industrial site/location/plant
das Industrieunternehmen (–) industrial undertaking/company, conglomerate
der Industrieverband (⸚e) industrial association
der Industriezweig (– e) sector of industry, sector, industry
infolge due to, as a result of
die Information (– en) information, data
der Informationsaustausch (– e) information exchange
das Informationsmaterial (–ien) information (material), product literature, documentation
die Informationsmöglichkeit (– en) opportunity for information
der Informationsstand level/amount of information (available)
das Informieren information
informieren to inform
sich informieren (über) to find out (about)
der Ingenieur (– e) engineer
der Inhaber (–) proprietor
der Initiator (–) initiator
das Inland interior, country, at home, inland; im Inland in Germany; tief vom Inland from deep inland; Versand im Inland erfolgt within Germany goods are dispatched
der Inlandtransport (– e) (in)land transport
inmitten in the middle of
innen inside, interior
der Innenausbau interior fittings
die Innenausstattung (– en) interior furnishings and fittings, cabin layout
der Innendienst (– e) (sales) office staff
das Innenleben interior; das reichhaltige Innenleben generously equipped interior
der Innenraum (⸚e) interior (space)
innerhalb inside (of)
die Innovation (– en) innovation
die Innovationssummen (pl) venture capital
das Innovationsvorhaben (–) (plan for) innovation
innovativ innovative

ins = in das
insbesondere especially, particularly; denke ich insbesondere an I'm particularly thinking of
die Insel (– n) island, platform; Ekofisk-Insel Ekofisk platform
die Insel-Stadt (⸚e) island city
insg. = insgesamt
insgesamt altogether, in all, a total of, total
insofern in so far
das Inspektionsbett (– en) inspection bed/bank
installieren to install
das Institut (– e) institution, institute, bank
die Institute (pl) institutions, institutes, banks
das Instrument (– e) instrument
das Instrumentarium (–ien) mix; absatzpolitisches Instrumentarium marketing mix
integrieren to integrate
integriert integrated (see integrieren)
der or das Interchange interchange, transhipment
der Intercity (– s) intercity (train)
interessant important, interesting
das Interesse (– n) interest
die Interessengemeinschaft (– en) syndicate (lit. community of interests), partnership, association, combine; Interessengemeinschaft Damenoberbekleidungs-Industrie association of companies in the ladies' outerwear industry
sich interessieren (für) to be/become interested (in)
interessiert (from interessieren) interested; interessiert sein an to be interested in
die INTERKAMA = Internationaler Kongreß mit Ausstellung für Meßtechnik und Automatik
intern internal(ly)
international international(ly)
der, die, das internationale (the) international (one)
die InternorGa = Internationale Fachausstellung für die nordische Gastronomie
investieren to invest
die Investition (– en) investment
die Investitionsgüter (pl) capital goods
inzwischen now
irgend some, any; vor irgendeinem Hintergrund against some background or other; in irgendeiner Form in some (other) way
irgendein, irgendeine, irgendeinem, irgendeinen, irgendeiner, irgendeines (to/from/for/of) some/any
irgendwann some/any time, at some point
irgendwelche some/any
irgendwie somehow
irgendwo some/anywhere, somehow, roughly
Irland Ireland
der Irrläufer (–) wrongly addressed mail; Irrläufer not known here
die Isar River Isar
ISH = Internationale Ausstellung Sanitär-Heizung-Klima
das Isolieren insulation
die ISPO = Internationale Sportartikelmesse
ist is, can, has (see sein); es ist nicht so, daß it isn't the case that; das ist that's; ist ... da there is ...; ist zu gewährleisten can be guaranteed
Italien Italy
der Italiener (–) Italian (person)
italienisch Italian
der IVG = Industrieverband Gartenbau

J

ja yes, what's more, after all, of course, well; Geld hat er ja (after all) he's got money
die Jagd (– en) hunting, shooting
das Jahr (– e) year; im Laufe der Jahre over the years; in früheren Jahren in the past; übers Jahr hinweg in the course of the year; im Jahr a year
der Jahresabschluß (–schlüsse) year-end accounts, annual accounts, (annual)

financial statement
die Jahresabschlußunterlagen (pl) annual financial statements, financial information
die Jahresausgabe (– n) annual edition; aus dieser Jahresausgabe from this year's edition
die Jahreszeit (– en) season
das Jahrhundert (– e) century
die Jahrhundertwelle (– n) wave of the century
jährlich annual(ly)
das Jahrzehnt (– e) decade
die Jakobsmuschel (– n) scallop
die Jalousie (– n) roller shutter; Jalousien-Schränke roller-shuttered cupboards/units, cupboards/units with roller shutters
der Januar January; im Januar in January
Japan Japan
japanisch Japanese
jawoll yes
der Jazz Jazz
je the; je ... desto the ... the; je besser ... desto besser the better ... the better; je nach according to; je ländlicher ... desto weniger the more rural ... the less
jede, jedem, jeden, jeder, jedes (to/from/for/of) any/each/every/every body/everyone
jederzeit at any time
jedoch however, but
jemand someone, anyone
jemanden (to) someone, anyone
jetzt now, still
jeweilig in question, particular
jeweils each time, in each case, all
der Job (– s) job
der Juli July; im Juli in July
jung young
die Jungfer virgin; der Neue Jungfernstieg street in Hamburg (lit. new virgin's path)
der, die, das jüngste (the) youngest/latest (one)
der Juni June; im Juni in June
juristisch legal(ly); juristische Person legal person/entity
die Jus juice

K

die Kabine (– n) booth
der Kaffee (– s) coffee
der Kaffeeautomat (wk m) (– en) coffee machine
die Kaffeemaschine (– n) coffee machine
die Kaffeemaschinen (pl) coffee machines
der Kaiser (–) emperor
der Kaisersaal (–säle) imperial hall (now a museum)
die Kaiserstraße imperial street
kam came (see kommen)
kamen (pl) came (see kommen)
die Kammer (– n) chamber (of commerce) (see Industrie)
der Kampf (⸚e) fight, confrontation
kämpfen to fight, contend with, confront; werden zu kämpfen haben (mit) will be confronted (with)
der Kandis sugar-candy
kann can (see können)
das Kännchen (–) (small) pot (of coffee/tea)
die Kanne (– n) (tea) pot
kannst can (see können)
die Kapazität (– en) capacity
das Kapital capital
der Kapitalbedarf capital requirement
der Kapitaleigner (–) shareholder, investor
der Kapitalgeber (–) investor
die Kapitalgesellschaft (– en) incorporated company, company
die Kapitalseite (– n) shareholders (lit. capital side)
der Kapitalstrom (⸚e) flow of capital
der Karneval (-e or -s) carnival
die Karosse (– n) body
die Karosserie (– n) bodywork
der Karosserie-Rohbau body shell, body in white, body(work) assembly line/plant
das Karosseriegerippe (–) bodywork skeleton/frame
die Karotte (– n) carrot
die Kartoffel (– n) potato
die Kartoffel-Krustel (– n) potato croquette
das Kartoffelpüree mashed potato, puréed potato

118 DEUTSCHES BUSINESS-MAGAZIN

der Kartoffelsalat (– e) *potato salad*
die Kartoffelsuppe (– n) *potato soup*
die Kartonnage (– n) *packaging, box*
die Kasse (– n) *cash (desk)*
der Katalog (– e) *catalogue*
die Kataphorese (– n) *cataphoresis*
der Katheter (–) *catheter*
der Kauf (∺e) *purchase*; beim Kauf im Geschäft *when purchased in the shop*; für den Kauf einer Bleibe *for purchasing a home*
kaufen *to buy*
der Käufer (–) *buyer*
die Käufergruppe (– n)
die Kauffrau (– en) *sales assistant, clerk, clerical worker (f)*
das Kaufhaus (∺er) *department store*
die Kaufleute (pl) *sales people, representatives, staff*
der Kaufmann (∺er) *sales clerk, trader, merchant*
kaufmännisch *commercial, for business purposes*; kaufmännisches Rechnen *maths for business purposes*; kaufmännische Lehre *commercial apprenticeship/training*; kaufmännischer Angestellter *salesman, sales manager*; kaufmännische Fächer *commercial subjects, vocational subjects*
kauft: kauft ... zu *see* zukaufen
der Kaufvertrag (∺e) *contract of sale, contract*
kaum *hardly, scarcely*
der Kautschuk (– e) *rubber*
kein, keine, keinem, keinen, keiner, keines *(to/from/for/of) no, none, no one*
keinerlei *no, none*; keinerlei Führungsfunktionen *no management functions whatsoever*
die Kelterei (– en) *winemaker*
kennen, a, a *to know*
die Kenntnisnahme (– n) *attention*; Mit der Bitte um: Kenntnisnahme *for information*
die Keramik (– en) *ceramics*
der Keramikkörper (–) *ceramic cartridge*
die Kernforschung *nuclear/atomic research*
der Kernteil (– e) *core*
die Kernzeit (– en) *core time*
das Kfz = Kraftfahrzeug
der Kfz-Mechaniker (–) *car mechanic*
die Kfz-Versicherung (– en) *motor insurance*
kg = Kilogramm
die KG (– s) = Kommanditgesellschaft
das Kilo (– s) *kilo*
das Kilogramm (– e) *kilogram*
der Kilometer (–) *kilometre*
das Kind (– er) *child*
der Kindergarten (∺) *kindergarten*
die Kirche (– n) *church*
die Kirchensteuer (– n) *church tax*
die Kirmes *funfair*
kl. = kleine, kleiner, kleines
klar *clear, simple*; das ist klar *that's clear*; klar werden *to become clear*
klassifiziert *(from klassifizieren) classified*
die Klassik *classical period*
klassisch *classic(al)*
das Klavier (– e) *piano*
kleben *to glue, stick, bond*
das Kleben *gluing*
die Kleidung *clothing*
klein *small, little, short*
der Kleinaktionär (– e) *small shareholder*
der, die, das Kleine (– n) *(the) little thing/one*, *(the) small thing/one*; daß sich der Bedarf des Kleinen entwickelt *that the small company develops the need*
kleiner (als) *smaller (than)*
der Kleinkunde (wk m) (– n) *small customer, person in the street*
das Klima (– s) *climate, air-conditioning*
die Klinik (– en) *medical centre, hospital*
der Kloß (∺e) *dumpling*
km = Kilometer
knacken *to crackle*
knapp *concise(ly), about, just*
knirschen *to crunch*
das Know-how *know-how, expertise, tricks of the trade, consultancy*
die Kö = Königsallee
der Koch (∺e) *cook, chef*
kochend *boiling*
der Kohl *cabbage*

die Köhlbrandbrücke *Köhlbrandbrücke (bridge in Hamburg)*
der Kollege (wk m) (– n) *colleague (m)*
die Kollektion (– en) *collection*
Köln *Cologne*
die Kolonie (– n) *colony*
kombinierbar *combinable*
der Komfort *convenience (lit. comfort)*
das Komma (– s) *comma, point*
die Kommanditgesellschaft (– en) *limited partnership*
der Kommanditist (wk m)(– en) *limited partner*
kommen, a, o * *to come, go, get, reach, arrive at*; kommen auf *to arrive at, get*; zu einem Fazit/Ergebnis kommen *to reach/arrive at a result/conclusion*; kommt jeder an den Punkt, an dem *everybody reaches the point at which*
kommen: kommen ... zurück *see* zurückkommen
die Kommission (– en) *committee, central purchasing committee*
kommt: kommt ... an *see* ankommen; kommt ... herum *see* herumkommen
die Kommunikation (– en) *communication*
die Kommunikationsanlage (– n) *communication system*
das Kommunikationsgerät (– e) *communication unit*
das Kommunikationsmittel (–) *communications medium*
das Kommunikationssystem (– e) *communication system*
das Kommunikationszentrum (–zentren) *communication centre*
der Komplementär (– e) *general partner*
komplett *complete(ly), fully*
das Komplettprogramm (– e) *full range*
der Komplettzustand: im Komplettzustand *complete*
der Komplex (– e) *complex*
kompliziert *complicated, complex*
die Komponente (– n) *component, unit*
die Konferenz (– en) *conference*
der Konferenzdolmetscher (–) *conference interpreter*
der Konferenzraum (∺e) *conference room*
die Konferenztechnik (– en) *conference technology*
das Konferenzzentrum (–zentren) *conference centre*
die Konfiguration (– en) *configuration*
die Konfitüre (– n) *jam, preserve(s)*
der Kongreß (–sse) *congress*
der König (– e) *king*
das Königreich (– e) *kingdom*; Vereinigtes Königreich *United Kingdom*
die Königsallee *(lit. king's avenue) main shopping street in Düsseldorf*
konkret *concrete(ly)*
der Konkurrent (wk m) (– en) *competitor*
die Konkurrenz (– en) *competition, competitor*
das Konkurrenz-Produkt (– e) *rival product*
der Konkurrenzkampf (∺e) *competition*
können *can, to be able, may*; das können wir gar nicht *we can't do that anyway*; die früher in den Boden gelangen konnten *which could in the past/used to be able to get into the ground*; ich habe Italienisch gekonnt *I could speak Italian*
konnte *could (see* können)
könnte *could (subjunctive, see* können)
konnten *could, used to be able to (see* können)
könnten *could, would be able (see* können)
konsequent *consistent(ly), purposeful(ly)*
die Konsequenz (– en) *consequence, conclusion, result, step*
konservativ *conservative*
konserviert *(from konservieren) preserved, sealed*
konstant *constant(ly)*
die Konstruktion (– en) *design, construction*
das Konstruktionssystem (– e) *design system*
der Konsum *consumption*
die Konsumgüter (pl) *consumer goods*
die Konsumgüterindustrie (– n) *consumer-goods industry*
der Kontakt (– e) *contact*
die Kontaktvermittlung (– en) *contact mediation, contacts*
das Konto (Konten) *account*

Kontoabfrage: Kontoabfrage *balance enquiry*
die Konto-Nummer (– n) *account number*
das Kontor (– e) *counting-house, merchant's office*
die Kontrolle (– n) *check, inspection, control, monitoring, supervision*
kontrollieren *to check, supervise*
die Konzentration (– en) *concentration*
sich konzentrieren (auf) *to concentrate on, focus on*
konzentriert *concentrates, concentrated (see* konzentrieren)
das Konzept (– e) *concept, design, idea*
die Konzeption (– en) *design(ing), concept, conception*
der Konzern (– e) *concern, group*
konzipieren *to conceive, design*
die Kooperation (– en) *cooperation*
die Koordination (– en) *coordination, coordinating*
der Kopf (∺e) *head*; Pro-Kopf *per capita*
der Kopfstand (∺e) *head stand (three sides open)*
das Kopiergerät (– e) *photocopier*
das Korn *corn, grain, schnapps*; Vollkorn *wholegrain*
die Korrektur (– en) *correction*
die Korrekturtaste (– n) *correction key*
kosten *to cost*; zu viel Zeit kosten *to take up too much time*
die Kosten (pl) *costs*
kostenlos *free of charge*
kostenmäßig *related to costs*; um kostenmäßig günstiger zu sein *to reduce costs*
der Kostenvorteil (– e) *cost benefit*
kostet *see* kosten
die Kraft (∺e) *force, power*; mit eigener Kraft *under its own power/steam*
das Kraftfahrzeug (– e) *(powered) vehicle*
das Krankenhaus (∺er) *hospital*
die Krankenkasse (– n) *health-insurance scheme*
der Krankenschein (– e) *health-insurance voucher*
die Krankenversicherung (– en) *health insurance*
die Krankheit (– en) *disease, illness*
das Kraut (∺er) *herb*
die Kräuterpilze (pl) *mushrooms with herbs*
der/die Kreative (– n), ein Kreativer *(the) creative person*
krebserregend *carcinogenic*
der Kredit (– e) *credit, loan*
der Kreditantrag (∺e) *credit application*
das Kreditinstitut (– e) *bank, credit institution*; öffentlich-rechtliche Kreditinstitute *public-sector banks*; genossenschaftliche Kreditinstitute *cooperative banks*
die Kreditkarte (– n) *credit card*
das Kreditwesen *banking (see* Bundesaufsichtsamt*)*
der Kreis (– e) *circle, group*
der Kreislauf *circulation*; ein guter Kreislauf *optimum flow of information*; wir machen einen guten Kreislauf *we have a good flow of information/feedback*
die Krise (– n) *crisis*
das Kriterium (Kriterien) *criterion*
kritisieren *to criticize*
kritisiert *criticizes, criticized (see* kritisieren)
krumm *hunched, uncomfortable (–ly)*
die Küche (– n) *kitchen, cuisine*
die Küchenlösung (– en) *kitchen solution, complete fitted kitchen*
das Küchenmodell (– e) *kitchen (model)*
die Küchentechnik *kitchen technology/equipment*
der Kuckuck (– e) *cuckoo*
das Kühlaggregat (– e) *cooling unit*
das Kühlbett (– en) *cooling bed/bank*
kühlen *to cool*
der Kühl-Container (–) *refrigerated container*
die Kultur (– en) *culture*
das Kulturzentrum (–zentren) *arts/cultural centre*
sich kümmern (um) *to deal with, bother about, look after*
der Kunde (wk m) (– n) *customer*; auf den Kunden *to the customer's requirements*
der Kundenauftrag (∺e) *customer order*; Herstellung im Kundenauftrag

custom manufacturing; nach Kundenauftrag *to the customer's order/specification*
die Kundenberatung (– en) *customer service/care*
die Kundenbuchhaltung (– en) *customer accounts (department), accounts receivable (department)*
der Kundendienst (– e) *customer service, customer care, after-sales service, customer service department*
die Kundendienstwerkstatt (∺en) *customer service centre*
der Kundenkontakt (– e) *customer/client contact*
der Kundenkreis (– e) *client list, clientele, customers*
das Kundenpersonal *customer's personnel*
der Kundenwunsch: der Kundenwunsch ist Befehl *the customer is king*
die Kündigung (– en) *dismissal*
künftig *future, prospective*
die Kunst (∺e) *art*
künstlich *artificial*
die Kunstsammlung (– en) *art collection*
der Kunststoff (– e) *plastic(s)*
kunststoffbeschichtet *plastic-coated*
die Kunststoffbeschichtung (– en) *plastic coating*
der Kurier (– e) *courier*
kurz *brief(ly)*; kurz und gut *in a nutshell*
kurzfristig *short-term*
die Kurzmitteilung (– en) *memo/compliments slip*

L

das Labor (– s) *laboratory*
das Laboratorium (Laboratorien) *laboratory*
der Laborraum (∺e) *lab(oratory) space, laboratory facility*
der Lachs (– e) *salmon*
der Lack (– e) *paint*
der Lackfehler (–) *paint defect, flaw in the paintwork*
das Lackieren *spray-painting*
lackieren *to paint*
der Lackierer (–) *paint-sprayer*
die Lackiererei (– en) *paint shop*
lackiert *painted*
die Lackierung (– en) *paint shop, painting process, paint, paintwork, lacquer*
die Lackschicht (– en) *coating of paint*
der Ladehafen (∺) *port of loading, freight terminal, sea terminal*
laden, (lädt), lud, geladen *to load*
der Laden (∺) *shop, boutique*
der Ladenschluß *(shop) closing time*
das Ladenschlußgesetz (– e) *law governing shop closing times*
die Ladung (– en) *cargo, consignment*
der Ladungseigentümer (–) *owner of the shipment*
die Lage (– n) *site, position, situation, location*
das Lager *stock, warehouse*; auf Lager *in stock*; im Lager *in the warehouse*; ab Lager *ex works*
der Lagereinkauf (∺e) *stock buying*
lagerhaltig *ex-stock*
die Lagerkapazität (– en) *warehouse/warehousing capacity*
das Lagerpersonal *warehouse staff*
das Land (∺er) *country, state, land, Land (second of two levels of state government)*
die Landeshauptstadt (∺e) *Land/state capital*
ländlich *rural*
ländlicher (als) *more rural (than)*
der Landtransport (– e) *land transport*
die Landung (– en) *landing*
der Landverkehrsträger (–) *road/rail transport*
die Landwirtschaft (– en) *farming, agriculture*
lang *long*; lang, länger als, der/die/das längste *long, longer than, the longest*; so lange *while*
die Länge (– n) *length*
länger (als) *longer (than)*
langfristig *long-term*
langjährig *long-standing, well-established*
langsam *slow(ly)*
längst *for a long time, long ago*; in längst

Glossary

vergangenen Tagen *in days gone by*
der, die, das längste *(the) longest (one)*
am längsten *longest*
der, die, das Langweiligste *(the) most boring thing/one*
lassen (läßt), ließ, gelassen *to let, leave, allow, have something done;* ob sich das Material umformen läßt *whether the material can be deformed*
läßt *see* lassen
der Lastkraftwagen (–) *truck, lorry*
die Lastschrift (– en) *direct debit*
das Lastspektrum (–spektren) *load spectrum*
der Lauch (– e) *leek*
Laufe: im Laufe der Jahre *over the years;* im Laufe ihres Betriebes *in the course of their operation*
laufen (äu), ie, au * *to run, walk, go, be on, go on, happen;* wir laufen über die Messe *we go round the fair;* laufen im Direktimport *are imported directly*
laufend *continuously, running (machine)*
läuft: läuft ... ab *see* ablaufen
das Laufwerk (– e) *disk drive*
die Laufzeit (– en) *duration*
laut *loud, noisy*
lawinenartig *like an avalanche*
leben (mit) *to live (with)*
das Leben (–) *life*
die Lebensfreude *joie de vivre, zest for life*
das Lebensmittel (–) *food(stuff)*
der Lebensmitteleinzelhandel *retail food trade*
das Lebensmittelgesetz (– e) *food law governing additives and preservatives*
der Lebensmittelhandel *food and drink/grocery trade, food and drink/grocery retailers*
die Lebensversicherung (– en) *life assurance/insurance*
das Leder *leather*
leer *empty*
der Leercontainer (–) *empty container*
die Leercontainergestellung (– en) *delivery of an empty container*
legen *to put, lay, attach;* darauf/auf etwas Wert legen *to value, attach importance to, set store by sth.*
legt: legt ... an *see* anlegen
die Lehre (– n) *apprenticeship*
der Lehrling (– e) *trainee, apprentice*
das Lehrlings-Gehalt (¨er) *apprentice's wage*
lehrreich *educational*
leicht *easy, light;* leicht, leichter als, der/die/das leichteste *easy, easier than, the easiest;* sich die Sache leicht machen *to take the easy option;* leicht durchschaubar *transparent*
leichter (als) *easier, lighter (than)*
leisten *to achieve, make (payment), offer, provide, carry out, afford;* Ihre Zahlung ist innerhalb 14 Tagen zu leisten *payment shall be made within 14 days (lit. is to be made), accounts are payable within 14 days;* wir können uns das nicht leisten *we cannot afford that*
die Leistung (– en) *power, performance, benefit(s), achievement, efficiency*
leistungsfähig *successful, powerful, high-power*
die Leistungsmöglichkeit (– en) *need*
das Leistungsspektrum (–spektren) *range of services*
das Leitbild (– er) *image*
leiten *to run, direct, chair, be in charge of;* ich leite die Controlling-Abteilung *I am head of the controlling department*
das Leiten *management*
leitend *managerial;* leitender Angestellter *member of the middle management*
der Leiter (–) *manager, head* (lit. *leader);* Leiter Öffentlichkeitsarbeit *head of the public relations department;* Leiter der Abteilung Offshore *head of the offshore department*
der Leitfaden (¨) *guide, manual*
der Leitstand (¨e) *control console*
die Leitung (– en) *management, (pipe)line;* Leitung Maschinenbau *manager of engine construction*
das Leitungswasser *tap water, water from pipes and apparatus*
lenken *to direct, steer*
das Lenkrad (¨er) *steering wheel*
lernen *to learn;* ich habe Exportkaufmann gelernt *I trained as an export salesman;* lesen lernen *to learn to read*
das Lesen *reading*
lesen (ie), a, e *to read*
der, die, das letzte *(the) last (one), past, recent(ly);* in letzter Zeit *recently*
letztendlich *in the end, finally*
letztlich *finally, in the end, in the final analysis*
die Leute (*pl*) *people, staff, personnel*
das Licht (– er) *light*
die Lichttechnik *lighting* (lit. *lighting technology)*
lieben *to love*
lieber (als) *rather, preferably, prefer;* lieber möchten *prefer;* tragen lieber *prefer to wear*
der, die, das liebste *(the) favourite (one)*
am liebsten *best of all, ideally;* am liebsten noch *best of all, ideally*
der Lieferant (*wk m*)(– en) *supplier*
die Lieferbedingung (– en) *delivery condition (see* Versand*)*
lieferfähig *available for delivery, able to make delivery, operational*
das Lieferlos (– e) *batch, delivery*
die Liefermöglichkeit (– en) *delivery conditions*
liefern *to provide, supply, deliver;* Leistung liefern *to provide benefits*
liefern: liefern ... aus *see* ausliefern; liefern ... zu *see* zuliefern
liefert *provides (see* liefern*)*
der Liefertermin (– e) *delivery date/time/deadline*
die Liefertreue *reliable delivery*
die Lieferung (– en) *delivery, supply*
die Lieferverzögerung (– en) *delay in delivery*
die Lieferzeit *delivery time*
die Lieferzuverlässigkeit *reliability of delivery*
liegen, a, e *to lie, be (situated/located);* daneben liegen *to be off the mark*
liegengeblieben *broken down*
Lieschen: Lieschen Müller *individual consumer, "punter"*
ließ *see* lassen
Lingua: die Lingua franca *lingua franca*
die Linie (– n) *line, route*
der Liniendienst (– e) *liner service*
der Linienverkehr *scheduled flights*
links *(on/to the) left*
die Liquidation (– en) *winding up;* eine Liquidation durchführen *to wind up a company*
liquidieren *to wind up (a company)*
die Liste (– n) *list*
die Listung (– en) *listing*
die Literatur (– en) *literature*
die Lizenz (– en) *licence*
der Lkw (– s) = Lastkraftwagen
das Loch (¨er) *hole*
locker *loose, light*
der Löffel (–) *spoon*
logisch *logical(ly)*
die Logistik *logistics*
logistisch *logistical(ly)*
der Lohn (¨e) *wage, pay;* Lohn– und Gehaltsabrechnung *wage and salary statement, pay statement/advice;* Lohn– und Gehaltsbüro *wages and salaries office, pay office/department*
die Lohnsteuer (– n) *income tax*
das Lokal (– e) *tavern, pub, restaurant*
los *away, off, loose;* das geht los bei *it starts/begins with*
der Lösemittelanteil (– e) *solvent content*
lösen *to solve, remove, loosen*
die Losgröße (– n) *batch size*
die Lösung (– en) *solution, feature;* zur Lösung *to solve*
loswerden (*sep.*) (wird los), wurde los, losgeworden * *to get rid of*
die Lücke (– n) *gap, hole*
lud *see* laden
lud: lud ... aus *see* ausladen; lud ... ein *see* einladen
Ludwig *Ludwig, Louis*
die Luft (¨e) *air, atmosphere*
die Luftfahrt *aviation;* Luft– und Raumfahrt *aerospace*
die Lufthoheit (– en) *air sovereignty*
Luxemburg *Luxemburg*

M

m = Meter
machen *to do, make, give, set, transact, open up, carry out, produce;* ein Geschäft machen *to do business;* richten sich danach aus, ... zu machen *are geared to making ...;* Mut machen *to give encouragement;* das macht mir Spaß *I enjoy it/that;* die Leute machen jetzt Brotshops *people are now opening "bread shops";* sich selbständig machen *to start one's own business;* das Sekretariat machen *to carry out secretarial duties, run the office*
die Macht (¨e) *power, might*
macht: macht ... aus *see* ausmachen
die Machtposition (– en) *position of power*
made: made in Europe *made in Europe*
das Magazin (– e) *magazine*
mager *lean*
magnetinduktiv: magnetinduktives Prüfverfahren *magnetic particle inspection/testing*
der Mai *May;* im Mai *in May*
Mailand *Milan*
das Mailing (– s) *mailing, mail-shot*
der Main *(River) Main*
Mainhattan *Mainhattan (play on the words (River)* **Main** *and* **Manhattan***)*
die Mainmetropole *Main metropolis*
die Maintenance *maintenance*
der Makler (–) *broker*
das Mal (– e) *time*
mal = (*coll.*) einmal *once*
der Maler (–) *painter*
das Malz *malt*
man *one, you, we, they, people;* die man zu verspüren meint *which people think they can detect*
das Management (– s) *management*
der Manager (–) *manager*
manchmal *sometimes*
die Mandel (– n) *almond*
die Mandelbutter *almond butter*
der Mangel (¨) *defect*
der Mann (¨er) *man*
männlich *male*
mannshohe: eine mannshohe Blechrolle *a metal coil 6 feet high*
der Mantel (¨) *coat*
manuell *manual(ly)*
die Marine *navy, marine*
die Mark (–) *mark (German currency);* deutsche Mark *Deutschmark, German mark, D-Mark*
die Marke (– n) *brand (name)*
der Markenartikel (–) *brand product*
der Markenartikler (–) *brand manufacturer*
der Markenhersteller (–) *brand-name manufacturer, brand manufacturer*
das Markenimage (– s) *brand image*
das Markenzeichen (–) *trademark*
das Marketing *marketing*
der Marketing-Manager (–) *marketing manager;* Marketing-Manager International *international marketing manager*
die Marketing-Seite (– n) *marketing side*
die Marketingaktivität (– en) *marketing activity*
die Marketingkommunikation (– en) *marketing communication*
das Marketingmedium (–medien) *marketing medium*
der Markt (¨e) *market, (super)store, centre;* auf dem freien Markt *in the free/open market*
der Marktanteil (– e) *market share*
das Marktbedürfnis (– se) *demands/requirements (of the market)*
die Märkte (*pl*) *markets*
die Markteinführung (– en) *market launch*
der Markterfolg (– e) *market success*
die Marktforschung (– en) *market research*
der Marktführer (–) *market leader*
marktgerecht *competitive*
der Marktleiter (–) *store manager*
die Marktnische (– n) *market niche*
die Marktnischenüberlegung: wir haben Marktnischenüberlegungen geführt *we considered the market niches available*
die Marktöffnung (– en) *opening up of the market, market opening*
das Marktsegment (– e) *market segment*
die Marktuntersuchung (– en) *market research, market study*
die Marktwirtschaft (– en) *market economy;* soziale Marktwirtschaft *social market economy*
der März *March;* im März *in March*
die Maschine (– n) *machine, machinery*
der Maschinenbau *mechanical engineering;* Stahl–, Maschinen– und Anlagenbau *steel, machinery and plant construction*
der Maschinenpark (– s) *machinery, equipment, production facilities*
der Maschinenschlosser (–) *engine fitter, mechanic, machinist*
das Maschinenteil (– e) *machine part*
das Maß (– e) *measure, dimension, degree;* in zunehmendem Maße *increasingly*
die Maß (–) *measure, litre (of beer)*
die Masse (– n) *mass, material/substance, majority;* die Masse der Kunden *the majority of customers*
die Massengüter (*pl*) *bulk goods*
maßgeblich *decisive*
maßgeschneidert *tailor-made*
die Maßnahme (– n) *measure*
das Material (–ien) *material*
der Materialfluß (flüsse) *flow of materials*
die Materiallieferung (– en) *delivery of material(s)*
die Materialqualität (– en) *quality of material(s)*
die Materialstärke (– n) *material thickness*
Math. = Mathematik(er)
der Mathematiker (–) *mathematician*
der Maurer (–) *bricklayer*
maximal *maximum*
MBB = Messerschmitt-Bölkow-Blohm
die Mechanik *mechanical structure(s), enclosure(s)*
der Mechaniker (–) *mechanic*
die Mechanikerlehre (– n) *apprenticeship as a machinist*
mechanisch *mechanical;* mechanische Fertigung *machine shop*
das Medaillon: Medaillons vom Schweinefilet *fillets of pork*
der Media-Turm (¨e) *media tower*
die Medien (*pl*) *media*
das Meer (– e) *sea*
der Meeresboden *sea bed*
die Meerestechnik *marine engineering/technology*
das Meeting (– s) *meeting*
mehr (als) *more (than);* mehr oder weniger *more or less;* nicht mehr *no longer;* viel mehr als *much more than;* mehr und mehr *more and more*
mehrere *several, a number*
die Mehrwertsteuer (– n) *Value-Added Tax*
der Meilenstein (– e) *milestone*
mein, meine, meinem, meinen, meiner, meines *(to/from/for/of) my*
meinen *to think*
die Meinung (– en) *opinion;* meiner Meinung nach *in my opinion*
der Meinungsbildner (–) *opinion leader(s)*
meist *most(ly)*
der, die, das meiste *(the) most;* die meisten Banken *most banks*
die meisten (*pl*) *most*
der Meister (–) *master craftsman, supervisor, foreman*
die Menge (– n) *quantity;* eine ganze Menge *a wide range*
der Mensch (*wk m*) (– en) *person; (pl) people*
die Mentalität (– en) *mentality*
die Messe (– n) *trade fair;* die Messe Frankfurt *the Frankfurt Fair*
der Messebau *exhibition-stand construction*
die Messebeteiligung (– en) *trade-fair exhibition* (lit. *participation)*
das Messegelände (–) *trade-fair complex*
das Messeland (¨er) *country for trade fairs*
der Messeplatz (¨e) *trade-fair centre/complex*
der Messestand (¨e) *trade-fair stand*
die Messestände (*pl*) *trade-fair stands*
der Messeturm *trade-fair tower,* Messeturm
die Messe-Werbung *trade-fair advertising*
die Messezeit (– en) *trade-fair period;* zu Messezeiten *when trade fairs are on*
das Meßgerät (– e) *measuring instrument*
die Meßtechnik *metrology, instrumentation, measuring technology;* Meß- und Automatisierungstechnik *instrumentation and automation (engineering)*

das Metall (– e) *metal, metal-working industry, metal-workers*
metallic *metallic*
die Metallindustrie (– n) *metal industry*
metallverarbeitend *metal-processing*; metallverarbeitende Industrie *metal-processing industry*
der *or* das Meter (–) *metre*
die Metropole (– n) *metropolis*
die Metzgerei (– en) *butcher*
mich *me*
die Miete (– n) *rent, rental*
mieten *to rent*
der Mieter (–) *tenant*
der Mietwagen (–) *car hire, rented/hire car*
die Mikroelektronik *microelectronics*
die Milch *milk*
Mill. = Million
die Milliarde (– n) *1,000,000,000, thousand million, billion, milliard*
millimetergenau *millimetre precision*
die Million (– en) *1,000,000, million*
mindestens *at least*; mindestens haltbar bis *best before*
die Mineralölverarbeitung *oil refining/processing*
minimieren *to minimize*
minus *minus*; konstant gehaltene Minus-Temperaturen *constant refrigeration*
die Minute (– n) *minute*
die Minuten (*pl*) *minutes*
Mio. = Million
mir *to me*
die Mischware (– n) *mixed fabric(s)*
mit *with*; mit Verlassen des Werks *when (goods) leave the factory*
der Mitarbeiter (–) *colleague (m), employee (m), personnel, staff, human resources (lit. co-worker)*; Mitarbeiter im Außendienst *sales representative*
der Mitarbeiterstamm *workforce*
die Mitarbeiterzahl (– en) *number of employees*
die Mitbestimmung *(worker) participation in management, co-determination*
das Mitbestimmungsgesetz (– e) *Co-determination Act*
mitbringen (*sep.*), brachte mit, mitgebracht *to bring with (him/her/them ...)*
miteinander *together*; miteinander verbunden *connected (together)*
das Mitglied (– er) *member*
die Mitgliederberatung (– en) *members' advisory department*
das Mitgliedsland (–̈er) *member country*
der Mitgliedstaat (– en) *member state*
mitintegriert (*from* mitintegrieren) *integrated*
mitnehmen (*sep.*) (nimmt mit), nahm mit, mitgenommen *to take along*; zum Mitnehmen *takeaway*; Speisekarte zum Mitnehmen *takeaway menu*
das Mittagessen (–) *lunch*
die Mitte (– n) *middle, mid*
das Mittel (–) *means, resources*
Mittel-Amerika *central America*
Mitteleuropa *central Europe*
mittelgroß *medium-sized*
der Mittelstand (–̈e) *small and medium-sized companies, middle class*
mittelständisch *medium-sized*; mittelständisches Unternehmen *medium-sized company*
mitten *in the middle of*; mitten in der Nordsee *in the middle of the North Sea*
der Mittenstand (–̈e) *centre point*
der, die, das mittlere *medium-sized*
der Mittwoch (– e) *Wednesday*; am Mittwoch *on Wednesday*
mittwochs *on Wednesdays*
mitübernehmen (*sep.*) (übernimmt mit), übernahm mit, mitübernommen *to take over*
mitübernommen *taken over (see* mitübernehmen)
ml = Milliliter
mm = Millimeter
Mo = Montag
die Möbel (*pl*) *furniture*
mobil *mobile, active*
möchte (*from* mögen): ich möchte *I'd like*
möchten *see* möchte
die Mode (– n) *fashion*; anspruchsvolle Mode *high fashion, haute couture*
das Modell (– e) *model*
die Modemesse (– n) *fashion fair*
die Modemetropole (– n) *fashion metropolis/centre*
modern *modern*
modernisieren *to modernize*
die Modernisierung (– en) *modernization*
der, die, das modernste *(the) most modern/up-to-date (one), latest, extremely modern/up-to-date*; modernste Technik/Technologie *the latest technology*
modifizieren *to modify*
die Modifizierung (– en) *modification*; nach der Modifizierung der Basis *after the basic systems have been modified*
modular *modular*
mögen (mag), mochte, gemocht *to like to*
möglich *possible*; so viel wie nur möglich *as much as possible*
die Möglichkeit (– en) *possibility*; nach Möglichkeit *if possible*; besteht die Möglichkeit *it is possible*
möglichst: möglichst das Risiko zu verhindern *to prevent the risk if/as far as possible*
der Moment (– e) *moment*; im Moment *at the moment, now*
momentan *at the moment, at present*
der Monat (– e) *month*
monatig *monthly*; 6monatig *6 month*
monatlich *monthly*
das Monatsgehalt (–̈er) *monthly salary*; dreizehntes Monatsgehalt *thirteenth month's salary, annual bonus*
der Montag (– e) *Monday*; am Montag *on Monday*
die Montage (– n) *assembly, erection*
der Montagefehler (–) *assembly error/defect*
der Montageschaum *assembly foam*
montags *on Mondays*
die Montanindustrie (– n) *coal and steel industry*
montieren *to assemble, mount*
das Montieren *mounting, assembling*
montiert *assembled (see* montieren*)*
Moos *moss*
morgen *tomorrow, on the next day*
morgens *in the morning(s)*
die Motivation (– en) *motivation*
motivieren *to motivate*
motiviert *motivates, motivated (see* motivieren*)*
der Motor (– en) *engine*
der Motorblock (–̈e) *cylinder block*
der Motorenbau *engine construction*
die Motorensteuerung (– en) *timing gear*
der Motorenteil (– e) *engine component*
die Motormontage (– n) *engine assembly*
das Motorsegment (– e) *motor segment*
das Motto (– s) *motto*
Mrd. = Milliarde
das MTZ = Münchner Technologiezentrum
mühelos *effortless(ly)*
die Müllbeseitigung (– en) *refuse collection*
multinational *multinational(ly)*
München *Munich*
Münch(e)ner *of Munich, Munich*
das Museum (Museen) *museum*
die Musik *music*
muß *must, have to, got to*; man muß you have to; das muß nicht sein *it's/that is not necessary*
müsse *had to (subjunctive) (see* müssen*)*
müssen (muß), mußte, gemußt *to have to*
mußte(n) *had to*
müßten *had to, would have to (subjunctive) (see* müssen*)*
das Muster (–) *sample*
das Musterziehen *sampling, ordering samples*
der Mut *encouragement*; Mut machen *to give encouragement*
die Muttergesellschaft (– en) *parent company (lit. mother company)*
der Mutterschutz *maternity leave* (coll.)
muttersprachlich *mother-tongue*
die MwSt. (= Mehrwertsteuer) *VAT*

N

nach *to, after, according to, in accordance with, in conformity with, following, about, for, in*; je nach *according to*; nach wie vor *still, now as ever*; unserer Erfahrung nach *in our experience*; nach denen *according to which*; die Nachfrage nach dem Deutschen *the demand for German*
nachbarlich *neighbouring*; nachbarliches Umfeld *surrounding regions/countries*
nachdem *since, after*
die Nachfrage (– n) *demand*; die Nachfrage nach dem Deutschen *the demand for German*
nachgeschaltet (*from* nachschalten) *later, at a later stage*
nachher *after(wards), later*; bis nachher *until finally*
die Nachnahme *cash on delivery*; per Nachnahme *cash on delivery*
die Nachricht (– en) *news*
die Nachspeise (– n) *dessert*
der, die, das nächste *(the) next/nearest (one)*
der, die, das nächstgelegene *(the) nearest (one)*
der Nachteil (– e) *disadvantage*
der Nachtisch (– e) *dessert*
die Nachverbrennungsanlage (– n) *afterburning system*
nackt *empty, naked*; nackte Fläche *floorspace*
nah *near*; nah, näher als, der/die/das nächste *near, nearer than, the nearest*
näher (als) *nearer (than)*
nahezu *nearly*
nahm *see* nehmen
nahm: nahm ... auf *see* aufnehmen
Nahost *Near East*
die Nahrung *nutrition, food*; die Nahrungs– und Genußmittelindustrie *food, drink and tobacco industry*
der Name (*wk m; genitive* –ns) (– n) *name*
namhaft *well-known*
der, die, das namhafteste *best-known*
nämlich *that is, i.e., you see*
national *national*
die Natur (– en) *nature*
naturgemäß *naturally, by its very nature*
natürlich *of course, natural(ly)*; natürliche Person *natural person, individual*
die Navigation *navigation*
die Navigationsanlage (– n) *navigation system*
das Navigationsgerät (– n) *navigation instrument*
der Nebel (–) *fog, mist*
neben *next to, in addition to, apart from*
nehmen (nimmt), nahm, genommen *to take, use*; man nehme *you take*; ernst nehmen *to take seriously*; sich Zeit nehmen *to take time*
nehmen: nehmen ... ab *see* abnehmen; nehmen ... an *see* annehmen
die Neigung (– en) *tendency, preference*
nennen, nannte, genannt *to call, name*
nervös *nervous(ly), apprehensive(ly)*
netto *net(t)*
das Netto-Einkommen (–) *net income*
der Nettolohn (–̈e) *net wage, net pay*
der Nettopreis (– e) *net price*
das Netz (– e) *net(work), mains*
neu *new*; neu eingeben *re-enter, enter again*
der, die, das Neue *(the) new thing/one*; etwas Neues *something new*
neuer (als) *newer, more recent (than)*
der, die, das neuere *(the) newer (one)*
der, die, das neu(e)ste *(the) newest/latest (one)*
neugestalten *to rearrange*
neugestaltet *rearranged (see* neugestalten*)*
die Neugründung (– en) *founding, establishment, start-up*
die Neuheit (– en) *innovation, new product*
neun *nine*
der, die, das neunte *(the) ninth (one)*
neunzehn *nineteen*
neunzig *ninety*
neunziger: die neunziger Jahre *the nineties*
der Neupreis (– e) *new/purchase price*
neutral *neutral*; neutrales Mitglied *neutral member*
die NGG = Gewerkschaft Nahrung-Genuß-Gaststätten (*see* Gewerkschaft)
nicht *not, none*; nicht nur ... sondern auch *not only ... but also*
nichts *nothing*; während das nichts ausmacht *while that doesn't matter*
nie *never*
die Niederlande *Netherlands*
die Niederlassung (– en) *subsidiary*
Niedersachsen *Lower Saxony*
der Niederschlag (–̈e) *precipitation*
niedrig *low, compact*
die Niere (– n) *kidney*; auf Herz und Nieren *down to the last detail*
der Nieselregen *drizzle*
das Nietsystem (– e) *riveting system*
die Nischengestaltung (– en) *niche design, room divider system*
das Nitrat (– e) *nitrate*
das Niveau (– s) *level*
noch *still, even, as well, yet*; nur noch *the only thing, only, (from now on) only*; auch noch mal *still*; noch nicht *not yet*; immer noch, noch immer *still*; weder ... noch *neither ... nor*
nochmal *again, once more, further*
nochmals *again, once more*
die Nocke (– n) *cam*
die Nockenform (– en) *cam shape/form/profile*
die Nockenwelle (– n) *camshaft*
Nord *north, North*
Nord-Amerika *North America*
das Nord-Süd-Gefälle (–) *north-south divide*
der Norden *north, North*; im Norden *in the North*
nordisch *northern*
Nordrhein-Westfalen *North Rhine-Westphalia*
die Nordsee *North Sea*
die Nordsee-Bohrinsel (– n) *North-Sea drilling rig/platform*
die Norm (– en) *standard*; Deutsche Industrie-Norm *German industry standard*
normal *normal*
der Normalablauf (–̈e) *normal procedure*
normalerweise *normally*
die Normung (– en) *standardization*; Deutsches Institut für Normung *German Institute for Standardization*
Norwegen *Norway*
norwegisch *Norwegian*
die Notenbank (– en) *central bank, bank authorized to issue banknotes*
nötig *necessary*
notwendig *necessary*
der November *November*; im November *in November*
Nr. = Nummer
nüchtern *sober*
die Nudelsuppe (– n) *noodle soup*
null *zero, nil, nought*
die Nummer (– n) *number*
das Nummernschild (– er) *number plate*
nun *well, now*
nunmehr *now*
nur *only, just, solely*; nicht nur ... sondern auch *not only ... but also*; nur noch *the only thing, only*
Nürnberg *Nuremberg*
Nürnberger *of Nuremberg, Nuremberg*
der Nürnberger (–) *person from Nuremberg*
nutzen *or* nützen *to use*
der Nutzen *benefit*
nützlich *useful*
die Nutzung (– en) *use*
das Nylon *nylon*

O

ob *whether*
obenauf *on top*
Oberbayern *Upper Bavaria*
der Oberbegriff (– e) *generic term*
das Oberteil (– e) *top part*
objektiv *objective*
obwohl *although*
der Ochse (*wk m*) (– n) *ox, bullock*
OCR = optical character recognition (optische Zeichenerkennung)
oder *or*; entweder ... oder *either ... or*; oder aber *or alternatively*
offen *open(ly)*

Glossary

öffentlich *public;* öffentliche Dienste *public services*
öffentlich-rechtlich *public-sector, public-law;* öffentlich-rechtliche Kreditinstitute *public-sector banks*
die Öffentlichkeitsarbeit *public relations (work)*
offiziell *official(ly)*
öffnen *to open (up)*
das Öffnen *opening*
die Öffnungszeit (– en) *opening time*
der Offshorebereich (– e) *offshore sector*
die Offshoretechnik *offshore engineering/technology*
oft *often*
ohne *without*
ohnehin *in any case*
der OHP = Overheadprojektor
der Oktober *October;* im Oktober *in October*
das Oktoberfest (– e) *Oktoberfest (beer festival in Munich)*
das Öl *oil;* Öl-Bohrfeld *oil (drilling) field*
der Oldtimer (–) *veteran car, old timer*
oliv *olive*
der Olympiaturm *Olympic Tower (television tower in Munich)*
die Operation (– en) *operation*
operativ *operational*
die Optik *visual/optical effect, appearance*
optimal *optimum*
optimieren *to optimize*
optimiert *optimized (see optimieren)*
die Optimierung (– en) *optimization, optimizing*
optisch *optical(ly), visual(ly);* optisch eindrucksvoll *spectacular*
die Order (– s) *order, ordering*
die Ordermöglichkeit (– en) *opportunity for ordering*
die Ordnung (– en) *order;* in Ordnung *in order, satisfactory, conform to our requirements*
die Organisation (– en) *organization*
die Organisationsabteilung (– en) *organization department*
die Organisationsentwicklung (– en) *organization development*
organisatorisch *organizational*
organisieren *to organize*
organisiert *organized (see organisieren)*
orientieren *to orient(ate)*
orientiert *oriented (see orientieren)*
der Ort (– e) *place, site;* vor Ort *on site (lit. at the coalface), on the spot*
örtlich *local(ly)*
der Ortstarif (– e) *local rate*
Ost *east, East*
Ost-Europa *Eastern Europe*
der Osten *east, East;* im Osten *in the East*
Österreich *Austria*
Osteuropa *Eastern Europe*
Ostfriesland *East Friesland*
die ÖTV = Gewerkschaft Öffentliche Dienste, Transport und Verkehr *(see Gewerkschaft)*
der Overheadprojektor (– en) *overhead projector*
ozonschädigend *damaging to the ozone layer*

P

das Paar (– e) *pair, couple*
paar: ein paar *some, a few*
die Packetfahrt *see HAPAG*
das Packmittel (–) *packaging*
die Packung (– en) *packing*
die Packungsdichte (– n) *packing density*
das Paket (– e) *package, parcel*
das Paketgewicht (– e) *package weight*
die Palette (– n) *range*
der Pannendienst (– e) *breakdown service*
die Papaya (– s) *paw paw, papaya*
das Papier (– e) *paper*
die Parfümerie (– n) *perfumer's, shop selling perfumes and cosmetics*
parken *to park*
der Park (– s) *park*
die Parkgebühr (– en) *parking fee*
das Parkhaus (:er) *multi-storey car park*
das Parkhotel *park hotel*
der Parkplatz (:e) *car park*
der Parmaschinken (–) *Parma ham*
die or das Partikel (–n or –) *particle*
der Partner (–) *partner*
das Partnerland (:er) *partner (country)*

die Partnerschaft (– en) *partnership* partnerschaftlich *as partners, mutual*
der Passagier (– e) *passenger*
der Passagierraum (:e) *passenger compartment, saloon*
passen (paßt) *to fit, suit*
passieren* *to happen*
passiert *happens, happened (see passieren)*
paßt *see* passen; paßt sich ... an *see* anpassen
das Patent (– e) *patent*
das Patentamt (:er) *patent office*
das Patentrecht (– e) *patent law*
der Patient (wk m) (– en) *patient (m)*
pauschal *flat rate*
der Pauschalpreis (– e) *flat rate (price)*
der PC (– s) = Personal Computer *PC*
die PC-Station (– en) *PC workstation*
der PC-Wagen (–) *PC trolley*
die Penetranz (– en) *penetration*
die Pension (– en) *retirement (old-age), boarding house, pension*
per *by virtue of, by, on;* per Gestellungsdatum *on the delivery date;* per Post *by post;* per Nachnahme *cash on delivery*
perfekt *perfect(ly)*
periodisch *periodic(ally)*
das Perlon *perlon*
permanent *permanent*
das Persil *Persil (washing powder)*
die Person (– en) *person*
das Personal *personnel*
die Personalabteilung (– en) *personnel/human-resource department*
die Personalentwicklung *personnel/human-resource development, personnel/human-resource training department*
die Personalschulung (– en) *personnel/human-resource training*
die Personengesellschaft (– en) *partnership, unlimited company*
die Personenversicherung (– en) *personal insurance*
persönlich *personal(ly)*
der Petersfisch (– e) *(Saint) Peter's fish*
die Petersilie (– n) *parsley*
die Petersilienkartoffel (– n) *parsley potato*
das Petroleum *petroleum*
der Pfennig (– e) *pfennig*
die Pflicht (– en) *obligation*
die Pflichtversicherung (– en) *compulsory/obligatory insurance*
phantastisch *fantastic(ally)*
die Phase (– n) *phase*
die Philosophie (– n) *philosophy*
das Physiklabor (– s) *physics laboratory*
das Pilotprojekt (– e) *pilot project*
der Pilz (– e) *mushroom*
die Pinakothek: Alte Pinakothek *Alte Pinakothek (art gallery in Munich)*
das Planen *planning*
planen *to plan*
planerisch *planning, of a planning nature*
die Planung (– en) *planning*
das Plastik *plastic;* Plastik-Geld *plastic money*
die Platine (– n) *printed circuit board, PC board*
die Platte (– n) *panel*
die Plattform (– en) *platform*
das Plattformbein (– e) *platform leg*
der Platz (:e) *square, place, space*
plazieren *to place;* einen Auftrag plazieren *to place an order*
plaziert *places, placed (see plazieren)*
der Plotter (–) *plotter*
plötzlich *suddenly*
plus *plus;* konstant gehaltene Plus-Temperaturen *temperatures constantly maintained above zero*
die Pneumatik *pneumatic systems*
Polen *Poland*
die Police (– n) *policy*
die Politik *policy, politics*
die Polizei (– en) *police*
das Polyamid *polyamide*
das Polyäthylen *polyethylene*
die Polyäthylenverpackung (– en) *polyethylene packaging*
der Polyester *polyester;* Polyester-Polykondensations-Anlage *polyester polycondensation plant*

die Polykondensation *polycondensation (see* Polyester*)*
populär *popular, strong demand*
Portugal *Portugal*
die Position (– en) *position*
das Positionieren *positioning;* Positionieren der Produkte *product positioning*
positiv *positive(ly)*
die Post *post, postal workers, postal industry*
das Postamt (:er) *post office*
der Posten *post (place to stand)*
das Postfach (:er) *post box (PO box)*
die Postleitzahl (– en) *post code, zip code*
prägen *to stamp, shape, determine*
die Prägung (– en) *recess, position, characteristic, feature*
praktisch *more or less*
praktizieren *to practise, pursue, apply;* vertriebsstrategisches Denken praktizieren *to apply marketing principles;* anders zu praktizieren *to pursue a different policy/strategy*
praktiziert *practises, practised (see* praktizieren*)*
die Präsentation (– en) *presentation*
präsentieren *to present*
sich präsentieren *to present oneself*
präsentiert *presents, presented*
das Präservativ (– e) *condom*
die Praxis *practice, experience;* in der Praxis *in practice*
präzis(e) *precise(ly)*
die Präzision *precision*
der Preis (– e) *price*
das Preis-Abschlußgespräch (– e) *final discussion to establish price*
die Preisänderung (– en) *change in price*
preisgünstig *cost-effective, low-cost, cheap*
preisgünstiger (als) *more cost-effective (than), lower-cost (than), cheaper (than)*
preiswert *value for money, low-cost, cheap*
preiswerter (als) *more cost-effective (than), better value for money (than)*
die Premiere (– n) *launch*
die Presse (– n) *the press*
die Presse-Betreuung (– en) *press relations*
die Presse-Information (– en) *press release*
die Pressekonferenz (– en) *press conference*
der Pressekontakt (– e) *press contact*
pressen (preßt), preßte, gepreßt *to press*
die Pressenstraße (– n) *press line*
das Preßwerk (– e) *press works, press shop, pressings plant*
das Preßwerkzeug (– e) *press(ing) tool*
prima *great, splendid, first-class*
das Prinzip (–ien) *principle;* im Prinzip *in principle*
prinzipiell *in/on principle, basically*
die Priorität (– en) *priority;* absolute Priorität *top priority*
privat *private(ly)*
privatisieren *to privatize*
die Privatperson (– en) *private person/individual*
pro *per;* pro Kopf *per capita;* pro Tag *per/a day;* ein Abend pro Woche *one evening a week;* Pro-Kopf-Umsatz *sales per capita*
die Probe (– n) *test, sample;* Proben ziehen *to take samples*
die Probelieferung (– en) *sample delivery/amount*
das Problem (– e) *problem*
die Probleme (pl) *problems*
die Problemstellung (– en) *problem (formulation)*
das Produkt (– e) *product, material;* Portex-Produkte *Portex product range;* das Produkt Portex *the Portex product range;* aus natürlichen Produkten *made of natural materials*
die Produkt-Präsentation (– en) *product presentation*
die Produktaufnahme (– n) *integration of the products*
das Produktdesign (– s) *product design*
die Produktentwicklung (– en) *product development*
die Produktgruppe (– n) *product group*
die Produktion (– en) *production, shop floor*
der Produktionsablauf (:e) *production process*
die Produktionsaufnahme (– n) *starting up production*

produktionsbegleitend *during the production process*
die Produktionsleitung (– en) *production pipework*
die Produktionsplanung (– en) *production planning*
der Produktionsprozeß (–prozesse) *production process*
der Produktionsraum (:e) *production space/premises*
der Produktionssektor (– en) *production (sector)*
die Produktionszusammenlegung (– en) *merging production operations*
der Produktkontakt (– e) *product contact;* Produktkontakt zur Spitze *leading-edge products*
die Produktqualität *product quality*
produzieren *to produce*
produziert *produces, produced (see* produzieren*)*
der Profit (– e) *profit*
das Profit Center (– s) *profit centre*
das Profit-Center-Wesen *profit-centre concept, profit centres*
die Prognose (– n) *forecast*
prognostizieren *to forecast*
prognostiziert *forecasts, forecast (see* prognostizieren*)*
das Programm (– e) *programme, program, (product) range*
programmierbar *programmable*
das Projekt (– e) *project*
die Projektfinanzierung (– en) *project financing*
das Projektmanagement (– s) *project management*
der Projektor (– en) *projector*
der Prokurist (wk m) (– en) *authorized signatory*
die Promotion *promotion*
promotionsmäßig: promotionsmäßig unterstützen *to promote*
promovieren *to do a doctorate*
promoviert: ich habe promoviert *I did a doctorate*
der Propeller (–) *propeller*
der Prospekt (– e) *brochure*
das Protokoll (– e) *report*
die Provision (– en) *commission*
das Prozent (– e) *percent*
der Prozentsatz (:e) *percentage*
der Prozeß (–sse) *process*
die Prüfdokumentation (– en) *inspection/test reports/documentation*
prüfen *to audit, inspect, examine, test*
der Prüfstand (:e) *test stand/bench*
die Prüfstrecke (– n) *test section/track*
die Prüfung (– en) *exam(ination), audit*
der Prüfungsassistent (wk m) (– en) *trainee auditor (m)*
das Prüfverfahren (–) *test procedure, testing, inspection;* magnetinduktives Prüfverfahren *magnetic particle inspection/testing*
die Psychologie *psychology*
psychologisch *psychological(ly)*
die Public Relations (pl) *public relations*
publizieren *to publish*
der Puffer (–) *buffer*
der Punkt (– e) *factor, point, dot;* mit ein wesentlicher Punkt *one essential factor;* kommt jeder an den Punkt *everybody reaches the point*
pünktlich *on time, punctual(ly)*
die Pünktlichkeit *punctuality*
das PVC *PVC*

Q

der Quadratkilometer (–) *square kilometre*
der Quadratmeter (–) *square metre*
der Qualifikationsspiegel (–) *qualification profile*
die Qualität (– en) *quality;* in bester Qualität *top quality*
qualitativ *qualitative(ly)*
die Qualitätsanforderung (– en) *quality requirement/demand*
das Qualitätsgefälle (–) *quality scale (falling from ... to ...)*
qualitätsmäßig *from the quality aspect;* qualitätsmäßig hochstehend *high quality*
die Qualitätsprüfung (– en) *quality test/inspection*
die Qualitätsprüfungsorganisation (– en)

quality-inspection organization
das Qualitätssicherungssystem (– e) quality-assurance system
die Qualitätssicherung (– en) quality assurance
der Qualitätsstandard (– s) standard of quality
das Qualitätssystem (– e) quality system
die Qualitätsverbesserung (– en) quality improvement
die Quantität (– en) quantity
die Quelle (– n) source
querbeet (right) across the board

R

das Rad (¨er) wheel
das Radfahren cycling
das Radhaus (¨er) wheel arch; hinteres Radhaus rear wheel arch
das Radio (– s) radio
der Rahmen (–) frame; im Rahmen in the course of/context of, during, in, with
die Raiffeisenbank (– en) agricultural credit cooperative
der Rat advice
rational rational(ly)
der Raum (¨e) room, area
raus = heraus or hinaus
rausfliegen (sep.), o, o * to fly out
rausgehen (sep.), ging raus, rausgegangen * to go out
rauskommen see rauskommen
rauskommen (sep.), a, o * to come out, emerge
rauskriegen (sep.) to find out
rauszukriegen see rauskriegen
reagieren to react
die Reaktion (– en) reaction
rechnen to calculate, count (amount)
das Rechnen maths; kaufmännisches Rechnen maths for business purposes
die Rechnung (– en) bill, invoice, account; auf eigene Rechnung on (our) own account
das Rechnungsdatum (–daten) invoice date
das Rechnungswesen accountancy
recht rather, quite
rechtlich legal (see öffentlich-rechtlich)
rechts (on/to the) right
die Rechtsform (– en) legal form
die Rechtsschutzversicherung (– en) legal insurance (costs and expenses)
rechtzeitig in good time
reden to talk
reduzieren to reduce
reduziert reduces, reduced (see reduzieren)
die Reederei (– en) shipping company, shipping line
die Reeperbahn Reeperbahn (red-light district in Hamburg)
das Regal (– e) shelf
die Regel (– n) rule, convention; regelmäßig regular(ly); in aller Regel normally
regelmäßig regular(ly)
der Regen rain
die Region (– en) region
regional regional
die Registratur (– en) filing department
die Regularien (pl) rules, principles; betriebswirtschaftliche Regularien principles of business administration
reich rich
reichen to extend, be sufficient
reichhaltig extensive; das reichhaltige Innenleben generously equipped interior
der Reifen (–) tyre
die Reihe (– n) row, series, a number of; eine Reihe von Dingen a number of things; in einer Reihe Regionen in a number of regions
der Reihenstand (¨e) row stand
rein pure(ly), clean
reinfliegen (sep.), o, o * to fly in
die Reinigung cleaning
die Reise (– n) journey
die Reisegepäckversicherung (– en) baggage/luggage insurance
das Reisen travel(ling)
der/die Reisende (– n), ein Reisender traveller, field staff
der Reiz (– e) incentive, impetus, attraction, appeal
reizen to excite, attract
die Reklamation (– en) complaint, customer service/care (department)
reklamieren to complain, query (sth.)
die Relation (– en) relation
relativ relative(ly)
der or das Relaunch (–(e)s) relaunch
die Religion (– en) religion
die Rentenversicherung (– en) pension insurance
die Reparatur (– en) repair
das Reparieren repair(s)
die Reserve (– n) reserve; als Reserve in reserve
die Reservierung (– en) reservation
die Residenzstadt (¨e) residence town, seat of a royal court
die Responsezeit (– en) response time
das Restaurant (– s) restaurant
restriktiv restrictive(ly)
resultieren (in) to result (in)
resultiert results, resulted (see resultieren)
die Rezeptur (– en) recipe, formula
der Rhein River Rhine
der Rheinturm Rhine Tower (television/telecommunications tower in Düsseldorf)
richten to direct, gear
sich richten (nach) to be determined, calculated; danach richtet sich is determined by that
richtig right, proper(ly), correct(ly)
die Richtlinie (– n) directive, guideline
die Richtung (– en) direction; in Richtung Gartenschmuck gehen to move towards/in the direction of garden accessories; Verantwortlichkeit in Richtung Umwelt responsibility towards the environment, environmental responsibility
riechen, o, o to smell
riesig huge
der Rinderbraten roast beef
die Rinderroulade beef olive
der Ring (– e) ring, coil
der Ringmotor (– en) ring motor
das Risiko (Risiken) risk
die Risikobetrachtung (– en) risk assessment
das Risikokapital venture capital
der Riß (Risse) crack, tear
der Roboter (–) robot, automated manipulative machine
der Rohbau body(work) assembly line/plant, body(work), structural shell
der Rohbauzustand: im erweiterten Rohbauzustand structural shell with utilities connected
der Rohling (– e) blank
das Rohmaterial (–ien) raw material
das Rohr (– e) tube, pipe
die Röhre (– n) tube, pipe
die Röhren-Werke (pl) tubing works
die Röhrenproduktion (– en) tubing production
die Rohrleitung (– en) pipeline
der Rohstoffvorrat (¨e) reserves of raw materials
das Rohteil (– e) blank
die Rolle (– n) role, roll
rollen to roll
rollend rolling
der Rollenprüfstand (¨e) roller test stand
der Römer old town hall in Frankfurt (lit. Roman)
der Römerberg hill by the town hall (see Römer)
der Römersaal (–säle) coronation hall in the Römer (now a museum)
das Röntgenverfahren (–) X-ray procedure, X-ray/radiographic testing
rosa pink; rosa gebraten rare
der Rost rust
rot red
die Rôtisserie carvery, restaurant
der Rotwein (– e) red wine
die Rückgabe (– n) return; Mit der Bitte um: Rückgabe Please return
der Rückgang decline; im Rückgang befindlich declining
rückläufig declining
der Rückruf (– e) return (phone) call; Mit der Bitte um: Rückruf please ring back
die Rückseite (– n) reverse, back page; siehe Rückseite see reverse/over
der Rückversicherer (–) re-insurer
die Rückversicherung (– en) re-insurance
der Ruf (– e) reputation
der Ruhetag (– e) rest day, day of rest
die Ruhezeit (– en) slack period
die Ruhr (River) Ruhr
das Ruhrgebiet Ruhr (area)
der Rumpf (– e) fuselage
das Rumpfheck (– s) fuselage (section)
die Rumpfheckausrüstung equipping the fuselage (section)
die Rumpfheckmontage (– n) fuselage (-section) assembly
rund about, around, approximately; rund um ... herum around
die Rundfahrt (– en) tour
die Rundfunkwerbung radio advertising
die Rundsicht (– en) tour
runtergeschrieben (from runterschreiben) wrote, typed
runtersetzen (sep.) to lower, reduce
das Russisch Russian
rüsten: rüsten ... um see umrüsten
das Rüstzeug equipment, tools, outfit

S

's = es
Sa = Samstag
der Saal (Säle) hall
der Sachbearbeiter (–) clerk, clerical worker (m)
die Sachbearbeiterin (–nen) clerk, clerical worker (f)
die Sache (– n) thing
das Sachgebiet (– e) area of responsibility
sachlich objective(ly), factual, matter-of-fact
Sachsenhausen Sachsenhausen (district in Frankfurt with traditional taverns)
die Sachversicherung (– en) non-life insurance, property insurance
der Sack (¨e) sack
der Safran saffron
die Safrannudeln (pl) noodles with saffron
sagen to say, pass on; um nicht zu sagen not to say; sagen Sie es weiter pass it on
sah saw (see sehen)
die Sahne cream
die Saison (– s) season
das Saisongemüse vegetable(s) of the season
der Salat (– e) salad
das Salz (– e) salt
der Samstag (– e) Saturday; am Samstag on Saturday
samstags on Saturdays
samt including (all)
sämtlich(e) all
Sanitär sanitation
die Sauce (– n) sauce
sauer sour; süß-saure Sauce sweet-and-sour sauce
der Sauerbraten sauerbraten (beef marinated in vinegar)
saugen to suck
der Sauger (–) sucker; Staubsauger hoover (lit. dust-sucker)
die Säule (– n) column, pillar; Drei-Säulen-System three-column system
die Sauna (–s or Saunen) sauna
saure see sauer
die S-Bahn (– en) suburban rail network
der Scanner (–) scanner
schade shame, pity; da ist uns die Mark nicht zu schade we think every penny's well spent
die Schadenversicherung (– en) property and liability insurance
der Schadstoff (– e) pollutant
die Schadstoffreduzierung (– en) reduction of pollutants
schalldicht soundproof
schalldichter (als) more soundproof (than)
der Schaltkreis (– e) circuit
die Schaltung (– en) circuit
der Schaltungshersteller (–) circuit manufacturer
schauen to look, see
schauen: schauen ... an see anschauen
das Schaufenster (–) shop window
das Schaufensterdekorationsmaterial (–ien) decoration material for shop windows/window-dressing, window display(s)
schaut: schaut ... an (see anschauen)
der Scheck (– s) cheque; Zahlen Sie gegen diesen Scheck Pay against this cheque the sum of
die Scheck-Nr. cheque number
die Scheck-Nummer (– n) cheque number
der Schecktext (– e) cheque text
die Scheibe (– n) slice, window
scheibenweise by the slice
der Scheinwerfer (–) headlamp
scheitern * to founder
schenken to give
der Schenk-Tip (– s) gift tip
die Schicht (– en) coating, shift
schicken to send
die Schickeria jet-setters (similar to Sloane rangers/yuppies)
schiefgehen (sep.), ging schief, schiefgegangen * to go wrong
schier sheer, quite
das Schiff (– e) ship
die Schiffahrt shipping
der Schiffbau ship-building
der Schiffsraum cargo space
die Schiffsreise (– n) sea voyage
schimmernd shimmering
der Schinken (–) ham
die Schlachterei (– en) butcher
der Schlachtermeister (–) master butcher
schlagartig suddenly, at a stroke
schlagen (ä), u, a to strike, beat
schlagen: schlagen ... drauf see draufschlagen
schlecht bad
das Schleifen grinding
schleifen, schliff, geschliffen to rub down, grind
Schleswig-Holstein Schleswig Holstein
schließen, o, o to close, conclude; wenn der Kaufvertrag geschlossen wird when a contract of sale is concluded; auf das Lieferlos schließen to infer the quality of the batch
das Schließen filling, closing
schließlich finally
schließt: schließt ... ab see abschließen
das Schloß (¨sser) castle
der Schnee snow
schnell fast, quick(ly), rapid
die Schnellauszahlungstaste (– n) fast-cash key
schneller (als) faster (than)
der, die, das schnellste (the) quickest/fastest (one); schnellste Materiallieferung delivery of materials as fast as possible
schnellstens as fast/soon as possible, ASAP
schnellstmöglich as soon as possible; ASAP
der Schnickschnack accessories, ornaments
das Schnitzel (–) schnitzel, escalope, scallop, cutlet (may be breaded or unbreaded)
die Scholle (– n) plaice, flounder
schön nice, beautiful
schon already
schöner (als) more beautiful/nicer (than)
der Schrank (¨e) cupboard, cabinet, unit
die Schraube (– n) screw; eine Schraube, die ins Unendliche geht unlimited expenditure (lit. a screw which turns and turns to infinity)
der Schrebergarten (¨) allotment, garden (at a site with other gardens)
die Schreibarbeit (– en) correspondence
der Schreibdienst (– e) typing service
das Schreiben (–) letter; Ihr Schreiben vom your letter of
schreiben, ie, ie to write; etwas großschreiben to attach great importance to sth.
schreibend writing
die Schreibkraft (¨e) copy typist
die Schreibmaschine (– n) typewriter
schreibt: schreibt ... vor see vorschreiben
der Schreibtisch (– e) (writing) desk; Schreibtisch des Ruhrgebiets administrative centre/headquarters of the Ruhr
schrieb wrote (see schreiben)
die Schriftenlesesoftware (– s) OCR software
schriftlich written, in writing
der Schritt (– e) step
schrittweise step-by-step
die Schule (– n) school

schulen to train, carry out training; das Kundenpersonal wird geschult the customer's personnel is trained, vendor training is carried out; an ... geschult trained in the mould of ...
die Schulung (– en) training
das Schüttgut (¨er) bulk goods
der Schutz protection
schützen to protect
schwarz black, dark
der, die, das Schwarze (the) black thing/one, bull's eye; ins Schwarze treffen to hit the bull's eye
Schweden Sweden
das Schwein (– e) pig, pork
das Schweinefilet (– s) fillet of pork
die Schweinshaxe (– n) knuckle of pork
das Schweinswürstel (–) pork sausage
die Schweißanlage (– n) welding system/plant
das Schweißen welding
schweißen to weld
die Schweißfachtechnik welding engineering
der Schweißpunkt (– e) weld spot/point
schweißtechnisch: schweißtechnisch bearbeiten to weld (see schweißen)
die Schweiz Switzerland
Schweizer Swiss
der Schweizer (–) Swiss (person)
schwer heavy(–ily), difficult, severe(ly)
das Schwergut heavy cargo
der Schwerpunkt (– e) main focus/target, emphasis; Schwerpunkte des Unternehmens focus of a company's activities
die Schwester (– n) sister
die Schwesterfirma (–firmen) sister company
der Schwiegersohn (¨e) son-in-law
schwierig difficult
schwieriger (als) more difficult (than)
die Schwierigkeit (– en) difficulty
der, die, das Schwierigste (the) most difficult thing/one, (the) most difficult task
das Schwimmbad (¨er) swimming bath
das Schwimmen swimming
sechs six
der, die, das sechste (the) sixth (one)
das/ein Sechstel (–) (a) sixth
sechstens sixthly, number six
sechzehn sixteen
sechzig sixty
sechziger: die sechziger Jahre sixties
der See (– n) lake
der Seelauf (¨e) sea transport
der Seetransport (– e) sea transport
die Seeverladung (– en) sea transport
die Seezunge (– n) sole
das Seezungenfilet (– s) fillet of sole
das Segeln sailing
das Segment (– e) segment, section
sehen (ie), a, e to see, conceive; so wäre ... zu sehen this might permit ...; wir würden uns gerne sehen wollen we'd like to see ourselves
die Sehenswürdigkeit (– en) sight
sehr very, so much, a lot; nicht so sehr darum not about that so much; sehr viel a lot (of); sehr viel besser far better; das hat sehr geholfen that helped a lot
sei (from sein) is (subjunctive), was (reported speech); es sei denn unless; sei es erforderlich it was necessary
die Seife (– n) soap
sein (ist), war, gewesen * to be; bin am; ist is, has; sind are, have; war was; gewesen been, gone; stolz darauf, „Aniliner" zu sein proud of being employees of BASF
sein, seine, seinem, seinen, seiner, seines his, (to/from/for/of) him
seit since, for; seit 18 Jahren for 18 years; seit Mitte der 70er Jahre since the mid seventies
seitdem since (then)
die Seite (– n) side, page; auf der anderen Seite on the other hand
der Seitenrahmen (–) side frame
die Seitenverkleidung (– en) side panel(s), wall(s)
seitlich side, at the side
das Sekretariat (– e) secretarial duties; das Sekretariat machen to carry out secretarial duties, run the office
die Sekretärin (–nen) secretary (f)
der Sektor (– en) sector
die Sekunde (– n) second
selber or selbst myself, yourself, himself, herself, itself, etc.
selbst even (see also selber)
selbständig independent(ly), autonomous; dann habe ich mich selbständig gemacht I then started my own business
selbständiger (als) more independently (than)
die Selbständigkeit independence
der Selbstkostenpreis (– e) cost price
selbsttätig self-acting, automatic
selbstverständlich naturally, of course
das Selbstverständnis identity
das Seminar (– e) seminar
senken to sink
sich senken to come down, descend
sensibel sensitive
sensibilisieren to sensitize
der September September; im September in September
die Serie (– n) (mass) production, series, product line; geht in Serie goes into production
der Service service
die Service-Palette (– n) range of services
die Serviceleistung (– en) service; Serviceleistungen (pl) service package
der Serviceleiter (–) service manager
der Servicetechniker (–) service engineer
setzen to use, set; setzt Akzente sets trends; außer Kraft setzen to repeal
setzen: setzen sich ... durch see durchsetzen
setzt: setzt... voraus (see voraussetzen)
setzte: setzte ... ein see einsetzen
das Shampoo (– s) shampoo
der Shrimp (– s) shrimp
sich (to/from/for/of) oneself, himself, herself, itself, yourself, yourselves; an und für sich really, actually; also used as a reflexive pronoun
sicher certain(ly), safe(ly), secure(ly), reliable (–ly), no doubt
die Sicherheit (– en) safety, security, protection, reliability, safety margin; geprüfte Sicherheit safety-tested; Sicherheit von security against
der Sicherheitsabstand (¨e) safety distance
der Sicherheitsgurt (– e) safety/seat belt
das Sichern security
sichern to secure
sie she, her, it, they, them
Sie you (polite)
sieben seven
der, die, das siebte (the) seventh (one)
siebzehn seventeen
siebzig seventy
siebziger: die siebziger Jahre the seventies
siehe see (from sehen); siehe Rückseite see reverse/over
sieht see sehen
sieht: sieht .. aus see aussehen
das Silicon silicon
das Silicon-Valley (– s) Silicon Valley
sind are, have (see sein)
der Sinn (– e) meaning, point, sense; im weitesten Sinne in the widest sense
sinnvoll sensible, practical
die Situation (– en) situation
der Sitz (– e) seat, headquarters
sitzen, saß, gesessen to sit
die Sitzung (– en) meeting
Skandinavien Skandinavia
skifahren (sep.) (ä), u, a * to ski
das Skifahren skiing
der Skisack (¨e) ski sack
das Skiwandern ski hiking, cross-country skiing
der or das Skonto (– s) discount
die Skulptur (– en) sculpture
die Skyline (– s) skyline
der Slogan (– s) slogan
der or das Smalltalk (– s) small talk
die SMD-Schaltung (– en) SMD circuit
SMM = Schiff, Marine, Meerestechnik
so so, thus, such (that), (like) this, about, as; so lange while; so ..., daß ... in such a way that; so daß so that; und so weiter etc.; so ... wie as ... as; so viel ... wie nur möglich as much ... as possible
die or das Soda soda, sodium carbonate
die Sodafabrik (– en) soda factory (see BASF)
sofern provided (that), if
sofort immediately
die Sofortbuchung (– en) immediate booking
die Software (– s) software
sogar even
sogenannt so-called, (often non-pejorative), known as, called
der Sohn (¨e) son
solch, solche, solchem, solchen, solches such; für solche Dimensionen on such a scale
die Solidität solidity, reliability
soll should, is/has to (see sollen)
das Soll debit; Soll und Haben debit and credit
sollen (soll), sollte, gesollt to be supposed/intended/destined to, to be, should
sollte(n) should, ought to (see sollen)
somit thereby, therefore
der Sommer summer
das Sonderangebot (– e) special offer
die Sonderausstattung (– en) extras, optional/special equipment
die Sonderlackierung (– en) special paint job/finish
die Sonderlegierung (– en) special alloy
sondern but, on the contrary (used after negations in which an idea is excluded); nicht nur ... sondern auch not only ... but also
der Sonnabend (– e) Saturday; am Sonnabend on Saturday
sonnabends on Saturdays
die Sonne (– n) sun
der Sonnenschein sunshine
der Sonntag (– e) Sunday; am Sonntag on Sunday
sonntags on Sundays
sonst otherwise, usually, else
sonstig other
sorgen (für) to take care (of)
sorgte: sorgte für caused (see sorgen)
die Sorte (– n) make, variety, type, kind
sortiert (from sortieren) sorted
das Sortiment (– e) (product) range, products
die Souveränität sovereignty
sowie as well as, and
sowieso anyway
sowohl: sowohl ... als auch both ... and
sozial social; soziale Marktwirtschaft social market economy
die Sozialkunde social studies
die Sozialpartner (pl) unions and management
die Sozialversicherung (– en) social insurance, national insurance (UK)
der Sozialversicherungsbeitrag (¨e) social-insurance contribution
die Soziologie sociology
die Spachtelmasse (– n) filler
Spanien Spain
die Spareinlage (– n) savings deposit
sparen to save
die Spargelcrème (– s) cream of asparagus soup
die Sparkasse (– n) savings bank
die Sparte (– n) division, product group
der Spaß (¨e) fun, enjoyment; das macht mir Spaß I enjoy it/that
spät late
später later, future; seinen späteren Kunden its future customer/owner
der, die, das spätere (the) later (one)
spätestens at the latest, not later than, maximum
der Speck bacon
der Spediteur (– e) freight forwarder
die Spedition (– en) freight forwarder, forwarding agent, carrier, haulage company
der Speicher (–) warehouse
die Speicherstadt warehouse city (warehouse area in Hamburg)
die Speise(n)karte (– n) menu
spektakulär spectacular
sperrig bulky
sich spezialisieren (auf) to specialize (in)
spezialisiert specialized, specialist
die Spezialisierung (– en) specialization
der Spezialist (wk m) (– en) specialist
die Spezialität (– en) speciality
speziell special
der, die, das Spezielle (the) special thing/one
spezifizieren to specify
der Spiegel (–) mirror
das Spiegelei (– er) fried egg
das Spiel (– e) game
spielen to play
die Spielwaren (pl) toys
das Spielwarenhaus (¨er) toy shop
die Spielwarenmesse (– n) toy fair
das Spielzeug (– e) toy, toys
der Spieß (– e) (roasting) spit
der Spinat spinach
die Spitze (– n) pinnacle, top; an der Spitze top of the league; Produktkontakt zur Spitze leading-edge products
der Sport sport; Sport treiben to go in for sport
die Sportartikelmesse trade fair for sports equipment
der Spot (– s) (advertising) spot, commercial
sprach(en) spoke (see sprechen)
die Sprache (– n) language
die Sprachenschule (– n) language school
das Sprachgewirr babble of tongues; babylonisches Sprachgewirr confused babble of tongues, babel
die Sprachkultur (– en) language culture
das Sprachstudium language course
sprechen (i), a, o to speak
spricht speaks (see sprechen)
spritzen to spray
sprudelnd bubbling
das Spülzentrum (–zentren) sink unit; Funktions-Spülzentrum multifunction sink unit
die Spur (– en) trace, track, lane, wheel alignment; die Spur wird eingestellt the wheels are aligned
die Spureinstellung (– en) wheel alignment
St. Pauli St Pauli (district of Hamburg with the notorious Reeperbahn)
staatlich government-owned, state; staatliches Geld state/government money; staatliche Einrichtungen state authorities, the state
die Stabilität stability
das Stadium (Stadien) stage
die Stadt (¨e) town, city
die Stadtmitte (– n) city/town centre
der Stadtstaat (– en) city state (Hamburg, Bremen, Berlin)
der Stahl (¨e) steel
der Stahlbau steel construction
das Stahlblech (– e) steel sheet, sheet steel, steel strip
die Stahlerzeugung (– en) steel production
die Stahlindustrie (– n) steel industry
die Stahlkrise (– n) steel crisis
der Stahlschrank (¨e) steel rack/cabinet
das Stahlstück (– e) steel section
stammen (aus/von) to originate (from)
das Stammhaus (- er) parent company, headquarters
der Stammlieferant (wk m) (– en) regular supplier
das Stammwerk (– e) main plant/factory, head office, headquarters
stand stood (see stehen)
der Stand (¨e) stand; Stand 1988 as at 1988
die Stand-Organisation (exhibition) stand organization
der Standard (– s) standard (see Norm)
die Standardausbildung (– en) orthodox education/training
die Standardzusammenstellung (– en) standard assembly/configuration, standard components
die Standhilfe (– n) stand assistant
die Standkosten (pl) stand costs
die Standreinigung stand cleaning
das Standtelefon (– e) stand telephone
stark strong (ly), powerful(ly) highly, heavy (–ily); stark, stärker als, der/die/das stärkste strong, stronger than, the strongest; wir verkaufen sehr stark we sell a lot of
die Stärke (– n) strength, thickness
der, die, das stärkste (the) strongest (one)
der Starnberger See Lake Starnberg
der Start (– s) start, take-off
die Startchance (– n) start-up opportunity
starten to start, launch
die Station (– en) station
die Statistik (– en) statistic(s)
statt instead of
statten: statten ... aus see ausstatten

124 DEUTSCHES BUSINESS-MAGAZIN

stattfinden (*sep.*), a, u *to take place*
stattgefunden *taken place (see stattfinden)*
der Staub *dust*
der Staubsauger (–) *hoover, vacuum cleaner*
die Steckdosenleiste (– n) *socket strip*
der Steckerlfisch (– e) *fish barbecued/grilled on a skewer*
stehen, stand, gestanden (*auxiliary* sein *or* haben) *to stand, be, be laid down;* ähnlich stehen *to be on the same level*
der Stehimbiß (–imbisse) *snack bar*
stehlen (ie), a, o *to steal;* die Zeit stehlen *to waste time*
steht *is laid down*
steigen, ie, ie * *to increase*
der Stein (– e) *stone*
der Steinbutt (– e) *turbot*
die Stelle (– n) *place, point, job*
stellen *to put, be, deliver, set;* zur Verfügung stellen *to provide;* an etwas hohe Anforderungen stellen *to make great demands on sth.;* es werden an viele Fügetechniken ... gestellt *many joining methods have to meet ...*
stellen: stellen ... aus *see* ausstellen
der Stellenwert (– e) *status*
stellt: stellt ... fest *see* feststellen; stellt ... her *see* herstellen
stellte: stellte ... dar *see* darstellen; stellte ... fest *see* feststellen
die Stellung (– en) *standing, position, status*
die Stellungnahme (– n) *comment;* Mit der Bitte um: Stellungnahme *for comment*
der Stellvertreter (–) *deputy (chairman)*
der Stereolautsprecher (–) *stereo loudspeaker*
stetig *constant(ly), continuous(ly)*
die Steuer (– n) *tax*
der Steuerabzug (¨e) *tax deduction;* Steuerabzüge insgesamt *total tax deductions*
der Steuerberater (–) *tax adviser, book-keeper*
das Steuerberaterexamen (–) *exam(s) to become a tax adviser, accountancy exams*
die Steuerberatungsgesellschaft (– en) *tax consultancy company*
die Steuererklärung (– en) *tax return*
die Steuerklasse (– n) *tax schedule/class*
die Steuerlast (– en) *tax burden*
steuerlich *(relating to) tax*
steuern *to control, tax*
die Steuerung (– en) *control*
der Stichentscheid (– e) *casting vote*
die Stichprobe (– n) *random test, spot check, sample;* Stichproben machen *to take samples*
stichprobenmäßig *random(ly), at random;* stichprobenmäßig prüfen *to carry out random tests/spot checks*
die Stiftung (– en) *foundation;* Stiftung Warentest *German Consumer Council*
der Stil (– e) *style*
stimmen *to be true, correct, right, to fix, be OK;* stimmt das Arbeitsklima *if the atmosphere is right;* ob der Sinn stimmte *whether the meaning was correct*
der Stoff (– e) *substance, material*
die Stoffe (*pl*) *substances, materials*
stolz *proud*
die Stomaversorgung (– en) *stoma care*
stören *to disturb*
der Stoß (¨e) *batch;* im Stoß fertigen *to manufacture in batches*
stoßen (ö), ie, o (auf) * *to hit, encounter*
die Stoßstange (– n) *bumper*
die Straße (– n) *road(way), street*
der Straßenkarneval (–e/–s) *street carnival*
die Strategie (– n) *strategy*
strategisch *strategic(ally)*
der Streik (– s) *strike*
die Streuverluste (*pl*) *waste coverage*
der Strich (– e) *line;* unter dem Strich *the bottom line, in the final analysis*
die Strickwaren (*pl*) *knitware*
die Strickwarenindustrie (– n) *knitware industry*
der Strom (¨e) *stream, flow, current*
der Stromstoß (¨e) *surge current*
die Struktur (– en) *structure*
strukturell *structural(ly)*
der Strukturwandel *structural change, restructuring*
das Stück (– e) *unit, piece;* 300 Stück Steckerlfisch *300 Steckerlfisch*
der Stückgutbahnhof (¨e) *freight station*
die Studie (– n) *study*
studieren *to study, go to university*
das Studio (– s) *studio*
das Studium (Studien) *(course of) study, studies*
stufenweise *incremental(ly), gradual(ly), in stages*
die Stunde (– n) *hour*
stündig: 24-stündig *24-hour*
der Sturm (¨e) *storm*
subjektiv *subjective(ly)*
suchen *to search, look for*
Süd *south, South*
Süd-Amerika *South America*
das Süd-Nord-Gefälle *south-north divide ('falling off' from south to north)*
süddeutsch *south German*
der Süden *south;* im Süden *in the south*
Südfrankreich *southern France*
südlich *south(erly)*
Südosteuropa *south-eastern Europe*
die Summe (– n) *sum, total, amount, fee*
super *super, great*
die Suppe (– n) *soup*
süß *sweet;* süß-saure Sauce *sweet-and-sour sauce*
die Süßwaren (*pl*) *sweets, confectionery*
die Süßwarenmaschine (– n) *sweet machine*
swinging *swinging*
das Symbol (– e) *symbol, logo*
die Synthesefaser (– n) *synthetic fibre(s)*
das System (– e) *system*
systematisch *systematic(ally)*
die Systeme (*pl*) *systems*
die Systemtechnik *systems engineering*
die Systemzentrale (– n) *head office*

T

der Tag (– e) *day;* eines Tages *one of these days;* jeden Tag *every day;* pro Tag *per day;* auf den Tag *to the day*
die Tage (*pl*) *days*
tagen *to hold a conference*
das Tagen *holding a conference*
das Tagesgeschäft (– e) *day-to-day business*
täglich *daily, every day, per day*
die Tagung (– en) *conference*
der Tank (– s) *tank*
die Tante (– n) *aunt*
der Tante-Emma-Laden (¨) *corner shop*
der Tanz (¨e) *dance*
die Tapete (– n) *wallpaper*
der Tarif (– e) *pay scale*
die Tarifautonomie *free collective bargaining*
die Tarifpartner (*pl*) *unions and management*
die Tarifpolitik *policy for pay and working conditions*
der Tarifvertrag (¨e) *collective agreement, pay contract*
die Tasche (– n) *pocket (see* greifen*)*
die Taskforce *taskforce*
die Tasse (– n) *cup*
der Tastaturauszug (¨e) *keyboard drawer*
tätig *active;* tätig sein *to be, be employed;* beratend tätig sein *to advise on, give advice, provide consultancy services*
die Tätigkeit (– en) *job, occupation;* berufliche Tätigkeit *job, occupation*
tatsächlich *in fact, in practice, actual*
tausend *thousand*
tausende *thousands*
die Technik *engineering, technology, technique;* modernste Technik *the latest technology*
der Techniker (–) *(service) engineer, technical representative, technician*
technisch *technical, technically;* Technischer Überwachungsverein (TÜV) *German Technical Inspectorate;* technische Voraussetzung *technical prerequisite/facilities;* technischer Vertreter *technical representative*
technisiert *sophisticated, technological*
die Technologie (– n) *technology*
der Technologievorsprung (¨e) *technological advance/progress/lead*
das Technologiezentrum (–zentren) *technology centre*
technologisch *technological(ly)*
der Tee (– s) *tea*
der Teelöffel (–) *teaspoon*
der *or* das Teil (– e) *part;* zum Teil *(in) part, partly*
teilbezogen *part-related*
teilen *to share, divide*
sich teilen *to divide (itself)*
teils *partly;* teils ... teils *partly ... partly*
die Teilschale (– n) *shell assembly*
teilweise *partly*
Tel. = Tel. *(see* Telefon*)*
das Telefax (– e) *telefax, fax;* per Telefax *by fax*
das Telefon (– e) *telephone;* Tel. *Tel.;* Telefon-Service-Büro *telephone services office*
das Telefon-Service-Büro (– s) *service helpline (lit. telephone services office)*
der Telefondienst (– e) *telephone answering service*
telefonisch *by telephone*
das Telefonmarketing *telephone marketing*
die Telefonmarketingaktion (– en) *telephone marketing campaign*
das Telefonnetz (– e) *telephone network*
die Telefonvermittlung (– en) *switchboard*
die Telefonvorwahl (– en) *(telephone) dialling code*
das Telegramm (– e) *telegram*
das Telex (– e) *telex*
die Temperatur (– en) *temperature*
der Temperaturbereich (– e) *temperature range*
tendieren (auf) *to tend, incline (to)*
das Tennis *tennis*
der Teppich (– e) *carpet*
der Teppichboden (¨) *carpeting*
der Termin (– e) *appointment*
das Terminal (– s) *terminal*
die Terminologieliste (– n) *terminology list*
die Terminologiestelle (– n) *terminology point/centre*
der Tesafilm *Tesa tape/strip (generic comparable with Sellotape)*
der Tesafilmstreifen (–) *Tesa strip, strip of adhesive tape*
das Tesaklebeband (¨er) *Tesa adhesive tape, Tesa masking tape*
der Test (– s) *test*
der Text (– e) *text*
die Texterkennung *text recognition*
die Textilien (*pl*) *textiles*
die Textverarbeitung (– en) *word processing*
der Theaterbesuch (– e) *going to the theatre*
das Thema (Themen) *theme, subject*
tief *deep;* tief in die Tasche greifen *to dig deep in your pocket*
die Tiefgarage (– n) *underground car park*
die Tiefziehpresse (– n) *deep-drawing press*
die Tierstation (– en) *(animal) cage, accommodation for animals*
der Tisch (– e) *desk, table*
die Tischplatte (– n) *table top, top shelf*
das Titan *titanium*
der Titel (–) *title*
der Toaster (–) *toaster*
die Tochter (¨) *subsidiary (company), daughter*
die Töchter (*pl*) *subsidiaries, daughters*
die Tochtergesellschaft (– en) *subsidiary company*
der Tod (– e) *death*
die Toilette (– n) *toilet, lavatory*
die Toiletten (*pl*) *toilets*
die Toilettenartikel (*pl*) *toiletries*
tolerant *tolerant*
toll *great, wild, crazy*
der Tomatenspiralstab (¨e) *spiral tomato stakes*
der Ton (¨e) *shade, tone, sound*
das Tor (– e) *gate, gateway*
das Torhaus (¨er) *gatehouse*
tosend *raging*
der Tourismus *tourism;* Tourismus-Zentrale *tourist office;* Touristen-Zentrale *tourist office*
der Tourist (*wk m*) (– en) *tourist*
tourniert *(from* tournieren*) shaped*
die Tradition (– en) *tradition*
traditionell *traditional(ly);* traditionell begründet *based on tradition*
traditioneller (als) *more traditional (than)*
tragen (ä), u, a *to carry, bear, wear, finance;* das Risiko tragen *to bear the risk*
der Träger (–) *support, underwriter, insurer*
das Training *training*
der Transport (– e) *transport, shipment*
das Transportflugzeug (– e) *transport aircraft, transporter*
transportieren *to transport*
transportiert *transports, transported (see* transportieren*)*
die Transportkette (– n) *transport chain*
das Transportsystem (– e) *transport system*
die Transportversicherung (– en) *transport insurance*
traumhaft *fabulous, unbelievable*
treffen (i), a, o *to meet*
sich treffen (i), a, o *to congregate, meet*
der Treffpunkt (– e) *meeting point*
treiben, ie, ie: Sport treiben *to go in for sport;* Handel treiben *trade and commerce*
das Treibgas (– e) *propellant*
der Trend (– s) *trend;* auf diesem Trend weiterfahren *to continue this trend*
trennen *to separate*
die Trennwand (¨e) *divider, partition*
treu *true, loyal*
der Triebwerksbau *power plant/engine construction*
trifft *see* treffen
trinken, a, u *to drink*
das Trinkwasser *drinking water*
das Trinkwassernetz (– e) *drinking-water supply*
das Trinkwasserwerk (– e) *potable water complex*
trist *sad*
der Trockentunnel (–) *tunnel drier*
das Trocknen *drying*
der Trüffel (–) *truffle*
das Trüffelgelee (– s) *truffle garnish* (lit. *jelly*)
die Tschechoslowakei *Czechoslovakia*
die Tugend (– en) *virtue*
tun, tat, getan *to do, deal with;* die mit Elektronik zu tun haben *connected with electronics*
die Tür (– en) *door*
das Türblatt (¨er) *door panel*
der Turm (¨e) *tower*
die Türzarge (– n) *door-frame*
der TÜV (= Technischer Überwachungsverein (*see* technisch)) *MOT (German equivalent of the MOT test)*
der Typ (– en) *type*
typisch *typical(ly)*
der, die, das Typische *(the) typical thing/one*

U

u. = und *and*
die U-Bahn (– en) *underground, subway*
über *over, above, more than, about, away;* über etwas hinaus *in addition to sth.;* über etwas hinauskommen *to get away from*
überall *everywhere*
der Überblick (– e) *overview*
der Überbringer (–) *bearer*
die Überbrückungsphase (– n) *bridging period;* eine Überbrückungsphase finanzieren *to provide redundancy/severance pay*
überdenken, überdachte, überdacht *to review*
die Übergabe (– n) *transfer*
der Übergang (¨e) (zu) *transfer (to), delivery (to), transition;* bei Übergabe der Ware an den Spediteur *when the goods are transferred to the freight forwarder*
übergehen (*sep.*), ging über, übergegangen * (zu) *to transfer (to), go over (to)*
übergroß *oversized*
überhaupt *at all, single;* überhaupt ein Strich *a single stroke*
das Überleben *survival*
überlegen *to debate, consider*
das Überlegen *debate*
die Überlegung (– en) *consideration;* wir haben Marktnischenüberlegungen geführt *we considered the market niches available*
übernehmen (übernimmt), übernahm, übernommen *to take over*
übernommen *see* übernehmen
überprüfen *to test, inspect, examine, check*
überprüft *see* überprüfen
die Überprüfung (– en) *test, inspection*
die Überraschung (– en) *surprise*
übers = über das
überschwemmt *(from* über-

schwemmen) *flooded*
Übersee *overseas*
übersenden *to enclose, send*
der Übersetzer (–) *translator*
die Übersetzung (– en) *translation*
die Übersetzungsarbeit (– en) *translation work*
übersichtlich *clear(ly), manageable, straightforward*
übersichtlicher (als) *more clearly (than)*
übersteigen, ie, ie *to exceed*
der Überstrom *overcurrent*
die Überstromdiode (– n) *overcurrent diode*
überwachen *to monitor, supervise*
überwacht *monitored (see* überwachen*)*
die Überwachung (– en) *monitoring*
der Überwachungsverein (– e) *inspectorate (lit. inspection organization (see* technisch*))*
die Überweisung (– en) *credit transfer*
überwiegend *generally, principally, primarily*
(sich) überzeugen *to convince, ascertain;* man hat sich davon überzeugt, daß *we (have) ascertained/concluded that;* wo wir uns über mehrere Teile überzeugen *where we test several components (*lit. *satisfy ourselves)*
überzeugt *convinced, ascertained (see* überzeugen*)*
üblich *usual, standard, common, ordinary*
übrig *remaining*
die UdSSR *USSR*
die Uhr (– en) *clock, watch;* 8 Uhr *8 o'clock*
der Ultraschall *ultrasound*
das Ultraschallverfahren *ultrasound procedure, ultrasound testing*
um *for, in;* um zu *in order to;* um 9,2% zunehmen *to increase by 9.2%;* rund um ... herum *around*
der Umfang (⸚e) *scope;* im Umfang von 192 Seiten *192 pages long*
umfangreich *comprehensive*
umfassen *to include, cover, comprise*
das Umfeld *environment;* das nachbarliche Umfeld *the surrounding regions/countries*
umformen (*sep.*) *to deform*
die Umformschwierigkeit (– en) *deformation difficulties/problems*
die Umgebung (– en) *surroundings, environment*
die Umgebungsbedingung (– en) *ambient condition*
umgekehrt *the other way round*
umgestellt *changed (see* umstellen*)*
umgestiegen *changed (see* umsteigen*)*
der Umlaut (– e) *sound shift, umlaut*
umrüsten (*sep.*) *to retool*
ums = um das
der Umsatz (⸚e) *turnover, sales*
der Umsatzerlös (– e) *sales (revenue)*
das Umsatzvolumen (–) *sales volume*
die Umsetzung (– en) *conversion, transformation*
der Umstand (⸚e) *condition, circumstance;* unter Umständen *potentially*
umsteigen (*sep.*), ie, ie * (auf) *to change over, switch (to)*
umstellen (*sep.*) *to change;* umstellen von ... auf *to change from ... to*
die Umstellung (– en) *adjustment*
die Umstrukturierung (– en) *restructuring*
die Umwelt *environment*
das Umweltbedürfnis (– se) *environmental requirement*
der Umweltschutz *environmental protection*
die Umweltschutzüberwachungszentrale (– n) *environmental-protection monitoring (control) centre/station*
die Umwelttechnik *environmental technology*
unabhängig *independent(ly)*
unbedenklich *safe;* unbedenklich für die Umwelt *environmentally safe*
unbedingt *necessarily, really, absolutely*
unbegrenzt *unlimited*
und *and;* und so weiter (usw.) *and so on, etc.*
die Unebenheit (– en) *unevenness, infelicity*
das Unendliche *infinity (see* Schraube*)*
unentbehrlich *indispensable*
der Unfall (⸚e) *accident*
die Unfallversicherung (– en) *accident insurance*
Ungarn *Hungary*
ungefähr *about, approximately*
ungeheuer, ungeheu(e)re *huge, high(ly)*
ungestört *undisturbed*
ungestützt *unprompted;* ungestützte Bekanntheit *unprompted level of awareness*
ungewöhnlich *unusual(ly)*
der, die, das ungewöhnlichste *(the) most unusual (one)*
der, die, das Unglaubliche *(the) unbelievable thing/one, impossibility/impossibilities*
unheimlich *really, tremendous(ly)*
universal *universal(ly)*
die Universalbank (– en) *universal bank*
universell *universal(ly)*
die Universität (– en) *university*
unkontrolliert *unchecked, uncontrolled*
unmöglich *impossible*
uns *(to) us, for us, ourselves*
unser, unsere, unserem, unseren, unserer, unseres *(to/from/for/of) our*
unseriös *casual, lacking in a serious approach*
unter *under, beneath, among(st), on, in with;* unter Telefon 089/323009-30 *on 089/323009-30*
der Unterbodenschutz *underbody sealing, sealing compound*
die Unterbringung *accommodation;* Unterbringung von Hunden möglich *dogs allowed (*lit. *accommodation for dogs possible)*
untereinander *between them/us;* Kommunikation untereinander *communication between the partners*
der Untergang (⸚e) *loss*
untergebracht *accommodated*
unterhalten (ä), ie, a *to entertain*
sich unterhalten (ä), ie, a (mit) *to talk, converse (with)*
die Unterlage (– n) *document;* Unterlagen (*pl*) *documentation*
unterm = unter dem
das Unternehmen (–) *company, enterprise, undertaking, operation*
der Unternehmensbereich (– e) *department, division;* Unternehmensbereich Logistik und Einkauf *logistics and purchasing department*
die Unternehmensführung (– en) *management*
der Unternehmensgründer (–) *founder (of a company), entrepreneur*
die Unternehmensgruppe (– n) *group (of companies)*
unterscheiden, ie, ie *to distinguish*
sich unterscheiden, ie, ie *to distinguish (itself/oneself), be distinct*
der Unterschied (– e) *difference*
unterschiedlich *variable, different, differing;* regional unterschiedlich *regional differences*
unterschreiben, ie, ie *to sign*
die Unterschrift (– en) *signature*
unterstützen *to support*
unterstützt *supports, supported*
die Untersuchung (– en) *examination, study, investigation*
das Unterteil (– e) *bottom part*
unwahrscheinlich *improbable (-ly);* unwahrscheinlich viel *an incredible number*
der Urlaub (– e) *holiday(s)*
der Ursprung (⸚e) *origin*
ursprünglich *original(ly)*
die USA *United States of America, USA*
usw. (= und so weiter) *etc.*

V

variabel *variable*
die Variante (– n) *variant, version*
variierbar *variable*
variieren *to vary*
variiert *varies, varied (see* variieren*)*
der VDE = Verband der Deutschen Elektrotechniker (*see* Verband*)*
die VEDES = Vereinigung der Spielwaren-Fachgeschäfte (*see* Vereinigung*)*
das Ventil (– e) *valve*
das Verankern *anchoring*
die Verankerung (– en) *anchoring, loyalty, anchorage, anchorage point;* die starke Verankerung mit Ludwigshafen *the deep roots in/strong loyalty to Ludwigshafen*
der Veranstalter (–) *organizer*
die Veranstaltung (– en) *event*
verantwortlich *responsible (to), answerable (to);* den Aktionären verantwortlich *responsible to the shareholders;* dem Aufsichtsrat verantwortlich *answerable to the supervisory board*
der/die Verantwortliche (– n), ein Veranwortlicher *(the) responsible person;* die Verantwortlichen *those responsible, the management*
die Verantwortlichkeit (– en) *responsibility*
verarbeiten *to process*
verarbeitet *processes, processed (see* verarbeiten*)*
der Verband (⸚e) *association, union, federation, society;* Verband der Deutschen Elektrotechniker *Association of German Electrical Engineers*
verbessern *to improve*
die Verbindung (– en) *connection, link;* er wird in Verbindung gebracht *it's associated with*
die Verbindungsbrücke (– n) *connecting bridge*
das Verbindungselement (– e) *fastener*
der Verbleib: zum Verbleib *for your files*
verbracht (*from* verbringen) *spent*
der Verbraucher (–) *consumer*
das Verbraucherbedürfnis (– se) *consumer requirement*
der Verbrauchermarkt (⸚e) *superstore/hypermarket*
verbreitet *widespread, common*
der Verbund (– e) *association, cooperation*
verbunden (*from* verbinden) *connected, linked, bound;* verbunden mit *bound up with;* miteinander verbunden *connected together*
verchromen: wenn sie ein Bauteil verchromen sollen *if a component has to be chrome-plated*
verdeutlicht: verdeutlicht es *sets the scene*
verdienen *to earn*
der Verdiener (–) *earner, wage-earner*
verdoppelt (*from* verdoppeln) *doubled*
die Verdoppelung (– en) *doubling*
das Verdübeln *inserting rawlplugs*
vereidigt: vereidigter Buchprüfer *certified accountant*
vereinbart *agreed;* vertraglich vereinbart *contractually agreed*
die Vereinbarung (– en) *agreement;* gemäß vorheriger Vereinbarung *by prior agreement*
vereinigt *united*
die Vereinigung (– en) *association, union, federation, society;* Vereinigung der Spielwaren-Fachgeschäfte *association of specialist toy shops*
das Verfahren (–) *process*
die Verfahrenstechnik *process engineering*
die Verfassung (– en) *constitution*
der Verfassungsgerichtshof (⸚e) *constitutional court*
verfolgen *to pursue, follow, observe;* während der Abpressung wird verfolgt *during the pressing we observe*
die Verfolgung: systematische Verfolgung der Termine *systematic scheduling*
verfügen (über) *to have access (to), have (at one's disposal)*
die Verfügung: zur Verfügung stellen *to provide;* zur Verfügung stehen *to be available*
vergangen: im vergangenen Jahr *last year (see* vergehen*);* in längst vergangenen Tagen *in days gone by*
vergehen, verging, vergangen * *to go by, pass by;* es vergeht manchmal ein Jahr *a year sometimes goes by*
der Vergleich (– e) *comparison* im Vergleich zu *in comparison with;* im europäischen Vergleich *in comparison with the rest of Europe*
vergleichbar *comparable*
das Vergnügen *pleasure, enjoyment, festivity, entertainment;* zum Vergnügen *for pleasure*
verhaftet *attached;* verhaftet sein *to be attached*
das Verhältnis (– se) *ratio, relation(ship), (pl) circumstances, (pl) conditions*
verheiratet *married*
verhindern *to prevent, avoid*
der Verkauf *sales, sales off.*
das Verkaufen *selling;* Verkaufen in den Handel hinein *wholesale;* Verkaufen vom Handel aus an den Endverwender *retail*
verkaufen *to sell*
die Verkaufsförderung *sales promotion*
der Verkaufskollege (*wk m*) (– n) *sales colleague*
der Verkaufsleiter (–) *sales manager*
der Verkaufsmarkt (⸚e) *(sales) market*
die Verkaufsstelle (– n) *sales office, sales outlet*
verkauft *sells, sold (see* verkaufen*)*
der Verkehr *traffic, transport*
die Verkehrs-Service-Versicherung (– en) *breakdown insurance*
das Verkehrsamt (⸚er) *tourist office*
das Verkehrsflugzeug (– e) *commercial aircraft*
das Verkehrsmittel (–) *means of transport*
der Verkehrsverein (– e) *tourist office*
der Verkehrsweg (– e) *mode of transport*
verknittert (*from* verknittern) *crumpled*
verkürzt (*from* verkürzen) *shortened, abbreviated*
die Verlademöglichkeit (– en) *possible modes of transport*
verladen (ä), u, a *to load, ship, have loaded/shipped*
die Verladung (– en) *shipment, transport*
verlagern *spread, postpone; (see* zeitlich*)*
verlangen *to demand, ask for*
verlängert (*from* verlängern) *extends, extended*
verlassen (ä), ie, a *to leave;* etwas verlassen *to leave something;* sich auf etwas verlassen *to rely on sth.*
das Verlassen: mit Verlassen des Werks *when (goods) leave the factory*
die Verläßlichkeit *reliability*
verläßt *leaves (see* verlassen*)*
der Verleih (– e) *hiring (out), borrowing*
verlieren, o, o *to lose*
verloren *diminished, lost (see* verlieren*);* haben an Bedeutung verloren *have diminished in importance*
verlöten *to braze, solder*
verlötet *brazed, soldered (see* verlöten*)*
der Verlust (– e) *loss;* Gewinn- und Verlustrechnung *profit and loss account*
die Verlustrechnung (– en) *see* Verlust
vermarktet (*from* vermarkten) *markets, marketed*
die Vermietung (– en) *rental, lease*
vermindern *to reduce*
vermindert *reduced (see* vermindern*)*
vermittelt (*from* vermitteln*) communicated*
der Vermittler (–) *intermediary, go-between*
die Vermittlung (– en) *mediation, communication*
das Vermögen (–) *wealth, fortune*
die Verpackung (– en) *packaging*
die Verpackungskosten (*pl*) *packaging costs*
die Verpackungsmaschinen (*pl*) *packaging technology*
verringern *to reduce*
sich verringern *to be/become reduced*
verringert *reduced (see* verringern*)*
der Versand *mail order, dispatch, carriage;* Versand- und Lieferbedingungen *conditions of dispatch and delivery*
der/die Versandbeauftragte (– n), ein Versandbeauftragter *carrier, forwarding agent*
der Versandhandel *mail-order trade*
das Versandunternehmen (–) *mail-order company*
verschicken *to send (off/in)*
verschieden *various, different*
der, die, das verschiedenste *(the) most varied (one), a wide variety of*
die Verschlechterung (– en) *deterioration*
verschmutzt (*from* verschmutzen) *polluted*
verschrauben *to screw, bolt*
verschraubt *bolted (on) (see* verschrauben*)*
verschwanden *disappeared (see* verschwinden*)*
verschweißt (*from* verschweißen) *welded*
verschwinden, a, u * *to disappear*

versegeln * to sail
versehen (mit) to be provided with, have; das Amateurgärtnern ist mit einem Süd-Nord-Gefälle versehen amateur gardening has a north-south divide
versicherbar insurable
der Versicherer (–) insurer/assurer
versichern to insure/assure
sich versichern to insure/assure oneself
versichert insures/assures, insured/assured
der/die Versicherte (– n), ein Versicherter (the) assured/insured (person)
die Versicherung (– en) insurance/assurance; Versicherungen insurance/assurance policies
die Versicherungshauptstadt (⸚e) insurance capital
der Versicherungskaufmann (⸚er) insurance clerk/salesman
der Versicherungsschutz insurance protection
das Versicherungsunternehmen (–) insurance/assurance company
die Versicherungswirtschaft insurance industry; Gesamtverband der Deutschen Versicherungswirtschaft German Insurance Association (association of the German insurance industry)
versiegeln to seal
versinken, a, u * to sink
die Versorgungsleitung (– en) supply line
die Verspätung (– en) delay
versprechen (i), a, o to promise
versprühen to spray (on), apply
verspüren to detect
verstand see verstehen
verständig sympathetic
verstehen, verstand, verstanden to understand
sich verstehen, verstand, verstanden (als) to be understood, regard oneself; alle Preise verstehen sich all prices shall be understood
das Verstehen understanding, comprehension
versuchen to try, attempt
die Verteilung (– en) distribution
vertippt (from vertippen): Vertippt? Incorrect entry?
der Vertrag (⸚e) contract
vertraglich contractual(ly); vertraglich vereinbart contractually agreed
die Vertragsstrafe (– n) contractual penalty
die Vertragswerkstätte (– n) authorized service centre
vertreiben, ie, ie to distribute, sell
vertreten (vertritt), a, e to represent, act as an agent for
vertreten represented (see vertreten)
der Vertreter (–) representative; technischer Vertreter technical representative
die Vertretung (– en) agent, representative
der Vertrieb (– e) sales, selling, sales organization/department, distribution, marketing
vertrieben distributed, sold (see vertreiben)
die Vertriebsaktivität (– en) sales activity
das Vertriebsbüro (– s) sales office
die Vertriebsfirma (–firmen) sales company, distributor
die Vertriebsgesellschaft (– en) sales company, distributor
der Vertriebsinnendienst (– e) (in-house) sales department/office
das Vertriebsprogramm (– e) sales/product range
vertriebsstrategisch: wir haben vertriebsstrategisches Denken praktiziert to apply marketing principles
vertritt see vertreten
vertrödeln to waste (time)
die Verwaltung (– en) administration, management, local authority
der/die Verwaltungsfachangestellte (– n), ein Verwaltungsfachangestellter clerk, administrator
verwechselbar confusable; der Name ist verwechselbar the name can be confused
verwenden to use
verwendet uses, used (see verwenden)
verzehrt (from verzehren) consumes, consumed

das Verzeichnis (– se) register
verzinkt (from verzinken) zinc-plated, galvanized, zinc-passivated
das Video (– s) video
der Videokonferenzraum (⸚e) video conference room
viel much, many; viel, mehr als, der/die/das meiste much/many, more than, the most; sehr viel a lot (of), a great deal of; so viel ... wie nur möglich as much ... as possible; viel mehr als many/much more than
viel(e) many, all
vielleicht perhaps, may; der Urlaub, der vielleicht gerade bevorsteht the holiday which may be coming up
der Vielpunktautomat (wk m) (– en) automatic multiple-spot welder
vielversprechend promising, with potential
vier four
das/ein Viertel (–) (a) quarter, district
das Vierteljahr (– e) quarter (year); alle Vierteljahr(e) every three months
viertens fourthly
vierzehn fourteen
vierzig forty
der Vierzylinder (–) four-cylinder (engine)
die Visitenkarte (– n) business card, visiting card
die Volksbank (– en) industrial credit cooperative (lit. people's bank)
die Volksrepublik: Volksrepublik China People's Republic of China
die Volkswirtschaft economics
voll full(y)
vollautomatisch fully automatic(ally)
vollbracht (from vollbringen) completed
vollendet perfect(ly)
völlig complete(ly)
das Vollkornbrot wholegrain bread
vollständig complete(ly), entire(ly)
vollzogen (from vollziehen) completed
das Volt (–) volt
vom = von dem of/from the, date
von of, from, by, lasting; vom of/from the, date; von den Aktionären gewählt elected by the shareholders; von etwas bis zu from sth. through to; von etwas her in terms of sth.; von den Farben her where colours are concerned; vom Preis her regarding price; von der Ausbildung her by training; vom Portex-Produkt auf ein Konkurrenz-Produkt from the Portex product range to a rival product; von sich aus on its own
vor before, in front of, on, ago; vor allem above all, mainly, first and foremost, particularly; vor Ort on site (lit. at the coalface); vor vielen Jahren many years ago; vor allen Dingen especially; nach wie vor still, now as ever; vor 20 Jahren 20 years ago
die Voranmeldung (– en) appointment
voraus in front (see also vorausetzen)
voraussetzen (sep.) to require, demand, presuppose
die Voraussetzung (– en) prerequisite, basis, facilities; technische Voraussetzung technical prerequisite/facilities
vorbehalten reserved; bleiben uns vorbehalten we reserve the right to
das Vorbild (– er) model, example
vorbildlich exemplary
die Vorbildung previous education
die Vorderachsbremse (– n) front brake
die Vorderachse (– n) front axle
der Vordergrund (⸚e) foreground
der Vorgang (⸚e) operation, event, procedure, document, file; geschäftliche Vorgänge business documents/files
vorgeben (sep.) (gibt vor), gab vor, vorgegeben to specify, prescribe, set; sich etwas vorgeben to set oneself
vorgedruckt (from vordrucken) (pre)printed
vorgeprägt (from vorprägen) predetermined; war die Industrie branchenmäßig vorgeprägt the industrial sectors were predetermined
vorgeschritten (from vorschreiten) advanced; die sich in einem technologisch sehr vorgeschrittenen Stadium befinden which are operating at the leading edge of technology

vorgesehen conceived, planned, provided, laid down (see vorsehen)
vorgestanzt (from vorstanzen) prestamped
vorgibt sets (see vorgeben)
vorhanden available
der, die, das vorhandene (the) existing (one)
das Vorhandensein presence, existence
vorherig previous, prior; gemäß vorheriger Vereinbarung by prior agreement
der Vorlauf land transportation, road/rail transport
der Vorname (wk m; genitive –ns) (– n) first name, forename
vornherein: von vornherein from the start/outset
das Vorprodukt (– e) initial product
vorschreiben (sep.), ie, ie to specify, prescribe
die Vorschrift (– en) regulation, specification, standard; Vorschriften und Bedingungen regulations and conditions
vorsehen (sep.) (ie), a, e to plan, conceive, provide, lay down
der/die Vorsitzende (– n), ein Vorsitzender chairman, chairperson
die Vorsorge (– n) provision; staatliche und private Vorsorge state and private insurance/provision
die Vorspeise (– n) starter, hors d'œuvre
der Vorsprung (⸚e) advance, progress, lead
der Vorstand (⸚e) board of management
das Vorstandsmitglied (– er) member of the board of management, director
vorstellen (sep.) to present; das, was sie an Produkten vorstellen the products they present
sich vorstellen (sep.) to introduce oneself, present
die Vorstellung (– en) requirement, idea
der Vorteil (– e) advantage
die Vorwahl (– en) dialling code
der Vulkan (– e) volcano

W

wachsen (ä), u, a * to grow, expand; um 33% wachsen to grow by 33%
das Wachsen growing; im Wachsen begriffen ist is growing
das Wachstum growth
das Wachstumsfeld (– er) growth area
der Wagen (–) car, trolley
das Wagniskapital venture capital
die Wahl (– en) choice
wählen to elect; von den Aktionären gewählt elected by the shareholders; wählen ... aus to select
wahnsinnig fantastic(ally)
während during, while, whereas
wahrscheinlich probably, very likely
die Währung (– en) currency
das Währungsrisiko (–risiken) currency exposure/risk
die Wand (⸚e) wall
das Wandern hiking, rambling
die Wandfuge (– n) crack in the wall, wall joint
war(en) was/were (see sein)
wäre would be, might (see sein); wie es wäre such as
die Ware (– n) product, goods, merchandize; Waren goods, merchandize; die ganze Ware the entire delivery/batch
die Wareneingangsinspektion (– en) incoming-goods inspection
die Wareneingangsprüfung (– en) incoming-goods inspection
das Warenhaus (⸚er) warehouse; das Warenhaus auf der grünen Wiese out-of-town hypermarket/superstore
die Warenprüfung (– en) product testing, quality control
der Warentest (– s) comparative testing; Stiftung Warentest German Consumer Council
warm warm; warme Küche hot meals
wärmer (als) warmer (than)
warnen to warn, alert
warten to service, wait
die Wartung (– en) maintenance
der Wartungsvertrag (⸚e) maintenance/service contract
warum why
was what, that, something; das/dessen,

was of what; was für what kind of
das Waschbecken (–) wash basin
das Waschmittel (–) detergent
das Wasser water, schnapps
der Wasseranschluß (–üsse) water supply
wassergelöst: wassergelöster Lack paint in aqueous solution
der Wasserinstallateur (– e) plumber
der Wasserkessel (–) kettle
die Wassertechnik water products (lit. water technology)
das WC WC
der Wechsel (–) change
wechseln to change, vary, switch allegiance; hat sich entschieden, zu wechseln had decided to switch allegiance
das Wechseln: Wechseln Change
weder: weder ... noch neither ... nor
der Weg (– e) way, path, route, method
wegen because of
weiblich female
weil because
weiß know (see wissen)
weiß white
das Weiß white
das Weißbier (– e) weiss beer (beer made with top-fermented yeast)
das Weißbrot white bread
weißerstarrt chilled
die Weißwurst (⸚e) white sausage (made from veal)
weist ... hin see hinweisen
weit far, wide; wie weit how far, to what extent
weiter further, more, continued; und so weiter etc; sagen Sie es weiter pass it on
weitere other(s)
weiterentwickeln (sep.) to develop further
weiterentwickelt developed further (see weiterentwickeln)
weiterfahren (sep.) (ä), u, a * to drive on, continue; auf diesem Trend weiterfahren to continue this trend
weitergebaut (from weiterbauen) built/constructed (further)
weiterhin largely, to a great extent, continue(d)
weiterveredelt (from weiterveredeln) further processed, refined
weiterzuentwickeln see weiterentwickeln
weiterzufahren see weiterfahren
der, die, das weiteste (the) widest/furthest (one)
welche, welchem, welchen, welcher, welches (to/from/for/of) which, some, them; welchen Beitrag sie verlangt the size of subscription it asks for
die Welle (– n) wave, shaft
die Welt (– en) world; in aller Welt all over the world
der Weltflughafen (⸚) world airport
die Weltkarte (– n) map of the world
der Weltkongreß (–sse) world congress
der Weltmarkt (⸚e) world market
die Weltstadt (⸚e) world city, cosmopolitan city
weltweit worldwide
die Weltwirtschaftskrise (– n) world economic crisis
der Wendelstein Wendelstein (mountain in the Bavarian Alps)
sich wenden (an) to turn (to), approach; sich an jemanden wenden to contact/approach someone
wenig little, few; wenig, weniger als, der/die/das wenigste little/few, less/fewer than, the least/fewest; ein wenig a little; mehr oder weniger more or less
weniger (als) less (than)
wenigstens at least
wenn if, when
wer who; wer ist wer who is who, who's who
die Werbeaktion (– en) advertising campaign
die Werbefläche (– n) advertising space
das Werbemittel (–) advertising, advertisement
werben (i), a, o to advertise
werblich: werblich unterstützen to advertise
die Werbung (– en) advertising,

Glossary

advertisement
werden (wird), wurde, worden * *auxiliary verb used to form passive and future;* werden kritisiert *are criticised*
werden (wird), wurde, geworden * *to become, turn out*
die Werft (– en) *dock, shipyard, hangar*
der Werftchef (– s) *shipyard owner/manager*
das Werk (– e) *company, factory, works*
die Werkbank (:-e) *bench, workbench*
der Werker (–) *worker*
die Werksfläche (– n) *works/factory area*
die Werkstatt (:-en) *workshop*
die Werkstätte (– n) *workshop*
der Werkstoff (– e) *material*
die Werkstoffleute (pl) *technicians/engineers in the materials-testing department (lit. materials people)*
die Werkstoffprüfung (– en) *materials test(ing)*
die Werkstofftechnik *materials engineering*
der Werktag (– e) *working day*
das Werkzeug (– e) *tool*
der Werkzeugmacher (–) *toolmaker*
der Wert (– e) *importance;* darauf/auf etwas Wert legen *to value, attach importance to sth., set store by sth.*
das Wertpapier (– e) *security*
das Wesen *nature, concept*
wesentlich *important, essential, much*
wesentlicher (als) *more important (than)*
der Weserraum *area round the River Weser*
West *west, West*
Westen *west, West;* im Westen *in the West*
West-Europa *Western Europe*
der Wettbewerb (– e) *competition*
wettbewerbsfähig *competitive*
der Wettbewerbsvorteil (– e) *competitive advantage*
das Wetter *weather*
wichtig *important*
der, die, das Wichtige *(the) important thing/one*
wichtiger (als) *more important (than)*
der, die, das wichtigste *(the) most important (one);* das wichtigste ..., das es überhaupt gibt *the most important ... there is*
wie *how, as, like, as if;* nach wie vor *still, now as ever;* wieviel/wie viele *how much/many;* so ... wie *as ... as;* so viel ... wie nur möglich *as much ... as possible;* wie es ... zeigt *as shown in ...;* wie weit *how far, to what extent*
wieder *again, back;* fließt wieder ein *flows back into;* hin und wieder *now and then;* immer wieder *again and again*
wiederherstellen (sep.) *to restore*
wiederholen *to repeat*
wiederholt *repeated(ly) (see wiederholen)*
wiegen, o, o *to weigh*
Wien *Vienna;* Wiener Art *à la Viennese*
die Wiener (–) *Wiener, sausage made from smoked meat*
die Wiese (– n) *field, meadow;* das Warenhaus auf der grünen Wiese *out-of-town hypermarket/ superstore*
wieso *why;* wieso denn *why*
wieviel *how much/many;* wie viele *how many*
Wilhelm *William*
will *wants (to) (see wollen)*
die Windschutzscheibe (– n) *windscreen*
der Winter *winter*
wird *is (see werden)*
wirken *to work, affect, have an effect*
wirklich *really, in fact*
wirkt: wirkt sich ... aus (see auswirken)
die Wirtschaft *economy, trade and industry;* gewerbliche Wirtschaft *industry*
wirtschaftlich *economic, financial(ly), cost-effective*
wirtschaftlicher (als) *more cost-effective (than)*
die Wirtschaftlichkeitsrechnung (– en) *profitability calculation, capital budgeting, investment appraisal*
die Wirtschaftlichkeitsstudie (– n) *feasibility study*
die Wirtschaftslehre (– n) *economics and business studies*
das Wirtschaftsprüferexamen (–) *exam(s) to become an auditor, accountancy exams*
die Wirtschaftsprüferkammer *Chamber of Auditors*
der Wirtschaftsprüfer (–) *auditor (comparable with chartered accountant)*
die Wirtschaftsprüfungsgesellschaft (– en) *auditing company*
der Wirtschaftsverband (:-e) *industrial association*
das Wissen *knowledge, expertise*
wissen (weiß), wußte, gewußt *to know (a fact);* wußten Sie schon? *did you know?*
die Wissenschaft (– en) *science(s)*
wissenschaftlich *academic*
der Wissensstand *knowledge, expertise*
wo *where*
die Woche (– n) *week*
die Wochen (pl) *weeks*
die Wochenarbeitszeit *working week*
wog *weighed (see wiegen)*
wohingegen *whereas*
wohnen *to live*
das Wohnen *living*
der Wohnort (– e) *residential area*
das Wohnortprestige *prestigious residential areas*
die Wohnung (– en) *flat, dwelling, place*
der Wohnungsmarkt (:-e) *housing market;* auf den Wohnungsmärkten der europäischen Gemeinschaft *in the housing markets of the European Community*
wollen (will), wollte, gewollt *to want to;* wir würden uns gerne sehen wollen *we'd like to see ourselves*
wollte *wanted (to) (see wollen)*
worden *was/were (used to form the passive, from werden)*
das Worksharinggespräch (– e) *work-sharing discussion*
die Wortbildung (– en) *word (formation), words*
der Wortschatz *vocabulary*
der Wunderheiler (–) *faith-healer*
der Wunsch (:-e) *wish, desire, request, requirement;* nach seinen Wünschen *in accordance with his requirements;* auf Wunsch *available with, option/choice of, on request*
wunschgemäß *as requested*
wurde(n) *was/were (see werden)*
würde(n) *would (see werden)*
die Wurst (:-e) *sausage*
die Wurstsorte (– n) *type/kind of sausage*
wußte(n) *knew;* wußten Sie schon? *did you know?*

Z

z.B. (= zum Beispiel) *e.g.*
die Zahl (– en) *number, digit;* Zahlen und Fakten *facts and figures*
zahlen *to pay;* Zahlen Sie gegen diesen Scheck *Pay against this cheque the sum of*
zählen *to count, number*
die Zahlung (– en) *payment;* Ihre Zahlung ist innerhalb von 14 Tagen zu leisten *payment shall be made within 14 days (lit. is to be made), accounts are payable within 14 days*
die Zahlungsfrist (– en) *term of payment*
der Zahlungsverkehr *payments*
die Zahnbürste (– n) *toothbrush*
die Zahnklinik (– en) *dental clinic*
die Zahnpasta (–pasten) *toothpaste*
zehn *ten*
der, die, das zehntausendste *ten thousandth*
der, die, das zehnte *(the) tenth (one)*
das Zeichen (– e) *sign, symbol, logo, reference, ref.;* Ihr Zeichen *your ref.;* Unser Zeichen *our ref.*
die Zeichnung (– en) *drawing*
zeigen *to show;* wie es ... zeigt *as shown in ...*
sich zeigen *to emerge;* es zeigt sich immer wieder *it keeps emerging*
zeigt *shows, emerges (see zeigen, sich zeigen)*
die Zeit (– en) *time, period;* zu jeder Zeit *at all times;* zu der und der Zeit *at such and such a time;* zu gegebener Zeit *in due course;* zur Zeit *at present, at the moment;* mit der Zeit *in time;* nach einiger Zeit *after some time*
der Zeitabstand (:-e) *interval*
zeitaufwendig *time-consuming*
zeitaufwendiger (als) *more time-consuming (than)*
die Zeiten (pl) *times*
das Zeitintervall (– e) *time interval, period*
zeitlich *over time;* zeitlich verlagern *to spread over time, defer*
der Zeitmotor (– en) *time motion/machine*
der Zeitpunkt (– e) *point in time;* zum gleichen Zeitpunkt *at the same time*
zeitraubend *time-consuming*
die Zeitschrift (– en) *magazine*
die Zeitung (– en) *newspaper*
die Zeitungsbeilage (– n) *newspaper insert*
der Zentimeter (–) *centimetre*
zentral *central, centralized*
die Zentrale (– n) *headquarters, head office, (control) centre, station, reception*
der Zentraleinkauf *central purchasing (department)*
das Zentrieren *centring*
das Zentrum (Zentren) *centre*
zerstören *to destroy*
zerstörend *destructive*
zerstört *destroys, destroyed (see zerstören)*
zerstörungsfrei *non-destructive*
ziehen, zog, gezogen *to pull, order, take, brew, steep;* Proben ziehen *to order samples;* Muster ziehen *to order/take samples*
das Ziel (– e) *aim, target, goal, objective*
die Zielrichtung (– en) *objective, aim, purpose, target*
ziemlich *fairly, rather, quite*
das Zimmer (–) *room*
das Zimmertelefon (– e) *room telephone*
die Zimmervermittlung (– en) *accommodation service*
die Zinkphosphatierung (– en) *zinc phosphating*
zirka *about, approximately, roughly*
das Zivilflugzeugprogramm (– e) *civil/ commercial aircraft programme*
der Zoll (–) *inch*
der Zoo (– s) *zoo*
zu *to, at, too, on;* um ... zu *in order to ...;* braucht ... zu arbeiten *... needs to work;* zum *for (doing);* zum Schließen *for filling;* zu Messezeiten *when trade fairs are on;* zu der und der Zeit *at such and such a time;* zu Hause *at home, domiciled/based*
das Zubehör *accessory, accessories*
das Zubehörteil (– e) *accessory*
zubereitet *(from zubereiten) prepared*
der Zucker *sugar*
zuerst *(at) first*
zufällig *fortuitous(ly), by accident, accidental(ly)*
zufolge *according to;* der Studie zufolge *according to the study*
zufrieden *satisfied*
zufriedenstellen (sep.) *to satisfy*
zufriedenzustellen see zufriedenstellen
der Zugang (:-e) *access;* Zugang zu *access to*
zugeben (sep.) (i), a, e *to add, admit*
zugehörig *accompanying*
zugenommen *increased (see zunehmen)*
zugeschickt *(from zuschicken) sent, dispatched*
zukaufen (sep.) *to buy in, source*
die Zukunft *future*
zukünftig *future*
zukunftsorientiert *future-oriented*
zukunftsträchtig *with growth potential, future-oriented*
die Zulassung (– en) *approval, certification*
der Zulieferer (–) *supplier*
die Zulieferindustrie (– n) *component-supply industry*
zuliefern (sep.) *to supply*
zum = zu dem
zumindest *at least, at any rate*
zunächst *initial(ly), first of all, to start with;* zunächst einmal *initial(ly), first(ly)*
zunehmen (sep.) (nimmt zu), nahm zu, zugenommen *to increase;* um 9,2% zunehmen *to increase by 9.2%*
zunehmend *increasing(ly)*
zur = zu der
zurechtkommen (sep.), a, o * *to manage, find one's way around/through*
zurück *back*
zurückblicken (sep.) *to look back*
zurückerhalten (sep.) (ä), ie, a *to receive, regain*
zurückführen (sep.) (auf) *to be based (on)/due (to)*
zurückgehen (sep.), ging zurück, zurückgegangen * *to decrease, decline, return, go back*
zurückgekommen *returned (see zurückkommen)*
das Zurückgewinnen *recovering, recovery*
zurückkommen (sep.), a, o * *to come back, return*
zurückschrauben (sep.) *to reduce (lit. screw back)*
zurückzuführen see zurückführen
zusammen *(put) together*
die Zusammenarbeit (– en) *cooperation*
zusammenarbeiten (sep.) *to work together, work with, cooperate*
das Zusammenfügen *(final) assembly*
zusammengebaut *(from zusammenbauen) assembled*
die Zusammengehörigkeit *unity, synergy*
zusammengerückt *(from zusammenrücken) moved together*
zusammengestellt *assembled (see zusammenstellen)*
zusammengezogen *(from zusammenziehen) brought together*
zusammenhalten (sep.) (ä), ie, a *to hold together*
der Zusammenhang (:-e) *connection, context;* in Zusammenhang mit *in connection with/the context of*
zusammenhängen (sep.), i, a (mit) *to be linked/connected (with);* die Abwicklung, die damit zusammenhängt, einen Service durchzuführen *the processing which is connected with carrying out a service*
zusammenhängend *coherent, integrated*
zusammenhängend mit *connected with*
die Zusammenlegung (– en) *combination, combining, merging*
zusammenrücken (sep.) * *to move together*
der Zusammenschluß (:-sse) *merger, merging, assembly*
die Zusammensetzung (– en) *composition, combination*
(sich) zusammenstellen (sep.) *to put together, assemble*
zusammenzuarbeiten see zusammenarbeiten
zusammenzustellen see zusammenstellen
zusätzlich *additional(ly), extra;* zusätzliche Mitarbeiter *temporary staff*
zuständig (für) *responsible (for)*
zuverlässig *reliable (–ly)*
die Zuverlässigkeit *reliability*
zuzüglich *plus*
zwangsläufig *inevitable(-ly)*
zwanzig *twenty*
der, die, das zwanzigste *(the) twentieth (one)*
zwar *indeed, although, actually, in fact;* zwar ... aber *although ... but;* und zwar *that is*
der Zweck (– e) *aim*
zweckmäßig *functional, practical*
zwei *two*
zweieinhalb *two and a half*
zweimal *twice*
der, die, das zweite *second*
zweiteilig *two-part*
zweitens *secondly*
der, die, das zweitgrößte *(the) second largest (one)*
zweiundachtzigtausend *eighty-two thousand*
zwischen *between*
das Zwischenstück (– e) *spacer*
zwölf *twelve*
der Zylinderkopf (:-e) *cylinder head*

HOW SAXBY STREET GOT ITS NAME

WORLD WAR ONE AND THE PEOPLE OF SOUTH HIGHFIELDS

Researched and written by the people who live here

Designed by Sophie Hardwicke

First published in Great Britain in 2015 by South Highfields Neighbours

© South Highfields Neighbours

ISBN 978-0-9931180-0-5

Printed by..

Funded by the Heritage Lottery Fund and Leicestershire Archaeological and Historical Society

For more information about South Highfields Neighbours see www.wearesouthhighfields.co.uk